Con 102 082 818 8 n Systems

This book is due for return on or before the last date shown below.

Antoni Olivé

# Conceptual Modeling of Information Systems

With 185 Figures

 Springer

*Author*

Antoni Olivé
Universitat Politècnica de Catalunya
Department of Software (LSI)
Jordi Girona 1-3,
E-08034 Barcelona
Catalonia, Spain
olive@lsi.upc.edu

ACM Computing Classification (1998): D.2.1, D.2.2, H.2.1, I.6.5, F.3.1

ISBN  978-3-642-07256-7      e-ISBN  978-3-540-39390-0

Springer is a part of Springer Science+Business Media

springer.com

© Springer-Verlag Berlin Heidelberg 2010

Cover design: KünkelLopka Werbeagentur, Heidelberg

# Foreword

It is now more than fifty years since the first paper on formal specifications of an information system was published by Young and Kent. Even if the term "conceptual model" was not used at that time, the basic intention of the abstract specification was to a large extent the same as for developing conceptual models today: to arrive at a precise, abstract, and hardware independent model of the informational and time characteristics of a data processing problem. The abstract notation should enable the analyst to organize the problem around any piece of hardware. In other words, the purpose of an abstract specification was for it to be used as an invariant basis for designing different alternative implementations, perhaps even using different hardware components.

Research and practice of abstract modeling of information systems has since the late fifties progressed through many milestones and achievements. In the sixties, pioneering work was carried out by the CODASYL Development committee who in 1962 presented the "Information Algebra". At about the same time Börje Langefors published his elementary message and e-file approach to specification of information systems. The next decade, the seventies, was characterized by the introduction of a large number of new types of, as they were called, "data models". We saw the birth of, for instance, Binary Data Models, Entity Relationship Models, Relational Data Models, Semantic Data Models, and Temporal Deductive Models. At this time, most of the researchers in the modeling field had, essentially, a data-base orientation. I believe the first time the term "conceptual schema" was used was by the ANSI/X3/SPARC, Study Group on Data Base Management Systems, in 1975 when they formulated the "three schema approach" to data-base management. The conceptual schema was seen as the "essential schema", depicting the content of the database in an implementation, and external representation independent way.

The term *conceptual modeling* gradually gained general acceptance, perhaps largely due to the use of the term conceptual schema in the ISO working group's TC97/SC5/WG5 preliminary report, *Concepts and Terminology for the Conceptual Schema* edited by J.J. van Griethuysen, et. al. in 1982. At about the same time information system researchers began to use the term "conceptual modeling" for modeling of information systems in an implementation independent way. Usually, this kind of modeling was carried out during the requirements elicitation and specification phase of systems development. The last two decades of conceptual modeling practice have been dominated by two main trends. The first is the spread and use of the UML object oriented language and approach, including its language OCL (Object Constraint Language) for formulating business rules and constraints. The second trend, in my opinion, is the change of mode of modeling towards a way where users and stakeholders are very much more involved – participatory modeling. This trend points to the importance of modeling skills and knowledge becoming important not only for system development professionals but also for stakeholders and users.

Antoni Olivé has written an impressive book that brings and puts together knowledge of conceptual (and data-) modeling, produced in research spanning more than half a century. In doing so it summarizes, and puts in context, research on conceptual modeling presented in more than 220 references. It deals with all essential aspects of conceptual modeling, thoroughly explained and illustrated in detail. Structural as well as behavioral conceptual modeling concepts are explained in detail. Every chapter is concluded with a bibliographical note that gives the research-oriented reader the possibility of further study through references to works on that particular topic. Each chapter also gives students a challenge to test their newly acquired knowledge by solving a number of problems. A fairly large chapter at the end, describing a case study, illustrates the use of modeling constructs presented earlier. Of practical interest are the frequent translations into UML and OCL of the modelling concepts that are introduced. The book concludes with a chapter on "Metamodeling" and a chapter on "Meta-metamodeling" and Metadata Interchange (XMI), a standard that enables the exchange of data about schemas as well as about schema instances. Metamodeling is also an important mechanism for reasoning about conceptual schema languages of different types and for integrating conceptual models with other kinds of models, such as business and enterprise models.

The book is one of the most informative and comprehensive texts on conceptual modeling published to date. It is very appropriate for students of advanced level university courses in information systems, requirements engineering, or in data base design, as well as for qualified practitioners in the field.

Lund in May, 2007                                    Janis Bubenko
Prof. em., Dr Techn, Dr. Techn. h.c., ACM Fellow
Department of Computer and Systems Science
Royal Inst. of Technology, Stockholm, Sweden

# Foreword

Antoni Olivé has taken the time to create a book that is certain to become essential reading for students of conceptual modeling in Information Systems Engineering. Despite the title, this is not just "another book" on conceptual modeling, data bases and information systems. Antoni Olivé has succeeded in creating a text that brings formalization together with the essentials of information systems engineering in a way that encourages the understanding of both.

The most common modeling approaches in Information Systems Engineering may be classified into approaches that are process-oriented, data-oriented, rule-oriented or object-oriented. Antoni Olivé has been a staunch supporter of rule-oriented approaches in his scientific work. It is impressive to see how he has managed to adopt a holistic method in relating his rule-oriented attitude and background to the other three "schools" of thought.

His objective of explaining in detail the use of the standard Object Constraint Language (OCL) of the Universal Modeling Language (UML) was essential in providing an elegant harmonization of the four approaches. To achieve this he starts out with the very simple assumption that an information system has three main functions: a memory to maintain a representation of the state of a domain, an informative function to provide information on the state of the domain, and an activity function to perform actions that change the state of the domain. This initial assumption rests heavily on his own scientific research on rule-oriented approaches to Information Systems Engineering. He has, nevertheless, managed to explain the essentials of UML/OCL within this framework.

Antoni Olivé has placed more emphasis on formalizing the end result of the process of developing an information system than on the stages leading to the detailed end result. The intermediate stages between the initial conception of a system, through its requirement engineering stage and into the finalization stage where the detailed system solution is hammered out, have been given less emphasis. Much of this is well treated in the literature. Most of the known approaches are not based on well-defined specification languages. It may very well be that Antoni Olivé's explanation of the formal basis of UML/OCL will encourage a re-examination of the requirements engineering phase associated with object-oriented approaches to information systems design, as well as a re-examination of process oriented approaches.

We cannot expect in the future to have only one universal modeling language for Information Systems Engineering. There will always be a need for introducing domain-specific language constructs into the information system's specific modeling language, so we will always be challenged by different modeling languages. Hopefully they may in the future be seen as various dialects of a common family of Information Systems Engineering languages. In order to relate the dialects to each other, we need meta-modeling languages. Antoni Olivé's text is rounded off with a treatise on meta-modeling, and he thus prepares the reader for the future need of being able to model the modeling languages.

Trondheim May, 2007                                        Arne Sølvberg
Professor
The Norwegian University of Science and Technology – NTNU
Dean of Faculty of Information Technology,
Mathematics and Electrical Engineering

To those who are happy to see this book,
and to those who would be happy to see it,
if they were still with us.

# Preface

If an information system is able to perform useful actions for persons working in a given domain, it is because the system knows something about that domain. The more knowledge it has, the more useful it can be to its users. Without that knowledge, the system is useless.

Most of the knowledge a system has is concrete or particular. It refers to concrete objects and the relationships they have in the domain at some point in time. Given that many systems work in domains with a very high number of objects and relationships, it is hardly surprising that the concrete knowledge they have is very large. Think, for instance, of bank management systems, where it is usual to find a large number of accounts, loans, etc. for which many details must be known (account holders, balances, transactions, etc.).

However, it is not possible to have concrete knowledge about a domain without a prior *general* knowledge about that domain. A bank management system may know the balances of accounts once it knows that there are accounts in the domain, and that accounts always have a balance. Similarly, the system may know the holders of accounts because it knows that accounts do have holders. Concrete knowledge requires prior general knowledge, which is independent of the concrete objects and relationships existing at any point in time.

This general knowledge also includes rules that must be obeyed (for instance, balances may not be negative), definitions that allow new knowledge to be obtained from existing knowledge (for instance, what is understood as the return on investment), and details of the actions that the users want the system to perform when some condition is satisfied (for example, how to calculate the interest earned by savings accounts).

In the information systems field, we use the name *conceptual modeling* for the activity that elicits and describes the general knowledge a particular information system needs to know. The main objective of conceptual modeling is to obtain that description, which is called a *conceptual schema*. Conceptual schemas are written in languages called conceptual modeling languages. Conceptual modeling is an important part of requirements engineering, the first and most important phase in the development of an information system.

The elicitation of the general knowledge required by an information system is a necessary activity. Information systems cannot be designed or programmed without prior elicitation of the knowledge they need to know. This is captured by one of the principles that guide this book, called the *principle of necessity*: "to develop an information system, it is necessary to define its conceptual schema".

The only option we have is whether or not to explicitly describe that knowledge. That is, whether or not to write the conceptual schema. Sometimes, system development projects choose not to write the conceptual schema, or they do not have the time to do so. In these cases, the general knowledge is in the designers' heads only. This has many disadvantages. If there are several designers, they must share this knowledge without an explicit description. User participation is hampered. Once the system has been built, it is likely that the general knowledge will be forgotten. The future evolution of the system will require that general knowledge to be rediscovered. The explicit description of the conceptual schema brings many advantages, especially when it is done in a machine-readable language.

Furthermore, many researchers have put forward, many times, a vision in which the conceptual schema is the only important description that needs to be created in the development of an information system. According to this vision, the building of information systems is completely automated. The only things to be done are to determine the functions that the information system has to perform and to define its conceptual schema (and, probably, the design and construction of the input/output user interface). The huge potential economic benefit of this vision justifies the research and development efforts currently devoted to it, which are being made mainly in the framework of OMG's Model Driven Architecture. The progress made in other branches of computer science (especially in the field of databases) makes this vision feasible in the mid-term. On the day when the vision becomes a reality we shall be able to say that "to develop an information system it is necessary and sufficient to define its conceptual schema".

## Objectives

The main objectives of this book are:

1. To describe the principles of conceptual modeling independently of particular methods and languages.
2. To describe these principles in the detail required to correctly apply them in real projects and to be able to assess the methods, languages, and tools that are most suitable in those projects.
3. To describe the formal bases of conceptual schemas. However, in this book, the logical formalization is only sketched and is not pushed too far. The book describes the formal bases with extensive use of intuitive ideas and examples.
4. To describe in detail the use of standard UML/OCL as a particular conceptual modeling language.
5. To provide exercises for readers who want to practice and deepen their knowledge by solving exercises.
6. To give bibliographical references for the concepts presented in the book and for the extensions suggested to readers, including further formalizations.

## Audience

The book has two intended audiences:

1. Computer science and information systems students who, after an introduction to information systems, databases, and UML, want to know more about conceptual modeling in their preparation for professional practice.
2. Professionals with some experience in the development of information systems who feel a need to formalize their practical experiences or to update their knowledge, as a way to improve their professional activity.

Some prerequisite knowledge is assumed – and necessary – in order to benefit from the book:

1. Knowledge of the fundamental concepts of the language of first-order logic.
2. Knowledge of fundamental concepts of object technology, such as classes, operations, and inheritance.

3. Knowledge of the fundamental constructs of ER and UML for information modeling. A basic knowledge of OCL is necessary from Chap. 8 onwards.

## Structure of the Book

The 18 chapters of this book are divided into five logical parts:

- *Chapter* 1: *introduction*. Here we give a general view of conceptual modeling. Readers with prior knowledge about the field may skip this chapter, but it may be useful to those who want to recall concepts and terms learnt long ago.
- *Chapters* 2–10: *structural modeling*. Here we study the concepts of entity types, relationship types, constraints, derivation rules and taxonomies.
- *Chapters* 11–15: *behavioral modeling*. Here we describe the concepts of events, their constraints, and their effects. We also describe behavioral modeling with state machines and statecharts. We include a review of the concept of the use case and its relationship to the conceptual schema.
- *Chapter* 16: *a case study*. In the preceding chapters, we follow a bottom-up approach, starting with the basic elements of entity and relationship types, and then proceeding to more complex elements until we reach state transition diagrams and statecharts. In this chapter, we provide an integrated view of conceptual modeling by means of a case study.
- *Chapters* 17 and 18: *metamodeling*. Here we introduce the main concepts of metamodeling and describe their use. We study two important standards related to metamodeling: the MOF and XMI.

Figure I.1 shows the main precedence relationships among the chapters of this book.

The book also includes a companion website (http://www-pagines.fib.upc.edu/~modeling) where students and professionals can find additional exercises, case studies, reading material and presentations on selected topics. If you have any comments on the book, any typos you have noticed, or any suggestion on how it can be improved, I would like to hear from you. The companion website includes information on how to contact me.

For the convenience of the reader, in this book I use "he" to refer to both genders.

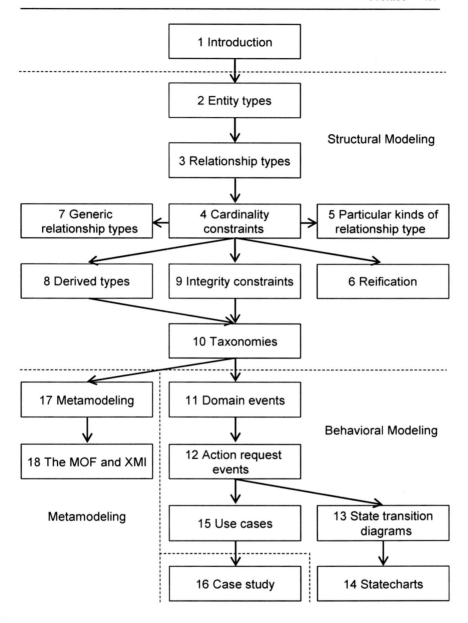

**Fig. I.1.** Main precedence relationships among the chapters of this book

## Acknowledgements

This book explains part of what I have learnt over the years that I have dedicated to the study of conceptual modeling. I have learnt a lot from other people's work. The extensive bibliography shows clearly enough how the ideas and realizations of others have contributed to this book. My first thanks to all these people. I also express my gratitude to the members and friends of the IFIP WG8.1, CAiSE, and ER communities for the many opportunities they have given to me to share and discuss views on what this book is about.

Many people contributed directly and indirectly to bringing this text into existence. First and foremost, I would like to thank my colleagues of the GMC group (whose current composition is: Jordi Cabot, Jordi Conesa, Dolors Costal, Cristina Gómez, Enric Mayol, Joan Antoni Pastor, Anna Queralt, Ruth Raventós, Maria Ribera Sancho, and Ernest Teniente) for providing a friendly environment in which I have been able to discuss many ideas that have helped me to sharpen and focus this book, and for the many comments and suggestions they have given to me over the years.

During the thirteen-year period in which the ideas expressed in this book were developed, from their first expression as lecture notes in Catalan until their current form and language, many friends, colleagues and students have reviewed, read and commented on previous drafts of this book or its chapters. Their help is gratefully acknowledged. Among them, I specially thank Carles Farré, Oscar Díaz, Juan Ramón López, Elena Planas, Carme Quer, Sudha Ram, Keng Siau, Albert Tort and Toni Urpí. Preliminary versions of this book have been used in several courses on conceptual modeling. I deeply appreciate the many comments made by the students. Any remaining errors are, of course, mine.

I would like to thank my university, the Technical University of Catalonia, for the continued support that it has provided to me during these years, and the research agencies that have funded part of my research. Finally, I would also like to thank Ralf Gerstner, from Springer, for his continued interest and help in this book.

Barcelona, June 2007

Antoni Olivé

# Contents

# 1 Introduction

In this chapter we review the basics of the conceptual modeling of information systems. We explain that conceptual modeling is a necessary activity in the development of an information system, the objective of which is to define the conceptual schema of the system. We also explain that conceptual modeling must be preceded and followed by other activities.

We begin by reviewing the concept of an information system. In particular, we are interested in the functions that these systems perform. This is the subject of Sect. 1.1. In order to perform their functions, information systems require some knowledge, which must be defined in each case. In Sect. 1.2, we explain that a conceptual schema is the definition of the knowledge an information system needs to perform its functions. The explanation is introductory and somewhat informal. We also refer to the chapters of the book in which the various concepts are studied in more depth. Section 1.3 shows the role of conceptual schemas in the architecture of information systems. Section 1.4 presents the activity of conceptual modeling in the wider context of the development of information systems. Once we have defined conceptual schemas and their role in the architecture and development of information systems, we describe in Sect. 1.5 the properties that conceptual schemas must have if they are to fulfill their roles effectively. Section 1.6 concludes the chapter with a brief history of conceptual modeling.

## 1.1 Functions of an Information System

The concept of an *information system* began to emerge around the year 1960, and although it may be considered a well-established concept it remains difficult to define precisely. Part of the difficulty stems from the fact that information systems can be analyzed from at least three different, but complementary, perspectives:

1. The contribution they make.
2. Their structure and behavior.
3. The functions they perform.

From the first perspective, information systems are defined as a means that allows wider systems to achieve their objectives. This type of definition emphasizes that information systems are subsystems that contribute to wider systems. An information system does not exist for its own purposes. Examples of this kind of definition are "An information system is a system designed to support operations, management, and decision making in an organization", and "An information system is a system that facilitates communication among its users".

For our purposes, the main problem with this kind of definition is that it does not clearly establish what an information system actually is. The wider system of which an information system is a part may also require means other than information systems to achieve its objectives. Furthermore, there are other instruments that can provide similar contributions without actually being information systems. For example, there are various ways of facilitating communication among users, including working in close proximity to each other or participating in meetings.

Even if it is difficult to define information systems in terms of the contribution they provide, it is very important to realize that this consideration is essential during their development. The requirements of an information system are determined by the objectives of the organization for which the system is being designed and built.

Definitions from the second perspective emphasize the structure and behavior of the physical and abstract elements that make up an information system. Both structure and behavior may be characterized in greater or lesser detail.

For the purposes of conceptual modeling, the most useful definitions are those based on the functions performed by information systems. That is, definitions that focus exclusively on what information systems do, without considering why and how they do it.

From this perspective, the classic definition states that "An information system is a system that collects, stores, processes, and distributes information". This is a commonly accepted definition, because of both its simplicity and its generality. However, some further comments may be necessary in order to make it more precise.

Firstly, in information systems engineering, we should restrict the definition to designed systems, that is, systems that are designed and built by an engineer. The restriction is necessary because there are natural systems that perform information-processing functions, which are beyond the scope of our study. For example, in cognitive science, the human mind is viewed as a complex system that receives, stores, processes, and distributes information.

Secondly, the above definition is too general with regard to the kind of information an information system may deal with. In fact, the definition places no constraints on the possible type of information and thus encompasses systems that many people would not in fact consider to be information systems. For example, a fax machine could be considered an information system according to this definition, since it can be regarded as a system that receives documents (which contain data representing information), stores them (even if only for a short time), translates them (that is, changes the representation of the information), and sends the result across telephone lines.

The usual constraint on the kind of information handled by an information system is that it must refer to the state of a certain *domain* (also called the *object system* or *universe of discourse*). The nature of this domain does not influence the definition of an information system. For many systems, the domain is an organization, but the definition does not exclude other domains, such as a vehicle, the atmosphere, or a chess game.

According to this definition, a fax machine is not an information system. A fax does not consider the documents it sends as information about the state of a particular domain. To a fax machine, documents are merely uninterpreted data.

We have therefore established that an information system is a designed system that collects, stores, processes, and distributes information about the state of a domain. This book focuses on this type of information system, and for the sake of simplicity, and when no confusion is likely to arise, we refer to such systems as information systems, or just as systems.

It is easy to agree on the above functions, but the problem remains that they are too general. For this reason, some authors prefer to use a more specific definition of these functions, one that captures the nature of information systems more precisely. A system is therefore considered to have three main functions (Fig. 1.1):

1. *Memory*: to maintain a representation of the state of a domain.
2. *Informative*: to provide information about the state of a domain.
3. *Active*: to perform actions that change the state of a domain.

In the following sections, we shall analyze each of these functions.

## 1.1.1 The Memory Function

The objective of the memory function is to maintain an internal representation of the state of the domain. This representation is needed by the other functions of the system. The state of the domain usually changes fre-

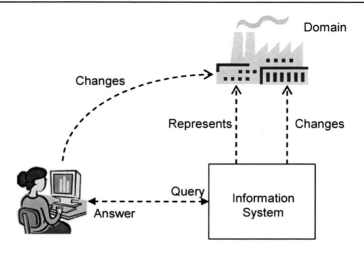

**Fig. 1.1.** Functions of an information system

quently and in many different ways. The system must keep track of the state changes and update the internal representation accordingly.

The memory function may be performed in two modes: *on request* or *autonomously*. In the first mode, when the state changes the users inform the system about the change that has occurred and request the system to update the representation of the state. For example, a system may know customers' addresses because whenever a customer changes its address, someone informs the system about the new address and expects the system to remember it. The information system is therefore totally reliant on human input in order to know customer addresses.

In the second, *autonomous* mode, the system memorizes the state of the domain without an explicit request from a user. The system is able to autonomously observe the state of the domain. An example of this is a system that periodically reads a device that gives the temperature of a building. In this case, the system can maintain a representation of the temperature because it is able to obtain the reading directly from the environment.

### 1.1.2 The Informative Function

By means of the informative function, the system provides users with information about the state of the domain. The state of the domain can often be observed directly in the domain, while at the same time it is represented in the information system. For example, the quantity of a given product on the shelves of a retail store may be directly observed when necessary, and can be simultaneously represented in the information system. In general, it is easier to request the information from the system than to observe the domain directly.

Sometimes the state is represented only in the information system and it is very difficult, if not impossible, to observe it directly in the domain. For example, in a retail store it is not possible to observe how many units of a product have been sold up to a given moment. As a further example, consider account balances in the banking domain. The balance of an account at a given point cannot be obtained by observing the account holders or the particular branch where the account is held. The only place in which balances can be viewed is in the information system. In these cases, the information system is the only source of information about the state, and the system thus becomes indispensable to its users.

In the most frequent case, users pose a query, which is then answered by the system. Both query and answer are made in a language understood by the users and the system. Queries may be extensional (the most frequent case) or intensional. An extensional query requests information about the state of the domain, to which the system gives an extensional or intensional answer. An extensional answer, which is the most common type, consists of information about the state of the domain in more or less detail. An intensional answer characterizes the state of the domain, but it does not describe the state explicitly.

Examples of simple extensional answers might be:

- Laura is taking the Conceptual Modeling course.
- Eighty students are taking the Software Engineering course.

Some extensional answers need to be much more detailed, and may require statistical analysis, simulation, or execution of a decisional model. Examples of such answers might be:

- Ninety percent of customers who buy books also buy CDs.
- No customer has bought more than 200 books.

As we have said, the answer to an extensional query may be intensional. For example, the system's answer to the question "Who earns more than 100K euros?" might be "The managers."

Intensional queries concern the type of information the system knows, rather than particular information. For example:

- What do you know about students?
- What is the maximum number of courses a student can take simultaneously?
- What is a student?

The informative function can also be performed in two modes. The most frequent is *on request*: users receive information when they ask for it explicitly. In contrast, in the *autonomous* mode, users define a condition for the state of the domain and order the system to inform them when this condition is satisfied. For example, the condition might be "the temperature is above a given level", and users expect that the system will issue a signal when the condition is satisfied.

The informative function does not change the state of the domain. The system merely provides the information requested by users. It is the users who will take actions that change the domain, if they wish to do so.

## 1.1.3 The Active Function

With the active function, the system performs actions that modify the state of the domain. In order to perform this active function, the system must know the actions it can take, when they can be taken, and how they will affect the state of the domain.

The active function also operates in the two modes mentioned above. In the *on request* mode, users delegate the system to perform an action that may modify the state of the domain. For example, users may ask the system to calculate the interest on bank accounts and credit the required amounts to the accounts.

In the *autonomous* mode, users delegate the system to perform an action that may modify the state of the domain when a particular condition is satisfied. The system will monitor the state of the domain and, when the condition is satisfied, perform the requested action.

A variety of actions may be delegated to the system (in both modes). These may be simple and clearly defined, or actions for which only the objectives are defined, leaving the system free (or *autonomous*) to decide how best to achieve them.

The classic example of the active function, in *autonomous* mode, is the automatic replenishment of a store. For each product, users define a reorder point and a quantity to be ordered. The system maintains the available quantity of each product and users give it the task of issuing replenishment orders when the quantity on hand is below the reorder point.

In the above example, we assumed that the state of the domain represented in the system changed when a new order was issued. If the orders were not part of the state of the domain represented in the system, then the automatic replenishment would not be an example of the active function. It would instead be an example of the informative function. Outputs from the system could require action by users, but the state of the domain would not be altered.

Table 1.1 is a summary of the three functions and the two modes.

**Table 1.1.** Examples of functions in the two modes

| Functions | Modes | |
| | On request | Autonomous |
| --- | --- | --- |
| **Memory** | Change of customer address | Temperature reading |
| **Informative** | What courses is a student taking? | Signal when temperature is above a given level |
| **Active** | Credit interest to accounts | Automatic replenishment of a store |

## 1.1.4 Examples of Information Systems

All conventional information systems perform a memory function and an informative function. We shall not give any specific examples, since they are already well known and the functions they perform are easily identified. However, it may be useful to discuss some particular types of system in order to see that, although one might question whether they are actually information systems, they do in fact perform the functions we have seen in this section.

### 1.1.4.1 Chess-Playing System

Let us imagine a chess-playing system. We shall see that this system can be considered an information system.

The domain consists of the board, the pieces, the position of the pieces on the board, and the player. At any given moment, the domain is in a particular state, which varies over time. The system must maintain a representation of the state of the domain; otherwise, it would be unable to play. When a move is made, the system must somehow be made aware of it so that it can update the representation of the state. This is a simple example of the memory function of an information system.

The system has to display the state of the game on a screen. When a game starts, the system shows the initial distribution of the pieces. After every move, the system must show the new distribution. This is therefore an example of the informative function in the *autonomous* mode.

Once the player has made a move, it is assumed that the system will consider the alternatives that will allow it to achieve its objective (using the current state of the game and the knowledge that the system may have), and that, after a certain amount of time, it will make its own move. In making this move, the system changes the state of the domain. This is therefore a complex example of the active function.

If the system were naive enough to offer the player genuine advice about the next move, this would be an example of the informative function in the *on request* mode.

### 1.1.4.2 Intranet Email System

Let us consider an intranet email system. The domain is made up of users (who send or receive messages), distribution lists, messages, folders created by users to organize their messages, and other components. Each message has a given content, a subject, a sender, a date, and one or more recipients. Normally, the content and subject of a message are data that cannot be interpreted by the system.

The memory function maintains a representation of the state of the above domain. The main part of the state will be represented only within the system and cannot be directly observed in the domain. The state of the domain changes when a user issues a message, receives a message, deletes a message, creates a folder, puts a message in a folder, removes a message from a folder, or deletes a folder.

One use of the informative function is to allow users to view their messages and the contents of their folders in more or less detail.

The active function consists in sending messages created by users to the respective recipients. The sent message is put in the corresponding inbox of each recipient. This function is performed in the *on request* mode.

### 1.1.4.3 Real-Time Systems

The final example is not a concrete system but a type of system: a real-time system. There is no consensus on precisely what real-time systems are, but they can generally be identified by a set of common characteristics, which we analyze below.

Firstly, a real-time system monitors and controls an environment (that is, it issues controlling commands that change the environment). In our terminology, monitoring the environment is a memory function and controlling it is an active function. Secondly, real-time systems interact with users, for whom they perform a required function. Such a function may be either informative or active. Real-time systems frequently have various sensors and intersystem interfaces that provide continuous or periodic input. These are the mechanisms that allow the system to know the state of the environment for the memory function. Finally, a real-time system has a set of actuators, or intersystem interfaces, which must be driven periodically. These correspond to the mechanisms the system uses to send the output to the environment from the active function.

A real-time system has other characteristics that are related not to the essential functions it has to perform, but to how it must perform them, for example sampling intervals for sensors, response time, simultaneous processing of multiple inputs, high reliability, and resource (main or secondary memory, processor capacity, etc.) limitations. These characteristics are very important but they do not change the fact that real-time systems may be considered as information systems.

## 1.2 Conceptual Modeling

In the previous section we reviewed the main functions of an information system. To be able to perform these functions, a system requires knowledge about its domain and about the functions it has to perform. This section describes the main types of knowledge required by most information systems. The line of reasoning we follow is:

- If the memory function of an information system maintains a representation of the state of the domain, we must define the particular state that must be represented.
- The state of most domains varies over time, so potential changes must be defined.
- The representation of the state in the information system must be consistent. Therefore, it is necessary to define when a representation is consistent.
- Answering queries posed by users often requires an inference capability on the part of the information system. This capability uses derivation rules, which must be defined.

In the reminder of this section, we develop the reasoning outlined above. As part of our explanation, we shall offer an informal introduction to the terminology, give an intuitive idea of the basic concepts and identify the chapters of the book in which these concepts are studied in greater depth.

## 1.2.1 The Structural Schema

The objective of the memory function of an information system is to maintain a representation of the state of its domain. The state of a domain consists of a set of relevant properties.

The question of what the relevant properties of the domain of a system are depends on the purpose for which the system is built. We have already mentioned that an information system is always a means through which a wider system can achieve its objectives. The relevant properties depend on these objectives and on the anticipated contribution of the information system. We intend to focus here on what the relevant properties are, rather than how to determine them. This, of course, does not mean that the latter aspect is less important.

In the field of information systems, we make the fundamental assumption that a domain consists of a number of objects and the relationships between them, which are classified into concepts. The state of a particular domain, at a given time, therefore consists of a set of objects, a set of relationships, and a set of concepts into which these objects and relationships are classified. For example, in the domain of a company, we may have the concepts of a customer, a product and a sale. At a given moment, we have objects classified as customers, objects classified as products, and relationships between customers and products classified as sales.

This underlying assumption is also shared by disciplines such as linguistics, (first-order) logic, and cognitive science. Unfortunately, these disciplines have not yet reached agreement regarding the terminology, concepts, and mechanisms that we use to distinguish between the objects and relationships in a domain. Consequently, we do not have a solid theoretical basis on which to base our study and, as is often the case when discussing information systems, we must adopt a humble and eclectic attitude.

The assumption that a domain consists of objects, relationships, and concepts is a specific way of viewing the world (a domain). At first glance, it seems an obvious assumption. The truth of the matter is, however, rather different. Other possible views exist that may be more suitable in other fields. To give a simple and well-known example, in propositional logic one assumes that domains consist of facts, which may be either true or false. The study of the nature and organization of the real world is a branch of philosophy called ontology.

When we assume that a domain consists of objects, relationships, and concepts we commit ourselves to a specific way of viewing domains. The term used in ontology to denote this commitment is *ontological commitment*. In the field of information systems, this commitment to viewing domains in a particular way is called the *conceptual model*. In principle, the same conceptual model can be applied to many different domains, and several conceptual models can be applied to the same domain.

The set of concepts used in a particular domain constitutes a *conceptualization* of that domain. The specification of this conceptualization is sometimes called an *ontology* of the domain. Note that the term *ontology* is used to denote two different ideas: a branch of philosophy and a specification of a conceptualization. In computer science, the latter is the usual meaning.

There may be several conceptualizations of the same domain and thus several ontologies. Additionally, an ontology is a concrete view of a particular domain. Therefore, it is also an ontological commitment for the people who observe and act on this domain.

In the field of information systems, ontologies are called *conceptual schemas*, and the languages in which they are written are called *conceptual modeling languages*.

The formal basis of conceptual modeling languages is logic. Any conceptual schema can be specified in some kind of logical language. In particular, the first-order logic (FOL) language is sufficient for the specification of most conceptual schemas. In the examples given in this introductory chapter, we use the FOL language only.

However, in many projects the use of logical languages is impractical, and specialized languages are more suitable. One such language is the Unified Modeling Language (UML). In this book, we shall explain in detail the use of UML as a conceptual modeling language.

As we shall see, conceptual models of information systems make more complex assumptions than simply considering that a domain consists of objects and relationships. A conceptual model assumes that a domain includes other "things" and that objects, relationships, and concepts have several properties that must be distinguished. A conceptual model also includes a view of how a domain changes.

There is great diversity in conceptual models, and they may be more or less useful in particular situations or for particular purposes. However, all of them are based on the fundamental assumption that we have mentioned, which we shall attempt to clarify in the reminder of this section.

We begin by trying to establish the distinction between a concept and an object. According to dictionary definitions, a *concept* is

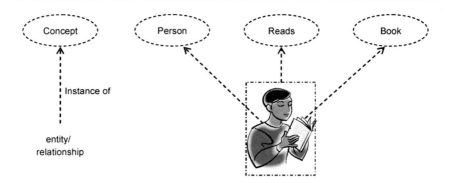

**Fig. 1.2.** Entities and relationships are instances of concepts

- "An abstract or generic idea generalized from particular instances."[1]
- "An idea or mental picture of a group or class of objects formed by combining all their aspects."[2]

These definitions fit our purpose here. A concept, then, is something that we have formed in our mind through generalization from certain instances. A concept has an extension and an intension. The extension of a concept is the set of its possible instances, while the intension is the property shared by all its instances.

As human beings, we use the concepts that we have to structure our perception of a domain. In this sense, concepts are like "spectacles" through which we observe a domain. Concepts allow us to classify the things that we perceive as exemplars of the concepts that we have. In other words, what we observe depends on the concepts that we employ in the observation.

*Classification* is the operation that associates an object with a concept. The inverse operation, *instantiation*, gives an instance of a concept. The set of objects that constitutes an instance of a concept at a given time is known collectively as the *population* of the concept at that time.

An *entity type* is a concept whose instances are individual, identifiable objects. Objects that are instances of an entity type are called *entities*. Figure 1.2 shows two examples of entities and entity types: a *person* and a *book*. In the FOL language, entity types are represented by unary predicates. We shall study entity types in the next chapter.

---

[1] Merriam-Webster Online Dictionary.
[2] Concise Oxford Dictionary.

All entities are an instance of an entity type, but an entity may be an instance of more than one entity type. For example, in Fig. 1.2, the person shown could also be an instance of *student.*

If there is a thing that we are interested in, but which we are unable to classify into any of the concepts we have, we then have to design a new concept of which this particular thing could be an instance. In contrast, there may be concepts without instances in the usual domains. The typical example is *unicorn*. In conceptual modeling, we do not show a practical interest in concepts without instances.

Some concepts are associative, in the sense that their instances relate to two or more entities. *Relationship types* are concepts whose instances are *relationships*. The set of relationships that are instances of a relationship type at a given time is called the *population* of the relationship type at that time. Figure 1.2 shows an example of this: the relationship type *reads* between a *person* and a *book*. In the FOL language, a relationship type whose instances relate *n* entities is represented by an *n*-ary predicate. We shall study relationship types in Chap. 3.

The set of entity and relationship types used to observe the state of a domain is the conceptualization of that state. The description of that conceptualization, as well as other elements that will be mentioned below, is sometimes referred to as the ontology of the state, the *conceptual schema of the state,* or simply the *structural schema*. The set formed by the structural schema and the behavioral schema, which will be described later, is called the *conceptual schema*.

Not all of the entities and relationships in a domain need to be represented in an information system. This leads us to the distinction between the conceptual schema of a domain and the conceptual schema of an information system. The former describes the conceptualization of the domain, which applies irrespective of which entities and relationships will be represented in the information system. In contrast, the latter describes only a fragment of the conceptualization such that its entities and relationships are represented in the information system. For example, the conceptual schema of the domain shown in Fig. 1.3 contains five concepts, but we want to represent only three of them in the information system (*person, book,* and *reads*).

If the memory function has to maintain a representation of the state of the domain, the system has to know which entity and relationship types are to be represented, as well as their current population. Some systems may also require knowledge of the population at some or all points in the past. The entity and relationship types of interest are general knowledge about the domain, whereas the time-varying population is particular knowledge.

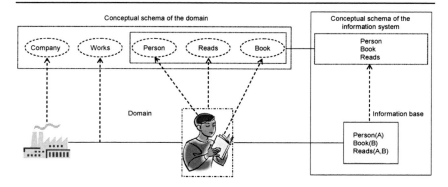

**Fig. 1.3.** Conceptual schema and information base

## 1.2.2 The Information Base

An *information base* is a representation of the entities and relationships of a domain, and their classification into entity and relationship types. The classification of an entity into an entity type or of a relationship into a relationship type is called a *fact*, and we say that the information base contains the facts about a domain.

In the FOL language, entities are represented by constants, and a fact is an atomic formula without variables. For example, let us imagine that we have a schema with two entity types, represented by the predicates *Person* and *Book*, and a relationship type, represented by the binary predicate *Reads*. Assume also that the domain contains only one person and one book and that the person is reading the book. Then, the information base will contain

- a constant *A* that represents the person;
- a constant *B* that represents the book;
- the fact *Person*(*A*), representing *A* as a person;
- the fact *Book*(*B*), representing *B* as a book;
- the fact *Reads*(*A*,*B*), representing person *A* reading book *B*.

Figure 1.3 illustrates the relationship between the conceptual schema and the information base. The conceptual schema is described in the FOL language. The information base contains three facts, described in the same language.

The information base does not exist physically. It is simply an abstract description that we use to help us analyze a schema and illustrate particular situations in a domain. Naturally, the system must maintain an internal description (e.g. in a database) of the entities and relationships in a domain, but the information base is a description closer to the conceptual schema and is not meant to be an internal description.

Unfortunately, the term *conceptual model* is not always used to mean the same thing in the literature. In addition to the meaning we have assigned to it, other meanings we have found are:

- Conceptual model = Conceptual schema
- Conceptual model = Conceptual schema + Information base

In this book, we shall use three distinct terms (conceptual model, conceptual schema, and information base) to distinguish three different concepts. The same distinction is well established in the field of databases: there are data models (for instance, relational data models), database schemas, which are written in a particular data model, and databases, which are instances of database schemas.

The term *information base* may be confused with the term *knowledge base*, which is used in the fields of deductive databases and artificial intelligence. A knowledge base is a set of representations of the knowledge about a domain. Normally, the language used to represent this knowledge is the FOL language. The knowledge may be simple facts, which are represented as atomic formulas, or general knowledge about a domain, which is represented as complex formulas. In conceptual modeling, the general knowledge about a domain is represented in the conceptual schema, while simple facts are represented in the information base. Therefore, the correspondence is knowledge base = conceptual schema + information base.

### 1.2.3 The Behavioral Schema

The *behavioral schema* specifies the valid changes in the domain state, as well as the actions that the system can perform. Changes in the domain state are domain events, and a request to perform an action is an action request event. We introduce these two event types below.

#### 1.2.3.1 Domain Events

In general, the state of the domain of an information system changes over time. Consequently, if the information base is a representation of this state, the facts of the information base will need to change over time.

We say that there is a *change* in the state of the domain at time $t$ if the entities or relationships that exist at $t$ are different from those existing at the previous point in time. More precisely, a state change is a change in the population of one or more entity or relationship types between two states: the new state (corresponding to time $t$) and the old state (corresponding to time $t - 1$).

A state change consists of a set of one or more structural events. A *structural event* is an elementary change in the population of an entity or relationship type. The precise number and meaning of structural events depend on the conceptual modeling language used. In the FOL language, there are only two kinds of structural event: insertion and removal of facts.

A *domain event* is a state change consisting of a set of one or more structural events that are perceived as a valid change in the domain. Any valid domain state change corresponds to one or more domain events. The concept of a domain event is akin to that of a transaction in the field of database systems. We shall study domain events in Chap. 11.

An example of a domain event could be a bank account transfer. Imagine that account balances are represented in the information base by the binary predicate *Balance*, and that there are two accounts with respective balances

> *Balance(Account_1,Money_1)*
> *Balance(Account_2,Money_2)*

A transfer of money $M$ from *Account_1* to *Account_2* entails the following four structural events:

> *Deletion of Balance(Account_1,Money_1)*
> *Deletion of Balance(Account_2,Money_2)*
> *Insertion of Balance(Account_1,Money_1 - M)*
> *Insertion of Balance(Account_2,Money_2 + M)*

### 1.2.3.2 Action Request Events

Information systems perform *actions*. The effect of an action is a change in the information base and/or the communication of a certain piece of information or command to one or more recipients. An *action request event* (or simply an action request) is a request to the information system to perform an action. We shall study action requests in Chap. 12.

Depending on the way in which they are initiated, action requests may be explicit, temporal, or generated. An *explicit* action request may be *external* or *induced*, depending on whether it is initiated explicitly by a user or by some other action, respectively. An external action request is initiated by a user in the context of a use case, as we shall see in Chap. 15. Most action requests are external.

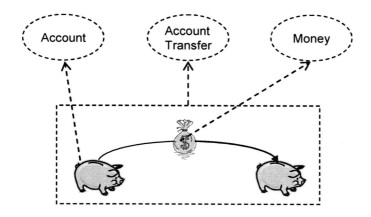

**Fig. 1.4.** Events are instances of concepts

Two important types of external action request are domain event notifications and queries. A *domain event notification* is an external action request whose only effect is a change in the information base that corresponds exactly to a single domain event. Through domain event notifications, users inform the system that a single domain event has taken place. The system has to change the information base to reflect the change in the domain.

A *query* is an external action request that provides information to the initiator of the action request. Queries do not change the information base.

A *temporal* action request is initiated simply by the passing of time. The action request occurs independently of the system.

A *generated* action request is initiated when a particular *generating condition* is satisfied. The system detects when the condition is satisfied and, at that point, generates the corresponding action request. For example, some banks offer an account with an automatic transfer service. This account is a savings account from which funds may be transferred automatically to the same account holder's checking account to cover a check or to maintain a minimum balance. In this example, the generating condition may be "the checking account balance is insufficient to cover a check or is below the minimum" and the action request generated is an account transfer.

### 1.2.3.3 Event Types

Events, either domain or action requests, are also instances of concepts. An *event type*, then, is a concept whose instances are events. Events have characteristics, which are relationships with other entities. In particular, all events have a relationship with an entity that is a time instant, which corresponds to the time at which the event occurs. Figure 1.4 is similar to Fig. 1.2, but it shows that events are also instances of concepts. The characteristics of the account transfer are the origin and destination accounts and the amount transferred.

The set of event types that are relevant to an information system and the effects of these event types are described in the behavioral schema.

The system must know the types of possible domain event. This is general knowledge about the domain. Similarly, the system must know the types of possible action request and their respective effects. This is knowledge about the functions that the system is required to perform.

## 1.2.4 Integrity Constraints

An information base is a representation of the state of a domain. An information system obtains and updates an information base from messages received through an input interface or from direct observation of the domain. In a perfect world, the information base would be an exact representation of the domain, input messages would always be correct, and the system would receive all relevant messages. In this perfect world, the information base would always contain only true facts and all relevant facts. An information base is *valid* if the facts it contains are true, and is *complete* if it contains all relevant facts.

Unfortunately, in reality it is likely that some of the input messages will communicate something that is not true. Also, the direct observation of the domain may be distorted. In such cases, some of the facts in the information base may not be true. It is also likely that the system will not receive all relevant messages, in which case the information base may not be complete.

Validity and completeness are the two components of the integrity of an information base. We say that an information base has *integrity* when all its facts are valid and it contains all relevant facts. Integrity is a very important property of an information base. Lack of integrity usually has negative consequences, which in some cases may be serious.

In most systems, total integrity can only be achieved through human intervention. In many cases, it is necessary to check the facts in the information base against the domain. For example, many retail stores need to make periodic checks to ensure that the products they have in stock actually correspond to the records in their system. It is not difficult to see that in some cases the cost of maintaining integrity will be very high and difficult to avoid.

However, it is possible to create mechanisms in a system that automatically guarantee some level of integrity. We can establish conditions for the information base such that, if they are satisfied, we may be reasonably confident of its integrity. These conditions are called *integrity constraints*, and are defined in the conceptual schema. We shall study integrity constraints in Chap. 9. An integrity constraint is a condition that may not be satisfied under some circumstances, although it is understood that the system will include mechanisms to guarantee that it is satisfied at any time. Integrity constraints are general knowledge about the domain.

For example, imagine a conceptual schema with a relationship type *assigned to,* involving the entity types *employee* and *project*. Suppose that, in the domain, all employees are always assigned to one or more projects. Then, an integrity constraint could be "all employees are assigned to a project". Once this has been defined in the conceptual schema, we may assume that the information base will always contain at least one relationship with a project for each known employee. This constraint does not guarantee total integrity (e.g. the information base could contain incorrect records of projects to which employees are assigned), but it is a condition that must necessarily be fulfilled.

An information base is *consistent* if it satisfies all the integrity constraints defined. A constraint is *violated* when it is not satisfied by the information base. When a constraint is violated, the system must produce a response to maintain consistency. Generally, violations are caused by the arrival of an incorrect message, and the response is usually to reject the message.

The set of integrity constraints defined in a conceptual schema must be *consistent* (or *satisfiable*). This means that there must be at least one state of the information base that satisfies these constraints. Some sets of constraints are only satisfiable when the information base is empty or infinite. A well-known example is the following set of constraints:

- Everybody works for somebody.
- Nobody works for himself.
- If x works for y and y works for z, then x works for z.

This set can be satisfied only by an empty or infinite information base. In conceptual modeling, we do not have a practical interest in empty or infinite information bases; therefore, we require that the set of constraints defined in a conceptual schema must be *strongly* satisfiable, that is, satisfiable in finite, nonempty information bases. If not stated otherwise, in this book we shall use the term "satisfiability" to mean *strong* satisfiability.

Most integrity constraints refer to the current population of entity and relationship types and are therefore part of the structural schema. Some constraints, however, refer to the population at two or more different time points, or to events; these are therefore part of the behavioral schema. An example of the latter possibility, which refers to events of the *account transfer* type, could be "the amount transferred must be at least 10 euros".

### 1.2.5 Derivation Rules

Through the informative function, information systems provide users with information about the state of a domain, either when they request it or under predefined circumstances.

If a system does not have an inference capability, it can provide only information received from the environment. In some cases, this may be all that is required, but users generally expect systems to have some ability to infer new facts from those already known. A very simple example is addition. If we give the system a sequence of numbers, we normally assume that it will at least be able to calculate the sum of them.

Most systems have a certain inference capability. This capability requires two main components: *derivation rules* and an *inference mechanism*. A derivation rule is a piece of general domain knowledge that defines an entity or relationship type in relation to others. Derivation rules are defined in the conceptual schema. The inference mechanism uses derivation rules to infer new information. The way in which the inference mechanism works may vary from one information system to another; it is considered to be part of the internal structure of the system and is therefore not specified in the conceptual schema. We shall study derivation rules in Chap. 8.

A derivation rule is an expression that defines how new facts can be inferred from others. The concrete form of this expression depends on the conceptual modeling language used. In many cases, the expressions are formulas expressed logically, but conventional algorithms can also be used. For example, imagine that we want to define the derivation rule corresponding to the concept *grandparent* from the concept *parent*. A logical expression might be "A person *gp* is the grandparent of a person *gc* if *gp* is a parent of a person *p* and *p* is a parent of *gc*." An equivalent algorithm that determines the four grandparents of person *gc* is:

1. Take the two parents *p1* and *p2* of *gc*.
2. Take the two parents *gp1* and *gp2* of *p1*.

3. Take the two parents *gp3* and *gp4* of *p2*.
4. The grandparents of *gc* are *gp1*, *gp2*, *gp3,* and *gp4*.

Derivation rules can be specific to a given domain (e.g. a bank), applicable to all domains of a certain class (e.g. banking), or general (e.g. statistical concepts). The conceptual schema must include all the derivation rules that can be used in a particular system, but we should explicitly define only those that are specific to our domain. The remaining derivation rules could be shared by all conceptual schemas for domains of the same class, or by all conceptual schemas.

In practice, most derivation rules infer facts about the current population of an entity or relationship type from other facts about the current population of different types, and the rules are then included as part of the structural schema. However, there is no reason why facts cannot be inferred from populations at previous points in time, or events inferred from other events, in which case the corresponding derivation rules are part of the behavioral schema.

## 1.2.6 The Principle of Necessity for Conceptual Schemas

A conclusion from the above analysis is that in order for an information system to perform its required functions, it must have some general knowledge about its domain and about the functions it has to perform. In the field of information systems, this knowledge is called a conceptual schema.

Every information system embodies a conceptual schema. Without a conceptual schema, a system could not perform any useful function. Therefore, developers need to know the conceptual schema in order to develop an information system. It is very important to realize that it is impossible to design an information system with no knowledge of its conceptual schema. The only available options are to explicitly define the schema or to have it in the minds of the designers.

Unfortunately, the need for conceptual schemas in the development of information systems is often overlooked or simply disregarded. The consequences are negative, both in theory and in practice. It is therefore useful to summarize the role of conceptual schemas in a simple principle called the principle of necessity:

> *To develop an information system it is necessary to define its conceptual schema.*

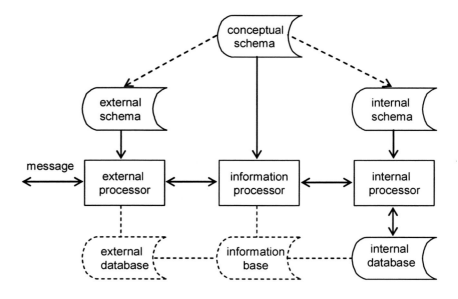

**Fig. 1.5.** ISO abstract architecture of an information system

The main purpose of conceptual modeling is to elicit the conceptual schema of the corresponding information system. Given that, as we have seen, any useful system needs a conceptual schema, we can easily reach the conclusion that conceptual modeling is an essential part of information system development.

## 1.3 The Abstract Architecture of an Information System

In the previous section, we introduced conceptual schemas. We shall now see the essential role that these schemas play in the architecture of information systems. The term *architecture* is used to refer to the main software components and their relationships. In principle, there are several possible architectures for a given system, and choosing the most suitable one for a particular system depends on several factors, including the preferred architectural style and the hardware and software platform on which it must operate. However, we do not need to consider all of these factors here. For

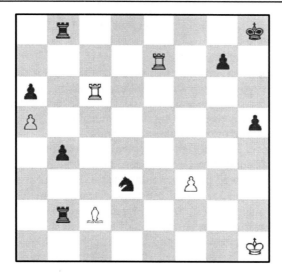

**Fig. 1.6.** A representation of the state of a chess game

our purposes, it will be sufficient to consider the abstract architecture proposed in an ISO report[3] (Fig. 1.5).

To illustrate this architecture and the role played by conceptual schemas, let us take the example of a chess-playing system that can play against human players or other systems. The conventional means of representing the state of a chess game is a drawing such as the one shown in Fig. 1.6. However, not everybody uses exactly the same representation. Different icons can be used to denote the same piece. Some users may prefer other graphical representations (e.g. a three-dimensional view), and in some cases text-based representations may be preferred (e.g. in machine–machine communication).

An *external schema* is a form of representation of the state of the domain, and an *external database* is a virtual representation of the state of the domain in this external schema. Figure 1.6 may be considered an external database. External databases are virtual, in the sense that they do not physically or permanently exist within the system.

In addition to a form of representation, external schemas also include aspects of the manipulation of this form, such as the language used to ask queries or to communicate events. In the above example, we again find a

---

[3] Griethuysen (1982).

number of possibilities. There are several textual (official) and graphical ways of representing a move (e.g. by a string such as "Rxc2" or by dragging a piece to the desired square).

There are usually several external schemas for a given domain, and it is not possible to single out one that satisfies all possible users and all possible uses. Therefore, the system must deal with several external schemas. To do so, the system needs to know the meaning of the representations used and the meaning of the alterations permitted.

Table 1.2 shows a simplified conceptual schema for the example. Each piece is of a particular type (king, queen, bishop, etc.), has a color (black or white), and is located on a particular square. Squares also have a color. For the sake of clarity, we shall use "board square" (or just "square") to denote a square that is part of the board, and "representation square" to denote a square drawn in a representation of the board (the external schema). A board square has a row code and a column code, which define its position on the board. The conceptual schema may also include a derivation rule establishing that a board square is *free* if no piece is placed on it; otherwise, it is *occupied*.

**Table 1.2.** Conceptual schema for the chess-playing example, in the FOL language

| Entity types | Relationship types |
| --- | --- |
| Piece | LocatedAt (piece,square) |
| Square | HasType (piece,pieceType) |
| PieceType | PieceColor (piece,color) |
| Color | SquareColor (square,color) |
| Row | SquareInColumn (square,column) |
| Column | SquareInRow (square,row) |
| RowCode | RowHasCode (row,rowCode) |
| ColumnCode | ColumnHasCode (column,columnCode) |

There is a single conceptual schema and there may be one or more external schemas. External schemas are defined in terms of the conceptual schema. For instance, the correspondence between the conceptual schema in Table 1.2 and the external schema in Fig. 1.6 is as follows:

- The board consists of 64 small representation squares corresponding to the board squares.
- Representation squares are given the same colors as the corresponding board squares.
- Each piece has a different icon, depending on its type and color.

- If a piece $p$ is located on a board square $s$, then the icon corresponding to $p$ is placed over the representation square corresponding to $s$.

The correspondence between manipulations and external events is defined similarly. For example, when the user drags a piece to a representation square, the conceptual meaning is a move of that piece to a board square, where it is then placed.

The *external processor* is the architectural component that interacts with users. In theory, there is an external processor for each external schema. These processors receive messages from users (in the language of the external schema), translate them into the language of the conceptual schema, and forward them to the information processor.

The *information processor* is the component that handles the messages sent by the users and performs any active function that may be delegated to the system. Specifically, if a message reports a domain event, the information processor applies the corresponding effect function and checks that the resulting state is consistent. In the example given here, if a new move is received, the information processor has to check whether the move is valid and, if so, update the state of the game.

To perform these tasks, the information processor needs to access and alter the state of the domain. It cannot use an external representation, since such representations are generally only partial and include aspects that bear no relation to the nature of the domain.

For example, if the system were to use the representation shown in Fig. 1.6 to check whether moving the black pawn to Column 2, Row 3 is a valid move, the information processor would have to check (among other things) that the representation square for Column 2, Row 3 does not have an icon on it. Neither "representation square" nor "icon" is a relevant concept in the chess domain. It is preferable for the information processor to ask questions such as "Is the board square in Column 2, Row 3 free?", where both "board square" and "free" are defined in the conceptual schema. For similar reasons, as we shall see in a moment, the information processor is also unable to use an internal representation.

The procedure that is most natural to the information processor involves using a representation based on the conceptual schema, which is the information base. The information base is virtual, however, since it does not exist physically within the system. When the information processor asks itself questions such as "Is the board square in Column 2, Row 3 free?", it behaves as if the information base really existed, when in reality the question will be sent to the internal processor, which will then answer it using the physical database.

The representation of the state that the system has to maintain internally must allow efficient execution, among other things. This means that the internal representation must be designed taking into account technical factors. The *internal schema* is the form used internally by the system to represent the state of the domain, and the *internal database* is the representation of the state in that schema. Only the internal database exists physically. The internal schema also comprises the set of operations that may be invoked on the database.

An internal schema for the example considered here that would be almost optimal in terms of the amount of space used (although not for other technical considerations) might be a file with the following record structure:

Pieces (PieceType, Color, Row, Column)

In a record, PieceType might use one character (K for king, Q for queen, R for rook, and so on), Color might use one bit (0 for white and 1 for black), and Row and Column might use a single byte (number 1…8). Internal schemas, like external ones, are defined with respect to the conceptual schema. In our example, the correspondence might be:

- The file has a record for each piece that is on the board.
- The first field indicates the piece type, the second its color, the third the row number of the board square on which the piece is located, and the fourth the column number.
- The color of the board square is not represented explicitly. The external processor may infer it by adding the numbers of the row and column: if the result is even, the board square is black; otherwise, it is white.

The internal processor receives the commands issued by the information processor and executes them, possibly accessing the internal database. For example, if it receives a command (in this case, a question) such as "Is the board square in Column 2, Row 3 free?", the internal processor will check whether there is a record in the above file such that Row = 3 and Column = 2. If there is no such record, the answer to the question will be positive; otherwise, it will be negative. In order to perform its task, the internal processor needs to know the internal schema, including its correspondence with the conceptual schema.

Modern architectures of information systems are designed with three logical layers: presentation, domain, and data management. The equivalent of the external processor is located in the presentation layer, that of the information processor in the domain layer, and that of the internal processor in the data management layer.

## 1.4 Requirements Engineering

In the previous section, we looked at the role of conceptual schemas in the architecture of information systems. Now we shall examine their role in the development of such systems.

Conceptual schemas are the common base of external and internal schemas and their processors. Therefore, it is clearly not possible to design the architecture of an information system without a conceptual schema. Conceptual modeling must precede system design.

The stage that precedes system design is called *requirements engineering*. One of the clearest definitions of this stage is:

> Requirements engineering is the branch of software engineering concerned with the real-world goals for, functions of, and constraints on software systems. It is also concerned with the relationship of these factors to precise specifications of software behavior, and to their evolution over time and across software families.[4]

Requirements engineering is a complex process, because it involves a number of parties (users, designers, managers, etc.) who may all have different views, needs, and interests. Requirements engineering consists of three processes:

- requirements elicitation;
- requirements specification;
- requirements validation.

During *requirements elicitation,* the future users and the designers of the system analyze their particular problems and needs and the characteristics of the domain. On the basis of this analysis, they decide on the changes to be introduced into the domain and the functions that should be performed by the new information system. Requirements elicitation is a crucial process, because it determines a significant proportion of the final success or failure of the overall project. In this phase, the configuration of the future system is decided, so any error in the decision often means that users will ultimately be presented with an inadequate system.

During this process, a conceptual schema of the existing and/or desired domain may be created if this is considered necessary to achieve a common understanding of the domain(s).

In the *requirements specification* process, the functional and nonfunctional requirements of the new system are defined. The result is a set of documents (called specifications) that precisely describe the system that

---

[4] Zave (1997).

the users require and that the designers have to design and build. Functional requirements describe what the system must do, while nonfunctional requirements describe the global properties of the system, such as response time or portability.

The conceptual schema of an information system is the specification of its functional requirements. The conceptual schema specifies all the functions (memory, informative and active) that the system must perform and, together with the specification of the nonfunctional requirements, corresponds to the system specification.

During *requirements validation*, the specifications are checked to ensure that they meet user requirements. In this phase, it is vital that the users understand exactly what the future system will be like before it is built. This is a crucial phase that can only be performed satisfactorily if the requirements have been precisely described.

Validation can be performed in several nonexclusive ways. Two of the best known are:

- To present the conceptual schema (and the system specification) in a language and form that are easily understood by users. If the conceptual modeling language used is not completely understandable to the users, it will be necessary to provide assistance in interpreting the language, to use more familiar languages (not excluding natural language), or to provide explanations of the schema and its behavior. When the conceptual schema is large, as is often the case, it may be necessary to divide its structure into fragments or views.

- To build (partial) prototypes of the system. If the conceptual modeling language used is formal, prototypes can be generated automatically. This form of validation is usually more effective than the above method, but also more expensive.

To summarize, then, conceptual schemas are created during the requirements engineering stage and form the basis of the next stage, system design.

## 1.5 Quality of Conceptual Schemas

Now that we have seen what conceptual schemas are and the role that they play in the architecture of a system and in the system development process, we shall provide details in this section of the properties that these schemas must have if they are to fulfill their roles effectively. The *quality* of a conceptual schema is the degree to which these properties are present.

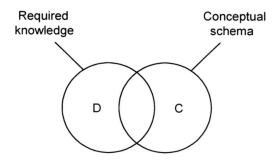

**Fig. 1.7.** Completeness and correctness

The quality of a conceptual schema should not be considered as an afterthought — it should be aimed for in each step of the conceptual modeling process.

A well-known property of conceptual schemas is the 100% principle, or completeness, which states that

> All relevant general static and dynamic aspects, i.e. all rules, laws, etc., of the universe of discourse should be described in the conceptual schema. The information system cannot be held responsible for not meeting those described elsewhere, including in particular those in application programs.[5]

A conceptual schema is *complete* if it satisfies this condition. The rationale behind this principle is that a conceptual schema is the definition of the general domain knowledge that the information system needs to perform its functions; therefore, the conceptual schema must include all the required knowledge. If the conceptual schema is executable or the system is generated automatically from it, it follows that the system cannot contain anything not included in the schema. The principle of necessity for conceptual schemas that we saw in Sect. 1.2.6 can be seen as a consequence of the 100% principle.

An important conclusion that can be drawn from this principle is that the conceptual modeling language used must enable all of the domain's relevant aspects, including structural and behavioral aspects, to be described.

A conceptual schema is *correct* if the knowledge that it defines is true for the domain and relevant to the functions that the system must perform. Figure 1.7 is a representation of the relationship between completeness and correctness. The left circle, D, represents the domain knowledge that the system needs to perform its functions. The right circle, C, represents the

---

[5] Griethuysen (1982).

knowledge defined in the conceptual schema. In a complete conceptual schema, D is a subset of C. In a correct conceptual schema, C is a subset of D. In a complete and correct conceptual schema, D = C.

Conceptual schemas are described in a particular conceptual modeling language. This language will have a set of rules that must be respected. A conceptual schema is *syntactically correct* if it respects all the rules of the language in which it is written. The syntactic correctness of a schema is independent of the domain.

A conceptual schema should be *understandable* to its relevant audience. All members of the relevant audience should be able to correctly understand the part of the conceptual schema that is relevant to them.

In some cases, the same piece of knowledge about a domain may be expressed in two or more ways in a given language. The condition of *simplicity* states that simple schemas are to be preferred, that is, schemas that use fewer language constructs or fewer complex constructs. Simplicity is related to understandability, because simple schemas are obviously easier to understand.

Another property that has become popular is the *principle of conceptualization*, which states that

> A conceptual model should only include conceptually relevant aspects, both static and dynamic, of the universe of discourse, thus excluding all aspects of (external or internal) data representation, physical data organization and access as well as aspects of particular external user representation such as message formats, data structures, etc.[6]

The justification for this is similar to that used in the previous point: if a conceptual schema is the basis for a system design, it should not include any design aspect, thus leaving the designers free to decide on all such characteristics. On the other hand, when a schema focuses only on conceptual aspects, it is simpler and therefore easier for users to understand. A conceptual schema that satisfies this condition is said to be *design-independent*.

Finally, we come to the property of *stability*, which is also referred to as flexibility, extensibility, or modifiability. A conceptual schema is stable if minor changes in the properties of the domain or in the users' requirements do not entail major changes in the schema.

---

[6] Griethuysen (1982).

# 1.6 A Brief History of Conceptual Modeling

The conceptual modeling of information systems, as we know it today, is the fruit of research and development that have been carried out since the 1960s. In this section we give a brief account of its evolution from early logical models to the current situation. We include a few references to key works. Many more are given in other chapters of the book.

## 1.6.1 Logical Models

Young and Kent (1958) presented what was probably the first specification language for information systems. Their objective was to define a system at an abstract level, independently of its implementation. To achieve this objective, they proposed a model consisting of input and output documents. Documents contain "information sets", which may be related. Output documents are produced when an input document is received or when a certain condition is satisfied.

The model proposed by Young and Kent was the first of the *logical* models. A committee of CODASYL formed in 1959 proposed a similar model, called "An Information Algebra" (Bosak et al 1962). These models view information systems as systems that receive inputs, apply a transformation to them, and produce outputs. The models are called logical because the inputs, outputs, and transformation are described without reference to their physical aspects, such as data representation or file organization. In logical models, the conceptual schema is embedded in the definition of the inputs, outputs and transformation.

Of the logical models, PSL (Problem Statement Language) made an impact on academia, in the early 1970s, mainly owing to its stated goal of automatically generating the physical system from its specification. This goal was not achieved, but a pioneer computer-aided software engineering (CASE) tool called PSA (Problem Statement Analyzer) was developed (Teichroew and Sayani 1971; Teichroew and Hershey 1977). A language that had a more substantial impact on the profession was SADT (Marca and McGowan 1988).

At about the same time, the work of Langefors (1974) came to prominence in European research circles. Langefors was concerned with the relationships between information systems and their domains. His work was the origin of what was termed "information analysis", a precursor to structured analysis.

Logical models were predominant in professional practice for more than 30 years. The most widely used variant was "structured analysis" (Gane and Sarson 1979; DeMarco 1979), a follow-up to "structured design", which in turn was a follow-up to "structured programming". Structured analysis appeared in the late 1970s, and until the 1990s formed the basis of most CASE tools. Over time, structured analysis partially converged with conceptual models by adopting elements of structural modeling and the concept of event.

### 1.6.2 Semantic Data Models

Database management systems started to appear during the 1960s. In the early 1970s, three data models dominated the field and competed among themselves: hierarchical, network, and relational models. All three were based on what Kent (1978) called the "record model", which allows efficient processing of data but is far removed from the conceptual model. Record models are to databases what logical models are to information systems.

In 1972, the ANSI/X3/SPARC committee established a study group with the aim of investigating the potential for standardization in the area of database management systems. The main result was a report (ANSI 1975; Tsichritzis and Klug 1978) that had a significant impact. For our purposes here, the main contribution of the report was to identify a new database description level between the external and internal levels, that is, the conceptual level:

> …the Study Group has taken note of the reality of a third level, which we chose to call the "conceptual", that has always been but never before called out explicitly. It represents the enterprise's view of the structure it is attempting to model in the data base. This view is that which is informally invoked when there is a dispute between the user and the programmer over exactly what was meant by program specifications. The Study group contends that in the data base world it **must** be made explicit and, in fact, made known to the data base management system. The proposed mechanism for doing this is the conceptual schema. The other two views of data, internal and external, must necessarily be consistent with the view expressed by the conceptual schema.[7]

The report appeared around the same time as the first semantic data models and fostered the development of many more during the 1970s and 1980s. Conceptual modeling of information systems has its origin in these semantic data models. From an academic perspective, one semantic model that had a significant impact was Abrial's binary model (Abrial 1974).

---

[7] ANSI (1975).

However, the most popular semantic model has proved to be Chen's ER (Entity–Relationship) model, published in Chen (1976). Codd (1979) provided an extension to the relational model (of his own invention) that allowed it "to capture more meaning".

Semantic data models have frequently been influenced by the area of artificial intelligence known as knowledge representation. The central problem in this area is how to represent knowledge about a domain in such a way as to make it possible to build machines that are able to act intelligently in the domain. This same problem affects semantic data models, so it is not surprising that there have been mutual influences. Modern knowledge representation languages have their roots in the semantic networks proposed by Quillian in 1966 (Quillian 1968). Later, Minsky introduced the concept of a *frame*, which formed the basis of several popular languages, such as KRL, KL-ONE and PSN (Mylopoulos and Levesque 1984, Brachman and Levesque 1985; Davis et al. 1993).

### 1.6.3 Conceptual Models of Information Systems

The ANSI/X3/SPARC report identified the need for a conceptual schema of databases. However, a database is only one of the components of an information system and the report was not specific about the principles and contents of the conceptual schema. As a result, in 1977 the ISO/TC97/SC5 committee created a study group with the aim of defining concepts for conceptual modeling languages. The work done by this group was reflected in a seminal report published in 1982 under the title *Concepts and Terminology for the Conceptual Schema and the Information Base* (Griethuysen 1982; Jardine 1984).

As was the case with the ANSI report, this ISO report appeared at the same time as several conceptual models, many of which were extensions of semantic data models, and prompted the development of new models. The large number of existing proposals needed to be analyzed and compared. With this aim, the IFIP WG8.1 work group launched a series of conferences called CRIS (Comparative Review of Information Systems Design Methodologies), which were held five times between 1982 and 1994 (Olle et al. 1982, 1983, 1986, 1988; Verrijn-Stuart and Olle 1994). At the 1982 conference, 13 methodologies representing the state of the art at that time were presented. The central element in each of these methodologies was the conceptual model.

The field of conceptual modeling has been influenced by related fields such as knowledge representation and software engineering. Indeed, these three areas have several points in common, which are often discussed in joint meetings. The first two of these meetings were held in the USA in 1980 and 1982 (Brodie and Zilles 1981; Brodie et al. 1984). One of the first conceptual modeling languages to explicitly acknowledge the influence of other fields was RML, a precursor of Telos (Borgida et al. 1985; Greenspan et al. 1994).

### 1.6.4 Object Orientation

The first effects of the object-orientation wave on the conceptual modeling of information systems appeared in the late 1980s. The idea of basing behavioral schema on entity types had a great impact on behavioral modeling.

During the 1990s, various object-oriented conceptual modeling languages appeared, often as part of information system development methods. This did not reflect a diversity of theories or concepts, but rather notational differences. A number of standardization initiatives emerged as a result, one of which was instigated by the Object Management Group (OMG) in 1996. The main result was the Unified Modeling Language (UML), adopted by the OMG in 1997.

## 1.7 Bibliographical Notes

Sundgren (1975, Chap. 5) and Le Moigne (1978) described the functions of information systems in detail, although the terminology they used is now a little outdated. Johannesson (1995) gave a more modern view. Jackson (2001) provided many reflections on system perspectives and the functions that systems may perform. There was a special issue of *Communications of the ACM* (ACM 1996) devoted to knowledge discovery in databases, an advanced component of the informative function. Motro (1994) analyzed the possible intensional answers to extensional questions. Papazoglou (1995) discussed the requirements for answering intensional queries. Nowadays, the *autonomous* execution mode of informative and active functions is often formulated using agents. Imam and Kodratoff (1997) gave an overall view of agents. There was a special issue of *Communications of the ACM* (ACM 1994) devoted to intelligent agents.

Each chapter of this book includes references to the most relevant work for the topic covered. Here, we mention only a few texts that provide an overview of conceptual modeling. An introduction can be found in Nijssen and Halpin (1989, Chap. 2) and Loucopoulos and Karakostas (1995, Chap. 4). (Boman et al. 1997) is a textbook on conceptual modeling. Borgida

(1985a) and Borgida et al. (1985) emphasized principles, with specific reference to languages. Loucopoulos (1992) and Rolland and Cauvet (1992) provided a complete overview of conceptual models and conceptual modeling, including numerous references. Mylopoulos (1998) offered a modern view of the field.

The term *ontology* is used to mean a number of different things. Guarino and Giaretta (1995) gave an analysis of these meanings. In this chapter, we have adopted the definition proposed by Gruber (1993). The principle of necessity for conceptual schemas was suggested by Olivé (2005).

Several conferences deal with the area of conceptual modeling. The most important series of conceptual modeling conferences is the *International Conferences on Conceptual Modeling* (known as *ER*), which was inaugurated in 1979, and these conferences have been held annually since 1985.[8]

There are several good textbooks on requirements engineering. (Davis 1993) is a classic, although it does not focus specifically on information systems. Loucopoulos and Karakostas (1997) emphasized the explanation of the three processes that we have mentioned. Sommerville and Sawyer (1997) gave many practical recommendations. Nuseibeh and Easterbrook (2000) provided an excellent overview of the field. Boman et al. (1997) offered a detailed explanation of the relationship between conceptual modeling and requirements engineering. Rolland and Prakash (2000) placed conceptual modeling in the general context of modern requirements engineering.

Bubenko (1977) was one of the first researchers to focus on the validation and verification of conceptual schemas. Gulla (1996) and Dalianis and Johannesson (1997) discussed the existing approaches to schema validation and described a prototype and the architecture of a schema explanation component.

The principles of 100% and conceptualization were first outlined in the ISO report mentioned above (Griethuysen 1982). Batini et al. (1992, Chap. 6) and Davis (1993, Chap. 3) gave a detailed description of the desirable properties of conceptual schemas. Lindland et al. (1994) developed an influential framework for quality in conceptual modeling, which was evaluated in (Moody et al. 2003). Moody (1998) completed a list of quality factors with metrics for measuring them. Katasonov and Sakkinen (2006) presented a framework for quality in the more general context of requirements engineering.

---

[8] The name was originally *International Conference on the Entity–Relationship Approach*.

Fry and Sibley (1976) gave an excellent summary of the evolution and state of the art of database management systems in the early 1970s. Kent (1978) provided a critical analysis of these systems. A similar summary of business system analysis techniques for the same period was given by Couger (1973). Hull and King (1987) and Peckham and Maryanski (1988) analyzed the general features of semantic data models and described and compared the best-known models at that time. Fowler (1997) included a historical description of object orientation in conceptual modeling. See (Booch et al. 1999) for a brief history of UML. Mylopoulos (1998) presented a brief history of conceptual modeling.

A partial, preliminary version of this chapter appeared in Olivé (2000a). The author gratefully acknowledges the permission given by Artech House to reuse that work here.

# 2 Entity Types

Determining the entity types that exist in a given domain and are relevant to an information system is a fundamental task in conceptual modeling. A clear understanding of entity types and their characteristics is therefore necessary. This is the focus of this chapter.

Entity types may be grounded in several disciplines. For the purposes of conceptual modeling, the most appropriate discipline is probably cognitive science and, more specifically, the concept and classification theories that have been developed in that science. The first section of this chapter briefly reviews these theories. Additional material may be found in the bibliographical references cited at the end of the chapter.

In the second section, we show that some concepts are natural, while others are human-made. An important task in information systems development is concept design.

In the third section, we define entity types. The concepts, as they are understood in cognitive science, are the starting point. In the fourth section, we study how to represent the classification of objects into entity types in an information system. The fifth section explains the concept of data types.

## 2.1 Introduction

Classification is an activity that we can perform efficiently and that we need in order to structure our perceptions of the world and our knowledge about it. It is a basic activity, because without it we can neither understand the world around us nor act on it in the way we do.

Classification is also fundamental for information systems, which, among other things, maintain a representation of the state of a domain. The same happens in the general field of computer science.

Classification assumes the existence of a concept and of an object to be classified. The classification operation consists in determining whether or not the object is an instance of the concept. Classification may seem to be a simple operation, but it becomes very complex when we ask ourselves what concepts are and when we try to explain how we determine whether or not an object is an instance of a concept.

In cognitive science, several theories have been developed about the nature of classification and concepts; they deserve to be reviewed, if only briefly, owing to their influence in conceptual modeling.

### 2.1.1 Definitional Concepts

The classical theory of concepts states that concepts, called *definitional* concepts, are sets of properties that we humans are able to observe in objects. This set of properties is called the *intension* of the concept. For example, the concept of a house could consist of the properties "is a building", "is a place where people live", "has a fixed geographical location", "has an owner", etc. According to the classical theory, an object is an instance of a concept if it has all the properties of that concept. Therefore, the classification operation consists in checking that the properties of the object include the properties of the concept.

The same object may be an instance of several concepts. For example, an object might be an instance of the concepts *book* and *gift*, if it has all the properties of *book* and *gift*.

Very often a property *P* of a concept is redundant, in the sense that if an object has all the other properties then it also necessarily has *P*. In the *house* example, the property "has a fixed geographical location" is redundant, because if an object is a building then it must have a fixed geographical location. For this reason, the properties of a concept are classified as defining or nondefining. The *defining* properties are the necessary and sufficient properties for an object to be considered an instance of the concept. The *nondefining* properties are redundant. If an object has the defining properties, it also has the nondefining ones. Therefore, the operation of classification simply involves checking that the properties of the object include the defining properties of the concept.

An instance of a concept has all its properties (defining and nondefining), but it may have other specific properties. For example, a given house may also have the properties "is located in Toronto", "is old", and "is expensive". In this respect, a concept is an abstraction of the properties of its instances, and classification is an abstraction operation, because it focuses only on some properties of the objects and ignores all the others.

## 2.1.2 Functions of a Concept

Classification serves several basic functions in our mental life. For our purposes, the most important ones are cognitive economy and inference ability. Classification provides *cognitive economy* because it allows us to structure knowledge about objects into two levels: concept and instance. At the concept level, we find the properties (both defining and nondefining) common to all instances of the concept. At the instance level, we find only the concept of which the object is an instance, and the particular properties of that instance. In the absence of classification, we would have to associate every instance with all of its properties. Classification reduces the amount of information we have to remember, communicate, and process; the extent to which it is reduced depends on the number of properties of the concept.

*Inference ability* is related to the fact that not all the properties of a concept need to be defining. There may be many nondefining properties which can be inferred without one needing to observe them directly. For example, the concept of a house includes the nondefining property "has an owner". Once we have classified an object as a house we may infer that it has an owner, even if we have not observed this directly.

## 2.1.3 Prototypical Concepts

The classical view of concepts has dominated scientific thought for many years. In recent decades, however, this view has been seriously undermined by the work of psychologists, linguists, and philosophers. The most important problem encountered is that we are not able to give a clear and precise definition of everyday concepts, even though we do not find it difficult to classify objects into those concepts. Take, for example, the concept of a *dog*. Except for biologists and other experts who are able to provide a precise definition based on its morphology or chromosomes, most people cannot give a definition of this kind and instead rely on nondefining properties (such as the shape or the sound) to define it, even though these properties may be shared by completely different objects.

The difficulties inherent in the classical view have led scientists to explore alternative theories that explain concepts which are not strictly definitional. One of these theories is based on a probabilistic view. In this view, there is a probability that each property of a concept will be present in the instances of that concept. Some properties will be typical of the concept, because they are shared by many instances. Other properties, however, will be atypical, in the sense that they are present only in a few instances. In this approach, the membership of an object in a concept will be more or less likely and not absolute as it was in the definitional view.

A probabilistic concept may be represented by a prototype. A *prototype* is a set of clearly perceivable properties that some instances of the concept, but not all of them, have. A prototype describes only the properties of the best exemplars of the concept. A concept represented by a prototype is called a *prototypical* concept. An object is classified into a prototypical concept if it shares a sufficient number of its properties. The degree of an object's membership in a concept will be a function of the number of properties shared with the prototype.

For example, the prototype of *bird* could be the set of properties "feathered", "flies", "small", "eats insects", and "sings". Not all objects that we classify as birds have these properties: the most popular example in our field is that of penguins, which do not fly. Many of the properties of a prototype are nondefining, but they are very effective in classification terms. The defining properties of the concept may not be easily perceivable. For example, the definition of *bird* will be based on biological facts that we cannot easily perceive.

### 2.1.4 Exemplar-Based Concepts

Both definitional and prototypical concepts are sets of properties that we should somehow store in our minds. However, some researchers challenge this mental association between a concept and a set of properties, and they prefer a theory of concepts based on *exemplars*. According to this theory, a concept is a set of exemplars, which may include all the known instances of that concept or only a subset of them. The theory holds that our minds store those exemplars associated with the name of the concept.

In the exemplar view, the classification of an object into a concept consists in comparing the object with the exemplars of the concept and calculating the degree of similarity of the object to the exemplars. The similarity determines the probability of classifying the object as an instance of the concept.

## 2.2 Design of Concepts

Many concepts may be considered natural, in the sense that their instances are objects that we consider natural in the world we live in, and are familiar to many people, such as the concepts of a tree, dog, temperature, hurricane, or meeting. Dictionaries give definitions of these concepts, which help us to learn them and are a basis for communication between people. Some of these concepts may be an object of study in a scientific field; in this case, they are given more precise definitions.

Often, however, the existing natural concepts are insufficient for people to act effectively in a concrete domain, or their definition is not precise enough. When this happens, it is necessary to invent new concepts or to give a more precise definition to an existing one. For example, in business it has been necessary to invent the concept of *leasing* in order to differentiate a particular kind of contract. Another example is the concept of a *customer*, which many companies need to define precisely in order to distinguish between people (or other companies) who buy, people who have bought in the past but not now, people who will possibly buy in the future but have not yet done so, etc. Different departments in a company may have different views on what a *customer* is. If they want to share the concept of a *customer*, they will need to agree on a common definition.

A further example is the concept of a *project*, as used by a company in the domain of project planning and control. Dictionaries give generic definitions of the concept, such as "a carefully planned piece of work to get information about something, to build something, to improve something, etc."[1] These are insufficient definitions. The company will need to design (or redesign) the concept to make it operational. The company may add, for instance, properties such as "it must be approved by an authorized body", "it must have a plan", or "it has a leader".

Defining new concepts and providing more precise definitions are design activities that require the participation and agreement of all the people who have to use those concepts in the corresponding domain. The design of concepts is a very important task in requirements engineering for information systems.

## 2.3 Definition of Entity Types

Entity types are one of the most important elements in conceptual schemas and they play a fundamental role in the memory, informative, and active functions of information systems. Defining the entity types that are relevant to a particular information system is a crucial task in conceptual modeling. In this section, we study what is meant by an entity type and what its characteristics are.

---

[1] Longman Dictionary of Contemporary English, 2005.

Entity types may be defined in several ways. A compact definition that captures their essence and is reasonably precise might be: "An entity type is a concept whose instances at a given time are identifiable individual objects that are considered to exist in the domain at that time." The objects that are instances of an entity type are called entities. An object may be an instance of several entity types.

First of all, this definition states that an entity type is a concept. Therefore, the concept theories developed in cognitive science are, in theory, applicable to entity types. However, most of the work in conceptual modeling is based on definitional concepts. In this book, we also adopt this view of concepts.

Secondly, the definition states that an instance of an entity type is an individual object. This excludes the possibility of entities that correspond to two or more objects in the domain. Normally, this aspect does not pose problems, but doubts may arise in some cases. For example, if *married couple* is an entity type, what are its instances? According to the definition, such an instance cannot be two objects (or people, in this particular example). It must be a single object: in this case, an abstract object that represents a couple. This object will be related to the two people who form the couple, but these relationships will be instances of relationship types, as we shall see in the next chapter.

Thirdly, the definition states that the instances of entity types must be identifiable objects. This means that there must be some mechanism in the domain that allows one object to be differentiated from another, and that this mechanism is known to the information system. Such mechanisms are the references, which are discussed in Chap. 5. According to the definition, domain objects that cannot be identified cannot be entities. This situation does sometimes arise: for example, in the domain of a forest we may have objects that are instances of a *tree*; if, however, we cannot differentiate between the (many) trees in the forest then *tree* cannot be an entity type.

Finally, the definition states that the instances of an entity type at a given time point are objects "... that are considered to exist in the domain at that time." This is the hardest aspect of the definition, but it is important in modeling dynamic domains. An object may be considered an instance of an entity type at one time point, but not so at another one.

The definition is neutral with respect to "who" believes an object exists in the domain at a given time, but we may assume that normally this is the people who observe and act in the domain. Doubts may sometimes arise because, although some people may believe that an object exists at a point in time, other people may believe that it does not (at least at that point). In such cases, an effort must be made to make the definition of the concept more precise and to reach agreement.

An example of a problem-free concept might be that of a *department* in the domain of a company. If an object is an instance of this entity type at a given time, it is because the object exists at that time. If the object has not been created (i.e. does not exist) at time *t*, it cannot be a department at *t*. If a department object existed previously but does not exist now, it is not a current instance of the department concept.

An example that might, in some situations, cause confusion is that of a *person*. According to the definition, an object may be considered an instance of a person at a given time if it exists at that time. But what exactly does existing at a given time mean? In some domains, people who have died do not exist anymore, but in other domains it may be reasonable to consider that, once born, people exist forever; if necessary, a distinction can be made between people who are *alive* and *dead*.

Another example that may cause confusion is the entity type *raise request*. An instance of this entity type is a request for an increase in salary by an employee, at some instant. Let us assume that a company takes into consideration the requests of its employees, that these requests are processed during a time interval in which managers study them, and that eventually a decision is made. In this example, a request may be considered to exist only at a given point in time (when the request is made), that it exists while it is being processed (until the decision is made), or that it exists forever. Which of these is the most suitable interpretation of the request must be defined in the domain. This decision will have an effect on the answer to questions such as "What raise requests do we have at this moment?"

A few additional examples of entity types are provided below to illustrate the explanation given above:

- *Stamp in collection*. In a system that records the state of a stamp collection, an instance of this entity type at a given time would be a stamp that is part of the collection at that time. A specific stamp will be an instance of *Stamp in collection* while it is part of the collection. Stamps must be identifiable, even when there are two or more exemplars of the same issue. If it is not possible to distinguish between two stamps of the same issue, then it will be necessary to define a different entity type, such as *Stamp issue in collection*. An instance of this type would therefore be a stamp issue of which there are one or more exemplars in the collection.

- *Project team*. An instance of this type is an abstract object. It could be considered that, in the domain, at a given time, there is an instance of *Project team* for each project existing at that time. This instance may be related to each person who has worked on the project for a certain time. It can also be related to the person who manages the team.

- *Software fault.* This may be an entity type if its instances are identifiable. We may assume that software faults have an identifier (a number, for example). It can be considered that an instance of this type exists at a given time if it has been reported at that time or before, and has not yet been solved. Alternatively, we may consider that a software fault exists because it has been reported and as a result exists forever. In this case, we might also have the entity type *Corrected software fault*, to represent the software faults that have already been corrected. Note that the answers to questions such as "Which software faults do we have?" will be quite different depending on the interpretation.

- *Metal.* An entity of this type is a specific metal, such as iron, copper, or gold.

### 2.3.1 Names

An entity type must have a name, which must be unique in a schema. The names must be significant to the persons who act in the domain. It is important to give "good" names to entity types. A useful guideline is that the name of an entity type must be a common noun in the singular form, possibly accompanied by one or more adjectives. When this guideline is followed, and $N$ is the name of an entity type, the following sentence is well formed:

> *An instance of this entity type is a (an) N.*

Note that the examples given up to now in this chapter follow this guideline (person, department, tree, married couple, etc.). However, the guideline would not be followed (and the sentence would not be well formed) by plural nouns (such as *customers* or *people*), adjectives (such as *expensive*), and verbs (such as *to buy a product*), etc.

Entity types should, when necessary, have an explicit definition in natural language. The definition must be comprehensible to both users and designers.

### 2.3.2 Population

The *population* of an entity type $E$ at a time $t$ is the set of instances of $E$ that exist in the domain at $t$. In general, the population of an entity type is time-varying during the lifetime of the information system. However, two cases of entity types are particularly noteworthy: constant and permanent entity types.

An entity type is *constant* if its population is the same at all times. For example, *Metal* and *River* are likely to be constant in most information systems.

An entity type is *permanent* if its instances never cease to be instances of it. The population of a permanent entity type cannot decrease. If $E$ is a permanent entity type and $e$ is an instance of $E$ at $t$, then $e$ will be an instance of $E$ at any later time (during the lifetime of the information system). For example, *Invoice* is likely to be permanent in most information systems. Once an invoice has been issued, it exists forever. It is easy to see that constant types are permanent too.

### 2.3.3 Subsumption

In general, the population of an entity type is independent of that of the other types defined in a schema. However, in some cases the population of an entity type must necessarily be included in that of another type. We say that $E_2$ *subsumes* $E_1$ if all instances of $E_1$ must also be instances of $E_2$. One can also say that $E_1$ is a *subtype* of $E_2$ and that $E_2$ is a *supertype* of $E_1$. For example, *Person* subsumes *Woman*: the population of *Woman* must necessarily be included in that of *Person*. *Woman* is a subtype of *Person* and *Person* a supertype of *Woman*.

It is interesting to see how subsumption is interpreted in the definitional theory of concepts, which we studied in Sect. 2.1. As stated in relation to that theory, a concept is defined by a set of defining properties, and an object is an instance of a concept if the object has the defining properties of that concept. Therefore, according to the definitional theory, a concept $C_2$ subsumes a concept $C_1$ if the defining properties of $C_2$ are a subset of those of $C_1$ (or, in other words, if $C_2$ has fewer properties than $C_1$). The concept of *Person* subsumes *Woman* because women have the defining properties of persons and of other concepts (such as being female).

The subsumption of entity types happens very often and has profound implications for conceptual modeling. A detailed study of subsumption is undertaken in Chap. 10.

## 2.4 Representation in an Information System

In order to be able to perform their functions, information systems must have a representation of their domain. With respect to the topics studied in this chapter, this means that an information system must have a representation of:

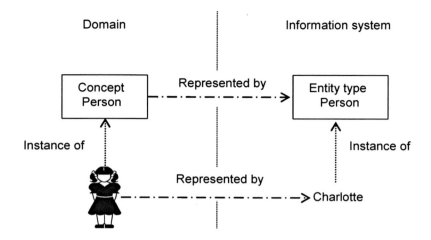

**Fig. 2.1.** Classification of objects in a domain

- the objects in the domain;
- the entity types;
- the classification of objects into entity types

(see Fig. 2.1).

The objects in the domain are represented in the information base. Recall that the information base is virtual (in the sense that it does not necessarily exist), but it is a representation of the knowledge that the system has of the state of the domain.

The information base contains a symbol (which is, in general, chosen arbitrarily) for each domain object represented in the information system. In Fig. 2.1, the person named *Charlotte* is represented in the information base by the symbol "Charlotte". We say that the object is represented by that symbol, or that the domain object has that symbol assigned to it in the information base, or that the symbol denotes the domain object. The concrete form of the symbol is irrelevant at the conceptual level. We only need to assume that such symbols do exist, and that there is a biunique correspondence between the domain objects represented in the information system and the symbols that represent them in the information base. In this book, we normally designate these symbols by words beginning with a capital letter. When confusion is unlikely to arise, however, we do not distinguish between objects and their symbols.

Entity types are represented in the conceptual schema. The schema contains a symbol (in general, chosen arbitrarily) for each relevant entity type. As before, the concrete form of the symbol is irrelevant at the conceptual level. We only need to assume that such symbols do exist, and that there is a biunique correspondence between the entity types represented in the information system and the symbols that represent them in the conceptual schema. In this book, we normally designate these symbols by words beginning with a capital letter. When confusion is unlikely to arise, however, we do not distinguish between entity types and their symbols.

The classification of an object into an entity type is represented in the information base. A classification of an object into an entity type is called a *fact*. A classification is represented by means of a relationship between the symbols representing the object and the entity type. At any time, every object represented in the information base must be classified into one or more entity types.

Internally, the representation of objects, entity types, and classifications may take many forms. At the conceptual level, we abstract from the details of the representation, but we need to define what must be represented and state some of the properties of the representation. To this end, we use a conceptual modeling language. There are several conceptual modeling languages, but all of them may be formalized in the language of first-order logic, with some extensions. Most professional languages have an associated textual and/or graphical representation. In this book, we sketch the formalization in first-order logic, and explain the use of UML to define conceptual schemas.

## 2.4.1 State of the Information Base

The *state* of an information base at a given time is the set of facts that it contains at that time. As we have seen, the classifications of objects into entity types are facts in the information base. Therefore, the state of the information base includes the set of classifications of objects. In the next chapter, we show that the state also includes relationships.

There are two kinds of information base, depending on the facts that they contain at a given time. A *current-state* information base contains at time $t$ only the facts that hold in the domain at $t$. A *temporal* information base contains at time $t$ the facts that hold in the domain at $t$ and the facts that have held at any time before $t$.

Current-state information bases are insufficient when the functions of the information system require that past facts be remembered. For example, an information system may be required to answer questions such as

"Who was a student a year ago?" Temporal information bases "remember" the facts that were true in the domain in the past, and are thus able to answer questions about the past.

A conceptual model is referred to as *current-state* or *temporal* if it assumes that the information base is, respectively, current-state or temporal. Most conceptual models, including UML, are current-state.

## 2.4.2 Logical Representation

In logic, we represent an entity type by a unary predicate, whose argument denotes an object[2]. We write predicate names starting with a capital letter and without blanks, for example the predicates *Woman* and *Student*. In the formulas, the variables start with a lowercase letter.

The classification of object $A$ into an entity type $E$ is represented by the formula $E(A)$, where $E$ is the unary predicate that represents the entity type. For example, *Woman(Charlotte)* means that *Charlotte* is an instance of *Woman*. In logic, formulas consisting of a single predicate with constant arguments are called *facts*, and that is why formulas such as $E(A)$ are called *entity facts*, or simply facts.

The same object $e$ may be an instance of several entity types at the same time. In this case, there will be a formula $E_i(e)$ in the information base for each $E_i$ of which $e$ is an instance at that time. For example, if *Charlotte* is also a student, the information base will also contain the fact *Student(Charlotte)*.

In logic, we represent the statement that $E_1$ is a subtype of $E_2$ by the formula[3]

$$E_1(e) \rightarrow E_2(e)$$

For example, to state that *Woman* is a subtype of *Person*, we write:

$$Woman(p) \rightarrow Person(p)$$

In current-state information bases, it is not possible to formalize the statement that a given entity type is constant or permanent. This is a constraint that can be formalized only in temporal information bases.

---

[2] In Chapter 17, we shall study an alternative logical representation of entity types.

[3] In order to simplify the notation, variables without quantifiers are assumed to be universally quantified in the front of the formula. The complete formula would be $\forall e \, (E_1(e) \rightarrow E_2(e))$.

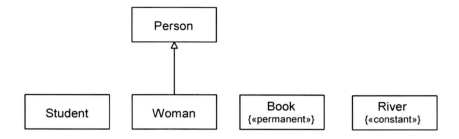

**Fig. 2.2.** Graphical representation of five entity types in UML. *Woman* in a subtype of *Person*

### 2.4.3 Representation in UML

The most widely used graphical representation of an entity type is un-doubtedly a rectangle with the name of the entity type inside. UML uses this representation too.[4] Usually, the name starts with a capital letter. Figure 2.2 shows an example of five entity types.

In UML, we represent the statement that $E_1$ is a subtype of $E_2$ by means of a solid-line path from $E_1$ to $E_2$ with a hollow triangle at the end of the path where it meets $E_2$. Figure 2.2 shows an example: *Woman* is a subtype of *Person*.

In UML, it is not possible to formally define that an entity type is constant or permanent. However, we can assume that there are two predefined constraints (constant and permanent) whose formalization is implicit: the tools that analyze schemas or generate code will understand their meaning and will behave accordingly.

We shall study in Chap. 17 the use of a UML mechanism, called a *stereotype*, to define new predefined constraints. For the moment, it suffices to say that to indicate that an entity type is constant or permanent we write {«constant»} or {«permanent»}, respectively, near the name of the entity type. In Fig. 2.2, we define in this way that *Book* is a permanent type, and that *River* is constant. A text string in braces {*C*} placed near the

---

[4] In strict terms, UML uses rectangles for object classes. Entity types should be defined as classes with the standard stereotype «type». A class-stereotyped «type» specifies a domain of objects without defining the physical implementa-tion of those objects. For the sake of readability, we assume in this book, unless stated otherwise, that UML rectangles without either keywords or stereotypes include the stereotype «type».

| Mary:Woman |
|---|

| Charlotte:Woman,Student |
|---|

**Fig. 2.3.** Graphical representation of a classification into entity types. *Mary* and *Charlotte* are instances of *Woman*. *Charlotte* is an instance of *Student* too

symbol of an entity type means that the population of that entity type must satisfy the constraint *C*. In this case, the constraint is stereotyped «constant» or «permanent», which means that it is a predefined constraint.

Normally, the classification of a concrete object into one or more entity types is not represented graphically. When it is done, UML uses the same notation as for entity types, but in place of the name of entity types there appears an underlined concatenation of the object symbol, a colon (":") and the name or names of the entity types. The convention for showing multiple entity types is to separate their names by commas. Figure 2.3 shows two examples. A diagram that shows entities and their relationships is called an *object diagram*.

### 2.4.4 Conceptual Models: Single or Multiple Classification

As we have said, in the general case an object may be an instance of two or more entity types at the same time. However, it is necessary to distinguish between two different cases, which leads to an important classification of conceptual models.

A *multiple-classification* model is one which allows an object to be an instance of two entity types, $E_1$ and $E_2$, such that

- $E_1$ does not subsume $E_2$;
- $E_2$ does not subsume $E_1$;
- no $E_3$ is subsumed by both $E_1$ and $E_2$

A *single-classification* model is one which does not admit multiple classifications. The logic language and UML are multiple-classification languages.

Figure 2.3 shows an example of a multiple classification. A person (*Charlotte*) is an instance of *Woman* and *Student*, but *Woman* does not subsume *Student*, nor does *Student* subsume *Woman*, and there is no entity type that is subsumed by both *Woman* and *Student*. There are women who are not students, and students who are not women.

Single-classification models do not allow a direct representation of situations such as those in Fig. 2.3. The solution is the *intersection* type, which we look at in Chap. 10. Informally, the idea consists in defining a new type, *FemaleStudent*, which is subsumed by *Woman* and *Student*. People who are instances of both *Woman* and *Student* (such as *Charlotte*) would be defined as direct instances of *FemaleStudent* and, therefore, they would also be instances of *Woman* and *Student*.

### 2.4.5 Conceptual Models: Static or Dynamic Classification

In the general case, an object may be an instance of different entity types at different times. However, this is not allowed in all conceptual models. We say that a *dynamic classification* model is one which allows objects to be instances of different entity types at different times. Otherwise, we say that it is a *static classification* model. Both logic and UML allow dynamic classification.

Static classification models assume that an object appears (is created) in the information base at some point in time and is classified as an instance of one or more entity types at that time, and that these classifications do not change during the object's lifespan. Once the object ceases to exist in the information base, it cannot reappear later on.

A static classification model would not allow us to define, for example, the entity types *Person*, *Student,* and *Employee*, assuming that a given person may at a given time be a student, and later an employee, who (possibly) ceases to be a student. In static classification models, a symbol is related to one or more entity types when it appears for the first time in the information base, and these cannot be changed.

### 2.4.6 Properties of the Representation

Regardless of the language that is used, the representation of objects and entity types in an information system, and the classification of objects into entity types (as shown in Fig. 2.1), must all satisfy certain properties. Completeness, correctness, a nonempty population, and nonredundancy are the most important of these properties. Below, we describe each of them in turn.

#### 2.4.6.1 Completeness

This property states that if, in the domain, an object $o$ is considered to be an instance of an entity type $E$ at a given point in time, and we want this fact to be represented in the information system, then the information base must contain a symbol representing $o$ and a representation of the classification of $o$ into entity type $E$ at that time.

Completeness requires that the information base includes a representation of the relevant classifications of the domain objects. This implies that the schema includes a representation of the entity types, and that the information base includes the relationships between the symbols and the representations of the entity types into which they are classified.

This property is necessary for the completeness of the conceptual schema. In general, completeness cannot be formally verified. It is part of the task of schema validation to ensure that this property is satisfied.

### 2.4.6.2 Correctness

This property states that if the information base contains a classification of a symbol $s$ into an entity type $E$ at a given instant, it must be considered that the object denoted by $s$ in the domain is an instance of entity type $E$ at that instant, and this fact should be represented in the information system.

Correctness requires that the representations in the information system (information base and conceptual schema) be correct and relevant. This property is necessary for the correctness of the conceptual schema. In general, correctness cannot be formally verified. It is part of the task of schema validation to ensure that this property is satisfied.

### 2.4.6.3 Nonempty Population

It must be possible for any entity type defined in the schema to have a nonempty population. Otherwise, an entity type would not have any instance during the system's lifetime. In information systems engineering, these entity types are not particularly relevant. An example of an entity type that would always have an empty population is *SingleAndMarried-Person*.

The inclusion in the schema of an entity type whose population must always be empty does not influence the completeness and correctness, but it does affect the simplicity of the schema, as it would contain a superfluous entity type.

In general, it is not possible to formally verify that an entity type *necessarily* has a nonempty population at a given time. Even if a conceptual schema includes an entity type $E$, this does not imply that users must communicate that some object is an instance of $E$ at a given time. They might never do so, and so $E$ would always have an empty population. It is part of the validation phase of a conceptual schema to ensure that there is an instance of an entity type at a certain time.

In some cases, however, it is possible to formally verify that an entity type *may* have a nonempty population at a given time. An entity type is *satisfiable* if it may have a nonempty population at a certain time. Similarly, an entity type is *unsatisfiable* if it must always have an empty population. The problem of the satisfiability of an entity type involves determining whether or not the entity type is satisfiable.

A simple example of an unsatisfiable entity type is *SingleAndMarried-Person.* If the schema includes the constraint that a person cannot be single and married at the same time, then *SingleAndMarriedPerson* is unsatisfiable. This type would always have an empty population, and should therefore not be part of the schema.

### 2.4.6.4 Nonredundancy

Two entity types are *redundant* if they must have always the same population. A schema should not include redundant entity types. For example, a schema could include the entity types *Person* and *Employee*. If the domain is interested only in employed people then, possibly, the population of the two entity types will be always the same. Redundancy must not be confused with the fact that a given entity type may have several alternative names (synonyms).

The inclusion in the schema of a redundant entity type does not influence the completeness and correctness, but it does affect the simplicity of the schema, as it would contain a superfluous entity type.

In general, it is not possible to formally verify that two entity types will or will not always have the same population. If a schema contains two entity types $E_1$ and $E_2$, it is possible that every time users communicate that an object is an instance of $E_1$ they will also communicate that it is an instance of $E_2$. The result of this would be that $E_1$ and $E_2$ have the same population during the system's lifetime. It is part of the validation phase of a conceptual schema to ensure that entity types normally have different populations at a given time.

In some cases, however, it is possible to formally verify that two entity types $E_1$ and $E_2$ must always have the same population. The entity types $E_1$ and $E_2$ are redundant if $E_1$ subsumes $E_2$ and $E_2$ subsumes $E_1$. The subsumption problem of two entity types involves determining whether or not an entity type is subsumed by another one.

As a simple example of a redundant entity type, let us consider the type *TechnicalDirector*. If a given person is a *Director* and a *Technician* he will be also an instance of *TechnicalDirector*. If, however, the schema includes the constraint that all directors must be technicians, *TechnicalDirector* and *Director* become redundant, and one of the two should not be in the schema.

## 2.5 Data Types

A *lexical entity type* is an entity type whose instances are words (the lexicon) in the language used in the domain, which may be written or spoken (i.e. uttered). The lexicon includes not only the words that appear in dictionaries, but also those that have been invented for a particular use in the domain.

In theory, it would seem that we need only one lexical entity type, whose instances would be all possible words. In fact, many conceptual schemas include such a type, named *String* or similar. The instances of *String* may be any concatenation of characters from a predefined set, which includes letters, digits, and several special characters. However, it is often necessary to define types that are more specific than *String*. For example, in a domain that deals with books, we might define the type *ISBN code*, whose instances are all valid ISBN codes. In a domain dealing with Web pages, we might define the type *URL*, whose instances are all syntactically valid URLs.

Most conceptual models use data types rather than lexical entity types. Data types may be seen as an extension of lexical entity types. Essentially, a *data type* consists of a set of *values* and a set of lexical representations, or *literals*. The set of values is the population of the data type, and is called the *value space* of the type. The set of lexical representations is called the *lexical space* of the type. Each value in the value space is denoted by one or more literals of the lexical space. Values are represented in an information base by means of one of their literals. The value space of a data type does not change over time. For this reason, data types are constant entity types.

For example, consider the data type *Decimal*, which is used to represent decimal numbers with an arbitrary precision. The value space of *Decimal* is the set of values $i \times 10^{-n}$, where $i$ and $n$ are integers and $n \geq 0$. The lexical space of *Decimal* is the set of finite sequences formed by the decimal digits (from 0 to 9) with a point, optionally preceded by a sign. For example, the literals -1.23, +1.543233, and 210 denote values of *Decimal*.

Conceptual models include a predefined set of data types and a mechanism for defining new ones. The examples used in this book use the data types defined in the XML Schema language. This language provides a rich set of data types and a powerful mechanism for defining new ones. The predefined XML Schema data types that we use include the following:

- *String.* The values are finite-length sequences of characters.
- *Boolean.* The values are {true, false}, represented by the literals {true, false, 1, 0}.
- *Decimal,* described above.
- *Integer.* Decimal values without digits in the fractional part. The space of values is the set {..., -2, -1, 0, 1, 2, ...}.
- *PositiveInteger.* Positive integers. The value space is the set {1, 2, ...}.
- *NonNegativeInteger,* which we shall call *Natural.* These are the positive integers and zero.

XML Schema also includes many data types related to time. The ones that we shall use most often in this book are as follows:

- *Date.* The space of values is the set of dates in the Gregorian calendar. The lexical representation of a date is CCYY-MM-DD, where CC represents the century, YY the year, MM the month, and DD the day.
- *Time.* The value space is the set of times in a day, starting from midnight. These times are represented by literals of the form HH:MM:SS, which denote the hour, minute, and second, respectively. Seconds may also be represented as a *Decimal,* thus allowing varying degrees of precision.
- *DateTime.* The values are specific instants. The value space comprises all valid combinations of *Date* and *Time.* These are represented by literals of the form CCYY-MM-DDTHH:MM:SS, where CCYY-MM-DD and HH:MM:SS are as before, and T is a separator.
- *gYearMonth.* The value space is the set of months in the Gregorian calendar. Normally, we omit the prefix *g* (for Gregorian) and write *YearMonth.* The lexical representation of a month is CCYY-MM.
- *gYear.* The value space is the set of years in the Gregorian calendar. Normally, we omit the prefix *g* (for Gregorian) and write *Year.* The lexical representation of a year is CCYY.
- *Duration.* The values are temporal durations. The value space is a six-dimensional space where the coordinates are the Gregorian year, the month, the day, the hour, the minute, and the second. Duration is represented by literals of the form

$$P n Y n M n D T n H n M n S$$

where $n$Y represents the number of years, $n$M the number of months, $n$D the number of days, $n$H the number of hours, $n$M the number of minutes, and $n$S the number of seconds; T is a separator. The number of seconds may contain decimal digits. In all cases, *n* may be any integer. An example of a duration is P1Y2M3DT10H30M.

### 2.5.1 Data Types in UML

UML assumes that there are primitive data types (such as *Boolean*, *Integer*, *UnlimitedNatural*, and *String*), which are defined outside UML. Other data types may be defined if necessary. Data types are not usually represented graphically, but if necessary they can be represented using the rectangle symbol and the keyword «dataType». Figure 2.4 (left) shows an example (*Date*).

An *enumeration* is a particular kind of data type whose values are enumerated in the model as enumeration literals. Figure 2.4 (right) shows an example. *DayOfWeek* is a data type comprising seven values. An enumeration may be shown using a rectangle and the keyword «enumeration». The name of the data type is placed in the upper compartment. A list of enumeration literals may be placed, one to a line, in the bottom compartment.

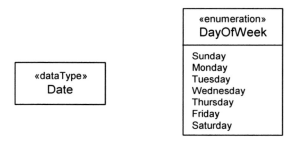

**Fig. 2.4.** Examples of data types in UML. *Left*: *Date* is a user-defined data type. *Right*: *DayOfWeek* is an enumeration

## 2.6 Bibliographical Notes

Smith (1988) provided an excellent brief explanation of the theories and functions of concepts in cognitive psychology. More details can be found in (Smith and Medin 1981). Stillings et al. (1995, Chap.3) also gave an explanation of these theories, which is more detailed in certain aspects, in the context of the more general field of cognitive science. (Lakoff 1987) is a must for a complete analysis of prototypical concepts and their implications. Chapter 2 of that book is especially relevant for its critical review of existing theories.

We have mentioned that entity types may be grounded in several disciplines. In this chapter, the option chosen has been cognitive science. A different option could be a branch of philosophy. (Artz 1997) is a short text that reviews several theories of concepts that have been proposed in philosophy and discusses their relevance to classification. Parsons and Wand (2000) provided a view based on Bunge's ontology.

Wegner (1987) gave a complete description of classification and dealt with aspects from the fields of biology, mathematics, logic, and programming. Booch (1991, Chap. 4) explained classification, mainly in the context of object-oriented software engineering.

Motschnig-Pitrik and Mylopoulos (1992) provided a detailed description of classification in the conceptual modeling of information systems, including an analysis of how it is dealt with in several languages. Parsons (1996) and Parsons and Wand (1997) directly related concept theories to conceptual modeling.

Most work in conceptual modeling has been based on definitional concepts, although some research, such as that carried out by Dubitzky et al. (1999), has been based on prototypical concepts.

Only a few books explain entity and relationship types in detail, independently of particular languages. Two noteworthy exceptions are (Kent 1978) and (Tsichritzis and Lochovsky 1982). There are, however, many books that focus on a particular language or method and explain specific concepts, such as (Nijssen and Halpin 1989), (Batini et al. 1992), and (Martin and Odell 1995). Chen (1983) gave one of the first analyses of the correspondence between entity types and parts of English sentences.

The first two properties of the representation of classification (correctness and completeness) are normally implicit, and very few authors mention them explicitly. Robinson (1979) was one of the first. A more recent work is (Martin and Odell 1995). An explicit formulation for object-oriented software engineering can be found in (Meyer 1997, p. 171). The nonempty population and nonredundancy properties were presented by Parsons and Wand (1997). The temporal properties of the populations of entity types were presented by Costal et al. (1997).

Section 2.5 is based on the W3C recommendation described in W3C (2004). Parent et al. (2006) provided a comprehensive set of data types for spatial and temporal applications.

## 2.7 Exercises

**2.1** Look up the definitions of the concepts *mother*, *book*, and *city* in your favorite dictionary. Analyze the properties included in these definitions, and determine whether the concepts are definitional or prototypical.

**2.2** Assume that you want to build a system that, among other things, records the broadcast schedule of several TV or radio channels on a daily basis. Design a set of categories (news, movies, etc.) that allows you to classify all the broadcasts. Try to define these concepts precisely enough so that other people will not find it too hard to classify a particular broadcast. Can the same broadcast be classified into two or more of the above categories?

**2.3** Assume that you have to develop a system that records the families who have existed or exist in a community (such as a town) and their time-varying composition. Try to design the concept of a *family* for this system. Check that your definition of *family* answers the following questions:
- When does a family start?
- When does a family cease to exist?
- When does a person become a member of a family?
- Can a person be a member of several families?

**2.4** Define the entity and data types needed by a system that has to store information about the papers published in a scientific journal.

**2.5** Give an example of an entity that is an instance of two entity types that are not mutually subsumed.

**2.6** We have seen that the population of an entity type may be constant, permanent, or unconstrained. In general, if $E_1$ is a subtype of $E_2$, the constraint of the population of $E_1$ is independent of that of $E_2$. Give an example of each of the nine possible combinations.

# 3 Relationship Types

Relationship types are another important element in conceptual schemas, because they also play a fundamental role in the memory, informative, and active functions of information systems. Determining the relationship types that are relevant to an information system is one of the most important tasks in conceptual modeling. In this chapter, we study the nature and general characteristics of a relationship type.

In the first section, we define relationship types similarly to the way in which entity types were defined in the preceding chapter. In Sect. 3.2, we explain how to represent relationships and their types in an information system, in both logic and UML. Attributes are a particular but important kind of relationship type, which is addressed in Sect. 3.3.

## 3.1 Definition

Relationship types can be defined in several ways. Here, we adopt a definition similar to that of entity types. The rationale is that there is a similarity between the operation of classifying an object into an entity type and that of classifying a relationship into a relationship type. For example, there is little difference between classifying the reader of this book as a *Person* and that of classifying what he does with the book as *Reads*. In both cases we abstract something: in *Person*, we ignore the differences that exist between people; in *Reads*, we ignore how, where, and why the book is being read, the reader's interest in the book, the level of difficulty, and so on. Thus, it would be reasonably accurate to use a definition of a relationship type that is almost identical to that of an entity type: "A relationship type is a concept whose instances at a given time are identifiable individual relationships that are considered to exist in the domain at that time."

However, the above definition is unsatisfactory because it ignores the fact that a relationship is always a relationship between objects. Although we can imagine isolated objects in a domain, it is impossible to imagine a relationship without the presence of objects. The *participants* in a relationship are the objects that participate in it. Each participant plays a *role* in the relationship. In the above example, the participants are *The reader of this book* and *This book*. The former plays the role of reader, and the latter the role of reading.

If we move on from instances to types, we can say that a relationship type consists of a set of $n$ participants, with $n \geq 2$. A participant is an entity type that plays a role in a relationship type. We write $R(p_1:E_1, \ldots, p_n:E_n)$ to denote a relationship type named $R$, with participant entity types $E_1, \ldots, E_n$ playing roles $p_1, \ldots, p_n$, respectively. Sometimes we omit the role $p_i$ played by participant $p_i:E_i$, either because it is obvious or because it is the same as the name of $E_i$. In these cases, it is assumed that $p_i$ is the same as $E_i$. For example, *Reads (reader:Person, Book)* is equivalent to *Reads (reader:Person, book:Book)*.

We say that $R(p_1:E_1, \ldots, p_n:E_n)$ is the *schema* of the relationship type $R$ and that $p_1:E_1, \ldots, p_n:E_n$ are its participants. Conceptually, the order of the participants in the schema is not significant. Two different participants can be of the same entity type, but there cannot be two participants with the same role. For this reason, we sometimes say simply that $p_1, \ldots, p_n$ are the participants of the relationship type.

Using the above notation and terminology, the following could be an acceptable definition: "A *relationship type* $R(p_1:E_1, \ldots, p_n:E_n)$ is a concept whose instances at a given time are distinct sets $\{<p_1:e_1>, \ldots, <p_n:e_n>\}$ formed by $n$ entities $e_1, \ldots, e_n$ that are instances of their corresponding type $E_1, \ldots, E_n$, and are considered to have a relationship $R$ in the domain at that time, playing the respective roles $p_1, \ldots, p_n$." The instances of a relationship type are called *relationships*.

This definition states, in the first place, that relationship types are concepts. Therefore, the concept theories developed in cognitive science are, in theory, also applicable to relationship types.

Secondly, the definition states that a relationship is a set $\{<p_1:e_1>, \ldots, <p_n:e_n>\}$ formed by exactly one pair $<p_i:e_i>$ for each of its $n$ participants. For example, the instances of *Supplies (Supplier, Part, user:Project)* must include an entity from each of the three entity types. If there were an instance of *Supplies* without, say, a *user* role then the relationship type would be incorrect. The definition requires each instance of *Supplies* to include a *user* role. Another incorrect case would occur if we were to accept that an instance of *Supplies* could consist of a supplier $S$, a part $P$, and user projects $A$, $B$, and $C$. The definition requires each instance of *Supplies* to include exactly one *user*; thus, we should consider that in this case there are three relationships, not one.

The fact that a relationship must include one entity for each participant should not be confused with the fact that two or more participants may be of the same entity type. A relationship type such as *IsParentOf (par-*

*ent:Person, child:Person*) is totally valid. An instance of this relationship type will include two persons, one for each participant (*parent* and *child*). A relationship type in which the same entity type plays two or more roles is called *recursive*.

Although it is rare, a relationship could include the same entity twice, as distinct participants. For example, the recursive type *Knows* (*Person, acquaintance:Person*) could have instances in which the two people are the same (if it were the case that a person knew himself).

Thirdly, the definition states that the instances of a relationship type must be distinct sets. It is not possible to have two relationships in the domain that are formed by exactly the same participants. In the *Supplies* example, there cannot be two relationships with the same *supplier, part,* and *project*.

Finally, the definition states that the instances of a relationship type *R* are sets of entities that are considered to have the relationship *R* in the domain at that time, playing their respective roles. It is important to note that the definition says that they "are considered to have the relationship *R*". As with entity types, this aspect does not cause difficulties in most relationship types, but there are cases that raise doubts because what some people may consider to exist at a given point in time, other people may consider not to exist (at least at that point in time). When this happens, an effort must be made to refine the definition and reach an agreement between the people involved.

An example of a relationship type that should not cause any problem in this respect is *Lives* (*resident:Person, placeOfResidence:Town*). If a person *p* and a town *to* are the participants in an instance of this type at some time, it is because *p* lives in *to* at that time.

An example that may raise some doubts is *IsMotherOf* (*mother:Woman, child:Person*). An instance of this type at time *t* involves a woman *m* and a person *p* if it is considered at *t* that *m* is the mother of *p*. Let us consider two people: Alice and Alan (see Fig. 3.1). Alice is born and dies at $T_1$ and $T_3$ respectively. At $T_2$, Alice gives birth to Alan, who dies at $T_4$. Figure 3.1 shows three possible interpretations of the relationship *IsMotherOf* (*Alice, Alan*):

(a) The relationship holds only while the child, *Alan*, is alive.
(b) The relationship holds only while both the mother and the child are alive.
(c) Once *Alice* has given birth to *Alan*, the relationship holds forever.

Which of these interpretations is best must be defined in the domain. The one that is chosen will have an impact on the answer to the question

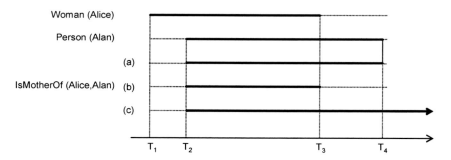

**Fig. 3.1.** Three interpretations, (a), (b) and (c), of the temporal existence of the relationship *IsMotherOf* (*Alice, Alan*) in a domain

"*who is p's mother now?*" In Fig. 3.1, the answer to this question at $T_3 < t < T_4$ and at $T_4 > t$ will depend on the interpretation chosen.

Note that the definition given above does not require that the entities participating in a relationship at time *t* must be an instance of their types at *t*. Although they usually will be, they might have been an instance at some previous time without being so at *t*. We can see the difference in the two previous examples. In *Lives* (*resident:Person, placeOfResidence:Town*), if person *p* lives in town *to* at time *t*, it is likely that *p* is required to be an instance of *Person* at *t*, and *to* to be an instance of *Town* at *t*. However, in *IsMotherOf* (*mother:Woman, child:Person*), it may be acceptable for woman *m* to be considered the mother of person *p* at time *t* even if *m* is not considered an instance of *Woman* at *t*. In interpretation (a) in Fig. 3.1, in the interval from $T_3$ to $T_4$ *Alice* is considered to be *Alan*'s mother even if *Alice* is no longer an instance of *Woman*. In interpretation (c), after $T_4$ *Alice* is also considered to be *Alan*'s mother, even if neither *Alice* nor *Alan* is an instance of its type at that time.

We say that $R(p_1:E_1, ..., p_n:E_n)$ is *synchronous* if, for each of its instances $r = \{<p_1:e_1>, ..., <p_n:e_n>\}$ at time *t*, the entities $e_1, ..., e_n$ participating in *r* are instances of their respective types at *t*; otherwise, *R* is *asynchronous*. In the examples above, *Lives* is synchronous, while *IsMotherOf* is asynchronous according to interpretations (a) and (c) in Fig. 3.1. Almost all relationship types are synchronous. Asynchronous relationship types can be defined only in temporal conceptual models. In this book, unless stated otherwise, we assume that relationship types are synchronous.

### 3.1.1 Degree

The *degree* of a relationship type is the number of participants in that type. Most relationship types have degree 2, and are called *binary*. Relationship types with a degree greater than 2 are called *n-ary*. The most common of the *n*-ary relationship types are those that have degree 3, which are referred to as *ternary*.

### 3.1.2 Pattern Sentence

Linguistically, a relationship is a fact that holds in a domain and can be expressed using a grammatical sentence. For example, an instance of *Reads (reader:Person, reading:Book)* with participants *Arnold* and *Alice in Wonderland* may be expressed using the sentence "Arnold reads Alice in Wonderland", while another with participants *Laura* and *Tirant Lo Blanc* could be expressed as "Laura reads Tirant Lo Blanc", etc.

The *pattern sentence* of a relationship type is a declarative sentence in which there is a placeholder for each participant. The sentence that linguistically expresses a relationship is obtained by filling in the placeholders with the names of the participants. In the above example, the pattern sentence could be

     *<Person>* reads *<Book>*

where *<Person>* and *<Book>* are slots that must be filled in with (the names of) a specific person and book respectively. If we wish to express that the first participant is a person and the second a book, we may use a longer pattern sentence:

     Person *<Person>* reads the book *<Book>*

which is instantiated as

     The person *Arnold* reads the book *Alice in Wonderland*
     The person *Laura* reads the book *Tirant Lo Blanc*

Pattern sentences help us to understand the meaning of relationship types and may be *implicit* or *explicit*. The former are built as explained below, and the latter are given by the designers. Every relationship type has one or more implicit pattern sentences. Explicit pattern sentences are optional.

Implicit pattern sentences are derived from the schema $R(p_1:E_1, ..., p_n:E_n)$. If we choose the names of the relationship types ($R$) and roles ($p_i$)

sensibly, the sentences derived may be enough, and we shall not need explicit pattern sentences.

The derivation of implicit pattern sentences depends on how roles are named. There are two approaches: *noun-based* and *verb-based*. In the noun-based approach, role names are nouns, while in the verb-based approach, role names are verbs. An example of the former is *R (reader:Person, reading:Book)*, where the roles (*reader* and *reading*) are nouns. The same example in the latter approach could be *R (reads:Person, is read by:Book)*, where the roles (*reads*, *is read by*) are verbs.

Firstly, we shall describe the derivation of implicit pattern sentences for binary types when the role names are nouns. In this case, there are three implicit pattern sentences. Before giving their general structure, we show the sentences for the example *Reads (reader:Person, reading:Book)*:

> The person *<Person>* reads the book *<Book>*
> The person *<Person>* is (a | the) reader of the book *<Book>*
> The book *<Book>* is (a | the) reading of the person *<Person>*

In the option (*a | the*) in the second sentence, we use *a* if a book may be read by several persons, and *the* if it can be read by one person at most.[1] In the third sentence, we use *a* if a person can read several books at the same time, and *the* if he or she can read one at most. The instantiation of these pattern sentences for a particular relationship could be as follows (assuming that a person reads several books and that the same book may be read by several persons):

> The person *Laura* reads the book *Tirant Lo Blanc*
> The person *Laura* is a reader of the book *Tirant Lo Blanc*
> The book *Tirant Lo Blanc* is a reading of the person *Laura*

Note that the first sentence is well formed when the name of the relationship type (*Reads*) is the verb of the sentence in third-person singular and the two participants in *R* appear in an appropriate order. The other two sentences are well formed when the role names are singular nouns.

The general structure of the three pattern sentences corresponding to a binary relationship type $R(p_1:E_1,p_2:E_2)$ is as follows:

> The $e_1 < E_1 >$ *R* the $e_2 < E_2 >$
> The $e_1 < E_1 >$ is (a | the) $p_1$ of the $e_2 < E_2 >$
> The $e_2 < E_2 >$ is (a | the) $p_2$ of the $e_1 < E_1 >$

---

[1] The information about how many people can read a book (or how many books can be read by a person) at the same time can be extracted from the cardinality constraints, which are considered in the next chapter.

We shall now go on to explain the derivation of implicit pattern sentences for binary types when the role names are verbs. In this case, the name of the relationship type is not used, and there are two implicit pattern sentences. Before giving their general structure, we show the sentences for the example *R* (*reads:Person, is read by:Book*):

> The person *<Person>* reads the book *<Book>*
> The book *<Book>* is read by the person *<Person>*

The instantiation of these pattern sentences for a particular relationship could be as follows:

> The person *Arnold* reads the book *Alice in Wonderland*
> The book *Alice in Wonderland* is read by the person *Arnold*

Note that the sentences are well formed when the role names are verbs in third-person singular.

The general structure of the two pattern sentences corresponding to a binary relationship type $R(p_1:E_1,p_2:E_2)$ is as follows:

> The $e_1 < E_1> p_1$ the $e_2 < E_2>$
> The $e_2 < E_2> p_2$ the $e_1 < E_1>$

For most binary types, at least one of the implicit pattern sentences captures the meaning of the corresponding relationship. When this happens, there is no need to define explicit pattern sentences.

In some cases, however, it may be difficult to find adequate names, making it necessary to define explicit pattern sentences. For example, consider the following popular relationship type found in online bookstores: "Customers who bought this book also bought this other book". It is difficult to choose names for the type and its two roles so that the implicit pattern sentences express the meaning of the relationships. A schema such as

> *CustomersAlsoBought* (*origin:Book, additional:Book*)

does not produce expressive sentences. Therefore, in this case it would be appropriate to define an explicit pattern sentence, such as

> Customers who bought book *<Book>* also bought book *<Book>*

An instance might be

> Customers who bought the book *Introduction to Conceptual Modeling* also bought the book *Advanced Conceptual Modeling*

For *n*-ary types, it is difficult to find names of relationship types and roles from which we can derive expressive pattern sentences. Normally, we need to define explicit pattern sentences for these types. For example, a pattern sentence for *Supplies* (*Supplier*, *Part*, *user:Project*) could be

> Supplier <*Supplier*> supplies part <*Part*> to be used in project <*Project*>

### 3.1.3 Unary Relationship Types

Normally, relationships are conceived of as having at least two participants. In fact, almost all conceptual modeling languages require that relationship types have a degree of at least two.

However, when we develop a conceptual schema for a domain, we find concepts that seem to be naturally modeled as unary relationship types. For example, we could have *IsThick* (*Book*) to represent the fact that a book is thick. Another example could be *IsManager* (*Person*).

In languages that do not allow unary relationship types, the above concepts can be modeled as new entity types. For example, we could define the type *ThickBook*, or the type *Manager*. This is a valid and elegant solution, but it adds new entity types to the schema.

Another solution involves modeling a unary type as binary, with an additional participant that may take two values: *true* and *false*. For example, if *Boolean* is a data type we could define *ThickBook* (*Book*, *Boolean*) and *Manager* (*Person*, *Boolean*). This is also a valid solution, and a practical one in some languages, but few people will find it elegant.

There is a third solution, which can be applied when we have two or more unary types with the same participant entity type *E*. An example of this situation might be when we have *IsManager* (*Person*) and *IsSalesman* (*Person*). In this case, we could define a binary type *P*(*E,E'*), where *E'* is an entity type with as many instances as the unary relationship types that we have. In this example, we could have *P* (*Person*, *JobCategory*), where *JobCategory* has the instances *Manager* and *Salesman*. In UML, *JobCategory* could be defined as an enumeration.

### 3.1.4 Population

The *population* of a relationship type *R* at time *t* is the set of its instances that exist in the domain at *t*.

In general, the population of a relationship type is time-varying during the lifetime of an information system. However, there are two particular cases that deserve special treatment: constant and permanent relationship types. Their definition bears some resemblance to that of entity types, but it is not the same.

A relationship type $R(p_1{:}E_1, ..., p_n{:}E_n)$ is *constant* with respect to a participant $p_i$ if the instances of $R$ in which an instance $e_i$ of $E_i$ participates are the same during the temporal interval in which $e_i$ exists. We shall illustrate this definition with two examples. The first is

*WasBorn (native:Person, birthplace:Town)*

We assume that *Town* is constant and that *Person* is not permanent, meaning that persons are born and die. *WasBorn* is constant with respect to *native* because the set of instances $r = \{<native{:}p>, <birthplace{:}to>\}$ in which a person $p$ participates is constant during $p$'s life. Note that *WasBorn* is not constant with respect to *birthplace*, because the set of people born in a town may change over time.

The second example is:

*Equivalence (source:Unit, conversionRate:Decimal, target:Unit)*

with the explicit pattern sentence

A *<Unit>* is equivalent to *<Decimal> <Unit>*

which produces sentences such as

An *inch* is equivalent to 2.54 *centimeters*

*Equivalence* is constant with respect to its three participants. The set of instances of *Equivalence* corresponding to a pair of *units* and a *decimal* is the same at any time.

A relationship type is *constant* if it is constant with respect to all its participants. *Equivalence* is constant, but *WasBorn* is not.

A relationship type $R(p_1{:}E_1, ..., p_n{:}E_n)$ is *permanent* with respect to a participant $p_i$ if the instances of $R$ in which an instance $e_i$ of $E_i$ participates never cease to exist during the temporal interval in which $e_i$ exists. In the example above, if *Person* were permanent, *WasBorn* would be permanent with respect to *birthplace*, because the set of people born in a town would never decrease. As another example, consider

*HasVisited (visitor:Person,Town)*

If we assume that *Town* is constant and that *Person* is permanent then *HasVisited* is permanent with respect to *visitor* and *town* because once a person has visited a town, he has visited it forever.

A relationship type is *permanent* if it is permanent with respect to all its participants. *HasVisited* is permanent, but *WasBorn* is not.

### 3.1.5 Subsumption

In general, the population of a relationship type is independent of that of the other types defined in a schema. However, in some cases the population of a relationship type must necessarily be included in that of another type. Using a definition similar to that of entity types, we say that $R_2$ subsumes $R_1$ or that $R_1$ is a subtype of $R_2$ if all instances of $R_1$ must also be instances of $R_2$. A formal definition is provided in the next section. For example, consider the following relationship types:

> *Works* (*employee:Person, employer:Company*)
> *Manages* (*manager:Person, Company*)

If we assume that the managers of a company are employees of that company, then *Manages* is a subtype of *Works*. We shall study the subsumption of relationship types in Chap. 10.

## 3.2 Representation in an Information System

As we already know, in order to be able to perform their functions, information systems must have a representation of their domain. In terms of the elements considered in this chapter, this means that an information system must have a representation of:

- the relationship types;
- the relationships in the domain;
- the classification of the relationships into relationship types.

The relationship types are represented in the conceptual schema. The schema contains a symbol (which is generally chosen arbitrarily) for each relevant relationship type. The concrete form of the symbol is irrelevant at the conceptual level. We need only to assume that the symbols exist and that there is a biunique correspondence between the relationship types represented in the information system and the symbols representing them in the conceptual schema. In this book, we normally designate these symbols with words beginning with a capital letter. When confusion is unlikely, however, we do not distinguish between relationship types and their symbols.

The relationships that exist in the domain and the classification of relationships according to their types are represented in the information base.

Below, we sketch the representation in first-order logic and describe the use of UML in more detail.

### 3.2.1 State of the Information Base

In the previous chapter, we defined the state of an information base at a given time as the set of facts it contained at that time. In that chapter, the facts were entity facts. We have now seen that there are also relationship facts. Therefore, the state of an information base consists of the entity and relationship facts represented in the information system. There are no other fact types.

### 3.2.2 Logical Representation

In logic, we represent a relationship type $R(p_1:E_1, \ldots, p_n:E_n)$, with degree $n$, using a predicate $R$ with the same degree, where the $n$ arguments are symbols denoting objects or values. The order of the arguments is conventional. We assume the order used in the schema. If the name $R$ is unique, then the name of the predicate is also $R$. Otherwise, given that there cannot be two predicates with the same name, we use some variation of the name $R$. We write the predicate's name starting with a capital letter and without blanks. Note that in this representation, the role names disappear.

A relationship $r = \{<p_1:A_1>, \ldots, <p_n:A_n>\}$ that is an instance of $R(p_1:E_1, \ldots, p_n:E_n)$ is represented using a formula $R(A_1, \ldots, A_n)$, where $R$ is the predicate corresponding to the relationship type and $A_1, \ldots, A_n$ are the symbols that denote the entities or the values of the participants. The formula $R(A_1, \ldots, A_n)$ indicates simultaneously that $A_1, \ldots, A_n$ are related in the domain and that the relationship they have is of type $R$. Note that, in logic, there cannot be duplicate formulas and therefore there cannot be duplicate relationships. In logic, the formulas consisting of a simple predicate with constant arguments are called facts. For this reason, formulas $R(A_1, \ldots, A_n)$ are called *relationship facts*, or simply facts.

For each synchronous relationship type $R(p_1:E_1, \ldots, p_n:E_n)$, the schema must include $n$ *referential* integrity constraints

$$R(e_1, \ldots, e_n) \rightarrow E_1(e_1)$$
$$\ldots$$
$$R(e_1, \ldots, e_n) \rightarrow E_n(e_n)$$

These constraints guarantee that each participant entity is an instance of its corresponding type. The referential constraint is the most important kind of constraint in conceptual modeling.

In logic, we represent that $R_1(p_{1,1}:E_1, \ldots, p_{1,n}:E_n)$ is a subtype of $R_2(p_{2,1}:E_1, \ldots, p_{2,n}:E_n)$ using the formula

$$R_1(e_1, \ldots, e_n) \rightarrow R_2(e_1, \ldots, e_n)$$

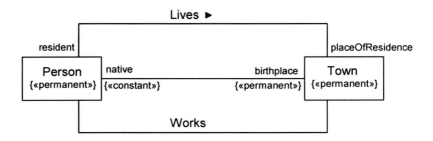

**Fig. 3.2.** Graphical representation of three relationship types as UML associations

For example, to state that

*Manages (manager:Person, Company)*

is a subtype of

*Works (employee:Person, employer:Company)*

we write

*Manages(p,c)* → *Works(p,c)*.

### 3.2.3 Representation in UML

In UML, binary relationship types can be represented in two ways: either as associations or as attributes. We consider associations here and attributes in the next section.

Binary associations are represented graphically by means of a line connecting the two entity types. The name of the association is shown near the line. The names of the roles are placed near their corresponding entity types. Although it is not explicitly prescribed in the official documentation, most users of UML define role names using nouns. Figure 3.2 shows the graphic representation of the associations corresponding to the following types:

> *Lives (resident:Person, placeOfResidence:Town)*
> *WasBorn (native:Person, birthplace:Town)*
> *Works (Person, Town)*

In the case of the first example, we show the names of the relationship types and those of the two roles. The solid arrowhead next to the name of the association that points toward a participant indicates the order of the participants used in the derivation of implicit pattern sentences. When the order is left to right or top to bottom, we usually omit the arrowhead. In this example, the implicit pattern sentences are:

>Person <*Person*> lives in town < *Town*>
>Person <*Person*> is a resident of town <*Town*>
>Town <*Town*> is the place of residence of person <*Person*>

These sentences are reasonably expressive.

In the case of the second example, we omit the name of the relationship type. There will only be two implicit pattern sentences, which are expressive enough:

>Person <*Person*> is a native of town <*Town*>
>Town <*Town*> is the birthplace of person <*Person*>

In the case of the third example, the names of the roles are the same as those of the entity types. The single implicit pattern sentence is also expressive:

>Person <*Person*> works in town <*Town*>

Given that the order of the participants is from left to right, an arrowhead is not needed in this case.

In UML, the name of an association is optional. When there is no name and we need to refer to an association, we use the names of the roles. An example is shown in the case of the association *native-birthplace* in Fig. 3.2.

Two or more associations may have the same name, but, conceptually, each association shown in a diagram is unique. The role names are optional; when they are missing, they are assumed to be the name of the entity type starting with a lowercase character.

In UML, it must be possible to unambiguously navigate from one entity type to the others with which it is connected using only the role names. In Fig. 3.2, we can navigate from *Person* to *Town* using the role names *placeOfResidence*, *birthplace*, and *town*. An ambiguity arises if we add a new association between *Person* and *Town*, such that the name of the role played by *Town* is one of the other three. For example, the following would not be admissible:

>*HasVisited* (*Person, Town*)

It must be defined with different role names, such as

>*HasVisited* (*visitor:Person, visitedTown:Town*)

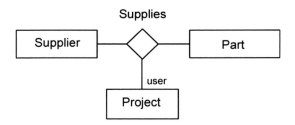

**Fig. 3.3.** UML representation of a ternary relationship type

Similarly, we can navigate from *Town* to *Person* using the role names *resident, native,* and *person.* As before, an ambiguity arises if we define a new association between *Person* and *Town*, with *Person* playing a role named *placeOfResidence, birthplace,* or *person.* Sometimes it is difficult to find good role names.

UML represents *n*-ary relationship types as associations. An association is drawn as a diamond, with a solid line for each participant connecting the diamond to the corresponding entity type. The name of the association is placed inside or near the diamond. The names of the roles are placed near their corresponding entity types. An example is shown in Fig. 3.3.

In UML, it is not necessary to explicitly define the referential integrity constraints. The symbol used to represent an association (either a line or a diamond and lines) connects the participating entity types, and from here those constraints are defined implicitly.

In UML, it is not possible to formalize whether a relationship type is constant or permanent.[2] However, as we did for entity types, we can assume that there are two constraint stereotypes (named *constant* and *permanent*), whose formalization is implicit. On the basis of this assumption, we have only to attach the constraint stereotype to the corresponding participant or association. In Fig. 3.2, we have defined that the association *native-birthplace* is constant with respect to *native* and permanent with respect to *birthplace.*

As with entity types, in UML we represent association $R_1$ as a subtype of $R_2$ using a solid-line path from $R_1$ to $R_2$ and a large hollow triangle at the end of the path where it meets $R_2$.

Normally, concrete relationships are not shown in diagrams. However, if needed, UML provides a notation that can be used for showing relation-

---

[2] UML 2.1 has a concept of changeability of association participants and attributes, but it is not expressive enough to capture the semantics of constant and permanent constraints.

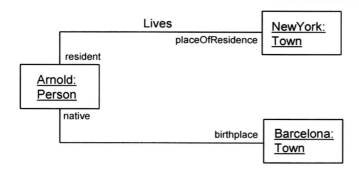

**Fig. 3.4.** Graphic representation of two links

ships in object diagrams. A concrete relationship is shown using the same notation as for an association, but the solid path or paths connect entities rather than entity types. In UML, instances of associations are called *links*. The graphic representation of relationships is useful to illustrate a fragment of complex schemas. Figure 3.4 shows two links of the associations defined in Fig. 3.2.

The UML graphical representation of relationships may not be practical when we want to show many links, because the figures become large. In these cases, a tabular representation may be a better choice.

### 3.2.3.1 Ordered Participants

Consider the relationship type

    *WaitingList* (*Flight, passenger:Person*)

shown in Fig. 3.5, with the pattern sentence

    The person *<Person>* is in the waiting list of flight *<Flight>*

If a given flight has several people in its waiting list, there will be an instance of *WaitingList* for each passenger in the list, but these instances are unordered. We cannot assume that there is a first instance corresponding to the first passenger in the list, a second one corresponding to the second, and so on.

**Fig. 3.5.** The passengers in the waiting list of a flight are ordered

If we are interested in representing the order of people in the list, we can add a third participant to the relationship type,

*WaitingList* (*Flight, passenger:Person, order:Ordinal*)

which now has a pattern sentence such as

The person *<Person>* is the *<Order>* in the waiting list of flight *<Flight>*

This is an acceptable solution, but it is difficult to maintain in an information base. One of the main problems is that when a passenger leaves a waiting list, the order of the people that follow him changes. Another problem is that we need to define an integrity constraint requiring that, in a list, the orders must be consecutive.

UML provides a construct that is useful in cases such as this one: *ordered* participants. In the above example, we would define a binary association and indicate that the passenger participant is ordered, using the keyword *ordered* in braces. The meaning is that the passengers in the waiting list of a flight are ordered. The passengers of a flight can be obtained in the order in which they are in the list. A passenger can be added in any position of the list. When a passenger leaves a list, the order of the people that follow him in the list is updated automatically. Using this construct, the above constraint is not needed.

## 3.2.4 Properties of the Representation

In the previous chapter, we saw that, independently of the language used, the representation of entities and their types in an information system must satisfy a few properties, mainly completeness, correctness, nonempty population, and nonredundancy. The same applies to the representation of relationships and their types. In the following, we briefly describe each of these properties.

### 3.2.4.1 Completeness

This property states that if a relationship *r* in the domain is considered to be an instance of *R* at a given time, and we want to represent this fact in an information system, then the information base must contain a representation of *r* and a representation of the classification of *r* into *R* at that time.

### 3.2.4.2 Correctness

This property states that if at some instant the information base contains a classification of a relationship *r* into relationship type *R*, then in the domain it must be considered that *r* is an instance of *R* at that instant, and this should be represented in the information system.

### 3.2.4.3 Nonempty Population

It must be possible for any relationship type defined in the schema to have a nonempty population. Otherwise, that type would not have any instance during the system's lifetime. An example of a relationship type that would always have an empty population is *Writes (author:Person, Machine)*. Assuming that nobody writes a machine, *Writes* would always have an empty population. No valid instance of *Writes* may exist in the domain such that its second participant is a machine.

A relationship type is *satisfiable* if it may have a nonempty population at a certain time. Similarly, a relationship type is *unsatisfiable* if it must always have an empty population.

### 3.2.4.4 Nonredundancy

Two relationship types are redundant if they must always have the same population. A schema should not include redundant relationship types. For example, a schema could include the following types:

> *Manages (boss:Employee, subordinate:Employee)*
> *Supervises (supervisor:Employee, Employee)*

If, using the logical representation, the following property must hold in the information base,

> *Manages(b,s)* ↔ *Supervises(b,s)*

then *Manages* and *Supervises* are redundant. One of them must be removed from the schema. Redundancy must not be confused with the fact that a given relationship type may have several alternative names (synonyms).

## 3.3 Attributes

Besides relationship types, most conceptual models contain the concept of an attribute of an entity type. Attributes are not strictly needed at a conceptual level,[3] and they are very similar to binary relationship types. Thus it is not clear whether attributes should be used or when.

In a binary relationship type there are two participants, each of which is an entity type playing a role in that type. The two participants must be considered as "colleagues" in the relationship type, because they perform the same function, and neither of them is subordinated to the other. This can be illustrated by a type such as *Reads* (*reader:Person, reading:Book*): a person cannot read without a text, nor can a book be read without a reader. The order of the participants in the schema does not imply a relationship of priority or subordination between them.

However, there are some relationship types in which users and designers may consider a participant as a "characteristic" of the other. For example, in the case of *HasBalance* (*Account, balance:Money*) someone might argue that the participant *balance* is a characteristic of *account* and is thus subordinate to *Account*. The concept of an attribute allows this (subjective) subordination of one participant to another to be defined.

An *attribute* is a binary relationship type $R(p_1:E_1,p_2:E_2)$ in which participant $p_2$ is considered to be a characteristic of $E_1$, or $p_1$ a characteristic of $E_2$. Therefore, an attribute is like a binary relationship, except that users and designers add the interpretation that one participant is a characteristic of the other. Sometimes we say that $E_1$ has attribute ($p_2:E_2$), that $E_2$ is the value of the attribute $p_2$ of $E_1$, or that ($p_2:E_2$) is an attribute of $E_1$.

We denote the schema of an attribute using $P(E_1,E_2)$, which must be understood as equivalent to a relationship type $R(E_1,p:E_2)$. In the above example, attribute *Balance* (*Account, Money*) is equivalent to the relationship type *HasBalance* (*Account, balance:Money*).

Data types may have attributes too. An attribute of a data type is considered to be an immutable characteristic of its instances (values).

### 3.3.1 Conceptual Models Based on Attributes

Some conceptual models use attributes instead of relationship types. The rationale, as we shall see in Chap. 6, is that all relationship types can be transformed into binary ones and that attributes are binary relationship types.

For any relationship type $R(p_1:E_1,p_2:E_2)$ we can define one or two attributes, $P_2(E_1,E_2)$ and/or $P_1(E_2,E_1)$. If we define two, then we must indicate that they correspond to the same relationship type; this can be done by de-

---

[3] There are conceptual modeling languages that do not use attributes. The most prominent one is ORM (Halpin 2001).

claring that one is the *inverse* of the other. For example, $A_1 = Reader$ (*Book, Person*) and $A_2 = Reading$ (*Person, Book*) would be the two attributes that correspond to *Reads* (*reader:Person, reading:Book*). To this we should add that $A_1$ is the inverse attribute of $A_2$, and vice versa.

### 3.3.2 Attribute Pattern Sentence

Linguistically, instances of attributes can also be expressed by grammatical sentences. The pattern sentence of an attribute gives the general structure of those sentences. For example, a pattern sentence of *Balance* (*Account, Money*) could be

The balance of account <*Account*> is the money <*Money*>

This produces sentences such as

The balance of account 12345 is the money 30_*euros*.

As we did for relationship types, we can also distinguish here between implicit and explicit pattern sentences. For attributes, there is only one implicit pattern sentence. If we choose the name of the attribute ($P$) sensibly, the implicit pattern sentence may be enough in most cases. The general structure of the implicit pattern sentence of attribute $P(E_1,E_2)$ is

(A | The) $P$ of $e_1 < E_1>$ is $e_2 < E_2>$

In this sentence, we use the indefinite article if an instance of $E_1$ could have several attribute values and the definite article otherwise.

Alternatively, the following structure might be preferable:

$e_2 < E_2>$ is (a | the) $P$ of $e_1 < E_1>$

which, applied to the previous example, gives

The money <*Money*> is the balance of account <*Account*>

### 3.3.3 Representation in UML

UML shows attributes in the middle compartment of the corresponding entity type. Thus, the attribute $P(E_1,E_2)$ is represented by including the expression $p:E_2$ in the middle compartment of $E_1$. Figure 3.6 shows an entity type *Customer* with three attributes. Textually, we sometimes use the notation $E_1::p$ to refer to attribute $p$ of $E_1$.

In UML, attributes may be marked as read-only, using the keyword {*readOnly*} in braces. In our terminology, this keyword corresponds ap-

| Customer |
| --- |
| name: String |
| birthday: Date |
| balance: Money |

| River |
| --- |
| {«constant»} |
| length:Length |
| {«constant»} |

**Fig. 3.6.** Representation of attributes in UML

proximately to attributes constant with respect to $E_1$. In Fig. 3.6, we indicate that the lengths of rivers are constant. We define that an attribute is permanent with respect to $E_1$ by attaching a constraint stereotyped *permanent* to it. Attributes of data types are always constant, and we may assume that there is a constraint stereotyped *constant* attached to them.

The attributes of a given entity type must have different names. For navigation purposes, the name of an attribute of entity type $E$ should not be the same as the role name of any of the participants of the associations in which $E$ participates.

When we want to depict a particular entity in an object diagram we can also show the value of its attributes, as illustrated in Fig. 3.7. The text attribute *name = value* defines the concrete attribute values of the entity.

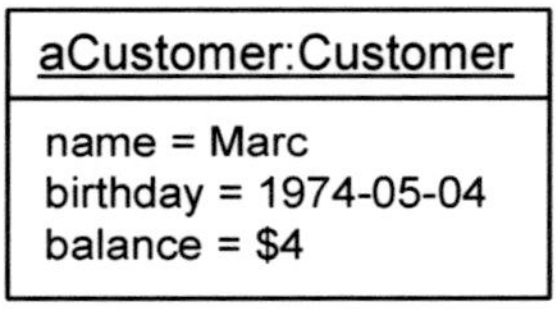

| aCustomer:Customer |
| --- |
| name = Marc |
| birthday = 1974-05-04 |
| balance = $4 |

**Fig. 3.7.** Representation of concrete entities and attribute values in UML

### 3.3.4 On the Use of Attributes

As we have seen, in the case of UML, when a conceptual model uses both relationship types and attributes their graphical representation is different. The graphical representations of relationship types show the entity types that participate in them. The whole schema shows clearly all the relationship types in which an entity type participates. This representation helps users and designers to understand the schema, especially when it is large.

The graphical representation of attributes, on the other hand, shows them in the context of the entity type of which they are a characteristic.

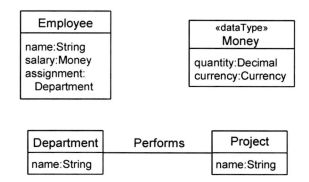

**Fig. 3.8.** An example of attribute misuse. The attribute *assignment* is best modeled by an association

This representation also helps one to understand the meaning of an entity type.

A problem arises when an entity type *E* is the value of the attribute of another type *E'*, because the diagram does not show a line connecting *E* and *E'*. The relationship between *E* and *E'* is not shown in the same way as the others. Figure 3.8 shows three examples. *String* is the value of the attribute *name* of *Employee*, *Department*, and *Project*. The diagram does not have three lines connecting *Employee*, *Department* and *Project* with *String*. In fact, *String* does not appear in the diagram. *Money* is the value of the attribute *salary* of *Employee*, but the diagram does not show this with a line connecting *Employee* and *Money*. There is a line connecting *Department* and *Project* to show the association *Performs*, but there is no line between *Employee* and *Department* to show the attribute *assignment*. The visual treatment of *String*, *Money*, and *Department* is different from that of *Employee* and *Project*.

This problem can be solved by distinguishing between two kinds of entity type: those that are specific to the domain being modeled and those that are independent of it. The former are entity types that must be defined completely in our schema: users and designers must reach agreement on their meaning. The latter are defined instead in other schemas, and they are only used (or reused) in our schema. In general, data types are domain-independent. In the example in Fig. 3.8, we assume that *String* and *Money* are domain-independent, while *Department* is considered particular to the domain being modeled.

On the basis of this distinction, a guideline for the use of attributes could be that the values of attributes should be entity types defined outside our schema. If we apply this guideline to Fig. 3.8, *name* can be an attribute in the three entity types and *salary* can be an attribute of *Employee*. However, *assignment* must be defined as an association between *Employee* and *Department*.

A variant of this guideline is to use attributes for data types and associations for ordinary entity types.

This is not a strict guideline, but it does help to make schemas easier to understand. We can define attributes whose values are entity types defined elsewhere, because their meaning must be sought outside our schema. In the above example, it does not seem sensible to assume that our schema must include a definition of what is meant by *String* and *Money*. On the other hand, we should not define attributes whose values are entity types particular to our domain (such as *Department*), because this makes it more difficult to see the relationships between these types and the others.

## 3.4 Bibliographical Notes

As we noted in the preceding chapter, only a few books describe relationship types in detail without focusing on particular languages. Two notable exceptions are (Kent 1978) and (Tsichritzis and Lochovsky 1982). In contrast, many books addressing a particular language or method give interesting explanations of particular topics, particularly (Nijssen and Halpin 1989, Batini et al. 1992, Martin and Odell 1995, and Halpin 2001). The material presented in this chapter is a synthesis of those texts and other journal and conference papers. One of the most seminal of these was Chen's paper (1976) on the entity–relationship language, which is the basis of this chapter. Wand et al. (1999) provided a thorough analysis of the relationship type concept based on Bunge's ontology.

Chen (1983) gave one of the first analyses of the correspondence between relationship types and English sentences. Rolland and Proix (1992) discussed the correspondence in both senses: from natural language to relationship types (and other schema constructs), and the generation of natural-language sentences from a schema. Hofstede et al. (1997) discussed the uses of verbalizations of fact types in conceptual modeling.

A few languages require a pattern sentence of relationship types to be defined, including OSA (Embley et al. 1992), YSM (Yourdon 1993) and ORM (Halpin 2001). Unary relationship types are allowed in ORM (Halpin 2001) (where they are called unary fact types) and HERM (Thalheim 2000).

The first two properties of the representation of classification (correctness and completeness) are normally implicit and very few works mention them explicitly. Two exceptions are Greenspan et al. (1994), who called them *property induction constraints*, and Martin and Odell (1995).

The nonempty population and nonredundancy properties are presented in Parsons and Wand (1997). The temporal properties of relationship types were presented by Costal et al. (1997).

The guideline on the use of attributes mentioned in Sect. 3.2.4 is well known in conceptual modeling. It has become part of the UML Reference Manual (Rumbaugh et al. 2005, p. 189)

## 3.5 Exercises

**3.1** Define at least ten relationship types found in the domain of a library that deal with books, authors, the order of the authors of a book, titles, publishers, number of pages, and so on. At least one of them must be *n*-ary. Give the implicit (and if necessary the explicit) pattern sentences. Give the representation of the relationship types in logic and in UML. Also, give the representation in logic and in UML of the relationship "*James Rumbaugh* is the *first* author of the book *The UML Reference Manual*".

**3.2** Define a schema with at least ten relationship types found in the domain of persons and their relatives. At least one of them must be *n*-ary. Give the implicit (and if necessary the explicit) pattern sentences. Give the representation of the relationship types in logic and in UML.

**3.3** Determine the schema of a relationship type whose instances can be expressed by sentences such as the following:

- Sudha was a General chair of the 25th edition of the ER conference.
- David was a Program chair of the 25th edition of the ER conference.
- Oscar was the Program chair of the 17th edition of the CAiSE conference.
- Colette was the General chair of the 13th edition of the RE conference.

Show the UML representation of this relationship type and of the four instances. Give an explicit pattern sentence.

**3.4** Determine the relationship types needed in a conceptual schema for a domain consisting of partially or completely filled-in Sudoku (also known as Number Place) puzzles. You will easily find the rules on the Internet. Each puzzle has a code that identifies it. Assume that the entity types needed include *Grid*, *Row*, *Column*, *Region*, and *Cell*. Other types may also be necessary. Give the implicit (and if necessary the explicit) pattern sentences. Give the representation of the relationship types in UML.

**3.5** The periodic table is a tabular display of the known chemical elements. Consider the data depicted in the standard table (to be found in Wikipedia, for example). Determine entity and relationship types in a schema that are able to represent the data depicted in the standard table. Define the schema in UML. Give the explicit pattern sentences where necessary. Show graphically the instantiation of your schema for the element californium (Cf, atomic number 98).

**3.6** The population of a recursive binary relationship type $R(p_1:E, p_2:E)$ can be constrained, like any other. Give an example of each of the following cases:

1. $R$ is permanent with respect to $p_1$ and constant with respect to $p_2$.
2. $R$ is permanent with respect to $p_1$ and $p_2$.
3. $R$ is constant with respect to $p_1$ and $p_2$.

Indicate in each case whether the population of $E$ is constant, permanent, or unconstrained.

# 4 Cardinality Constraints

Cardinality constraints are one of the most important kinds of constraint in conceptual modeling. In addition to constraining the population of relationship types, cardinality constraints help us to understand the meaning of the types involved, and they also play an important role in system design.

In the first section, we study cardinality constraints for binary relationship types, including attributes. We discuss the satisfiability of these constraints, and introduce a method for checking whether or not a schema with these constraints is satisfiable. In the second section, we study cardinality constraints for the $n$-ary case. Finally, in Sect. 4.3, we present an important guideline for the design of relationship types in conceptual schemas.

## 4.1 Cardinality Constraints of Binary Relationship Types

Let $R(p_1:E_1,p_2:E_2)$ be a binary relationship type. The *cardinality constraint* (or cardinality, for short) between $p_1$ and $p_2$ in $R$, written $Card(p_1; p_2; R)$, is a pair

$$Card(p_1; p_2; R) = (min,max)$$

that indicates the minimum and maximum numbers of entities of type $E_2$ that may be related, in $R$, to any entity of type $E_1$ at any time; $Card(p_2; p_1; R)$ is similarly defined. The minimum cardinality, *min*, must be equal to or greater than zero, and the maximum, *max*, must be greater than zero and not less than *min*.

For example, for the relationship type

> *Reads (reader:Person, reading:Book)*

the cardinalities

> *Card(reader; reading; Reads) = (0,3)*
> *Card(reading; reader; Reads) = (0,1)*

mean that a person may read between 0 and 3 books at any time, and that a book may be read by 0 or 1 person at any time.

Formally, $Card(p_1; p_2; R) = (min,max)$ if[1]

$$E_1(e_1) \rightarrow min \leq |\{e_2 \mid R(e_1,e_2)\}| \leq max$$

In this formula, $\{e_2 \mid R(e_1,e_2)\}$ is the set of entities $e_2$ that are related to the entity $e_1$. The formula states that, for any $e_1$, the cardinality of that set must be equal to or greater than $min$, and equal to or less than $max$.

We simplify the notation $Card(p_1; p_2; R) = (min,max)$ as follows:

- $Cmin(p_1; p_2; R)$ denotes the minimum cardinality ($min$).
- $Cmax(p_1; p_2; R)$ denotes the maximum cardinality ($max$).
- For $Card$, $Cmin$, and $Cmax$, we omit the third argument ($R$) when it is clear from the context that we are referring to $R$.

From the definition, we can see that if $Card(p_1; p_2) = (min,max)$, then $Card(p_1; p_2) = (min',max')$ for any $min' \leq min$ and $max' \geq max$. Usually we are interested only in the strongest $min$ and $max$ numbers, which are those such that if $Card(p_1; p_2) = (min,max)$ is valid, then $Card(p_1; p_2) = (min',max')$ is false for any pair or numbers $min'$ and $max'$ such that $min' > min$ or $max' < max$.

When $Cmin(p_1; p_2; R) > 0$, we say that the *participation* of $E_1$ in $R$ with role $p_1$ is *total* or *mandatory*, because all instances of $E_1$ must participate in some relationship of $R$, at any time. When $Cmin(p_1; p_2; R) = 0$, we say that the participation is *partial* or *optional*, because an instance of $E_1$ may not necessarily participate in $R$ with role $p_1$.

When $Cmax(p_1; p_2; R) = 1$, we say that there is a *functional correspondence* between $p_1$ and $p_2$ in $R$, or that there is a *functional dependency* between them, denoted by $\{p_1\} \rightarrow \{p_2\}$. When $Cmax(p_1; p_2; R) > 1$, the correspondence is *nonfunctional*.

Some cardinality constraints are not actually constraints. These are

$$Cmin(p_1; p_2; R) = 0$$
$$Cmax(p_1; p_2; R) = \infty$$
$$Card(p_1; p_2; R) = (0,\infty)$$

We say that these cardinalities are *unconstrained*. All other cardinalities are *constrained*.

Normally, cardinality constraints are shown graphically. The value of $Card(p_1; p_2; R) = (min,max)$ is shown next to the graphical element corresponding to $R$ in the form $min..max$. Some languages show $min..max$ near $p_1$, while others show it near $p_2$.

---

[1] In order to simplify the notation, variables without quantifiers are assumed to be universally quantified in the front of the formula.

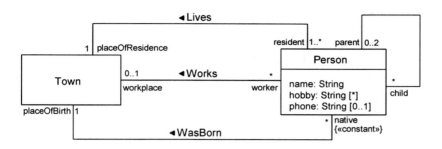

**Fig. 4.1.** Examples of cardinality constraints in UML

In UML, cardinality constraints are called multiplicities. The value of $Card(p_1; p_2; R) = (min,max)$ is shown near $p_2$. When $min = max$, we write just one number. If $max$ is unconstrained ($\infty$), this is denoted by an asterisk. When $min = 0$ and $max = \infty$, we write an asterisk only.

Figure 4.1 shows several cardinality constraints. A person may have between 0 and an unconstrained number (*) of children, and a person may have between 0 and 2 parents (0..2). In addition, all of the people were born and live in a town and, optionally, work in a town. At least one person lives in any given town, but it is possible that nobody works in it.

In Fig. 4.1 note that:

- There is a total participation of *Person* and *Town* in *Lives*.
- There is a total participation of *Person* in *WasBorn*.
- All the other participations are partial.
- There is a functional correspondence between *Person* and *Town* in *Lives*, *Works*, and *WasBorn*.
- All the other correspondences are nonfunctional.

The above definition of *Card* states that the value of $Card(p_1; p_2; R)$ is a single pair $(min,max)$. The definition may be easily generalized to a set of natural numbers *I*. The formal definition is then

$$E_1(e_1) \rightarrow |\{e_2 \mid R(e_1,e_2)\}| \in I$$

For example, if we want to state that a person may read 0, 2, or 4 books at the same time, then $Card(reader; reading; Reads) = \{0,2,4\}$. In practice, the sets *I* are often intervals $\{min_1, ..., max_1, ..., min_n, ..., max_n\}$, which explains why these constraints are called *interval* cardinality constraints, or *int-cardinality* constraints.

### 4.1.1 Existence Dependency Relationship Types

Let $R(p_1:E_1,p_2:E_2)$ be a binary relationship type. We say that $R$ is an *existence dependency* relationship type and that $E_1$ is *existence-dependent* on $E_2$ if the following conditions are satisfied:

- $Card(p_1; p_2; R) = (1,1)$
- $R$ is constant with respect to $p_1$.

In the example of Fig. 4.1, *WasBorn* is an existence dependency relationship type, and *Person* is existence-dependent on *Town*. Each instance of *Person* has one and only one *placeOfBirth*, which is always the same.

Existence dependency relationship types are important because, as we shall see in Chap. 6, any relationship type can be transformed into a set of existence dependency relationship types.

### 4.1.2 Attributes

Cardinality constraints can also be defined for attributes. An attribute $P(E_1,E_2)$, corresponding to a relationship type $R(e_1:E_1,p:E_2)$ is said to be *single-valued* if the correspondence between $e_1$ and $p$ is functional. Otherwise, the attribute is said to be *multivalued*. Moreover, the attribute is *total* if the participation of $E_1$ in $P$ is total; otherwise, it is *partial*.

For example, consider the attributes *Name (Person, String)* and *Hobby (Person, String)*. If a person has one name and may have any number of hobbies, then *Name* is single-valued and total, while *Hobby* is multivalued and partial.

In UML, the cardinality constraint of an attribute $P(E_1,E_2)$ is shown near the attribute name (see Figure 4.1). When the constraint is not shown, it is assumed to be (1,1), that is, the default cardinality constraint for an attribute is total and single-valued (as in the case of *name* in Fig. 4.1).

The cardinality constraint between $e_2$ and $e_1$ is not defined and is assumed to be unconstrained, if not specified otherwise elsewhere in the schema. If this assumption does not hold, an alternative could be to define an association instead of an attribute. Figure 4.1 states that there may be several persons with the same name, the same hobby, or the same phone. If, for example, we want to specify that there may not be two persons with the same name, we will need to define an explicit integrity constraint, as we shall see in Chap. 9. In this latter case, an alternative could be to define a binary association *HasName (Person, name:String)* with $Card(name; person) = (0,1)$, but this is rarely done. There is a trade-off between defin-

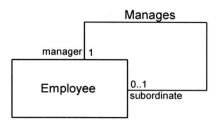

**Fig. 4.2.** A recursive relationship type with inconsistent cardinality constraints

ing an attribute and an explicit integrity constraint and defining a binary association and its two cardinalities.

### 4.1.2 Recursive Relationship Types

In general, the two cardinality constraints of a binary relationship types are independent of each other. However, it is interesting to observe that for recursive relationship types, some combinations are inconsistent, because one of the two cardinalities is either not valid in the domain or not defined with the strongest numbers.

Consider the example in Fig. 4.2. Each employee has exactly one manager and may have at most one subordinate. If these two cardinalities are valid, then we must (why?) have $Card(manager; subordinate) = (1,1)$, which is stronger than the $(0,1)$ shown in the figure: each employee must have exactly one subordinate. Also, note that $(1,\infty)$ would not be the strongest numbers of $Card(manager; subordinate)$.

In what follows, we give a set of consistency rules that the two cardinalities must satisfy.[2] Let $R(p_1:E,p_2:E)$ be a binary recursive relationship type, with $Card(p_1; p_2) = (min_1, max_1)$ and $Card(p_2; p_1) = (min_2,max_2)$. These cardinalities must satisfy the following consistency rules:

1. If $max_1 = max_2 = 1$, then $min_1 = min_2 = 0$ or $min_1 = min_2 = 1$. This rule is violated in the example in Fig. 4.2.
2. If $max_1 > 1$ and $max_2 = 1$, then $min_1 = 0$.
3. If $max_1 = 1$ and $max_2 > 1$, then $min_2 = 0$. This is symmetrical to rule 2.

---

[2] For proofs of these rules, see the references given at the end of the chapter.

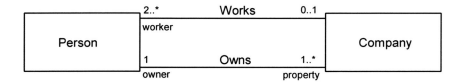

**Fig. 4.3.** Example of unsatisfiable cardinality constraints

## 4.1.3 Satisfiability of Cardinality Constraints

In general, conceptual schemas include many integrity constraints. The *legal* instances of an information base are those that satisfy all the constraints. A schema *S* is *satisfiable* if it admits at least one legal instance of an information base. For some constraints, it may happen that only empty or nonfinite information bases satisfy them. In conceptual modeling, the information bases of interest are finite and may be populated.

We then say that a schema *S* is *strongly satisfiable* if it admits at least one nonempty and finite legal instance of the information base. Schemas that are not strongly satisfiable are considered to be incorrect.

In this chapter, we examine whether or not a schema with a set of cardinality constraints is strongly satisfiable. Fortunately, there is a method that provides an answer to this question. The method is able to deal with the two cardinality constraints that we can define for binary relationship types. As we shall see in the next section, for *n*-ary types we can define many more cardinality constraints, but the method is not yet able to cope with all of them. We shall describe the binary case only. We omit the proof of the correctness of the method, which can be found in the references given at the end of the chapter.

Figure 4.3 shows an example that is not strongly satisfiable. The reader is invited to verify that no nonempty finite population of the four types (two entity types and two relationship types) satisfies the four cardinality constraints. The method described below enables us to detect the problem in a systematic way.

The method is based on building a directed graph *G* and checking that it does not contain cycles of a particular type. Figure 4.4 shows the graph corresponding to the example in Fig. 4.3. The graph *G* contains a vertex for each entity or relationship type in the schema. We have used diamonds to represent the relationship types. There are two arcs for each participant

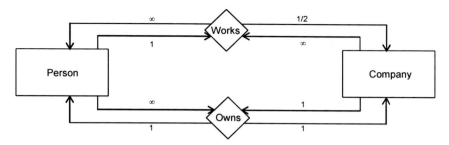

**Fig. 4.4.** The graph $G$ corresponding to the schema of Fig. 4.3

in a relationship type: one from the relationship type to the participant entity type and the other in the opposite direction.

Each arc has a weight, which is computed as follows. Let $R(p_1:E_1,p_2:E_2)$ be a binary relationship type with cardinalities $Card(p_1; p_2) = (min_{12},max_{12})$ and $Card(p_2; p_1) = (min_{21},max_{21})$. The arc from $R$ to $E_1$ has a weight $w_{12}$, where

- $w_{12} = \infty$ if $min_{12} = 0$;
- $w_{12} = 0$ if $min_{12} = \infty$;
- $w_{12} = 1/min_{12}$ otherwise.

The arc from $E_1$ to $R$ has a weight $max_{12}$.

In Fig. 4.3 we have $Card(company; worker) = (2,\infty)$. Therefore, the arc from *Works* to *Company* has a weight ½, and the arc from *Company* to *Works* has a weight $\infty$. The weights of the two arcs between $R$ and $E_2$ are computed in a similar manner.

It is obvious that $G$ contains cycles. A *critical* cycle of $G$ is a nonempty sequence of arcs $(v_0,v_1), (v_1,v_2), ..., (v_{k-1},v_k)$ such that

- $v_0 = v_k$ and
- $v_1, ..., v_k$ are mutually distinct, and
- the product of the weights of the arcs $(v_0,v_1), ..., (v_{k-1},v_k)$ is less than 1.

It can be proved that a schema is strongly satisfiable if the graph $G$ does not contain a critical cycle. In Fig. 4.4 there are some critical cycles, such as

(*Works*, *Company*), (*Company*, *Owns*), (*Owns*, *Person*),
(*Person*, *Works*)

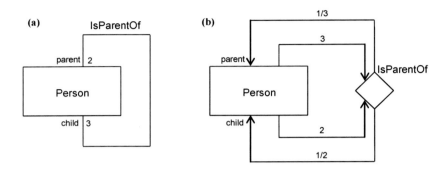

**Fig. 4.5.** A recursive relationship type with nonsatisfiable cardinality constraints

for which the product of the weights is ½. Therefore, the schema in Fig. 4.3 is not strongly satisfiable.

The method described above can also be applied to recursive types. An example is shown in Fig. 4.5. The schema (a) includes the constraints that each person must have two parents and three children. The corresponding graph (b) has a critical cycle, which proves that the schema is not strongly satisfiable.

## 4.2 Cardinality Constraints of *n*-ary Relationship Types

We have seen that for a binary relationship type $R(p_1:E_1,p_2:E_2)$ we have to define two cardinality constraints: $Card(p_1; p_2)$ and $Card(p_2; p_1)$. Let us now consider a ternary type, such as *Uses* (*Programmer*, *Language*, *Project*), shown in Fig. 4.6, with the explicit pattern sentence:

> The programmer *<Programmer>* uses the language *<Language>* in project *<Project>*

For ternary types, we can define up to 12 cardinality constraints. The constraints for the example are:

1. *Card(programmer; language)*, which gives the (minimum and maximum) number of languages that a programmer may use at a given time. A minimum of zero will indicate that there may be programmers who do not participate in any instance of *Uses* relationship.

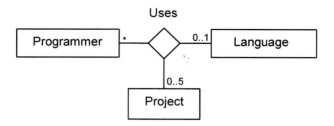

**Fig. 4.6.** Graphical representation of cardinality constraints in ternary associations

2. *Card*(*programmer*; *project*), which gives the number of projects in which a programmer may participate at a given time. As above, a minimum cardinality of zero means that there may be programmers who do not participate in any instance of the *Uses* relationship.
3. *Card*(*language*; *programmer*), which gives the number of programmers who may use a language. A minimum cardinality of zero means that some languages may not be used at some given time.
4. *Card*(*language*; *project*), which gives the number of projects that may use a language. A minimum cardinality of zero means that some languages may not be used at some given time.
5. *Card*(*project*; *programmer*), which indicates the number of programmers who may participate in a project. A minimum of zero means that not all projects participate in *Uses*.
6. *Card*(*project*; *language*), which indicates the number of languages that may be used in a project. As above, a minimum of zero means that not all projects participate in *Uses*.
7. *Card*(*programmer, language*; *project*). Note that the first argument is now a set of roles (which we write without braces) rather than just one role. The cardinality gives the number of projects in which a programmer may participate using a given language, that is, how many projects are allowed for a pair (programmer, language).
8. *Card*(*programmer, project*; *language*), which gives the number of languages a programmer may use in a project.
9. *Card*(*language, project*; *programmer*), which gives the number of programmers who may use a language in a project.
10. *Card*(*programmer*; *project, language*). Note that in this case the second argument is a set of two roles rather than just one role, as was the case before. The cardinality gives the number of project–language pairs in which a programmer may participate.

11. *Card*(*language*; *programmer*, *project*), which gives the number of programmer–project pairs that may be related to a language.
12. *Card*(*project*; *programmer*, *language*), which gives the number of programmer–language pairs that may be related to a project.

The formal definition of cardinality constraints for *n*-ary relationship types is as follows. Let the type be $R(p_1:E_1, ..., p_n:E_n)$, and let $p = \{p_1, ..., p_i\}$ and $q = \{p_{i+1}, ..., p_k\}$ be disjoint subsets of roles $\{p_1, ..., p_n\}$. We say that $Card(p; q) = (min,max)$ if

$$E_1(e_1) \wedge ... \wedge E_i(e_i) \rightarrow$$
$$min \leq |\{(e_{i+1}, ..., e_k) \mid R(e_1, ..., e_i, e_{i+1}, ..., e_k, ..., e_n)\}| \leq max$$

When $p = \{p_1:E_1\}$ is a single role, $q$ is a set of one or more roles, and $Cmin(p_1; q) > 0$ we say that there is total participation of $E_1$ in $R$ with role $p_1$, because all instances of $E_1$ always participate in some relationship of $R$. When $Cmin(p_1; q) = 0$, we say that the participation is partial, because not all instances of $E_1$ participate in $R$.

When $Cmax(p; q) = 1$, we say that there is a functional correspondence between $p$ and $q$ in $R$, or that there is a functional dependency $\{p\} \rightarrow \{q\}$. Note that $p$ and $q$ are one or more roles.

It is difficult to show all the cardinality constraints for *n*-ary types graphically. This is the reason why conceptual modeling languages choose to show only a few of them. The typical options are:

- To show $Card(p; q; R)$, where $q$ is a single role and $p$ are the remaining roles in $R$. The value is shown next to the line corresponding to role $q$. This is the option taken by UML.
- To show $Card(p; q; R)$, where $p$ is a single role and $q$ are the remaining roles in $R$. The value is shown next to the line corresponding to role $p$.

The other cardinalities must be shown separately, possibly using a general constraint definition language such as OCL in UML. Sometimes a cardinality is unconstrained; this can be considered to be the default value, if not stated otherwise.

In the previous example, the cardinalities could be:

1. *Card*(*programmer*; *language*) $= (0,2)$ if a programmer cannot use more than two languages at a given time.
2. *Card*(*programmer*; *project*) $= (0,5)$ if a programmer cannot participate in more than five projects at any time.
3. *Card*(*language*; *programmer*) $= (0,\infty)$. This is an example of unconstrained cardinality.

4. $Card(language; project) = (0,\infty)$.
5. $Card(project; programmer) = (1,\infty)$ if all projects must have at least one programmer at all times.
6. $Card(project; language) = (1,\infty)$ if all projects must use at least one language.
7. $Card(programmer, language; project) = (0,5)$ if a programmer cannot use a language in more than five projects at any time.
8. $Card(programmer, project; language) = (0,1)$ if a programmer can use at most one language in a project.
9. $Card(language, project; programmer) = (0,\infty)$.
10. $Card(programmer; project, language) = (0,5)$.
11. $Card(language; programmer, project) = (0,\infty)$.
12. $Card(project; programmer, language) = (1,\infty)$.

In UML we can represent only constraints 7, 8 and 9, as shown in Fig. 4.6. The remaining nine cardinality constraints, if they are not unconstrained, must be defined in the same way as for any other general constraint, as we shall see in Chap. 9.

### 4.2.1 Consistency and Inference Rules

The cardinality constraints corresponding to an $n$-ary relationship type $R(p_1{:}E_1, \ldots, p_n{:}E_n)$ are not completely independent of one another. There are *consistency* rules that must be satisfied. If these rules are not satisfied, some constraint is either not valid or not defined with the strongest numbers. Several of these rules are provided below. Their formalization and proofs can be found in the references given at the end of this chapter. In the rules, $p = \{p_1, \ldots, p_i\}$, $q = \{p_{i+1}, \ldots, p_k\}$ and $s = \{p_{k+1}, \ldots, p_l\}$ are disjoint subsets of roles $\{p_1, \ldots, p_n\}$ and $ps$ denotes the union of sets $p$ and $s$.

- CR1 (augmentation):

    $Cmin(p; q) \geq Cmin(ps; q)$
    $Cmax(p; q) \geq Cmax(ps; q)$

    For instance,

    $Cmax(programmer; language) = 2 \geq$
    $Cmax(programmer, project; language) = 1$.

- CR2 (transitive):

    $Cmin(p; q) * Cmax(q; s) \geq Cmin(p; qs)$
    $Cmax(p; q) * Cmax(q; s) \geq Cmax(p; qs)$

    For instance,

    $Card(project; programmer) = (1,\infty),$
    $Card(programmer; language) = (0,2),$
    $Card(project; programmer, language) = (1,\infty),$

    were $\infty*2 \geq \infty$ and $1*2 \geq 1$.

- CR3 (decomposition):

    $Cmin(p; qs) \geq Cmin(p; q)$
    $Cmax(p; qs) \geq Cmax(p; q).$

    For instance,

    $Cmax(programmer; project, language) = 5 \geq$
    $Cmax(programmer; language) = 2.$

- CR4 (union):

    $Cmin(p; q) * Cmax(p; s) \geq Cmin(p; qs)$
    $Cmax(p; q) * Cmax(p; s) \geq Cmax(p; qs)$

- CR5 (pseudotransitive):

    If $t \subseteq p$,
    $Cmin(p; q) * Cmax(qt; s) \geq Cmin(p; qs)$
    $Cmax(p; q) * Cmax(qt; s) \geq Cmax(p; qs)$

- CR6 (uniformity):

    If $Cmin(p; q) = 0$, then for any $q'$: $Cmin(p; q') = 0$

In the above example, $Cmin(programmer; language) = 0$. According to the uniformity rule, all cardinalities for which the first argument is the role *programmer* must have a minimum of zero.

The above rules can be used as *inference* rules, that is, rules that allow us to infer some cardinalities from others. The best known of these rules are the inference rules for functional dependencies, which are as follows:

- IR1 (augmentation):

    If $\{p\} \rightarrow \{q\}$ then $\{ps\} \rightarrow \{q\}$.

- IR2 (transitive):

    If $\{p\} \to \{q\}$ and $\{q\} \to \{s\}$ then $\{p\} \to \{s\}$.

- IR3 (decomposition):

    If $\{p\} \to \{qs\}$ then $\{p\} \to \{q\}$.

- IR4 (union):

    If $\{p\} \to \{q\}$ and $\{p\} \to \{s\}$ then $\{p\} \to \{qs\}$.

- IR5 (pseudotransitive):

    If $\{p\} \to \{q\}$ and $\{qs\} \to \{t\}$ then $\{ps\} \to \{t\}$.

Two useful inference rules related to the minimum cardinality are

- IMin1 (uniformity):

    If $Cmin(p; q) = 0$, for any $q'$: $Cmin(p; q') = 0$.

    (This is the same as CR6, the uniformity rule.)
- IMin2 (augmentation):

    If $Cmin(p; q) = 0$, for any $s$: $Cmin(ps; q) = 0$.

Two useful rules related to the unconstrained maximum cardinality are

- IMax1: If $Cmax(ps; q) = \infty$, $Cmax(p; q) = \infty$.
- IMax2: If $Cmax(p; q) = \infty$, $Cmax(p; qs) = \infty$.

## 4.3 Maximal Participation

Let us assume that in the domain of a university, we have the entity types *Person, Student, Teacher*, and *Course*, and the following relationship type (Fig. 4.7),

   *Takes* (*student:Person, Course*)

with partial participation of *student* in *Takes*, that is, *Cmin* (*student*; *course*) = 0. If we assume that only students can take courses, and that students are persons too, then the schema of *Takes* is unsatisfactory, owing to its lack of precision. It is not incorrect, because students are persons, but it lacks precision, because not all persons take courses. For this schema,

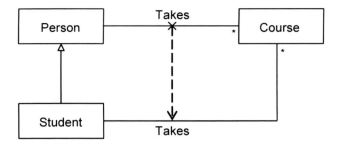

**Fig. 4.7.** Example of application of the maximal-participation guideline

therefore, we must define an additional constraint that guarantees that only instances of *Student* may take courses.

A simpler schema, which saves us the additional constraint, is *Takes (Student, Course)*, in which the participation of *Student* in *Takes* may be total if all students must take at least one course.

The above observation leads us to a guideline that we call the *maximal-participation* guideline. It has two variants, one simple and the other complex. The formalization of the simple variant is as follows. Let $R(p_1:E_1, ..., p_i:E_i, ..., p_n:E_n)$ be a type such that the participation of $p_i:E_i$ in $R$ is partial. If the schema includes an entity type $E'_i$ such that at any time the following conditions hold,

- $E'_i(e) \rightarrow E_i(e)$
- and the entities in the set $\{e_i \mid E_i(e) \wedge \neg E'_i(e)\}$ cannot participate in $R$,

then we should substitute $E'_i$ for $E_i$ in $R$.

Observe the application of the guideline to *Takes (student:Person, Course)*:

- Students are Persons: *Student (e)* $\rightarrow$ *Person (e)*
- *Persons* who are not *Students* cannot take courses.
- We should substitute *Student* for *Person* in *Takes.*

Note that the maximal-participation guideline requires that the entity type substituted for participant $p_i:E_i$ *already* exists in the schema. We might be tempted to apply the guideline by defining *new* entity types. For example, consider the type *Owns (owner:Person, Car)*, with the partial participation of *Person*. The participation could be made total by defining a new entity type *CarOwner*, whose population would be a subset of that of *Person*, and changing the relationship type schema to *Owns*

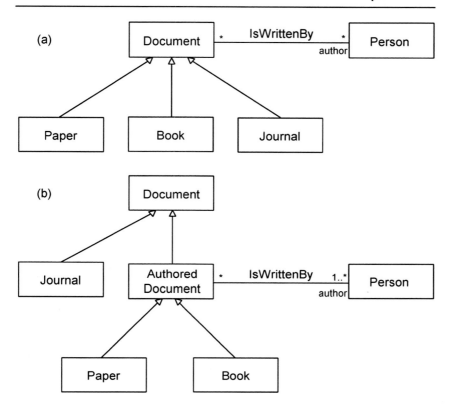

**Fig. 4.8.** Another example of application of the maximal-participation guideline

(*owner:CarOwner, Car*). However, this change is acceptable only if *CarOwner* is a concept that is already used in (or may be assimilated into) the domain. Otherwise, we would compromise the correctness property of the *CarOwner* representation: *CarOwner* could be considered an artificial concept.

The above simple variant of the guideline is almost a rule, because the resulting schemas are always simpler and do not incur any cost.

The case of the complex variant is not as clear. Let $R(p_1:E_1,\ldots, p_i:E_i,\ldots, p_n:E_n)$ be a type such that the participation of $p_i:E_i$ in $R$ is partial. If the conceptual schema contains a set of entity types $E_{i,1}, \ldots, E_{i,m}$ such that at any time the following conditions hold:

- $E_{i,j}(e) \rightarrow E_i(e)$ for $j = 1, \ldots, m$

- and the entities in the set $\{e \mid E_i \, (e) \wedge \neg \, (E_{i,1} \, (e) \vee \ldots \vee E_{i,m} \, (e))\}$ cannot participate in $R$,

then we should define a new entity type $E'_i$, whose population is the union of $E_{i,1}, \ldots, E_{i,m}$, and substitute $E'_i$ for $E_i$ in $R$.

This variant of the guideline is not as strong as the previous one. In some cases, designers or users may feel that the advantages of obtaining more precise participation do not compensate for the cost of defining a new entity type ($E'_i$).

For example, consider the schema shown in Fig. 4.8a, which has the entity types *Document*, *Book*, *Paper*, *Journal*, and *Person*, and the relationship type *IsWrittenBy* (*Document*, *author:Person*), with partial participation of *Document*. However, we know that

- *Book* (*e*) → *Document* (*e*)
- *Paper* (*e*) → *Document* (*e*)
- and the entities in the set $\{e \mid Document \, (e) \wedge \neg \, (Book \, (e) \vee Paper \, (e))\}$ cannot participate in *IsWrittenBy*.

If we were to apply the guideline, we would define a new entity type *AuthoredDocument*, whose population would be the union of *Book* and *Paper*, and we would substitute *AuthoredDocument* for *Document* in *IsWrittenBy*. The participation of *AuthoredDocument* in *IsWrittenBy* would now total, see Fig. 4.8b.

## 4.4 Bibliographical Notes

Apart from referential integrity constraints, cardinality constraints are the best known and more widely used constraints related to relationship types. They appeared in Chen (1976) and, since then, they have been adopted for almost all conceptual modeling languages. Liddle et al. (1993) presented a thorough study of the use of cardinality constraints in conceptual models. McAllister (1998) gave a detailed analysis of cardinality constraints in *n*-ary relationship types. Thalheim (2000) included a synthesis of most of the formal research that had been carried out on cardinality constraints. Siau et al. (1997) showed that cardinality constraints play a key role in the understanding of relationship types.

Consistency rules for recursive binary relationship types were presented by Dullea and Song (1999) and Dullea et al. (2003). McAllister (1998) gave rules for *n*-ary relationship types. Armstrong (1974) presented the inference rules for functional dependencies and showed that they were sound and complete.

The initial formulation of the problem of the satisfiability of cardinality constraints appeared in Lenzerini and Nobili (1990). That work also presented a method for discovering unsatisfiable constraints. Our Fig. 4.2 was inspired by an example given in that paper. The method was extended by Thalheim (1992) and generalized by Hartmann (1998).

The guideline on maximal participation was described by Batini et al. (1992), Boman et al. (1997), Dey et al. (1999), and Wand et al. (1999). An even stronger version of the guideline has been advocated by Bodart et al. (2001) and Gemino and Wand (2005).

## 4.5 Exercises

**4.1** Consider the domain of lists and their elements. A list is an ordered sequence of $n$ elements, with $n \geq 0$, and without duplicates. An element belongs to one, and only one, list. Figure 4.9 shows the two relationship types needed to represent the composition of lists, and to allow their traversal. Define the cardinality constraints of these relationship types.

**4.2** Consider a change in the domain of the previous exercise: now an element may be part of the list more than once (duplicates are allowed, not necessarily in consecutive positions). Make the corresponding change in Fig. 4.9, and determine the cardinalities of the resulting relationship types. Use only binary relationship types.[3]

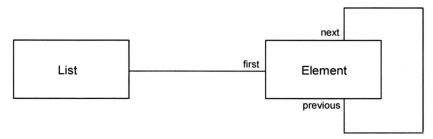

**Fig. 4.9.** Fragment of a conceptual schema for Exercise 4.1

---

[3] If you are already familiar with the concept of reification (association classes), refrain from applying it in this exercise.

**4.3** Consider another change in the domain in Exercise 4.1: now, an element may be part of one or more lists (and not just one) at the same time. As in Exercise 4.1, the lists do not contain duplicates. An element may occupy a different position in each list in which it participates. Make the corresponding change in Fig. 4.9, and determine the cardinalities of the resulting relationship types. Use only binary relationship types.[3]

**4.4** Consider again the domain of lists and their elements. A list is an ordered sequence of $n$ elements, with $n \geq 0$. Now, an element may be part of a list more than once (duplicates are allowed) and may be part of one or more lists at the same time. Figure 4.10 shows a ternary relationship type that represents the composition of such lists. Define the complete set (12) of cardinality constraints of this type.

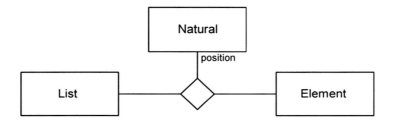

**Fig. 4.10.** Fragment of a conceptual schema for Exercise 4.4

**4.5** Assume a domain in which there are students, courses and teachers, and in which students take courses taught by teachers. In this domain, consider the relationship type *Takes (Student, Course, Teacher)*, shown in Fig. 4.11, with the following constraints:

- A teacher teaches one course at most. Some teachers may not teach courses.
- A course is taught by at least one and at most three teachers.
- A student may take six courses at most. All students take courses.
- A student has, at most, one teacher for a given course.
- A course has at least one student.

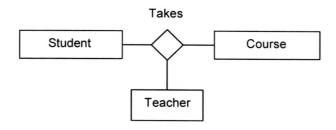

**Fig. 4.11.** Example of ternary association in UML for exercise 4.5

Define the 12 cardinality constraints of *Takes*. Check that they satisfy the consistency rules described in Sect. 4.2.1. Indicate which of these 12 cardinality constraints can be represented in the UML diagram shown in Fig. 4.11.

**4.6** We have seen that we can define up to 12 cardinality constraints for a ternary relationship type. How many can be defined for a quaternary relationship type?

**4.7** The cardinality constraints of the recursive relationship type shown in Fig. 4.5 are not strongly satisfiable. Check that if we change *Card(parent; child)* to (2,2) then it is strongly satisfiable. Give an instantiation of Fig. 4.5 that strongly satisfies the new cardinality constraints. Explain why this instantiation is implausible, and give the cardinalities of such a relationship type that you think are plausible.

**4.8** One kind of cardinality constraint for *n*-ary relationship types defined in (Liddle et al. 1993) is the *co-occurrence* constraint. Assume that there is a relationship type $R(p_1:E_1, ..., p_n:E_n)$ and let $p = \{p_1, ..., p_i\}$ and $q = \{p_{i+1}, ..., p_k\}$ be disjoint subsets of roles $\{p_1, ..., p_n\}$. A co-occurrence constraint

$$Co(p; q; R) = (min, max)$$

means that a tuple $(e_1, ..., e_i)$ that appears in some relationship of $R$ must co-occur (appear together) with at least *min* and at most *max* tuples $(e_{i+1}, ..., e_k)$. (Note that *min* > 0: why?) Formally, using the notation defined in Sect. 4.2, we have $Co(p; q; R) = (min, max)$ if

$$min \leq |\{(e_{i+1}, ..., e_k) \mid R(e_1, ..., e_i, e_{i+1}, ..., e_k, ..., e_n)\}| \leq max$$

1. Define the co-occurrence constraints of Exercise 4.5.
2. Justify the following relationships between *Co-card* and the *Card* studied in this chapter:

- *Cmax*($p$; $q$; $R$) = *Co-max*($p$; $q$; $R$).
- If *Cmin*($p$; $q$; $R$) > 0, *Cmin*($p$; $q$; $R$) = *Co-min*($p$; $q$; $R$).
- If *Cmin*($p$; $q$; $R$) = 0, *Cmin*($p$; $q$; $R$) < *Co-min*($p$; $q$; $R$).

# 5 Particular Kinds of Relationship Type

As we saw in Chap. 2, "entity types are concepts whose instances are identifiable objects ..." An entity is identifiable if there is a linguistic expression that denotes it. Most of these expressions are built from reference relationship types, a particular kind of relationship type described in Sect. 5.1. In Sect. 5.2, we discuss how to use reference relationship types to identify entities. Section 5.3 explains that in general the participants of a relationship type should be entity types rather than its identifiers.

In conceptual modeling, relationship types should be elementary, that is, it should not be possible to decompose them into a number of smaller relationship types without losing information. Section 5.4 describes the concept of elementary relationship types in detail. Bearing in mind that nonelementary relationship types should be decomposed, and that a relationship type may be nonelementary for several reasons, in Sect. 5.5 we describe the two most common cases, which are the result of functional and multivalued dependencies, and explain how they should be dealt with. In the next chapter we will study other kinds of decomposition.

## 5.1 Reference Relationship Types

A reference to an entity $e$ is an expression, written in some language, that denotes $e$. References are generally built from binary relationship types that have particular properties. For example, the type *HasCapital* (*Country*, *capital:Town*) shown in Fig. 5.1 allows references to countries to be built, such as "*the country whose capital is the town London*". Of course, not all relationship types serve to build references. In the present example, if a town could be the capital of several countries then *HasCapital* could not be used for that purpose.

There are three main ways of building references from binary relationship types. Starting with the most widely used way, we describe them below.

**Fig. 5.1.** *HasCapital* and *ISOcode* are simple references to *Country*. The attribute *name* is a simple reference to *Town*

### 5.1.1 Simple Reference

Let $R(p:E,p_1:E_1)$ be a binary relationship type. We say that $R$ is a simple reference relationship type for $E$ or, also, that $p_1$ is a reference to $E$ through $R$ if the following properties hold:

- The correspondence between $p_1$ and $p$ is functional.
- The participation of $E$ in $R$ with role $p$ is total.

Moreover, if $R$ is constant with respect to $p_1$, then we say that $R$ is an *immutable* simple reference to $E$; otherwise, it is a *mutable* one.

Observe that (Fig. 5.1)

*HasCapital* (*Country*, *capital:Town*)

is a mutable simple reference to *Country* (or, equivalently, *capital* is a reference to *Country* through *HasCapital*), because:

- The correspondence between *capital* and *country* is functional: a town may be the capital of one country at most.
- The participation of *country* in *HasCapital* is total: each country has one capital.
- *HasCapital* is not constant with respect to *capital*: a country may change its capital.

Note that if the participation of *Country* in *HasCapital* were not total, then there might be countries without capitals; therefore, we would not be able to reference all countries using their capitals.

Figure 5.1 shows another simple reference to *Country*: the *ISOcode* attribute of countries, which is a *String*. In this case, the reference is immutable.

Figure 5.1 also includes the relationship type (attribute)

*Name* (*Town*, *name:String*)

which is a mutable simple reference to *Town*, because:

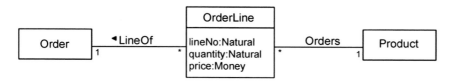

**Fig. 5.2.** The associations *LineOf* and *Orders* are a compound reference to *OrderLine*

- (We assume that) the correspondence between *name* and *town* is functional.
- The participation of *Town* in *Name* is total.
- *Name* is not constant: a town may change its name.

### 5.1.2 Compound Reference

References to an entity may sometimes be built using not one binary relationship type, but two or more. For example, from *LineOf* (*OrderLine, Order*) and *Orders* (*OrderLine, Product*), as shown in Fig. 5.2, we can build expressions such as *"The order line of product ABC in order 123"*. These expressions are references provided that orders do not have two order lines ordering the same product (although there may be order lines with the same product in different orders).

Let $R_1(p_1':E,p_1:E_1)$, ..., $R_n(p_n':E,p_n:E_n)$ be binary relationship types with $n \geq 2$. We say that the set $\{R_1, ..., R_n\}$ is a *compound reference* to $E$ if for each $i = 1, ..., n$:

- The correspondence between $p_i$ and $p_i'$ is nonfunctional.
- The participation of $E$ in $R_i$ with role $p_i'$ is total.
- Two instances $e, e'$ of $E$ cannot be related through $R_1, ..., R_n$ to exactly the same instances $e_1, ..., e_n$, that is,

$$R_1(e,e_1) \wedge R_1(e',e_1) \wedge ... \wedge R_n(e,e_n) \wedge R_n(e',e_n) \rightarrow e = e'$$

If all $R_i$ are constant with respect to $p_i'$, then the set $\{R_1, ..., R_n\}$ is an *immutable* compound reference to $E$; otherwise, it is a *mutable* one.

Figure 5.2 shows two compound references to *OrderLine*. One is the set $\{LineOf, Orders\}$ because:

- The correspondence between *order* and *orderLine* and between *product* and *orderLine* is non-functional.
- The participation of *OrderLine* in *LineOf* and in *Orders* is total.

- There are no two order lines *ol* and *ol'* with the same order *o* and the same product *p*:

  *LineOf(ol,o)* ∧ *LineOf(ol',o)* ∧
  *Orders(ol,p)* ∧ *Orders(ol',p)* → *ol* = *ol'*

The set {*LineOf*, *Orders*} is a mutable reference if an order line may change its order or its product.

Note that if an order may have two or more order lines ordering the same product (perhaps at different prices), then {*LineOf*, *Orders*} is not a compound reference to *OrderLine*.

The second compound reference is {*LineOf*, *LineNo*} because:

- The correspondence between *order* and *orderLine* and between *lineNo* and *orderLine* is nonfunctional.
- The participation of *OrderLine* in *LineOf* and *lineNo* is total.
- There are no two order lines *ol* and *ol'* with the same order *o* and the same line number *ln*:

  *LineOf(ol,o)* ∧ *LineOf(ol',o)* ∧
  *LineNo(ol,ln)* ∧ *LineNo(ol',ln)* → *ol* = *ol'*

The set {*LineOf*, *LineNo*} is a mutable reference if the order or the line number of an order line can be changed.

### 5.1.3 Set Reference

The third way of building references to entities is based on a single relationship type *R* (as for simple references), although here a reference to an entity uses several instances of *R* and not just one.

For example, consider the triangles defined in a schema by the relationship type *HasVertex* shown in Fig. 5.3. Assuming that there are no two triangles with exactly the same vertices, the set of vertices of a triangle is a reference to it. We can say, for instance, "the triangle consisting of the points A, B, and C".

**Fig. 5.3.** *HasVertex* is a set reference to *Triangle*

Formally, let $R(p:E,p_1:E_1)$ be a binary relationship type. We say that $R$ is a *set reference* relationship type for $E$ and also that $p_1:E_1$ is a set reference to $E$ through $R$, if:

- The correspondence between $p$ and $p_1$ is nonfunctional.
- The participation of $E$ in $R$ with role $p$ is total.
- Two instances $e$ and $e'$ of $E$ cannot be related through $R$ to exactly the same instances of $E_1$, that is, there exists at least one entity $e_i$ to which either $e$ or $e'$ is related, but not both:

$$E(e) \wedge E(e') \wedge e \neq e' \rightarrow \exists e_1 (R(e,e_1) \wedge \neg R(e',e_1))$$

Moreover, if $R$ is constant with respect to $p$, then we can say that $R$ is an *immutable* set reference to $E$; otherwise, it is a *mutable* one.

Let us see why *HasVertex* (*Triangle, vertex:Point*), shown in Fig. 5.3, is an immutable set reference to *Triangle* (or why *vertex* is a set reference to *Triangle*, through *HasVertex*):

- The correspondence between *triangle* and *vertex* is nonfunctional (a triangle has three vertices).
- The participation of *Triangle* in *HasVertex* is total (all triangles have vertices).
- Two different instances of *Triangle* must have at least one different vertex.
- *HasVertex* is constant with respect to *Triangle*.

## 5.2 Identification

Informally, an entity is identifiable if there is an expression formed by lexical entities that denotes it. For example, the expression "*The person called Mark*" is a reference to a person, formed from the lexical entity "*Mark*". An entity type is *identifiable* if all its instances are identifiable.

Entity types may be identified in six main ways. Below, we introduce each of them in turn.

First, all data types are identifiable. This is because their instances, which are values, are denoted by one or more literals, predefined by the corresponding data type. For example, in XML Schema, the data type *Integer* has a lexical representation consisting of a finite-length sequence of decimal digits with an optional leading sign, for instance -1, 0, 1267896754, or +100000. The same happens in more complex data types such as *DateTime*.

Second, an entity type $E$ is identifiable if the schema contains a simple reference $R(p:E,p_1:E_1)$ to $E$, and $E_1$ is identifiable. This is the most common case. For example, *Town* is identifiable if the schema contains the relationship type *Name (Town, String)*, which is a simple reference to *Town* (Fig. 5.1). Similarly, *Country* is identifiable if the schema contains the type *HasCapital (Country, capital:Town)*, which is a simple reference to *Country*, and *Town* is identifiable.

Third, an entity type $E$ is identifiable if the schema contains a compound reference $\{R_1 (p_1':E,p_1:E_1), ..., R_n (p_n':E,p_n:E_n)\}$ to $E$, and $E_1, ..., E_n$ are identifiable. Many entity types are identified in this way. For example, in Fig. 5.2, *OrderLine* is identifiable if the set

> *LineOf (OrderLine, Order)*
> *Orders (OrderLine, Product)*

is a compound reference to *OrderLine*, and both *Order* and *Product* are identifiable.

Fourth, an entity type $E$ is identifiable if the schema contains a set reference $R(p:E,p_1:E_1)$ for $E$, and $E_1$ is identifiable. For example, the entity type *Triangle* (see Fig. 5.3) is identifiable if the schema contains the type *HasVertex (Triangle, vertex:Point)*, which is a set reference to *Triangle*, and *Point* is identifiable.

The fifth identification method is the most complex. Consider a domain of personal objects, with a schema containing entity types *Book*, *CompactDisc*, and *Gift*. Let us assume that *Book* and *CompactDisc* are identifiable, but that *Gift* is not a data type, nor is there a reference to it. Therefore, in principle, *Gift* is nonidentifiable. However, let us also assume that a gift is necessarily a book or a compact disc, although not all books and compact discs are gifts. In this case, *Gift* is identifiable because its instances can be identified as books or as compact discs. Thus, we can say, *"The gift that is the book with ISBN code 84-7410-936-1"* or *"The gift that is the compact disc with code 0495-23 and editor AM"*.

Therefore, an entity type $E$ is identifiable if all its instances are also instances of another type that is identifiable. In particular, $E$ is identifiable if it is a subtype of an identifiable type.

Finally, an entity type $E$ is identifiable if its population always consists of a single entity. The rationale is that we may refer to that instance with an expression such as "the instance of type $E$", for example "the instance of type *Company*" or "the *Company*" in a domain in which there is just one company.

### 5.2.1 Identifiability of Entity Types

Each entity type defined in a conceptual schema must be identifiable, in (at least) one of the main ways defined above or in some other special way. The rationale behind this requirement is that when an entity type is identifiable, the users and the information system have a shared means to refer to its instances. If, on the other hand, an entity type is not identifiable, then the users and the information system will be unable to share information about instances of it.

For example, if the schema contains a nonidentifiable entity type *Customer*, then users will not be able to tell the system that a particular customer has bought a product. Similarly, if the system produces a report with details of the existing customers, users will not be able to relate the customers in the report to those that they know in the domain.

Note that the identifiability requirement is independent of the symbols used in the information base to denote the domain objects. These symbols are generated internally by the system and are not visible outside it; therefore, they cannot be used to identify entities externally.

## 5.3 Replacing Entities with Identifiers in Relationships

The participants of a relationship type $R(p_1:E_1, \ldots, p_n:E_n)$ are the $n$ entity types $E_1, \ldots, E_n$. Given that each entity type $E_i$ must be identifiable, we may be tempted to replace $E_i$ with its identifiers in $R$ and eliminate $E_i$ from the schema. The elimination of $E_i$ implies the elimination of all relationship types in which it participates. In general, however, it is not convenient to do this transformation.

Consider, for example, the following binary relationship type and cardinalities (see the UML representation in Fig. 5.4):

> *Name (Building, name:String)*
> *Card(building, name) = (1,1)*
> *Card(name; building) = (0,1)*

*Name* is a simple reference for *Building*: the instances of *Building* can be

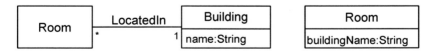

**Fig. 5.4.** The right part shows the replacement of *Building* by its identifier in *LocatedIn*

identified by its *name*. Consider now the relationship type *LocatedIn* (*Room*, *Building*), in which *Building* is a participant. Given that a building can be identified by its name, we may be tempted to apply the above transformation, replacing *Building* with *buildingName:String* in *LocatedIn* to obtain

LocatedIn (*Room*, *buildingName:String*)

and eliminating *Building* and *Name*. The advantage is that the new schema (see Fig. 5.4, right) is simpler: there is one fewer entity and relationship type (*Building* and *Name*). The drawbacks are that the semantics of *LocatedIn* is more obscure (it does not say that rooms are located in buildings), that a change in the name of a building requires changing the value of attribute *Room::buildingName* of all rooms located in that building, and that future changes requiring *Building* to be a participant in some new relationship type, such as

LocatedAt (*Building*, *Address*)

will have a significant effect on the previous schema.

Special care must be taken in the replacement of an entity type identified by a compound reference. For example, assume that *Room* is identified by the compound reference (see Fig. 5.5)

LocatedIn (*Room*, *Building*)
RoomNumber (*Room*, *Natural*)

That is, a room is identified by the building in which it is located and its room number. *Room* participates in the following two relationship types:

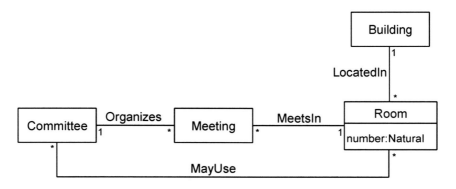

**Fig. 5.5.** Fragment of a schema in which *LocatedIn* and *Room::number* are a compound reference for *Room*

> *MeetsIn* (*Meeting, Room*)
> *MayUse* (*Committee, Room*)

which have the cardinalities shown in Fig. 5.5. If we want to replace *Room* by its identifiers, we obtain the ternary relationship types

> *MeetsIn'* (*Meeting, Building, number:Natural*)
> *MayUse'* (*Committee, Building, number:Natural*)

In the next section we shall see that *MeetsIn'* can be decomposed into two binary relationship types,

> *MeetsInBuilding* (*Meeting, Building*)
> *MeetsInRoomNumber* (*Meeting, number:Natural*)

but *MayUse'* cannot be decomposed, and therefore it remains ternary (why?).

## 5.4 Elementary Relationship Types

A relationship type $R$ of degree $n$ is *elementary* if it cannot be decomposed into $m$ relationship types $R_1, \ldots, R_m$ ($m \geq 2$) such that

- the degree of each $R_1, \ldots, R_m$ is less than $n$,
- the entity types participating in $R_1, \ldots, R_m$ are a subset of those participating in $R$, and
- the population of $R$ at any time can be obtained from the populations of $R_1, \ldots, R_m$ at that time.

The instances of elementary relationship types are called elementary relationships. Note that binary relationship types are always elementary.

An example of an elementary relationship type is

> *GetsGrade* (*Student, Grade, Course*)

with the pattern sentence

> The student *<Student>* gets grade *<Grade>* on the course *<Course>*

Assuming that it has only one functional dependency,

> {*student, course*} $\rightarrow$ {*grade*}

*GetsGrade* is elementary because it is not possible to decompose it into two or more binary relationship types $R_1, \ldots, R_n$, such that the population of *GetsGrade* can be obtained from that of $R_1, \ldots, R_n$.

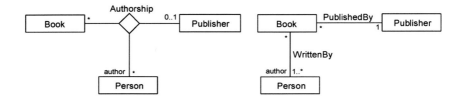

**Fig. 5.6.** *Authorship* is nonelementary and can be decomposed into *WrittenBy* and *PublishedBy*

An example of a nonelementary relationship type is (see Fig. 5.6, left)

*Authorship (author:Person, Book, Publisher)*

with the pattern sentence

The person *<Person>* is an author of the book *<Book>* published by publisher *<Publisher>*

and with the cardinalities shown in the figure and the additional functional dependency

$$\{book\} \rightarrow \{publisher\}$$

*Authorship* can be decomposed into the two types, *WrittenBy* and *PublishedBy*, shown in Fig. 5.6 (right). Figure 5.7 shows, in tabular form, an example of the populations of *Authorship*, *WrittenBy* and *PublishedBy*. It can be seen that we can obtain the population of *Authorship* from that of *WrittenBy* and *PublishedBy*.

It is strongly recommended that the relationship types defined in a conceptual schema be elementary. This recommendation is based on the following facts:

- Elementary relationship types are easier for users and designers to understand, because they are smaller than nonelementary ones.
- Elementary relationship types are easier to specify, because they have fewer cardinality constraints, their pattern sentences are shorter, etc.
- Elementary relationships cannot be represented in nonelementary relationship types. In the above example, we might need to represent the publisher of a new book before we know who the authors are. We cannot do this in *Authorship*, and it is possible only if we have the elementary type *PublishedBy*.
- In general, the occurrence of events may change the populations of relationship types. It is easier to specify the changes to elementary relation-

| Authorship | | |
| --- | --- | --- |
| Book | Author | Publisher |
| B1 | A1 | P1 |
| B1 | A2 | P1 |
| B1 | A3 | P1 |
| B2 | A3 | P2 |

| WrittenBy | |
| --- | --- |
| Book | Author |
| B1 | A1 |
| B1 | A2 |
| B1 | A3 |
| B2 | A3 |

| PublishedBy | |
| --- | --- |
| Book | Publisher |
| B1 | P1 |
| B2 | P2 |

**Fig. 5.7.** Examples of populations of the relationship types shown in Fig. 5.6

ship types than those to nonelementary ones. In the above example, we might have an event type that changes the publisher of a book. An instance might be a change in the publisher of *Book B*1 to *P*2. As we can see in Fig. 5.7, if we have the *Authorship* type we need to change three relationships (rows), while only one relationship must be changed in the elementary *PublishedBy*.

In the next section, we study how to decompose nonelementary relationship types into elementary ones.

## 5.5 Decomposing NonElementary Relationship Types

A nonelementary relationship type $R$ should be decomposed into a set $R_1$, ..., $R_m$ ($m \geq 2$) of elementary types. The decomposition must satisfy a goal called *information preservation*, which means that the population of $R$ at any time can be obtained from the populations of $R_1$, ..., $R_m$ at that time.

Nonelementary relationship types can be decomposed in several ways. In this chapter, we are only interested in decompositions such that

- the degree of each $R_1$, ..., $R_m$ is less than that of $R$, and
- the entity types participating in $R_1$, ..., $R_m$ are a subset of those participating in $R$.

In the next chapter we will study other kinds of decomposition.

A relationship type may be nonelementary for several reasons. In this chapter, we shall focus only on the two most common cases, which are the results of functional and multivalued dependencies. See the references given at the end of this chapter for other, less frequent cases.

### 5.5.1 Decomposition Based on Functional Dependencies

If a relationship type $R(p_1:E_1, ..., p_n:E_n)$ has a functional dependency $p \rightarrow q$ where $p = \{p_1, ..., p_i\}$ and $q = \{p_{i+1}, ..., p_k\}$ are disjoint subsets of roles $\{p_1, ..., p_n\}$, and $p \cup q \subset \{p_1, ..., p_n\}$, then $R$ can be decomposed into two new relationship types $R_1$ and $R_2$, with the schemas

$$R_1(p_1:E_1, ..., p_i:E_i, p_{i+1}:E_{i+1}, ..., p_k:E_k)$$
$$R_2(p_1:E_1, ..., p_i:E_i, p_{k+1}:E_{k+1}, ..., p_n:E_n)$$

Every functional dependency that satisfies the above conditions is a potential decomposition of $R$. If there are two or more, one of them should be chosen using the criteria described below. If the new relationship types are nonelementary then they should be decomposed again.

Let us illustrate this decomposition with a simple example that poses no particular problems: the relationship type *Authorship* (*author:Person, Book, Publisher*) shown in Fig. 5.6 (left). *Authorship* has two functional dependencies:

$\{book\} \rightarrow \{publisher\}$
$\{book, author\} \rightarrow \{publisher\}$

For the purposes of decomposing *Authorship*, the second functional dependency does not count, because it does not hold that[1]

$\{book, author\} \cup \{publisher\} \subset \{author, book, publisher\}$

Therefore, *Authorship* can be decomposed in only one way. The result is the following relationship types (see Fig. 5.6, right):

*PublishedBy* (*Book, Publisher*)
*WrittenBy* (*Book, author:Person*)

The cardinalities of *PublishedBy* and *WrittenBy* are four of the twelve cardinalities of *Authorship*. What happens to the eight remaining cardinalities? Two cases arise: they either can or cannot be inferred from those of *PublishedBy* and *WrittenBy*. In the former case, we say that the cardinalities are *preserved*. In the latter case, we say that some cardinality is not preserved. If some constrained cardinality is not preserved in the decomposition then we have to define it explicitly in an appropriate manner. In the example in Fig. 5.6, the constrained cardinalities of *Authorship* are:

*Card*(*book*; *publisher*) = (1,1)

---

[1] Recall that $A \subset B$ means that $A$ is a proper subset of $B$, that is, that $A$ is a subset of $B$, but $A$ is not equal to $B$.

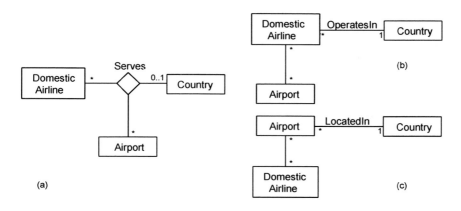

**Fig. 5.8.** Two alternative decompositions of the ternary relationship type *Serves*

$Cmin(book; author) = 1$
$Card(book; author, publisher) = (1,1)$
$Cmax(book, author; publisher) = 1$

It can be shown that these constraints are preserved in the decomposition given in Fig. 5.6 (right).

Figure 5.8 shows an example in which a constrained cardinality is not preserved in the decomposition. *Serves* is a ternary relationship type with the pattern sentence

The domestic airline *<DomesticAirline>* serves airport *<Airport>* located in country *<Country>*

*Serves* has the following three constrained cardinalities:

$Cmax(domesticAirline; country) = 1$
$Cmax(domesticAirline, airport; country) = 1$
        (shown in Fig. 5.6a))
$Cmax(airport; country) = 1$

Therefore, there are two potential decompositions:

- one based on {*domesticAirline*} → {*country*}, shown in Fig. 5.8b and
- one based on {*airport*} → {*country*}, shown in Fig. 5.8c.

In both cases, a functional dependency is not preserved: {*airport*} → {*country*} in the first case, and {*domesticAirline*} → {*country*} in the latter case.

When all potential decompositions preserve the same number of constraints, we can select any one of these decompositions; otherwise, we select the decomposition that preserves the greatest number of constraints. In the example in Fig. 5.8 both decompositions preserve the same number of constraints; therefore, choosing between (b) and (c) is a matter of personal taste. The constrained cardinalities that are not preserved in a decomposition must be defined some other way. In Chap. 9, which is devoted to integrity constraints, we look closely at how the cardinalities should be formally defined.

### 5.5.2 Decomposition Based on Multivalued Dependencies

If a relationship type cannot be decomposed on the basis of functional dependencies, we should then analyze whether it can be decomposed on the basis of multivalued dependencies. In the following paragraphs, we first introduce the concept of a multivalued dependency by means of an example, then we give a formal definition, and afterwards we explain how a relationship type that satisfies a multivalued dependency should be decomposed.

Figure 5.9a shows a ternary relationship type *Evaluates*. Its pattern sentence is

> In contest <*Contest*> juror <*Person*> evaluates
> participant <*Person*>

Let us assume that in a contest, each juror evaluates each participant and that a person may be a juror or a participant in several contests. None of the cardinalities of *Evaluates* is a functional dependency, but each contest determines two sets: a set of jurors and a set of participants. This is called a *multivalued dependency*, denoted by *contest ->> juror|participant*. The set of jurors in a contest is independent of the set of its participants. An instance of *Evaluates* such as

> *Evaluates (MusicContest, Salieri, Mozart)*

represents two independent facts: that *Salieri* is a juror in *MusicContest*, and that *Mozart* is one of its participants. If *Rossini* is another participant in the same contest, then we have the relationship

> *Evaluates (MusicContest, Salieri, Rossini)*

which correctly represents the fact that *Rossini* participates in *MusicContest*, although it does unfortunately "duplicate" the fact that *Salieri* is a juror in that contest. *Evaluates* can (and should) be decomposed into the two relationship types shown in Fig. 5.9b, as the duplication then disappears.

(a)                                                                                      (b)

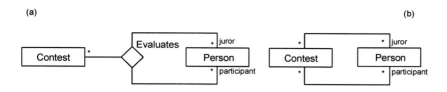

**Fig. 5.9.** *Evaluates* (a) satisfies the multivalued dependency *contest ->> juror|participant*, and can be decomposed into the two relationship types shown in (b)

We shall now formalize the multivalued dependencies for ternary relationship types $R(x:X, y:Y,z:Z)$. The extension to higher degrees is easy. We say that $R$ satisfies the multivalued dependency $x ->> y$ (or that $x ->> y$ holds for $R$) if

$$\forall x,z_1,z_2 \; (\{y|R(x,y,z_1)\} = \{y|R(x,y,z_2)\})$$

That is, $R$ satisfies the multivalued dependency $x ->> y$ if the set of values of $y$ that appear with a given $x$ and $z_1$ also appear with each combination of $x$ and $z_2$ in $R$. Therefore, this set is a function of $x$ alone and does not depend on the $z$-values that appear with $x$.

Whenever $x ->> y$ holds in $R(x:X, y:Y, z:Z)$, so does $x ->> z$. Hence $x ->> y$ implies $x ->> z$; therefore, it is often written as $x ->> y|z$.

The application of the formalization to the above example is as follows. The multivalued dependency $\{contest\} ->> \{juror\}|\{participant\}$ holds for *Evaluates* if the set of jurors related to a contest and a participant is the same as the set of jurors related to the same contest and any other participant in that contest. In other words, every participant in a given contest is evaluated by exactly the same jurors.

The multivalued dependencies that hold for a relationship type cannot be determined from the cardinalities, as they are additional constraints. This is a noteworthy difference with respect to functional dependencies, which can be determined from cardinalities.

If a relationship type $R(p_1:E_1, \ldots, p_n:E_n)$ satisfies the multivalued dependency $p ->> q|s$, where $p = \{p_1, \ldots, p_i\}$ and $q = \{p_{i+1}, \ldots, p_k\}$ are disjoint subsets of the roles $\{p_1, \ldots, p_n\}$, and $s = \{p_{k+1}, \ldots, p_n\} = R - p - q$, then $R$ can be decomposed into two new relationship types $R_1$ and $R_2$ with the following schemas:

$$R_1(p_1:E_1, \ldots, p_i:E_i, p_{i+1}:E_{i+1}, \ldots, p_k:E_k)$$
$$R_2(p_1:E_1, \ldots, p_i:E_i, p_{k+1}:E_{k+1}, \ldots, p_n:E_n)$$

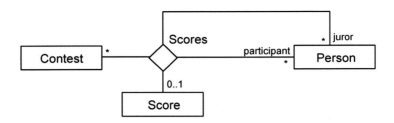

**Fig. 5.10.** *Scores* does not satisfy the multivalued dependency *{contest}* ->> *{juror}| {participant, score}*

This decomposition is information-preserving. Decomposing *Evaluates* (Fig. 5.9a) in this way gives the two relationship types shown in Fig. 5.9b.

It may be useful to analyze why a multivalued dependency that apparently holds for a relationship type may not in fact hold. Let us assume that we add to the example in Fig. 5.9 the score that a juror gives to a participant in a contest. We obtain the quaternary relationship type *Scores* shown in Fig. 5.10. The functional dependency is

$\{contest, juror, participant\} \rightarrow \{score\}.$

Apparently, the multivalued dependency

$\{contest\} \dashrightarrow \{juror\}|\{participant\}$

that holds for *Evaluates* also holds for *Scores*. Now we have four participants, and the multivalued dependency should be

$\{contest\} \dashrightarrow \{juror\}|\{participant, score\}.$

This will, however, hold only in the (unlikely) case that all jurors in a contest always give a participant the same score. If, for example, the following relationships were valid,

*Scores (MusicContest, Salieri, Mozart,* 5)
*Scores (MusicContest, Chopin, Mozart,* 10)

then the above multivalued dependency would not hold for *Scores*. If two jurors (*Salieri, Chopin*) can give different scores to the same participant (*Mozart*), then *{contest}* ->> *{juror}|{participant, score}* does not hold, and *Scores* cannot be decomposed.

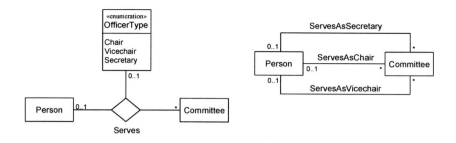

**Fig. 5.11.** Decomposition of *Serves* by absorbing *OfficerType*

### 5.5.3 Decomposition by Absorbing a Constant Entity Type

The above decompositions based on functional and multivalued dependencies should be applied whenever possible. In contrast, there is another kind of decomposition that should be applied only in special cases.

Consider the ternary relationship type *Serves* shown on the left in Fig. 5.11. An instance represents the fact that a person serves on a committee as an officer. There are three kinds of officer, given by the instances of *OfficerType*: chair, vice chair, and secretary.

*Serves* can be decomposed as shown in the right part of Fig. 5.11. There is a binary relationship type for each instance of *OfficerType*. We say that the constant entity type *OfficerType* is absorbed into the relationship type *Serves*, resulting in three relationship types, one for each instance of the absorbed type.

The advantage of this decomposition is that, like the others that we have seen before, it reduces the degree of a relationship type. However, it has several drawbacks:

- It increases the number of relationship types in the schema.
- It does not make it explicit that the resulting relationship types have the same underlying concept.
- The new schema is less stable: in the example shown in Fig. 5.11 the addition of a new officer type would induce a significant change into the schema.

## 5.6 Bibliographical Notes

The requirement that entity types must be identifiable is implicitly or explicitly stated in almost all conceptual modeling languages. Sundgren (1975) introduced the concept of reference and their variants. The ER model introduced by Chen (1976) deals extensively with entity identification. It includes the concept of a weak entity type, which corresponds to an entity type identified by means of a simple or compound reference involving one or more relationship types that are not attributes. See (Balaban and Shoval 1999) for a thorough analysis of weak entity types in ER schemas.

Kent (1978, Chap. 3) described some possibilities and difficulties in entity identification. Nijssen and Halpin (1989, Chap. 7) described simple and compound references; this description has been extended by De Troyer et al. (1988) and Halpin (2001). The work of Hofstede and Weide (1993) presented and formalized the concept of entity type identification. (Thalheim 2000, Chap. 8) provided a detailed explanation of identification in the HERM approach. Gogolla (2000) presented a unifying approach based on the so-called observation terms.

The replacement of entity types by their identifiers was discussed by Batini et al. (1992), Hainaut (1996) and Halpin (2001).

The need for elementary relationship types had already been recognized when conceptual modeling first began to be studied (Langefors 1974). The basic constructs of the entity–relationship model introduced by Chen (1976) are also elementary. Some languages, such as NIAM, by Nijssen and Halpin (1989) strongly emphasize elementary relationship types.

The theory of relationship type decomposition is based on the classical relational dependency theory developed in the field of databases for relational models. There are several good textbooks that provide a comprehensive description of this theory. (Ullman 1988) is a classic, while (Elmasri and Navathe 2003) is more recent. Multivalued dependencies were introduced by Fagin (1977).

In the ER model, (Ling 1985) is one of the earliest references to the decomposition of ER relationships in the context of a method for converting ER diagrams into relational database definitions. Jones and Song (1996) described the decomposition of ternary relationship types on the basis of an analysis of cardinality constraints. A synthesis of this work can be found in (Thalheim 2000). McAllister and Sharpe (1998) presented a detailed procedure for the decomposition of *n*-ary relationship types, which takes into account functional and multivalued dependencies, as well as join dependencies, a peculiar constraint only rarely found in practice. Decomposition by absorbing a constant entity type was presented in (Halpin and Proper 1995b, Assenova and Johannesson 1996); a thorough analysis was given in (Halpin 2001, Chap. 12.2).

## 5.7 Exercises

**5.1** Consider a schema for the domain of papers published in scientific journals. Suppose that the schema includes the entity types *Journal, Volume, Issue,* and *Paper.* Journals are identified by their name. Volumes are identified by the journal and the year of publication. Journal issues are identified by the volume and the number, or by the volume and the month of publication. Papers are identified by the journal issue in which they appear and their title, or by the journal issue and the initial page of the paper in the issue. Complete the schema with the necessary relationship types (associations or attributes), and explain how each entity type could be identified.

**5.2** Give an example of an existence dependency relationship type which is a simple reference, and another one which is not. State the condition that an existence dependency relationship type must satisfy to be a simple reference.

**5.3** Decompose the relationship type

> *HasAccount* (*holder:Person, Account, InterestRate*)

whose pattern sentence is

> The person *<Person>*
> is a holder of *<Account>* that pays the interest rate *<InterestRate>*

taking into account the functional dependency:

> {*account*} → {*interestRate*}

**5.4** Consider the following relationship type:

> *Represents* (*representative:Person, Country, Organization*)

whose pattern sentence is

> The person *<Person>*
> is the national representative of *<Country>* in *<Organization>*

Suppose that the functional dependencies that hold in *Represents* are

$$\{organization, country\} \rightarrow \{representative\}$$
$$\{representative\} \rightarrow \{country\}$$

Is *Represents* elementary? If it is not, how would you decompose it?

**5.5** Consider the following relationship type:

*Authorship (author:Person, Book, Paper)*

whose pattern sentence is

The person *<Person>*
is an author of the book *<Book>* and of the paper *<Paper>*

The only constrained cardinalities of *Authorship* are the following:

*Card(book; author)* = $(1, \infty)$
*Card(paper; author)* = $(1, \infty)$

Determine the multivalued dependency that holds in *Authorship*. How would you decompose this relationship type?

# 6 Reification

Reifying a relationship consists in viewing it as an entity. The word "reification" comes from the Latin word *res*, which means "thing". Reification has a well-known equivalent in natural language, nominalization, which basically consists in turning a verb into a noun. Reification is widely used in conceptual modeling; conceptual modelers must therefore have a good grasp of it. In Sect. 6.1, we define reification and explain its logical basis. Reification can easily be defined in UML, as we show in Sect. 6.2. In some languages, however, reification cannot be defined as easily, so one must instead use implicit reification, which is also described in Sect. 6.2. Implicit reification is an interesting schema transformation that can be used in other contexts.

In Sect. 6.3, we explain that reification may be partial; in this case, reification becomes a schema transformation that can improve the quality of a schema in given circumstances.

## 6.1 Definition

We shall introduce the concept of reification by means of an example, before giving its formal definition. Consider the relationship type *IsMemberOf* (*member:Person, Committee*). Figure 6.1 (left) shows an example population of *IsMemberOf* in tabular form. Person *P1* is a member of committees *C1* and *C2*. Person *P2* is a member of *C1* only.

An instance of *IsMemberOf* is a relationship that represents the fact that a person is a member of a committee. The same fact, however, could also be viewed as an entity. When we view a relationship as an entity, we say that the entity reifies the relationship. The reification of a relationship consists in viewing it as an entity. Like any other, this entity must be an instance of an entity type. In the present example, the entity type has been named *Membership*. For each instance of *IsMemberOf*, there is one and only one instance of *Membership*, and vice versa.

In linguistics, reification corresponds to a well-known phenomenon called nominalization, which consists in turning a verb into a noun (such as

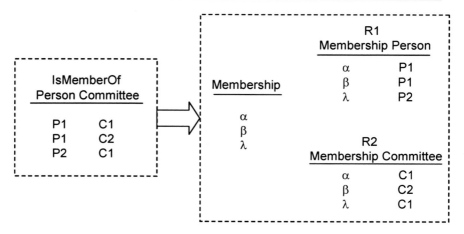

**Fig. 6.1.** *IsMemberOf* is reified into *Membership*. *R1* and *R2* are the intrinsic relationship types

"move" > "movement", "swim" > "swimming" or "be a member" > "membership").

Generalizing to the level of types, we say that *IsMemberOf* is reified into the entity type *Membership*. This entity type has a distinct instance for each instance of *IsMemberOf*, as illustrated in Fig. 6.1 ($\alpha$, $\beta$, $\lambda$). For example, the instance $\alpha$ of *Membership* corresponds to the instance (P1,C1) of *IsMemberOf*.

The instances of *Membership* must be related to the participant entities of *IsMemberOf*. Otherwise, we would not know which relationship is reified by a given instance of *Membership*. The correspondence between the instances of *Membership* and those of *IsMemberOf* is established by means of a binary relationship type for each participant of *IsMemberOf*. In the present example, we have two binary relationship types:

> *R1 (Membership, Person)*
> *R2 (Membership, Committee)*

These relationship types are called *intrinsic* because they can be seen as part of the new entity type. Figure 6.1 (right) shows the populations of *R1* and *R2*, which relate memberships to people and committees, respectively. It can be seen that we may obtain the instances of *IsMemberOf* from the instances of *Membership* and those of its two intrinsic relationship types.

The reification of a relationship type does not add any new knowledge to a schema, but it is necessary when we need to record additional facts regarding the instances of a relationship type. In the present example, the reification of *IsMemberOf* allows us to record the date on which a person becomes a member of a committee, the role (chair, secretary, etc.) that person plays in the committee, and so on.

Formally, the *reification* of a relationship type $R(p_1:E_1, ..., p_n:E_n)$ is an entity type $E$ and $n$ intrinsic binary relationship types $R_i(p:E,p_i:E_i)$, $(i = 1, ..., n)$, which have the following properties:

1. The $R_i$ are existence dependency relationship types. This means that they are constant with respect to $p$, that an instance of $E$ always refers to the same relationship of $R$, and that $Card(p; p_i; R_i) = (1,1)$. Therefore, the functional dependency $\{p\} \to \{p_i\}$ holds in $R_i$.
2. $Card(p_i; p; R_i) = Card(p_i; p_1, ..., p_{i-1}, p_{i+1}, ..., p_n; R)$.
3. There is a one-to-one correspondence[1] between the populations of $R$ and $E$:

$$R(e_1, ..., e_n) \to \exists!e(E(e) \land R_1(e,e_1) \land ... \land R_n(e,e_n))$$
$$R_1(e,e_1) \land ... \land R_n(e,e_n) \to R(e_1, ..., e_n)$$

The above definition guarantees that we can, at any time, obtain the instances of $R$ from the instances of $E$ and the instances of its intrinsic relationship types.

If, for some $R_i$, the functional dependency $\{p_i\} \to \{p\}$ holds, then $R_i$ is a simple reference to $E$. Otherwise, the set $\{R_1, ..., R_n\}$ is a compound reference to $E$.

Let us apply this definition to our present example. The reification of *IsMemberOf* (*member:Person, Committee*) is the entity type *Membership* and the two intrinsic relationship types $R1$ (*Membership, Person*) and $R2$ (*Membership, Committee*), with the following properties:

1. $R1$ and $R2$ are existence dependency relationship types. They are constant with respect to *membership*, and $Card(membership; person; R1) = Card(membership; committee; R2) = (1,1)$.
2. If $Card(person; committee; IsMemberOf) = (0,\infty)$ and $Card(committee; person; IsMemberOf) = (1,\infty)$, then $Card(person; membership; R1) = (0,\infty)$ and $Card(committee; membership; R2) = (1,\infty)$.
3. There is a one-to-one correspondence between the populations of *IsMemberOf* and *Membership*:

$$IsMemberOf(p,c) \to \exists!m(Membership(m) \land R_1(m,p) \land R_2(m,c))$$
$$R_1(m,p) \land R_2(m,c) \to IsMemberOf(p,c)$$

---

[1] Note that $\exists!e(\Phi(e,...))$ means that there is one and only one $e$ for which $\Phi(e,...)$ is true.

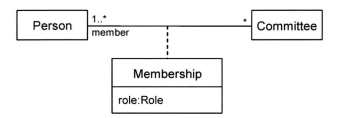

**Fig. 6.2.** *Membership* is an association class

The set {*R*1, *R*2} is a compound reference to *Membership*.

## 6.2 Representation in UML

We first study how reification should be represented in UML. We shall see that this language has a particular construct for that purpose; not all languages do, however. We shall show that when conceptual modelers use languages that lack reification constructs, they can define implicit reifications. This kind of reification is an interesting schema transformation, which we study at the end of the section.

### 6.2.1 Association Classes

UML provides the *association class* construct for defining reified relationship types. An association class is a single model element that is both a kind of association and a kind of entity type. The association and the entity type that reifies it are the same model element. Note that attributes cannot be reified.

An association class is shown as an entity type symbol attached to the reified association path by a dashed line. Logically, the association class and the association are the same semantic entity; they are, however, graphically distinct. In this representation, the intrinsic relationship types are implicit and are not shown graphically. Figure 6.2 shows in UML the example given in the previous section.

The association symbol and the association class symbol represent the same underlying model element, which has a single name. The name may be placed on the association path, in the entity type symbol, or in both positions, but the name must be the same. In this book, we place the name in the entity type symbol only; therefore, it follows the rules for entity type names. In Fig. 6.2, the name of the reified relationship type (*IsMemberOf*) is not shown.

Association classes may have attributes and may be related to other entity types. Figure 6.2 shows an example: *Membership* has an attribute *role*, which indicates the role played by a person in a committee. Note that, in UML, associations cannot have attributes. The only way to define an attribute of an association is by means of an association class.

Reification may also be applied to *n*-ary relationship types. Figure 6.3 shows the reification of a ternary association in UML. The pattern sentence of the association is

> The home team *<Team>* plays against the visitor team *<Team>* on *<Date>*

The association is reified into an entity type *Match*. This allows us to define three relationship types in which *Match* is a participant: two attributes (*score* and *spectators*), and an association with *Stadium*. Note that the attributes are optional, because their values are not known until a match has been played.

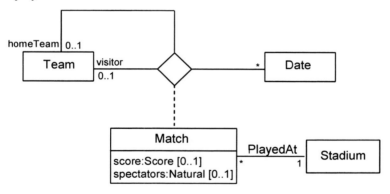

**Fig. 6.3.** Example of reification of a ternary association

## 6.2.2 Implicit Reification

Some conceptual modeling languages do not have a construct for explicitly defining the reification of a relationship type. The Logic language, for example, does not provide a construct to indicate that one predicate has been reified into another.

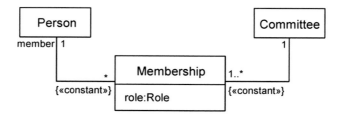

**Fig. 6.4.** *Membership* is an implicit reification of the association shown in Fig. 6.2

Conceptual schemas written in one of these languages cannot define the reification a relationship type *R* into an entity type *E*. In these cases, an alternative option is to define an *implicit reification*, as follows:

1. Define the entity type *E*.
2. Define the intrinsic relationship types.
3. Define the reification uniqueness constraint (see below).
4. Optionally, define *R* as a derived type.

Figure 6.4 gives the implicit reification of the relationship type *IsMemberOf* shown in Fig. 6.2. The two intrinsic relationship types that were implicit in the explicit reification (Fig. 6.2) are now explicit (Fig. 6.4).

The *reification uniqueness* constraint requires that for any pair (*person, committee*) there is at most one membership. This constraint is implicit in the explicit reification, because two links of type *IsMemberOf* cannot have exactly the same participants. In implicit reification, this constraint must be defined explicitly. We shall see in Chap. 9 how this constraint can be formally defined.

When the reification is implicit, the reified relationship type *R* is generally not shown. However, if desired, *R* may be defined as a derived relationship type. We shall see in Chap. 8 how to define derived relationship types.

The implicit reification of an *n*-ary relationship type has a side effect that is worth mentioning. We shall illustrate it by means of the example of a ternary association shown in Fig. 6.3, whose implicit reification is given in Fig. 6.5. The following constrained cardinalities have a graphical representation in Fig. 6.3, although unfortunately they are "lost" in Fig. 6.5:

$$Card(homeTeam, date; visitor) = (0,1)$$
$$Card(visitor, date; homeTeam) = (0,1)$$

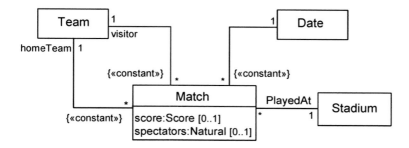

**Fig. 6.5.** *Match* is an implicit reification of the association shown in Fig. 6.3

Instead, the implicit reification shows three unconstrained cardinalities. The "lost" constrained cardinalities should be expressed in a general constraint definition language, as we shall explain in Chap. 9.

The reification uniqueness constraint requires that, for any tuple (*home team, visitor, date*), there is one match at most. This constraint is implicit in the explicit reification because two instances of type *Match* cannot be related to exactly the same home team, visitor, and date. In the implicit reification in Fig. 6.5, this constraint must be defined explicitly.

### 6.2.3 Implicit Reification as a Schema Transformation

A characteristic of implicit reification is that it transforms any relationship type into a set of existence dependency relationship types, which are binary, nonrecursive, constant with respect to a participant, and a functional dependency holds in them.

As a result of the above characteristic, implicit reification is an interesting schema transformation because it can transform any relationship type in a schema into a set of relationship types with particular properties. This result can be very useful for the analysis of certain properties of schemas and in system design.

The input to the transformation is the relationship type *R* with its complete set of cardinalities. The output is:

1. The new entity type *E*.
2. The intrinsic relationship types, including their cardinalities.
3. A set of integrity constraints corresponding to the constrained cardinalities of *R* not included in item 2.
4. The reification uniqueness constraint.

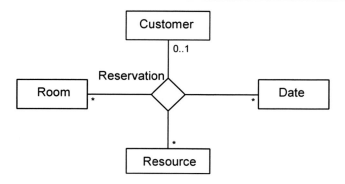

**Fig. 6.6.** *Reservation* is a nonelementary relationship type

The transformation preserves the information and the constraints of *R*. The population of *R* at any time can be derived from the population of *E* and that of the intrinsic relationship types at that time.

## 6.3 Partial Reification

Let us consider an example that will give us an intuitive understanding of partial reification. Assume the relationship type (Fig. 6.6)

> *Reservation (Room, Date, Customer, Resource)*

with the pattern sentence

> Room *<Room>* is reserved for day *<Date>* by customer *<Customer>*, who requires the room to be equipped with resource *<Resource>*

along with the functional dependency

> $\{room, date\} \rightarrow \{customer\}$

*Reservation* is nonelementary and should therefore be decomposed. Using the procedure described in the preceding chapter, *Reservation* may be decomposed into the following relationship types (Fig. 6.7):

> *Reserves (Room, Date, Customer)*
> *Requires (Room, Date, Resource)*

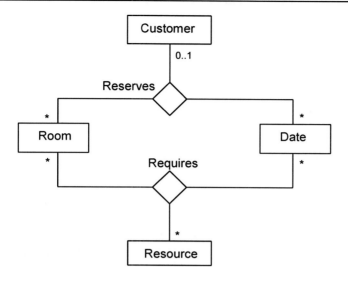

**Fig. 6.7.** *Reserves* and *Requires* have two common participants

The problem is that the populations of the two types are not independent. A pair (*room, date*) appearing in one of them must also appear in the other. For example, if *Reserves* has the relationship

{*<room:Room1>, <date:05/10/31>, <customer:ABC>*}

then *Requires* must necessarily have one or of the more relationships

{*<room:Room1>, <date:05/10/31>, <resource:_>*},

and vice versa. Therefore, there is a constraint involving the populations of *Reserves* and *Requires*: their projections to {*room, date*} must be the same.

Most languages (including UML) do not have a construct for easily defining constraints such as the one above; therefore, they must be defined in a general constraint definition language.

An alternative consists in reifying the common participants of the relationship types into a new entity type *E* and replacing those participants with *E*. This is called *partial reification* and is illustrated in Fig. 6.8. The association *room–date* is the projection of *Reserves* or *Requires* to {*room, date*}. This association is reified into a new entity type called *Reservation*. Then, *Reservation* replaces the participants {*room, date*} in *Reserves* and *Requires*. Now the common part of the two associations is clearly shown,

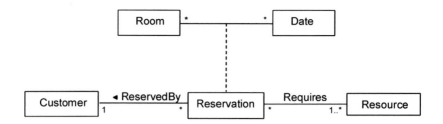

**Fig. 6.8.** Example of partial reification of the two common participants of the relationship types shown in Fig. 6.6

and the above constraint involving the populations of *Reserves* and *Requires* is not needed.

More precisely, the partial reification of a relationship type $R(p_1:E_1, ..., p_n:E_n)$ in the set of roles $\{p_1, ..., p_i\} \subset \{p_1, ..., p_n\}$ is a schema transformation whose output is

1. A relationship type $R'(p_1:E_1, ..., p_i:E_i)$ that corresponds to the projection of $R$ to $\{p_1, ..., p_i\}$.
2. The cardinalities of $R$ that apply to $R'$.
3. The reification of $R'$ into a new entity type $E$.
4. The relationship type $R''(E, p_{i+1}:E_{i+1}, ..., p_n:E_n)$.
5. The cardinalities of $R$ that apply to $R''$ and the cardinality $Cmin(e; p_{i+1}, ..., p_n; R'') = 1$. This new minimum cardinality comes from the fact that each instance of $E$ corresponds to a tuple $(p_1, ..., p_i)$ that appears in an instance of $R$ and that is therefore related to at least one tuple $(p_{i+1}, ..., p_n)$.

The transformation preserves the information and the constraints of $R$. The population of $R$ can be obtained from the populations of $R'$, $E$ (and its intrinsic relationship types), and $R''$.

Let us apply this transformation to *Reserves* (*Room, Date, Customer*) with the roles $\{room, date\}$. The output is:

1. The relationship type $R'(Room, Date)$ that corresponds to the projection of *Reserve* to $\{room, date\}$.
2. The two cardinalities of *Reserves* that apply to $R'$, which are shown in Fig. 6.7. In this case, both are unconstrained.
3. The reification of $R'$ into a new entity type *Reservation*.
4. The relationship type *ReservedBy* (*Reservation, Customer*).
5. The two cardinalities of *Reserves* that apply to *ReservedBy*, and $Cmin(reservation; customer; ReservedBy) = 1$, which are shown in Fig. 6.8.

In the example in Fig. 6.8, the constraint is that the projections of *Reserves* and *Requires* to {*room, date*} must be the same. However, partial reification can also be applied when one projection must be a subset of the other. A simple change to the example illustrates this well. Assume in Fig. 6.7 that a reservation need not require a resource in the room reserved. In this case, the constraint is that the projection of *Requires* to {*room, date*} must be a subset of the projection of *Reserves* to the same participants: a room may require a resource on a particular day only if that room is reserved by a customer for that day. Partial reification could be applied in this case as was done in the previous case. The result would be the same as that shown in Fig. 6.8, except that we would now have *Card*(*reservation*; *resource*; *Requires*) = (0,∞).

## 6.4 Bibliographical Notes

Many conceptual modeling languages provide a specific construct for relationship reification and give guidelines on its use. Among these languages are NIAM, presented in Nijssen and Halpin (1989), and YSM, described in Yourdon (1993). Martin and Odell (1995) discussed several graphical symbols for reification. In this book, we have adopted the symbol proposed for UML.

Most work on reification has been carried out in the context of a particular language, although the results are applicable to most languages. Nijssen and Halpin (1989, Sect. 10.3) discussed reification in detail in the context of NIAM. The discussion was continued (now in the context of ORM) in Halpin (2001, Sect. 12.3). Both gave an extensive coverage of reification. Rochfeld and Negros (1993) put forward an approach in which the participants in a relationship type may also be relationship types, which was followed in HERM (Thalheim 2000). Rosenthal and Reiner (1994) characterized the properties of intrinsic relationship types, and this work was extended in Snoeck and Dedene (1998), which explained in detail the (implicit) reification of any relationship type and gave a complete characterization of intrinsic relationship types. Olivé (1999) studied reification from a temporal perspective, and identified three kinds of temporal reification. Evermann and Wand (2005) analyzed reification from the perspective of Bunge's ontology and suggested several rules for its use.

Under the name of "pivoting", and in the context of the "participants may be relationship types" approach, partial reification was presented by Biskup et al. (1996). Hartmann (2001) extended that work by taking into account cardinality constraints. A different approach to partial reification was presented by Hainaut (1996).

## 6.5 Exercises

**6.1** Consider the schema fragment shown in Fig. 6.9. Assume that we now want to record the order of authors and the institution in which each author performed the work described in the paper. The association *WorksIn* represents the institution for which a person currently works. For example, the paper "Database abstractions: Aggregation and generalization" was written by John Miles Smith (first author) and Diane C. P. Smith (second author). For this paper, the authors' institutions are the same (University of Utah), but this is not the general rule.

1. Extend Fig. 6.9 to include this knowledge, using reification.
2. Extend Fig. 6.9 to include this knowledge, using implicit reification.

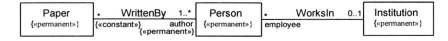

**Fig. 6.9.** A paper is written by one or more authors. A person may work in an institution

**6.2** In UML, define the implicit reification of the relationship type

*Manages* (*boss:Employee*, *subordinate:Employee*)

with the following cardinalities:

*Card*(*boss*; *subordinate*) = (0,10)
*Card*(*subordinate*; *boss*) = (0,1)

**6.3** Consider the schema fragment shown in Fig. 6.10, which is used to represent the (acyclic) composition of parts. Assume that we now want to record the quantity of a component required to make one unit of an assembly. For example, the assembly *WoodenChair* uses four units of the component *WoodenLeg*. Also, we want to record the alternative parts that an assembly may use when we run out of a given component. For example, if we run out of legs when assembling a wooden chair, we can use iron or plastic legs instead. Extend Fig. 6.10 to include this knowledge, using reification.

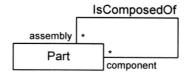

**Fig. 6.10.** A part may be composed of several component parts

**6.4** Assume that a conceptual schema includes the following relationship types:

> *IsEnrolled* (*Student, Course*)
> *TakesExam* (*Student, Course, Date, Mark*)

Students can take exams only for the courses in which they are enrolled. There is only one constrained cardinality: *Card*(*student, course, date; mark; TakesExam*) = (0,1). Using reification, define these relationship types and constraints in UML.

**6.5** Extend Fig. 6.3 to include the following relationship types,

> *Plays* (*Team, Player, Match, minutes:Natural, role:Role*)
> *Coaches* (*Team, Match, Coach*)

which have the following pattern sentences:

> As part of team *<Team>*, player *<Player>* plays in
> match *<Match>* during *<Natural>* minutes in
> role *<Role>*

and

> Coach *<Coach>* coaches team *<Team>* for match *<Match>*

A player may play in different teams for different matches. A coach may coach various teams for different matches. Assume that the populations of *Player* and *Coach* are disjoint.

*Plays* and *Coaches* satisfy the following cardinality constraints:

> *Card*(*player, match; team, minutes, role; Plays*) = (0,1)
> *Card*(*coach, match; team; Coaches*) = (0,1)
> *Card*(*team, match; coach; Coaches*) = (0,1)
> *Card*(*match; team; Coaches*) = (0,2)
> *Card*(*match; coach; Coaches*) = (0,2)

There are also the following constraints:

"If player $p$ plays in match $m$ as part of team $t$, then $t$ must be the home team or the visitor of $m$."

"If coach $c$ coaches team $t$ in match $m$, then $t$ must be the home team or the visitor of $m$."

Given that *Plays* is nonelementary (why?), it must be decomposed. If you find several (reasonable) solutions, describe only the one you prefer. Explain how the populations of *Plays* and *Coaches* can be obtained from the population of the entity and relationship types in your solution. How would you represent the above constraints in your solution? Note: do not change the reification shown in Fig. 6.3.

**6.6** Analyze whether or not the schema fragment of Fig. 6.5 can be automatically obtained from that of Fig. 6.3. Explain the result of your analysis.

# 7 Generic Relationship Types

In the four preceding chapters, we studied relationship types without taking into account their particular meaning. In general, the meanings of the relationship types existing in a schema are very diverse. However, there are some relationship types that appear in many schemas and even several times in the same schema. They are the subject of this chapter: in Sect. 7.1 we define them, and in Sect. 7.2 we show how they can be represented in an information system.

There are many generic relationship types. In this chapter, we study four of them. In Sect. 7.3, we describe the most important of these: the part–whole relationship. In Sects. 7.4, 7.5, and 7.6, we explore grouping, roles and materialization, respectively.

## 7.1 Definition

Some relationship types are ubiquitous. We find them in most schemas and often several times in the same schema. The most prominent example is the relationship type *IsPartOf* (*part:Entity*, *whole:Entity*). In the domain of books, for example, we find that chapters are part of books, paragraphs are part of chapters, exercises are part of chapters, and so on. Similarly, in the domain of regional planning, we find that towns are part of regions, regions are part of countries, districts are part of towns, and so on.

Another well-known example is the relationship type *IsMemberOf* (*member:Entity*, *group:Entity*). In some domains, we may find that a tennis player is a member of a tennis club, that a person is a member of a team, or that a person is a member of a committee.

From a conceptual modeling perspective, the two characteristics common to these relationship types are:

- The entity types of the participants are highly generic, such as *Entity* in the cases of *IsPartOf* and *IsMemberOf*.
- The participants in any of these relationships must be an instance of a valid combination of entity types, called a *realization*. In *IsPartOf*, the realizations in the above domains are *Chapter–Book, Paragraph–*

*Chapter, Exercise–Chapter, Town–Region, Region–Country* and *District–Town*. A relationship in which the two participants are not an instance of any of these realizations is not valid. Thus, a relationship in which *part* is a chapter and *whole* is an exercise would not be valid.

Relationship types that have the above characteristics are called *generic relationship types*. Formally, a generic relationship type $R$ is a relationship type $R(p_1{:}E_1, ..., p_n{:}E_n)$ that may have a set of $m$ realizations ($m \geq 0$) in a schema, and whose instances must satisfy a *realization constraint*. A realization is a set $\{p_1{:}E_{1,i}, ..., p_n{:}E_{n,i}\}$, where $p_1, ..., p_n$ are the roles of $R$, and $E_{j,i}$ are entity types. The realization constraint ensures that

- if the entities $e_1, ..., e_n$ participate in an instance of $R$, then
- they are an instance of a set $E_{1,i}, ..., E_{n,i}$ of entity types, such that
- $\{p_1{:}E_{1,i}, ..., p_n{:}E_{n,i}\}$ is a realization.

The general form of the realization constraint of a generic relationship type $R$ with $m$ realizations $\{p_1{:}E_{1,i}, ..., p_n{:}E_{n,i}\}$, $i = 1, ..., m$, is

$$R(e_1, ..., e_n) \rightarrow$$
$$[(E_{1,1}(e_1) \wedge ... \wedge E_{n,1}(e_n)) \vee ... \vee (E_{1,m}(e_1) \wedge ... \wedge E_{n,m}(e_n))]$$

The realization constraint is in addition to the referential integrity constraints that the instances of all relationship types must satisfy.

For example, the generic relationship type

$$IsPartOf\,(part{:}Entity, whole{:}Entity)$$

could have three realizations ($m = 3$) in a particular schema

$$\{part{:}Chapter, whole{:}Book\}$$
$$\{part{:}Paragraph, whole{:}Chapter\}$$
$$\{part{:}Exercise, whole{:}Chapter\}$$

The realization constraint is then

$$IsPartOf(p,w) \rightarrow [(Chapter(p) \wedge Book(w)) \vee$$
$$(Paragraph(p) \wedge Chapter(w)) \vee (Exercise(p) \wedge Chapter(w))]$$

This realization constraint is in addition to the referential constraints of *IsPartOf*, which are

$$IsPartOf(p,w) \rightarrow Entity(p)$$
$$IsPartOf(p,w) \rightarrow Entity(w)$$

Often, a participant $p_j$ is, in all realizations, an entity type $E_{j,i}$ that is a subtype of the corresponding participant $E_j$ in $R$. In this case, the referential integrity constraint on $E_j$ is redundant. This happens in the above example, because *Chapter*, *Book*, *Paragraph*, and *Exercise* are subtypes of *Entity*, but this need not be the case in general.

An ordinary relationship type can be seen as a generic relationship type without realizations. The realization constraint does not apply to ordinary types because they do not have realizations.

Besides *IsPartOf* and *IsMemberOf*, there are many more generic relationship types. All share the above characteristics (they must have realizations and must satisfy a realization constraint), but each may have its own additional characteristics. We shall study several generic relationship types in this chapter.

## 7.2 Representation in an Information System

A variety of methods may be used to represent generic relationship types. In this chapter we discuss some of these. Readers who are interested will find references to other methods in the bibliographical notes. We study the representation first in logic and then in UML.

### 7.2.1 Logical Representation

The simplest method for representing generic relationship types may be described as "one relationship type for each realization". Let $R(p_1:E_1, ..., p_n:E_n)$ be a generic relationship type with $m$ realizations. The method consists in defining, in the conceptual schema, a relationship type $R_i(p_1:E_{1,i}, ..., p_n:E_{n,i})$ for each realization $i = 1, ..., m$. A distinct predicate is used to represent each relationship type.

By way of example, consider the generic relationship type *IsPartOf* (*part:Entity*, *whole:Entity*), with the following three realizations:

> {*part:Chapter*, *whole:Book*}
> {*part:Paragraph*, *whole:Chapter*}
> {*part:Exercise*, *whole:Chapter*}

The representation in the conceptual schema would comprise the following relationship types:

> *ChapterOfBook* (*part:Chapter*, *whole:Book*)
> *ParagraphOfChapter* (*part:Paragraph*, *whole:Chapter*)
> *ExerciseOfChapter* (*part:Exercise*, *whole:Chapter*)

In this method, it is not necessary to explicitly define the realization constraint in the conceptual schema. This constraint is implicit because each realization has its own relationship type. For example, none of the above relationship types would allow one to define a chapter as part of an exercise.

Defining a new realization is straightforward: one need only define a new relationship type. Note that these relationship types are like any other in the schema; thus, there is no formal way of detecting that they are realizations of a generic relationship type. The lack of an explicit generic relationship type is a drawback of this method. In some applications, we may need to know which are the realizations of a generic relationship type or to define knowledge that is common to all realizations, such as integrity constraints and derivation rules.

Generic relationship types are explicit in a representation method that may be referred to as "realizations as subtypes". In this method, a generic relationship type $R(p_1:E_1, ..., p_n:E_n)$ with $m$ realizations ($m \geq 0$) is represented in the conceptual schema by $m + 1$ relationship types:

- The generic relationship type $R$ itself.
- A relationship type $R_i(p_1:E_{1,i}, ..., p_n:E_{n,i})$ for each realization $i = 1, ..., m$, with the same number ($n$) and name ($p_j$) of roles as it has in $R$ (as in the previous method).

The relationship type $R$ is defined as a derived type. Its derivation rule takes the general form

$$R(e_1, ..., e_n) \leftrightarrow R_1(e_1, ..., e_n) \vee ... \vee R_m(e_1, ..., e_n)$$

The $R_i$ are then subtypes of $R$.

Note that, in this method, there is a relationship type $R$ whose population comprises all the instances of the generic relationship type. The existence of this relationship type allows us to centralize the definition of the knowledge that is common to all realizations. For example, in relation to *IsPartOf*, we could define that no entity may be a direct or indirect part of itself.

## 7.2.2 Representation in UML

The two methods mentioned above can be applied directly in UML. However, there is a third method that is more appropriate to this language. This method may be described as "one marked relationship type for each realization".

The idea behind the method is to define a relationship type for each realization, similarly to what occurs in the "one relationship type for each realization" method. In this case, however, all the realizations of a generic relationship type have a mark that distinguishes them from the others. The effect of such a mark on the conceptual schema is predefined.

The best example of this is the generic relationship type *IsPartOf*. UML differentiates between two variants of this type: aggregation and composition. Aggregation associations are marked graphically by a hollow diamond attached to the entity type *whole*. Composition associations are marked graphically by a filled-in diamond.

In UML, the only predefined generic relationship type is *IsPartOf*. Others may be added using the stereotyping extension mechanism, as we explain later on in this chapter.

## 7.3 Part–Whole Relationships

### 7.3.1 Description

The best known generic relationship type is the part–whole relationship, also known as composition or aggregation. We shall call it *IsPartOf* here. Many relationships between two concrete entities may be considered to be instances of it. Informally, we define an instance of *IsPartOf* involving entities $P$ and $W$ by saying that

- $P$ is part of $W$, or that
- $W$ is a composite formed by $P$ (and possibly other entities).

*IsPartOf* is a binary relationship type in which one entity plays the role of a part, and the other the role of the whole. In some languages (including English), there are many different ways of expressing such relationships, which emphasize either the whole or the parts. The following are examples:

- The monitor is part of (is a component of) the computer.
- The computer has (includes) a monitor.

Part–whole relationships are important because they define the part–whole structure of domain objects. Given the fact that we view many objects as composites and that we tend to distinguish many parts in these objects, there is a definite need for part–whole relationships. Dictionaries define many concepts by their parts or by the wholes of which they are a part. For example, a definition of "chair" might be "a seat for one person, which has a back, usually four legs, and sometimes two arms".

Instances of *IsPartOf* are also called meronymic relationships (from the Greek word *méros*, which means "part"). If $P$ is part of $W$, then we say that

*P* is a meronym of *W* and that *W* is a holonym of *P*. In conceptual modeling, these relationships are usually called aggregations or compositions, although these terms have unfortunately become overloaded with a diversity of meanings and we shall not use them here.

It is usually accepted that *IsPartOf* is antisymmetric: if *P* is part of *W*, *W* cannot be part of *P*. It also seems natural to consider that *IsPartOf* is transitive: if *P* is part of *W* and *W* is part of *W2*, then *P* is part of *W2*. However, the transitivity of *IsPartOf* is controversial. Transitivity leads to acceptable results in many cases, but there are cases in which it does not hold. A popular example of this is

- the conductor's arm is part of the conductor, and
- the conductor is part of the orchestra.

We cannot, however, infer that "the conductor's arm is part of the orchestra". Therefore, whenever a conceptual schema uses *IsPartOf*, whether or not transitivity is assumed should be made clear.

### 7.3.2 Representation in UML

*IsPartOf* is the only generic relationship type for which UML provides a specific language construct. In fact, UML distinguishes between two kinds of *IsPartOf*, aggregation and composition, and provides two slightly different constructs for them. UML assumes that *IsPartOf* is both antisymmetric and transitive.

*Aggregation* conveys the thought that the whole is the sum of its parts. However, the only real constraint is that the aggregation relationship must be transitive and antisymmetric across all aggregation links in the information base.

Aggregation is shown by a hollow diamond adornment at the end of the association line which connects it to the whole. If there are two or more aggregations to the same whole, they may be drawn as a tree by merging the ends of the aggregation into a single segment (see a similar example for compositions in Fig. 7.2). The diamond should be noticeably smaller than the diamond notation for *n*-ary associations. The names of the roles need not be *part* and *whole*: we know that the role of *whole* is played by the entity type connected to the diamond.

Figure 7.1 shows three examples of aggregation. A bus line consists of a set of segments and a set of bus stops. Bus stops and segments may be part of several bus lines. A bus stop is part of a town.

*Composition* is a stronger form of aggregation that requires that a part be included in at most one whole at a time. The whole is called a *compos-*

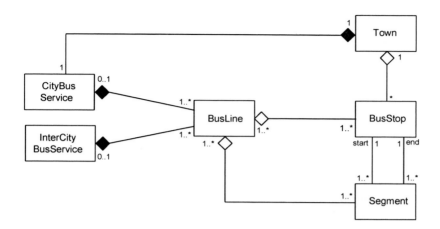

**Fig. 7.1.** Several examples of *IsPartOf* in a bus transportation system domain

*ite*. An entity may be part of different composites during its life, but only one at a time. In a composition, the multiplicity of the role of *whole* must be either 0..1 or 1. Composition is shown by a filled-in diamond adornment at the end of the association line which connects it to the composite.

Figure 7.1 shows three examples of composition. A bus line is part of a city bus service or of an intercity bus service. A city bus service is part of a town.

### 7.3.3 Part Sharing

Part sharing refers to the fact that an entity may be a (shared) part of several wholes. There are two kinds of sharing: local and global. Local sharing takes into account only one *IsPartOf* realization, whereas global sharing considers all of the *IsPartOf* realizations in a schema.

Let $R(part:P, whole:W)$ be a relationship type corresponding to an *IsPartOf* realization. We say that $P$ is *locally exclusive* in $R$ if the instances of $P$ may be parts of just one entity of type $W$ in $R$; otherwise, $P$ is *locally shared* in $R$.

Local sharing is expressed by means of $Cmax(part; whole; R)$. If $Cmax(part; whole; R) = 1$, then $P$ is locally exclusive in $R$; otherwise (if it is greater than one), $P$ is locally shared.

In Fig. 7.1 the parts are locally exclusive in four of the *IsPartOf* realizations, and locally shared in the other two. For example, a bus stop may be part of just one town (locally exclusive) but it may be part of several bus lines (locally shared).

Local sharing does not allow us to define an entity as part of at most one whole. Local exclusivity implies that an entity is part of at most one whole in a realization; that entity, however, could be a part of another whole in another realization.

Let $P$ be an entity type in a schema in which $P$ is a part in one or more *IsPartOf* realizations. We say that $P$ is *globally exclusive* in that schema if its instances can be a part in at most one of those realizations; otherwise, $P$ is *globally shared*. If an entity type is globally exclusive, then it must be locally exclusive in all realizations in which it is a part.

In UML, global exclusivity can easily be defined by means of the composition construct, as we have seen before. If an association is a composition, it is understood that the entity type that plays the role of the part is globally exclusive.

In Fig. 7.1, *BusLine* and *CityBusService* are globally exclusive. *BusLine* can be part of *CityBusService* or *InterCityBusSevice*, but not of both. *BusStop* and *Segment* are globally shared.

### 7.3.4 Part Dependency

Part dependency refers to the fact that the existence of the parts may depend on the existence of the wholes. Here there are also two kinds of dependency: local and global. Local dependency takes into account only one *IsPartOf* realization, whereas global dependency considers them all.

Let $R(part:P, whole:W)$ be a relationship type corresponding to an *IsPartOf* realization. We say that $P$ is *locally dependent* in $R$ if the instances of $P$ must be parts of at least one entity of type $W$ in $R$; otherwise, $P$ is *locally independent* in $R$.

Local dependency is expressed by means of $Cmin(part; whole; R)$. If $Cmin(part; whole; R) \geq 1$, then $P$ is locally dependent in $R$; otherwise, (zero) $P$ is locally independent.

In Fig. 7.1, the parts are locally dependent in four of the *IsPartOf* realizations, and locally independent in the other two. *BusLine* is locally independent in the two realizations of which it is a part. *BusStop* is locally dependent in the two realizations of which it is a part.

Local dependency does not allow us to define an entity as part of at least one whole. Local dependency implies that an entity must be part of a whole in a realization, but we could require an entity to be part of at least one whole in a given realization defined in a schema.

Let *P* be an entity type in a schema in which *P* is part of one or more *IsPartOf* realizations. We say that *P* is *globally dependent* in that schema if its instances must be parts of at least one of those realizations; otherwise, *P* is *globally independent*.

In Fig. 7.1, *BusLine*, *BusStop*, *Segment*, and *CityBusService* are globally dependent. In particular, *BusLine* is globally dependent because its instances must be part of an instance of either *CityBusService* or *InterCityBusService*.

If an entity type *P* is globally dependent and it is part of two or more *IsPartOf* realizations, then it must be locally independent in all of them. On the other hand, if an entity type *P* is part of just one *IsPartOf* realization in which it is locally dependent, then *P* must be globally dependent.

## 7.4 Grouping

### 7.4.1 Description

Another well-known generic relationship type is *Grouping*, also known as *association* or *membership*. We represent it here using the schema *IsMemberOf* (*member:Entity*, *group:Entity*). Many relationships between two concrete entities may be considered to be instances of it. Informally, we define an instance of *IsMemberOf* involving entities *M* and *G* by saying that

- *M* is a member of *G*, or that
- *G* is a collection that includes *M* (and possibly other entities).

*IsMemberOf* is a binary relationship type in which one entity plays the role of a member, and the other the role of a group. In some languages (including English), there are many different ways of expressing these relationships, which emphasize either the group or the members. The following are examples:

- A person is a member of (belongs to) a club.
- A team includes (has) a player.

*IsMemberOf* bears a resemblance to *IsPartOf*, but the differences between them are significant enough to warrant treating them differently. All members of a group perform the same function, whereas each part of a whole may play a different function. The members are always independent of the groups, because their existence does not depend on the existence of groups. Members are always shared by groups, because a member may be-

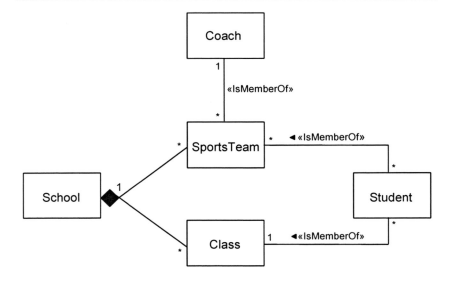

**Fig. 7.2.** Several examples of *IsMemberOf* in a school domain

long to several groups. Moreover, *IsMemberOf* is not considered to be transitive. For example, from

- Person is a member of PoliticalParty, and
- PoliticalParty is a member of Coalition

we cannot infer that "Person is a member of Coalition". Also, combinations of *IsPartOf* and *IsMemberOf* are not transitive, as illustrated by the following example,

- Bavaria is part of Germany,
- Germany is a member of the UN,

from which we cannot infer that Bavaria is part of or is a member of the UN.

Like *IsPartOf*, it is usually accepted that *IsMemberOf* is antisymmetric: if $M$ is a member of $G$, then $G$ cannot be a member of $M$.

## 7.4.2 Representation in UML

UML does not provide a built-in construct for defining an association as a realization of *IsMemberOf*. However, we can extend the language by means of stereotypes. We can define a new association stereotype such that the associations stereotyped by it correspond to the realizations of *Is-MemberOf*. By using this stereotype, we can easily identify the realizations of *IsMemberOf* in a schema.

We will assume that we have an association stereotype named «*IsMemberOf*». The stereotype may be used in binary associations. The first role of the association is the member role and the second is the group role. Figure 7.2 shows three examples of associations with this stereotype. In a school, a student is a member of a class and may be a member of several sports teams. A coach may be a member of several sports teams. Recall that for binary associations shown by a vertical line we follow the convention that the top role is the first, if not indicated otherwise (by means of an arrow).

### 7.4.3 Homogeneous Versus Heterogeneous Groups

An entity type $G$ is a homogeneous group when it plays the group role in one or more realizations such that the member role is played by only one entity type $M$. An entity type $G$ is a heterogeneous group when it plays the group role in two or more realizations such that the member role is played by two or more distinct entity types. Note that if $G$ plays the group role in only one realization, then it is homogeneous.

In Fig. 7.2, *Class* is a homogeneous group, whereas *SportsTeam* is a heterogeneous one.

## 7.5 Roles

### 7.5.1 Description

The concept of a role is one of the most controversial concepts in conceptual modeling. This is due partly to the fact that it is used with at least two different meanings, and partly to the fact that it can be represented in several different ways in conceptual schemas.

We have seen one meaning of "role" in Chap. 3: each participant in a relationship type plays a *role* in it. For example, in *Lives* (*resident:Person, placeOfResidence:Town*) the first participant plays the role of *resident* and the second the role of *place of residence*. In this meaning, a role is simply a name given to a participation of an entity type. In the logical representation of relationship types, roles are never used.

In this chapter, we study another meaning of "role", according to which it is not a name but a kind of entity type. It is unfortunate that we have to use the same term to convey two different meanings, although we are quite sure that the context will make it clear in which sense the term is being used in each case.

A role $r$ is a set of properties that characterize a situation which the instances of an entity type $E$ may be in at a given time. We say that $r$ is a role of $E$ or that $E$ plays the role $r$. Normally, the instances of $E$ are in a given situation only temporarily, and not all instances of $E$ need to be in the same situation. For example, "is a student" is a role of *Person*.

In conceptual modeling, roles are represented in two main ways: by subtyping and by surrogates. Representation by subtyping means defining an entity type $E_r$ as a subtype of $E$ such that the instances of $E_r$ are those of $E$ that play the role $r$. For example, we could define the entity type *Student* as a subtype of *Person*, such that the instances of *Student* are the persons that have the property "is a student". This representation of roles is analyzed in Chap. 10 (taxonomies).

Representation by surrogates means defining an entity type $E_r$ such that an instance $e_r$ of $E_r$ is a surrogate for an entity $e$ that plays the role $r$. For example, we could define the entity type *Student* thus: if $p$ is an instance of *Person* that "is a student", then there will be an instance $s$ of *Student* that will be a surrogate of $p$. In this case we can also say that $p$ plays the role $s$, or that $s$ is a role of $p$. Each instance of *Person* that is a student has a surrogate of $p$ in *Student*.

The correspondence between $e_r$ (the surrogate) and $e$ is a relationship that is an instance of the generic relationship type *IsRoleOf* (*role:Entity*, *player:Entity*). There is a realization of this type for each role/player combination in the schema, for example the realization {*role:Student*, *player:Person*}.

In a realization of *IsRoleOf*, the first participant entity type is called a role type, and the second a player type. The same entity type can be a player type in several realizations, but an entity type cannot be a role type in two or more realizations. A role type in a realization can be a player type in another one, but there cannot be cycles. For example, we may have the realizations {*role:Student*, *player:Person*} and {*role:GraduateStudent*, *player:Student*}.

*IsRoleOf* is antisymmetric: if $e_r$ is a role of $e$, then $e$ cannot be a role of $e_r$. Moreover, *IsRoleOf* is considered to be transitive. In the above example, a graduate student is also a role of a person.

An instance of a role type is the role of one, and only one, player. An instance of a player type may play several roles. Therefore,

$$Card(role; player; IsRoleOf) = (1,1)$$
$$Card(player; role; IsRoleOf) = (0,\infty)$$

Additionally, an instance of a role type is always the role of the same player. When an instance of a role type is created, it is related to its player by means of an *IsRoleOf* relationship, which cannot be changed. When an entity *e* ceases to play a role, its corresponding surrogate $e_r$ is deleted, and the *IsRoleOf* relationship $(e_r,e)$ is removed. Therefore, *IsRoleOf* is constant with respect to *role* and it is an existence dependency relationship type.

As we have seen, an instance of a player type can play several roles. In general, the roles played by an entity will belong to different role types. However, there are cases in which an entity is considered to play several roles of the *same* role type. An example might be the participation of persons in conferences, with the realization {*role:Participant, player:Person*}. A person may participate in several conferences at the same time. If we consider that each participation is a different role, then a person may have two or more roles (surrogates) in *Participant*.

### 7.5.2 Representation in UML

UML does not provide a built-in construct for defining an association as a realization of *IsRoleOf*. However, as in the previous case, we can extend the language by using stereotypes. We can define a new association stereotype such that the associations stereotyped by it correspond to the realizations of *IsRoleOf*. By using this stereotype, we can easily identify the realizations of *IsRoleOf* in a schema.

We shall assume that we have an association stereotype named «IsRoleOf». The stereotype may be used in binary associations. The first role of the association is the role type. It is not necessary to specify that the associations stereotyped by «IsRoleOf» are constant with respect to its role. It is understood that this constraint is part of the meaning of the stereotype, just like being antisymmetric and transitive.

Figure 7.3 shows five examples of associations with this stereotype that we might find in a conference management system. Persons may participate in conferences. An instance of *Participant* corresponds to the role played by a person in a conference. A person may participate in several conferences at the same time; he may therefore play several *Participant* roles. The set of associations {*person–participant, participant–conference*} is a compound reference to *Participant*.

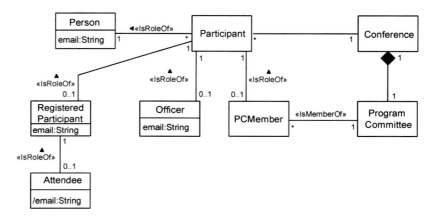

**Fig. 7.3.** Several examples of *IsRoleOf* in a conference management system domain

Being an officer at a conference is one way of participating in it. *Officer* is therefore a role of *Participant*. Note that *Participant* is an example of a role type that plays roles.

Each conference has a program committee. Being a program committee member (*PCMember*) is another way of participating in a conference. Thus, *PCMember* is a role of *Participant*.

Most participants register for a conference. *RegisteredParticipant* is therefore a role of *Participant*. When registered persons attend the conference they play the role of *Attendee*.

## 7.5.3 Propagation

When roles are represented by surrogates, roles do not "inherit" the attributes and associations of their players. For example, in Fig. 7.3, the instances of *Participant* do not have an *email address* attribute: the email address as an officer may be different from that as a person; and if a person plays several officer roles, the email addresses for each of these roles may be different.

If we want to propagate some of the attributes and/or associations of the player type to the role type, we can define them in the role type as derived attributes and/or associations. The derivation rule will state that their values are the same as those of the player type. In the example in Fig. 7.3, if we want to explicitly define that an attendee has an email address that is the same as the one he has as a registered participant, we define the derived attribute *email address* in *Attendee*. The derivation rule will state that the value of this attribute is the same as that of *RegisteredParticipant*.

## 7.6 Materialization

### 7.6.1 Description

Materialization has been studied less than the other generic relationship types described in this chapter. However, we do often find realizations of it in most domains and, for this reason, we feel it deserves as much attention as the other types. We represent it using the schema *Materializes* (*materialization:Entity, model:Entity*). A well-known example of realization is {*materialization:Car, model:CarModel*}. Informally, we define the model entity of an instance of *Materializes* as a model, a type, an abstract view or a specification of the materialization entity. For example, a car model has a set of attributes (such as the name or the number of doors) that are common to the cars of that model, and a set of constraints is specified that must be satisfied by all cars of that model (such as the set of available colors or the possible engine sizes).

Some other examples of realizations are

- *Production–Play*. A theater play may be produced in several ways. A production materializes the model given by the play: for example, the Lincoln Center Theater's production of Shakespeare's *Henry IV*.
- *Performance–Production*. A performance materializes a production on a particular date.
- *Seat–SeatType*. A theater classifies its seats by type. A seat type is a model for a number of seats. A seat materializes a seat type.
- *BookCopy–Book*. A library may have many copies of the same book. A book copy materializes a book.
- *FlightInstance–Flight*. A flight instance materializes a flight on a particular date.

*Materializes* is a binary relationship type in which one entity plays the role of the materialization, and the other the role of the model. *Materializes* is antisymmetric: if *mat* is a materialization of *mod*, then *mod* cannot be a materialization of *mat*. Moreover, *Materializes* is considered to be transitive. If a performance materializes a production and a production materializes a play, a performance is considered to materialize a play.

An instance of a materialization entity type is the materialization of one, and only one, instance of a model entity type. An instance of a model en-

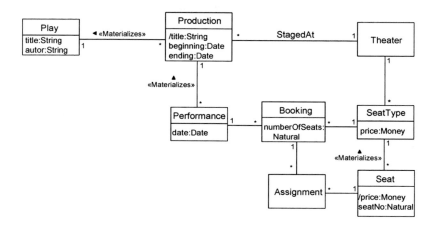

**Fig. 7.4.** Several examples of *Materializes* in a theater domain

tity type may be materialized in several instances of a materialization entity type. Therefore,

$$Card(materialization;\ model;\ Materializes) = (1,1)$$
$$Card(model;\ materialization;\ Materializes) = (0,\infty)$$

However, an instance of a materialization entity type always materializes the same model. When an instance of a materialization entity type is created, it is related to its model by a *Materializes* relationship, which cannot be changed. When a model entity *mod* ceases to exist, its corresponding materializations must also cease to exist, and the corresponding instances of *Materializes* are removed. Therefore, *Materializes* is constant with respect to *materialization* and it is an existence dependency relationship type.

## 7.6.2 Representation in UML

UML does not provide a built-in construct for defining an association as a realization of *Materializes*. However, as in the previous cases, we can extend the language by using stereotypes. We can define a new association stereotype such that the associations stereotyped by it correspond to the realizations of *Materializes*. By using this stereotype, we can easily identify the realizations of *Materializes* in a schema.

We shall assume that we have an association stereotype named «*Materializes*». The stereotype may be used in binary associations. The first role of the association is the materialization entity type. It is not necessary to specify that the associations stereotyped by «*Materializes*» are constant with respect to the first role. It is understood that this constraint is part of the meaning of the stereotype, just like being antisymmetric and transitive.

Figure 7.4 shows three examples of materialization. A production materializes a play, and a performance materializes a production. A production is staged at a theater. A theater classifies its seats into seat types. A seat materializes a seat type. A booking requests a number of seats of a given type for a particular performance. Specific seats will be assigned to it at a given time.

### 7.6.3 Inheritance

As we have seen, a model entity is a model, a type, an abstract view or a specification of a materialization entity. This means that materialization entities inherit attributes, associations and constraints from their models. Specifically, we can state the following:

- In UML, we can define the attributes and associations inherited by a materialization entity from its model in the materialization type as derived attributes and associations. The derivation rule will state that their values are the same as those of the model.
- The attributes and associations of a materialization entity may be constrained by the attributes and associations of its model.

Figure 7.4 shows two examples of attribute inheritance. The *title* of a *Production* is inherited from its *Play*. The derivation rule of *title* in *Production* will state that the *title* of a production is the title of its play. The *price* of a *Seat* is inherited from its *SeatType*. The derivation rule of *price* in *Seat* will state that the *price* of a seat is the price given by its seat type.

Figure 7.4 also shows an example of model attributes that constrain materialization attributes: the *date* of a performance must be in the interval between the *beginning* and *ending* dates of the production. In Chap. 9, we shall explain how these constraints should be formally specified.

## 7.7 Bibliographical Notes

Most of the work on generic relationship types has focused on particular types, mainly the part–whole. There has also been a lot of work for particular applications, mainly spatiotemporal applications; see, for example, MADS (Parent et al. 2006).

Storey (1993) provided one of the first analyses of the most widely used generic relationship types. More comprehensive analyses can be found in Goldstein and Storey (1999) and Dahchour et al. (2005). Olivé (2002) analyzed the methods of representation of generic relationship types in conceptual modeling.

Part–whole relationship types have been extensively studied in the fields of philosophy, linguistics, and cognitive science, although few texts other than Artale et al. (1996), published in a special issue of *Data and Knowledge Engineering* on "Modeling Parts and Wholes", have provided a unified view of these relationship types from a conceptual modeling perspective.

The work in the disciplines mentioned above that has had the most wide-ranging influence on the conceptual modeling field is that of Winston et al. (1987), and its continuation in Chaffin et al. (1988) and Chaffin and Herrmann (1988). In these publications, a classification of part–whole relationships was provided. Iris et al. (1988) provided a similar classification and commented on the problems of transitivity in these relationships. These works identified several kinds of part–whole relationship, and showed that in general transitivity holds when it is applied with relationships of the same kind. Martin and Odell (1995) described a method that adopts the classification given in Winston et al. (1987), with few changes.

The most relevant work on part–whole relationships has been in the field of object-oriented databases. A pioneering system was Orion, described in what are now considered classic texts by Kim et al. (1987, 1989). Orion was the first system based on a data model extended with part–whole relationships, which allowed global sharing and a variant of global dependency to be defined. Several research lines have continued this work. One of them is described in Halper et al. (1998), which deals with attribute propagation from the whole to its parts and vice versa.

In the conceptual modeling field, Motschnig-Pitrik (1993) and Motschnig-Pitrik and Kaasboll (1999) described sharing and dependency in terms of cardinality constraints, and gave a formalization in Telos. Henderson-Sellers and Barbier (1999) and Opdahl et al. (2001) extended the semantics of part–whole relationships by distinguishing between main and secondary characteristics. Lambrix (2000) described a representation of part–whole relationships in Description Logics.

(Brodie 1981) was the first paper that presented the concept of association in the context of conceptual modeling, which was analyzed further by Motschnig-Pitrik and Storey (1995).

The controversial nature of roles has given rise to an abundant literature on conceptual modeling. See (Steimann 2000) for a comprehensive literature survey. Pernici (1990) presented one of the first proposals of representation by surrogates. Cabot and Raventós (2006) analyzed the representation of roles in UML and proposed using a stereotype with attributes to define adopted properties.

Goldstein and Storey (1994) gave the first description of materialization. Pirotte et al. (1994) extended and defined the semantics of materialization in terms of other conceptual modeling constructs. Dahchour et al. (2002) presented an implementation of materialization.

## 7.8 Exercises

**7.1** Consider a domain of auctions in which there are articles, and lots of articles sold together. A lot consists of one or more articles. An article cannot be in two or more lots at the same time. The creation of a new lot includes the definition of the articles that it comprises. There may be articles that are not included in any lot. The composition of lots is immutable. Lots cease to exist at some time, but their articles may remain in the system and later become part of other lots. Design the conceptual schema of this domain in UML.

**7.2** Local sharing and local dependency are two orthogonal aspects of *IsPartOf* realizations. Four combinations are possible. Give an example in UML of each of them.

**7.3** Design a UML schema that represents the following knowledge about a flight management domain. Identify the associations in the schema that are realizations of the generic relationship types studied in this chapter. An airplane has an identifier, a name, and a type. Each airplane is owned by an airline. An airplane type has a name, and a number of seats. A flight is operated by an airline. Each flight has a code and one or more flight legs. A flight leg is a nonstop portion of a flight. For example, a Paris–Tokyo flight might consist of two flight legs: Paris–Frankfurt and Frankfurt–Tokyo. A flight leg leaves and arrives at an airport and has a scheduled departure time and arrival time. A flight leg is served by an airplane of a specific type. An airport has a name and a code and is located in a city. A flight instance is an occurrence of a flight on a particular date. A leg instance is an occurrence of a flight leg, served by a specific airplane. Two leg instances of the same flight may be served by different airplanes. The departure and arrival times of a leg instance may differ from the scheduled ones. Each leg instance has a crew, which consists of a pilot, one copilot or none, and one or more flight attendants. Each crew member has an identifier and a name. A person may be a crew member of several leg instances (whose schedules do not overlap, obviously).

**7.4** Although we have focused on four generic relationship types in this chapter, others are possible. Identify a new one that you think might be useful in a given project. For this new generic relationship type, provide

- its name;
- a description;
- several examples of realizations;
- the properties of the type and of its realizations;
- its representation in UML.

# 8 Derived Types

In this chapter we show that entity and relationship types may be base, derived, or hybrid (Sect. 8.1). The instances of base types need to be explicitly represented in an information base, while those of derived and hybrid types may be inferred by an information system, using derivation rules. Derivation rules are domain knowledge that an information system needs in order to derive certain facts; this knowledge must therefore be described in the conceptual schema. Section 8.2 describes the logical and the UML representations of derived and hybrid types and their derivation rules. In general, derivation rules are very diverse, although certain kinds appear very often. Section 8.3 describes some of these. Section 8.4 shows that the derivation rules of constant relationships require special interpretation. Section 8.5 explains how to define a particular kind of hybrid type in UML. Derived types add complexity to a schema, so their definition must be justified. Section 8.6 deals with the justification of derived types.

Formal definition of derivation rules requires the use of a formal language. In UML, the preferred language is OCL, and this is the language that will be used throughout this book. We assume that the reader is familiar with the basics of OCL. In Section 8.7 we give references to introductory and detailed texts on OCL.

## 8.1 Derivability

The *derivability* of an entity or relationship type means the way in which the information system knows the population of that type at any instant. According to its derivability, an entity or relationship type may be base, derived, or hybrid. These types are studied in the following sections.

### 8.1.1 Base Types

An entity or relationship type is *base* when its instances need to be explicitly represented in the information base, otherwise the information system could not know them.

For example, assume the entity type *Book*. In most systems, *Book* will be base because the information system knows its instances only if they are explicitly represented in the information base. Similarly, the relationship type *Reads* (*reader:Person, Book*) is base, for the same reason: the information system can only know who is reading which books if this is explicitly represented in the information base.

## 8.1.2 Derived Types

An entity or relationship type is *derived* when its instances need not be explicitly represented in the information base, because the information system may derive (i.e. infer or calculate) them at any time. For each derived type, there is a *derivation rule*, which is an expression that defines the necessary and sufficient conditions for an entity or a relationship to be an instance of the given type. It is assumed that the information system has an inference mechanism, by means of which it can derive the population of a derived type from its derivation rule and the population of other types. Each entity or relationship type whose population can be derived from that of other types should be defined as derived.

An example of a derived entity type might be *Quadrilateral*. Its derivation rule, written in natural language, would be "A quadrilateral is a polygon with four sides". An information system may derive the population of *Quadrilateral* from:

- The derivation rule indicated.
- The population of *Polygon*, which is explicitly represented in the information base.
- The population of the relationship type *HasSides* (*Polygon, sides:Natural*), which is also explicitly represented in the information base.

An example of a derived relationship type might be *Grandparent* (*grandchild:Person, grandparent:Person*). Its derivation rule, written in natural language, would be "A person *gc* is a grandchild of person *gp* if *gc* is a child of a *gp*'s child". An information system may derive the population of *Grandparent* from:

- The derivation rule indicated.
- The population of *Parent* (*child:Person, parent:Person*), which is explicitly represented in the information base.

### 8.1.3 Hybrid Types

An entity or relationship type is *hybrid* if several of its instances need to be explicitly represented in the information base but the others can be derived. The derived instances are defined by a derivation rule, which in this case is a partial rule, since it defines only part of the population of that type.

Let us assume that there are entity types *Document* and *Book*, and that *Book* is base. If books are documents, but there are documents that are not books (such as reports or theses), then *Document* is hybrid. The information system knows the complete population of *Document* from:

- The partial derivation rule "Books are documents".
- The population of *Book*, which is explicitly represented in the information base.
- The population of *Document* that is explicitly represented in the information base.

In the domain of a company, a simple example of a hybrid relationship type might be *MemberOfCommittee* (*Person, Committee*). Let us assume that employees may be members of committees, but that there is also a rule stating that the company's directors are members of all existing committees. The information system knows the complete population of *MemberOfCommittee* from:

- The partial derivation rule "Directors are members of all existing committees".
- The instances of *Director* and *Committee*, which are explicitly represented in the information base.
- The instances of *MemberOfCommittee* that are explicitly represented in the information base.

### 8.1.4 Transformation of Hybrid Types into Derived Types

Any hybrid entity type can easily be transformed into an equivalent derived type. Let $E$ be a hybrid entity type with a partial derivation rule $DR$. $E$ can be transformed into a derived type in the following two steps:

1. Define a new base type $E_{ext}$ such that its population at any time is the set of entities of type $E$ that is explicitly represented in the information base.
2. Define that $E$ is derived from the rule "An entity $e$ is an instance of $E$ if $e$ satisfies the derivation rule $DR$ or $e$ is an instance of $E_{ext}$".

Let us apply this transformation to the hybrid entity type *Document*.

1. We define a new base entity type *GeneralDocument* (or any other name that is considered appropriate to the domain). Documents that are not books are instances of this type.
2. We now define *Document* as a derived type using the derivation rule "An instance of *Document* is an instance of *GeneralDocument* or an instance of *Book*".

The above transformation can also be applied to relationship types. For example, the application to *MemberOfCommittee* (*Person*, *Committee*) would be as follows:

1. We define a new base relationship type *AssignedMember* (*Person*, *Committee*) (or any other name that may be more appropriate). The instances of *AssignedMember* are the explicit assignments of persons to committees.
2. We now define *MemberOfCommittee* as a derived type using the derivation rule "A person *p* is a member of committee *c* if *p* is a director or *p* is an assigned member of *c*".

As we have seen, hybrid types can be transformed into derived types. However, there is a price to pay, in the sense that a new, auxiliary type ($E_{ext}$) must be defined. Nevertheless, the transformation is important because most conceptual modeling languages (including UML) do not allow hybrid types, at least in the general case.

### 8.1.5 Design of Derivability

Derivability is not an intrinsic characteristic of an entity or relationship type. A type may be base in one information system and derived in another. For example, the entity type *Quadrilateral* may be derived in a system dealing with polygons and their number of sides, while it is likely to be base in a system dealing only with quadrilaterals.

In a given conceptual schema, we may have one or more types whose derivability is not predetermined. The typical example is that of the entity types *Person*, *Man*, and *Woman* and the attribute *Sex* (*Person*, *Sex*), to which there are at least two possible approaches:

- To define *Person* and *Sex* (*Person*, *Sex*) as base, and *Man* and *Woman* as derived.
- To define *Man* and *Woman* as base, and *Person* and *Sex* (*Person*, *Sex*) as derived.

There are no clear guidelines for designing derivability. In principle, it would seem that an important criterion should be user convenience. Derivability has an impact on the information that users have to provide to the system, and it is important to keep this information to a minimum or to require that it is expressed in the form that is most natural to users. The application of this criterion to the above example means choosing between the following options:

- If *Person* and *Sex* are base types, users need to inform the system of the existing persons and their *sex* attribute. *Man* and *Woman* can then be derived types.
- If *Man* and *Woman* are base types, users need to inform the system of the existing men and women. *Person* and *sex* can then be derived types.

## 8.2 Representation in an Information System

An information system needs to know the derivability of the entity and relationship types defined in the schema and, for derived and hybrid types, their corresponding derivation rules. Both the derivability and the derivation rules are defined in the schema. The form of representation depends on the conceptual modeling language used. In this section, we study the logical and UML representations.

### 8.2.1 Logical Representation

In the logical representation:

- The base types are those that do not have derivation rules. The system provides mechanisms by means of which users can inform the system of instances of these types.
- The derived types are those which have derivation rules. Users cannot tell the system that there are explicit instances of these types.
- The hybrid types also have derivation rules, but in this case the system provides mechanisms by means of which users can inform the system of additional instances of these types.

A derivation rule of a derived entity type $E$ is a closed formula

$$E(e) \leftrightarrow \phi(e)$$

where $\phi(e)$ is a subformula with a free variable $e$. The rule states that $e$ is an instance of $E$ if, and only if, the subformula $\phi(e)$ holds. For example, the derivation rule of *Quadrilateral* is

$$Quadrilateral(e) \leftrightarrow (Polygon(e) \land HasSides(e,4))$$

The partial derivation rule of a hybrid entity type $E$ is a closed formula:

$$\phi(e) \rightarrow E(e)$$

where $\phi(e)$ is, as before, a subformula with a free variable $e$. Note that an entity $e$ may be an instance of $E$ even if the subformula $\phi(e)$ does not hold. For example, the partial derivation rule of *Document* is

$$Book(e) \rightarrow Document(e)$$

Similarly, the derivation rule of a derived relationship type $R$ is a closed formula

$$R(e_1, \ldots, e_n) \leftrightarrow \phi(e_1, \ldots, e_n)$$

where $\phi(e_1, \ldots, e_n)$ is a subformula with free variables $e_1, \ldots, e_n$. The rule states that $e_1, \ldots, e_n$ is an instance of $R$ if, and only if, the subformula $\phi(e_1, \ldots, e_n)$ holds. For example, the derivation rule of *Grandparent* is

$$Grandparent(gc,gp) \leftrightarrow (Parent(gc,p) \land Parent(p,gp))$$

Finally, the partial derivation rule of a hybrid relationship type $R$ is a closed formula

$$\phi(e_1, \ldots, e_n) \rightarrow R(e_1, \ldots, e_n)$$

where $\phi(e_1, \ldots, e_n)$ is a subformula with free variables $e_1, \ldots, e_n$. The rule states that $e_1, \ldots, e_n$ is an instance of $R$ if the subformula $\phi(e_1, \ldots, e_n)$ holds. For example, the partial derivation rule of *MemberOfCommittee* is

$$(Director(p) \land Committee(c)) \rightarrow MemberOfCommittee(p,c)$$

### 8.2.2 Representation in UML

In general, UML allows derived attributes and associations to be defined. Derived attributes are represented graphically by placing a slash (/) in front of the name. The derivation rules are usually specified using the OCL language. The specification has the general form

```
context EntityType::attribute:Type
  derive: an OCL expression
```

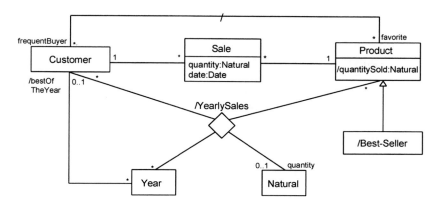

**Fig. 8.1.** Examples of derived entity types, attributes and associations

The **context** clause states the derived attribute whose derivation rule is specified by the expression given in the **derive** clause. This means that the evaluation of the expression for an instance of the entity type gives the value of the attribute for that instance. The value must conform to the type and multiplicity of the attribute. If the maximum multiplicity of the attribute is greater than one, the result of the expression is a set. If the minimum multiplicity is zero, the result may be the empty set. If the multiplicity is 0..1, the result may be a value or the empty set.

In the example in Fig. 8.1, *Product* has the derived attribute *quantitySold*, which is defined as the sum of the quantities of all sales of the product. The derivation rule is

```
context Product::quantitySold:Natural
  derive: sale.quantity->sum()
```

Derived associations are represented graphically by a slash either in front of the name of the association, in place of the name if no name is shown, or in front of the role names. Figure 8.1 shows three examples: the associations *frequentBuyer–favorite*, *YearlySales*, and *bestOfTheYear–year*.

Similarly to attributes, the derivation rules of associations are usually specified using the OCL language. The general form of the specification of a derived binary association is

```
context EntityType::Role:Type
  derive: an OCL expression
```

The **context** clause states one of the two roles of the association whose derivation rule is specified by the expression given in the **derive** clause. This means that the evaluation of the expression for an instance of the entity type provides the entities related to it in the role indicated. The result must conform to the type and multiplicity of the role. If the maximum multiplicity of the role is greater than one, the result of the expression is a set. If the minimum multiplicity is zero, the result may be the empty set. If the multiplicity is 0..1, the result may be an entity or the empty set.

The derivation rule of the association *frequentBuyer–favorite* shown in Fig. 8.1 might be

```
context Customer::favorite:Product
   derive: -- A product is one of self's favorites
           -- if self has bought more than 1000 units of it.
      Product.allInstances()->select(p:Product|p.sale->
        select(s:Sale|s.customer=self).quantity->sum() > 1000)
```

Note that the derivation rule can be specified for either of the two roles. In the above example, an alternative option might be

```
context Product::frequentBuyer:Customer
   derive: -- A frequent buyer has bought
           -- more than 1000 units of self.
      Customer.allInstances()->select(c:Customer|c.sale->
        select(s:Sale|s.product=self).quantity->sum() > 1000)
```

From a conceptual point of view, the two options are equivalent. The conceptual modeler may choose the option that he considers more natural or easier to specify.

### 8.2.3 Representation of Derivation Rules by Operations

In object-oriented languages such as UML, derivation rules may be represented by operations. One of the advantages of this form of representation is that it can be used for any kind of derived entity or relationship type. In general, in this book we use operations only when the standard representation is not possible or when using operations provides better representations of the derivation rules.

The idea is to associate each derived element with a query operation, called the *defining* operation. Query operations (also called query functions) return a value but do not alter the information base. In UML, the value is formally specified by an OCL expression defined in the **body** clause. The specification of the defining operation is the derivation rule. The signature of the defining operation and the details of its specification depend on the derived element, as we explain below.

For an attribute $A$ of entity type $E$ with values of type $E_1$, the defining operation is an instance operation in $E$ without arguments:

```
context E::A():[E₁|Set(E₁)]
```

where the result type is $E_1$ or *Set* $(E_1)$, depending on whether $A$ is single-valued or multivalued, respectively. The result of the operation is the value of the attribute $A$ for the corresponding instance entity.

For example, the defining operation corresponding to the attribute *quantitySold* of *Product* mentioned above is

```
context Product::quantitySold():Natural
  body: sale.quantity->sum()
```

Note that, for attributes, the `body` expression is the same as that of `derive`.

The defining operations are purely conceptual; they may or may not be part of the implementation. The only purpose of a defining operation is to specify the corresponding derivation rule. Normally, these operations are not shown in the class diagrams of conceptual schemas.

For a binary relationship type $R(p_1:E_1, p_2:E_2)$, the defining operation may take one of the following four forms:

- An instance operation of $E_1$ with signature $p_2()$: $[E_2 |$ *Set* $(E_2)]$. The result is $E_2$ or *Set* $(E_2)$, depending on the cardinalities of $R$. The result of the operation is the instance, or the set of instances, of $E_2$ related to an instance of $E_1$.
- An instance operation of $E_2$ with signature $p_1()$: $[E_1 |$ *Set* $(E_1)]$. This is similar to the above operation.
- An instance operation of $E_1$ with signature $p_1(p_2:E_2)$: *Boolean*. The result is *true* if there is a relationship of type $R$ between *self* and the instance given in the parameter, and *false* otherwise.
- An instance operation of $E_2$ with signature $p_2(e_1:E_1)$: *Boolean*. This is similar to the above operation.

From a conceptual point of view, the four options are equivalent. The place ($E_1$ or $E_2$) in which the operation is defined does not imply navigability. Conceptually, associations are navigable in all directions. The conceptual modeler may choose the place that he considers more natural or easier to specify.

For example, a specification of the defining operation of the association *frequentBuyer–favorite* defined in *Customer* might be

```
context Customer::favorite():Set(Product)
  body:
    Product.allInstances()->select(p:Product|p.sale->
      select(s:Sale|s.customer=self).quantity->sum() > 1000)
```

Similarly, a specification of the defining operation in *Product* might be

```
context Product::frequentBuyer():Set(Customer)
  body:
    Customer.allInstances()->select(c:Customer|c.sale->
      select(s:Sale|s.product=self).quantity->sum() > 1000)
```

Note that when the derivation rule of a binary association is specified in this way, the **body** expression is the same as that of **derive**.

An example illustrating the use of defining operations whose result indicates whether or not a relationship exists between *self* and an instance of the other role is the *bestOfTheYear–year* association shown in Fig. 8.1. Let us assume that customer $c$ is the best in year $y$ if $c$ is the customer with the greatest total quantity sold in $y$. A specification might be

```
context Customer::bestOfTheYear(y:Year):Boolean
  body:
    let customers:Sequence(Customer) =
        Customer.allInstances()->sortedBy(sale->
          select(date.year = y).quantity -> sum())
    in customers->notEmpty() and self=customers->last()
```

The derivation rule of a derived $n$-ary relationship type can also be specified by means of an operation. Let $R(p_1:E_1,\ldots, p_n:E_n)$ be a derived relationship type, with $n > 2$. We can host the defining operation in any of the $n$ participant entity types, and the result type may be any of the other $n$ - 1 entity types. Therefore, we may choose among $n^2$ defining operations, each of which is an instance operation of a certain $E_i$, $i \in \{1, \ldots, n\}$ and has either $n$ - 2 arguments and a return result of type $E_j, j \neq i, j \in \{1, \ldots, n\}$, or $n$ - 1 arguments and a return result of type *Boolean*.

In the first case, the general form of the instance operation for $i = 1$ and $j = 2$ is

```
context E₁::opname(p₃:E₃,…,pₙ:Eₙ) : [E₂|Set(E₂)]
```

where the result type is $E_2$ or *Set* $(E_2)$, depending on the cardinalities of $R$. The result of the operation is the set of instances of $E_2$ related to an instance of $E_1$ and to the instances of $E_3, \ldots, E_n$ given in the arguments.

In the second case, the general form of the instance operation for $i = 1$ is

```
context E₁::opname(p₂:E₂,p₃:E₃,…,pₙ:Eₙ):Boolean
```

The result is *true* if there is a relationship of type $R$ between *self* and the instances given in the parameters, and *false* otherwise.

It is difficult to define a general convention regarding the name *opname* of the operation. In many cases, the name of a role may be appropriate, but in other cases other names may be considered more appropriate. If necessary, the correspondence between the derived association and its defining operation can be documented with a comment.

For example, consider the derived quaternary association *YearlySales* shown in Fig. 8.1. An instance of this association gives the quantity of product *p* bought by customer *c* in year *y*, provided that *c* has made at least one sale of *p* during *y*. If we host the defining operation in *Customer*, the derivation rule in OCL is

```
context Customer::quantity(p:Product,y:Year):Natural
   body: let sales:Set(Sale) =
              sale->select(product = p and date.year = y)
         in
         if sales->notEmpty() then sales.quantity->sum()
         else Set{}
         endif
```

An alternative option might be to host the operation in *Product*. We would not normally host defining operations in data types (such as *Year* or *Natural* in the example above).

The derivation rule of a derived entity type *E* can also be specified by means of an operation. Here, the defining operation is a class operation of *E* without arguments, whose intended result is the set of instances of *E*. The OCL includes, for each entity type *E*, the predefined class operation of *E*,

```
context E::allInstances():Set(E)
```

which gives the set of all instances of *E* and of its subtypes at the time the operation is evaluated. For base entity types, this operation need not be specified, because its meaning is predefined. For derived entity types, it could be used (although it is not standard) as the defining operation of the corresponding derivation rule.

For example, consider the derived entity type *Best-Seller* shown in Fig. 8.1. Let us assume that a product is a best-seller if the quantity sold is greater than 10, 000 units. The derivation rule could be

```
context Best-Seller::allInstances():Set(Best-Seller)
   body: Product.allInstances()->select(quantitySold > 10000)
```

## 8.3 Particular Kinds of Derived Type

In general, derivation rules are very diverse, although certain kinds appear very often. In the following sections, we study several of the most popular derivation rules.

### 8.3.1 Derived by Union

An entity type *E* is *derived by union* of $E_1$, ..., $E_n$ ($n \geq 1$) if at any time its population is the union of the populations of $E_1$, ..., $E_n$. A classic example

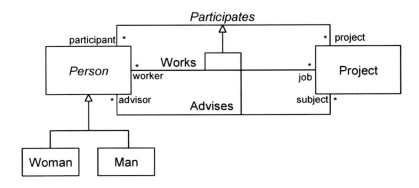

**Fig. 8.2.** *Person* and *Participates* are derived by union

is that of *Person*. Many systems define *Person* as derived by union of *Man* and *Woman*.

In UML, entity types derived by union are semantically equivalent to abstract entity types: the population of an abstract entity type is the union of the population of its subtypes. Thus, we can state that $E$ is derived by union of $E_1$, ..., $E_n$ by defining $E$ as abstract and $E_1$, ..., $E_n$ as subtypes of $E$. The name of an abstract entity type is shown in italic. An example is shown in Fig. 8.2.

A relationship type $R$ is *derived by union* of $R_1$, ..., $R_n$ ($n \geq 1$) if, at any time, its population is the union of the populations of $R_1$, ..., $R_n$. For example, if a person is said to participate in a project by either working on it or acting as an advisor, then

> *Participates (participant:Person, project:Project)*

is derived by union of

> *Works (worker:Person, job:Project)*
> *Advises (advisor:Person, subject:Project)*

Similarly to what occurs in the case of entity types, in UML we can state that $R$ is *derived by union* of $R_1$, ..., $R_n$ by defining $R$ as abstract and $R_1$, ..., $R_n$ as subtypes of $R$. The name of an abstract relationship type is shown in italic. An example is shown in Fig. 8.2.

UML offers an alternative representation of binary associations derived by union, which may sometimes be more practical than the one just described. In this representation, we define that an association $A$ is derived by union of the associations $A_1$, ..., $A_n$ using a property string *{union}* near

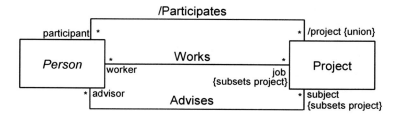

**Fig. 8.3.** Alternative representation of associations derived by union

to a role name $r$ of $A$ and a property string {*subsets $<r>$*} near to the corresponding role name of $A_1$, ..., $A_n$.

The two representations are semantically equivalent; instead of defining $A$ as abstract, we define that one of its roles $r$ is derived by union of the roles that are declared as its subsets. Figure 8.3 shows the example in Fig. 8.2 using this notation. One of the advantages of this representation is that it can also be applied to attributes.

### 8.3.2 Derived by Specialization

An entity type $E$ is *derived by specialization* of $E_1$, ..., $E_n$ ($n \geq 1$) when its derivation rule defines that $e$ is an instance of $E$ if $e$ is an instance of $E_1$, ..., $E_n$ and (optionally, if $n \geq 2$) if $e$ satisfies a specialization condition. If $E$ is derived by specialization of $E_1$, ..., $E_n$, then $E$ is a subtype of $E_1$, ..., $E_n$.

When $n = 1$, we say that $E$ is derived by *simple* specialization of $E_1$. In this case there must be a specialization condition; otherwise, $E$ and $E_1$ would be redundant. The instances of $E$ are those of $E_1$ that satisfy the specialization condition. For example, if a quadrilateral is defined as a polygon that has four sides, then *Quadrilateral* is derived by simple specialization of *Polygon*, with the specialization condition "has four sides". The formal derivation rule is

```
context Quadrilateral::allInstances():Set(Quadrilateral)
  body: Polygon.allInstances()->select(sides = 4)
```

Most derived entity types are derived by simple specialization. Another example is *Best-Seller*, shown in Fig. 8.1.

When $n > 1$, we say that $E$ is derived by *multiple* specialization of $E_1$, ..., $E_n$. In this case, the specialization condition is optional. If there is one, then the instances of $E$ at any time are the instances of $E_1$, ..., $E_n$ at that time that satisfy the specialization condition. An example might be the entity type

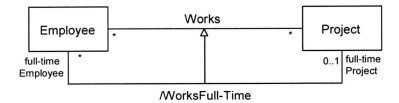

**Fig. 8.4.** *WorksFull-Time* is derived by specialization of *Works*

*AdultEmployeeStudent* if we assume that its instances are those individuals that are employees, students, and over 18 years old. The derivation rule is

```
context AdultEmployeeStudent::
        allInstances():Set(AdultEmployeeStudent)
  body: Person.allInstances->select
        (p:Person|p.oclIsTypeOf(Student) and
          p.oclIsTypeOf(Employee) and p.age > 18)
```

In this example, the specialization condition is "over 18 years old".

When $E$ is derived by multiple specialization of $E_1$, ..., $E_n$ but without a specialization condition, then we say that $E$ is derived by the *intersection* of $E_1$, ..., $E_n$. In this case, the population of $E$ at any time is the intersection of the populations of $E_1$, ..., $E_n$ at that time. For example, *Square* is derived by the intersection of *Rectangle* and *Rhombus*. Its formal derivation rule is

```
context Square::allInstances():Set(Square)
  body: Rectangle.allInstances()->
        intersection(Rhombus.allInstances())
```

Relationship types can also be derived by specialization. The definitions are similar to those of entity types. Figure 8.4 shows an example. An employee works full-time on a project if he works only on that particular project. *WorksFull-Time* is derived by simple specialization of *Works*, with the specialization condition "the employee works only on this project". The formal derivation rule of *WorksFull-Time* is

```
context Employee::full-timeProject:Project
  derive: if project -> size() = 1 then project->any(true)
          else Set{}
          endif
```

Most derived relationship types are derived by simple specialization.

### 8.3.3 Derived by Exclusion

An entity type $E$ is *derived by exclusion* if $E$ is derived by simple specialization of $E_1$ and the specialization condition is that the instances of $E$ are not instances of $E_2$, ..., $E_n$, with $n > 1$.

For example, if an instance of *UnemployedPerson* is a *Person* who is not an *Employee*, then *UnemployedPerson* is derived by exclusion. The formal derivation rule is

```
context UnemployedPerson::allInstances():
        Set(UnemployedPerson)
  body: Person.allInstances() - Employee.allInstances()
```

Relationship types may also be derived by exclusion. For example, assume the following types:

> *Actor* (*Movie*, *Actor*)
>
> *MainActor* (*Movie*, *mainActor:Actor*)
>
> *SupportingActor* (*Movie*, *supportingActor:Actor*)

If a supporting actor in a movie is an actor in that movie who is not a main actor, then *SupportingActor* is derived by exclusion. The formal derivation rule is

```
context Movie::supportingActor():Actor
  derive: actor - mainActor
```

### 8.3.4 Derived by Participation

Consider the relationship type $R(p_1:E_1, ..., p_n:E_n)$ and one of its participants $p_i:E_i$. Let us assume that the participation of $p_i$ in $R$ is partial. This means that there may be instances of $E_i$ that participate in a given relationship of type $R$ and others that do not. $E$ is an entity type *derived by participation* in $R$ if its population is defined as the instances of $E_i$ that participate in some relationship of type $R$. An entity type derived by participation is also derived by simple specialization. Observe that relationship types cannot be derived in this way.

For example, consider the association *Manages* shown in Fig. 8.5 and suppose that a manager is an employee that manages a department. *Manager* is therefore an entity type derived by participation in *Manages*. The formal derivation rule is

```
context Manager::allInstances():Set(Manager)
  body: Employee.allInstances()->
        select(department->notEmpty())
```

It may be useful to compare the representation shown in Fig. 8.5 with that in Fig. 8.6, in which *Manager* is a base entity type and a participant in *Manages*. The knowledge represented in Fig. 8.5 (including the derivation rule) is the same as that in Fig. 8.6. In principle, the representation shown in Fig. 8.6 is better, because it states clearly that only managers can manage departments and does not require a derivation rule. However, changes

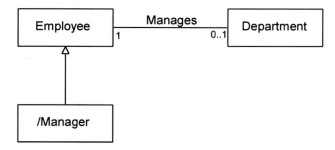

Fig. 8.5. *Manager* is an entity type derived by participation

to the information base become more complex. Consider, for example, a change of manager in a particular department. In the schema shown in Fig. 8.5, the change implies

- removing the *Manages* link between the current manager and the department, and
- adding a *Manages* link between the new manager and the department.

while in the schema in Fig. 8.6 the change implies

- removing the current department manager from *Manager*,
- removing the *Manages* link between the current manager and the department,
- adding the new manager to *Manager*, and
- adding a *Manages* link between the new manager and the department.

Clearly, the conceptual modeler must weigh up the benefits of a simple structural schema against those of a simple behavioral schema.

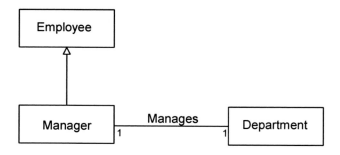

Fig. 8.6. An alternative representation of *Manager* and *Manages*

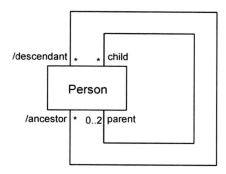

**Fig. 8.7.** The association *ancestor–descendant* is the transitive closure of *parent–child*

### 8.3.5 Transitive Closure

In mathematics, the transitive closure of a binary relation $R$ in a set $X$ is the smallest transitive relation in $X$ that contains $R$. In conceptual modeling, we often find binary associations that are the transitive closure of others. Such associations are derived.

Figure 8.7 shows an example of this. The association *ancestor–descendant* is the transitive closure of *parent–child*. The instances of *ancestor–descendant* are those of *parent–child* and those that can be obtained from them by transitivity. The formal specification is

```
context Person::descendant:Person
  derive: self.child->union(self.child.descendant)->asSet()
```

## 8.4 Derivation Rules for Constant Relationship Types

Like any other type, constant relationship types can be derived. However, their derivation rules require special interpretation. Consider the example in Fig. 8.8. A sale consists of a set of sale lines. Each sale line is for a given product. The attributes of a sale line are the amount sold, the unit price, and the line price. All of them are constant with respect to the sale line. In principle, it would seem that the unit price and the line price are derived. The derivation rule of the unit price might be as simple as

```
context SaleLine::unitPrice:Money
  derive: product.unitPrice
```

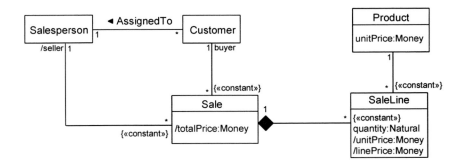

**Fig. 8.8.** Examples of derived constant attributes and associations

However, this derivation rule is incorrect because the unit price of the product sold may change after the sale line has been created, but this does not imply that the unit prices of the sale lines of that product must be changed. The correct form of the rule must define that the unit price of a sale line is determined by its product when the sale line is created.

A similar example, which is also shown in Fig. 8.8, is that of the *sale–seller* association, which is constant with respect to *sale*. If the seller of a sale is defined as the salesperson assigned to the customer of that sale, the derivation rule might be

```
context Sale::seller:SalesPerson
  derive: customer.salesPerson
```

However, as in the previous case, this derivation rule is incorrect because the salesperson assigned to a customer may change after the sale has been created, but this does not imply that the seller of the sales to a given customer must be changed. The correct form of the rule must define that the seller of a sale is determined by the customer of the sale when the sale is created.

These problems can be solved by applying a special interpretation to the derivation rules of constant relationship types. The idea is to adhere to the semantics of the constant constraint. As outlined in Chapter 3, if $R(p_1:E_1, ..., p_i:E_i, ..., p_n:E_n)$ is constant with respect to $p_i$, the set of instances of $R$ in which an instance $e_i$ of $E_i$ participates in the role $p_i$ is determined when $e_i$ is created and remains fixed during the lifetime of $e_i$. Therefore, it is natural to assume that, if $R$ is derived, $R(e_1, ..., e_i, ..., e_n)$ holds at a given time if $R(e_1, ..., e_i, ..., e_n)$ satisfied the derivation rule when $e_i$ was created.

According to this interpretation, the two derivation rules above are correct. The *unitPrice* attribute of a *SaleLine* exists when the sale line is created and it remains the same until the sale line ceases to exist. Evaluating the derivation rule at the time of creation gives the value of the attribute. Similarly, an instance of the association *sale–seller* starts to exist when the sale is created, and it continues to exist until the sale ceases to exist (if this occurs). The participants in the association are given by the evaluation of the derivation rule when the sale is created.

Figure 8.8 also shows the derived constant attribute *linePrice* of *SaleLine*. In this case, the derivation rule always gives the same value[1]:

```
context SaleLine::linePrice:Money
  derive: quantity * unitPrice
```

Note that in Fig. 8.8, the derived attribute *totalPrice* of *Sale* is not constant. It is assumed that sale lines can be added to and removed from a sale at any time. Therefore, this attribute is time-varying and its value is defined by the following derivation rule:

```
context Sale::totalPrice:Money
  derive: saleLine.linePrice->sum()
```

## 8.5 Hybrid Types in UML

Object-oriented languages (including UML) provide limited support for defining hybrid types. The general solution is then to transform these types into their derived equivalents. Unfortunately, as explained in Sect. 8.1.4, this transformation requires the definition of a new type, which may be considered artificial in many cases.

However, for a particular kind of hybrid type, there is a simple solution. Recall that in general a hybrid entity type $E$ has a partial derivation rule

$$\phi(e) \to E(e)$$

This means that the population of $E$ is given by the union of its explicitly given instances and those that satisfy $\phi(e)$.

This particular kind of hybrid type occurs when the partial derivation rule takes the form

$$E_1(e) \vee \ldots \vee E_n(e) \to E(e)$$

where $E_1, \ldots, E_n$ are entity types. That is, the population of $E$ is given by the union of its explicitly given instances and those of $E_1, \ldots, E_n$. To avoid

---

[1] In this book, we assume that *Money* and similar types support the + and the * operations.

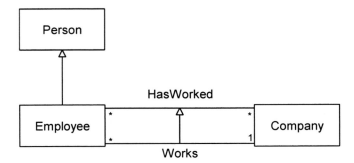

**Fig. 8.9.** *Person* and *HasWorked* are hybrid types

circularity, none of the $E_1$, ..., $E_n$ can be defined as being derived by specialization of $E$.

In object-oriented languages (including UML), the definition of this particular kind of hybrid type is very simple: define $E$ as nonderived and define $E_1$, ..., $E_n$ as subtypes of $E$. Figure 8.9 shows an example in UML. *Person* is a hybrid type with the partial derivation rule

$$Employee(e) \rightarrow Person(e)$$

The population of *Person* is the union of the set of employees and the set of instances explicitly classified as persons.

The same reasoning applies to hybrid relationship types. In the example in Fig. 8.9, *HasWorked* is a hybrid type with the partial derivation rule

$$Works(e,c) \rightarrow HasWorked(e,c)$$

The population of *HasWorked* is the union of *Works* and the set of relationships explicitly classified as *HasWorked*.

In Chap. 10, we describe an additional construct that can be used in UML to define another particular kind of hybrid relationship type.

## 8.6 Justification for Derived Types

The complexity of a conceptual schema depends on the number of entity and relationship types that it contains. Therefore, if the schema defines a type, there must be an agreed justification for it. Types without justification should not be included in a schema. The justification for base types must be that they are required by the functions of the information system,

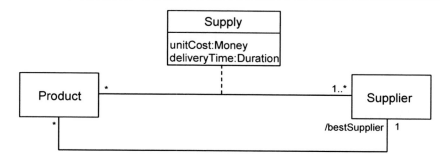

**Fig. 8.10.** Example of derived association (*product-bestSupplier*)

however the justification for derived types is not as clear. Below, we describe several of these justifications.

If we define a derived type, we can use it like a base type in any part of the schema and ignore the details of its derivation rule. If we do not define a derived type but need to refer to its instances in a given part of the schema, we have to write its derivation rule. Consequently, there is a trade-off between adding a derived type to the schema (including its derivation rule) and writing the derivation rule whenever it is needed.

For example, consider the schema fragment shown in Fig. 8.10. A product may be supplied by several suppliers. Each supply has a unit cost and a delivery time. Assume now that, in several parts of the schema, we need to know who is the best supplier of a given product. For instance, we may need this information when we have to issue purchase orders, when we have to specify an integrity constraint like "a supplier cannot be the best supplier of all products", or when we have to answer queries that request this information. In this scenario, we have two options. One is shown in Fig. 8.10 and consists in defining a derived association *product–bestSupplier* and its derivation rule. From this point on, we can use this association as a base type. If the best supplier of a product is the one that supplies it at the minimum cost, the formal derivation rule is

```
context Product::bestSupplier:Supplier
  derive: supply -> sortedBy(unitCost) -> first().supplier
```

The second option simply consists in writing an expression such as

```
aProduct.supply->sortedBy(unitCost)->first().supplier
```

whenever we need to know the best supplier of *aProduct*.

There are two additional arguments in favor of defining derived types in a schema. The first is that there is a unique definition of the derivation rule, which is always (implicitly) used in the same way. The second is related to schema evolution. We may need to change the definition of the best supplier to take into account the delivery time of the supply, for example. The evolution of derivation rules is much easier when they are defined in a single place.

## 8.7 Bibliographical Notes

Derived types and their rules have been considered fundamental components of the conceptual schemas of information systems since the early 1980s. See, for example, (Hull and King 1987). Derivation rules are sometimes classified as a type of business rule (Business Rules Group 2000).

In the field of deductive databases, the distinction between base, derived, and hybrid types and their logical representation have been well known since the early work of Nicolas and Gallaire (1978). In the same field, Bancilhon and Ramakrishnan (1986) described a procedure for transforming hybrid types into derived types. In conceptual modeling the distinction is well explained in (Martin and Odell 1995, Chap. 6).

Many conceptual modeling languages provide specific constructs for defining derived types and derivation rules. The early languages include DAPLEX (Shipman 1981), which provides a detailed justification for derived types, SDM (Hammer and McLeod 1981), which includes a detailed analysis of the kinds of derivation and provides constructs for defining them, and CIAM (Gustaffsson et al. 1982), which places a strong emphasis on derived types and the temporal perspective. Later languages include:

- The family of languages stemming from KL-ONE (see an overview in Brachman and Schmolze 1985) called Description Logics, which provide a specific formal syntax for defining derived entity and relationship types and strong reasoning capabilities (Bergamaschi and Sartori 1992, Borgida 1995).
- Chimera, as described by Ceri and Fraternali (1997), which includes deductive rules for data derivation and a set of mappings for the implementation of these rules as triggers or views in database systems.
- ORM, as described by Halpin (2001), which allows formal and informal versions of derivation rules.
- OO-Method, presented by Pastor et al. (2001).

The use of operations for the specification of derivation rules was presented in Olivé (2003a).

The main recognized justification for derived entity types is their participation in a given role of base relationship types. Among the texts that adopt this justification are (Nijssen and Halpin 1989, p. 130), (Yourdon 1993, p. 61) and (Parsons 1996). Other justifications were given by Shipman (1981) and Schreiber et al. (2000, p. 98).

The current version of the OCL specification is the document (OMG 2005b). Chapter 7 of that document is an informative introduction to the language. (Warmer and Kleppe 2003) is a practical guide to OCL.

## 8.8 Exercises

**8.1** Consider the schema in Fig. 8.11. An account is a materialization of an account type. In principle, all accounts of the same type have the same interest rate. However, there are exceptions: a bank may give an account an exceptional interest rate. The *numberOfExceptions* attribute gives the number of accounts of a given type that have exceptional interest rates (which may be zero). If the interest rate is not exceptional, the interest rate of an account is that of its type; otherwise, it is the exceptional rate. Define in OCL the derivation rules of the two derived attributes.

**Fig. 8.11.** Example with two derived attributes

**8.2** Consider an information system whose domain is a set of people and their family relationships. Assume that the schema includes the base entity type *Person* and the relationship types

> *Sex (Person, Sex)*
> *Parent (child:Person, parent:Person)*

Represent this schema in UML with the derived relationship types

> *Grandparent (grandchild:Person, grandparent:Person)*
> *Sibling (Person, sibling:Person)*
> *Uncle (Person, uncle:Person)*
> *Aunt (Person, aunt:Person)*
> *HasNumberOfChildren (Person, Natural)*

Define the derivation rules of the above types in OCL.

**8.3** Assume that in the domain of a school we have the entity type *Student*, the data type *Mark*, and the relationship type *Average* (*Student, Mark*) with the pattern sentence

> The average mark of the exams taken by student <*Student*> is <*Mark*>

Furthermore, assume that the school wants to define a new entity type named *GoodStudent*. Students will be an instance of this type if their average mark is higher than *goodMark* (a value of *Mark*). However, in particular cases, the school can designate students as good even if their average mark is less than *goodMark*. Therefore *GoodStudent* is hybrid.

1. Transform *GoodStudent* into a derived type. Explain its derivation rule.
2. Represent the resulting schema in UML and define the derivation rule of *GoodStudent* in OCL.

**8.4** Change the derivation rule of the *product–bestSupplier* association shown in Fig. 8.10, assuming that if, for a given product, there are two or more suppliers with the same *unitCost*, the best supplier is now (the) one that has the minimum *deliveryTime*.

**8.5** Figure 8.12 shows the schema of a system that records employees and their salary history. There is an instance of *SalaryChange* for each change in an employee's salary. The change comes into effect on the specified date. In this schema, an employee's current salary is a derived attribute whose value can be obtained from the last salary change in effect. The derived ternary association *HasSalary* gives the employee's salary on any date. Define the derivation rule of both types in OCL. You may assume that there is a variable, *CurrentDate*, which holds the current date.

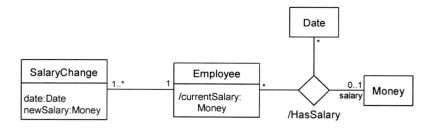

**Fig. 8.12.** Example with a derived attribute and a derived ternary association

# 9 Integrity Constraints

Section 9.1 studies the concept of an integrity constraint and its importance in conceptual modeling. Section 9.2 shows that integrity constraints can be classified from several points of view. These classifications help us in understanding the nature of integrity constraints. Section 9.3 describes the definition of static constraints in logic and in UML. In general, integrity constraints are very diverse, but there are some particular kinds that appear very often. Section 9.4 describes some of them. Section 9.5 identifies the creation-time constraint, an important particular kind of transition constraint, and explains a way to define it in conceptual schemas.

## 9.1 The Concept of an Integrity Constraint

### 9.1.1 Integrity = Validity + Completeness

An information base contains a representation of the knowledge that an information system has about the state of a domain. The information system obtains this knowledge from messages received through an input interface. In a perfect world, the information base would be an exact representation of the domain. Input messages would always be correct, and the system would receive all relevant messages. In this perfect world, the information base would always contain only true facts (it would be valid) and all relevant facts (it would be complete).

For example, an information base that contains the names of the employees of a company would be valid if the names it contained were all correct, and complete if it contained the names of all employees.

Unfortunately, in the real world, it is likely that some input messages may communicate something that is not true, and then some of the facts in the information base may be invalid. It is also likely that the system will not receive all relevant messages, and then the information base may be incomplete.

Validity and completeness are the two components of the integrity of an information base. An information base has integrity when the facts that it contains are valid and it contains all relevant facts. Integrity is an important property of an information base. Lack of integrity normally has negative consequences, which in some cases may be serious.

When we define a conceptual schema, we do not consider the case of a system malfunction, such as the accidental loss of data or the erroneous computation of false facts from valid ones. The possibility of malfunctioning does always exist, but we deal with this problem in the design and construction phases, and not in conceptual modeling.

### 9.1.2 Integrity Constraints

In most systems, total integrity can be achieved only by human intervention. To ensure integrity, we must systematically check the facts in the information base against the domain. For example, many retail stores need to check periodically that the products they have on the shelves correspond to their records in the information system. It is not difficult to see that in some cases the cost of integrity will be very high and hard to avoid.

However, it is possible to build mechanisms into an information system that automatically guarantee some level of integrity. We can define conditions on the information base and the events that change it such that, if satisfied, we can have some level of confidence on the integrity of the information base. These conditions, called integrity constraints, are defined in the conceptual schema. An integrity constraint is a condition that might not be satisfied in some states of the information base or by some events, but it is understood that the information system will include mechanisms to guarantee its satisfaction at any time.

For example, assume that our schema includes the relationship type

   *WorksIn* (*Employee, Project*)

Assume also that all employees work in one or more projects. A constraint could then be "Each employee works in some project", which is easily expressed by the cardinality $Card(employee; project; WorksIn) = (1,\infty)$. Once this has been defined in the schema, we may assume that for each employee $e$ in the information base there will be one or more relationships $WorksIn(e,p)$. This constraint does not guarantee full integrity (for instance, the information base may not have the correct assignment of employees to projects), but it is a necessary condition for it.

A constraint may be simple or compound. A constraint is compound if it can be decomposed into a conjunction of other constraints; otherwise, it is simple. For example, the constraint

   "Each employee works in some project"

is simple while

> "Each employee works in some project and each project has a name"

is compound. Given that a compound constraint is satisfied if and only if all of its component constraints are, we usually deal only with simple constraints.

We say that an information base is *consistent* if it satisfies all defined integrity constraints. We also say that a constraint is *violated* when the information base does not satisfy it.

### 9.1.3 Violation of Integrity Constraints

An integrity constraint is a condition that may be violated. Violations may be caused by

- the arrival of input messages;
- the absence of one or more input messages during a time interval.

The first case is the commonest. A new message violates a constraint when its facts, or the changes induced by them, do not satisfy the constraint.

As an example, consider an event *NewAccount*, which happens when a customer opens a new account in a bank, with some initial deposit. Assume also that the schema contains the following relationship types:

> *Holder(Account, Person)*
> *Balance(Account, balance:Money)*

An input message that communicates the occurrence of a *NewAccount* event could violate the following constraints:

1. "The initial deposit must be at least one euro". This constraint involves the event type *NewAccount*, and it can only be violated when an event of this type occurs.
2. "A customer cannot open two or more accounts on the same day". This constraint may be violated if a customer opens more than one account on a given day.
3. "A customer cannot have more than three accounts at the same time". This constraint may be violated if a customer tries to open a new account when he already holds three. The constraint involves the new event and the information base.
4. "A customer cannot open a new account if the total balance of the accounts he already has is negative".

In the same example, note that a condition such as

> "The initial balance of an account is the initial deposit of the event that opens it"

is *not* an integrity constraint. If we assume that the occurrence of a *New Account* event triggers the execution of an operation that inserts a relationship of type *Balance (Account, balance:Money)*, with a balance equal to the initial deposit, and that this is the only way to create a new account, then the condition will always hold. No input message can violate it. The condition must be interpreted as a requirement for the operation. Of course, the operation could be implemented in a way that does not satisfy the requirement (for instance, by assigning an initial balance of 1000 euros), and then the condition would fail. In such a case, however, the reason for the failure would be an error in the design and construction of the system, and not a constraint violation.

Likewise, derivation rules are not integrity constraints. Even if derivation rules can be seen as conditions relating facts in the information base, they are not violable by the presence or absence of input messages. Violation of a derivation rule may be due only to an error in the derivation process.

Less frequently, a constraint may also be violated by the nonarrival of an input message within some time interval. For example:

1. "All new employees are assigned to some department within 15 days". Assume an employee is hired on day *d*. The system must then receive an input message reporting an assignment of the employee to some department before *d* + 15. The absence of such a message violates the constraint.
2. "All employees report on their activities at least once per month". This constraint states that for each employee in the information base, there must be a *report* event at least once per month.

Some conditions requiring the presence of input messages are only violable (and therefore, may only be integrity constraints) if we assume that the system's lifetime is bounded. For example, with this assumption, the condition

> "All projects finish"

is an integrity constraint because it may be violated: when the system ends its lifetime, there may be one or more unfinished projects and then the constraint would be violated. However, if we assume that the system's lifetime is unbounded, then the condition is not violable.

Recall that an integrity constraint is a condition that must be satisfied at all times. Satisfaction of a constraint is not only a desirable property, it is mandatory. Therefore, if a condition expresses only a desirable behavior of the domain, it is not a constraint. A typical example is the condition

"A library user should return a book after at most six weeks"

Satisfaction of this condition requires, for each loan, the arrival of a return message within six weeks. However, in this case, the nonarrival of such a message does not mean that the information base has lost integrity. It means only that someone is not behaving as desired. In such cases, the condition specifies an output (an overdue letter) to be produced by the information system, rather than a constraint.

### 9.1.4 Violation Response Actions

When a constraint is violated, the system must produce some response to maintain consistency of the information base. In general, three classes of responses can be distinguished:

1. To refuse the message that produces the violation. This response is not applicable when the violation is due to the absence of an input message.
2. To execute a compensating action. This corresponds to extending the input message with new facts, such that the extended message maintains consistency. If the violation is due to the absence of an input message, this response corresponds to generating one.
3. To ask for the correction of some previous message. This may be applicable when the violation is caused by some incorrect previous message, or by the nonpresence in due time of some message.

More elaborate responses are also possible, such as marking input messages as an exception, or modifying the integrity constraint to accommodate the exception.

## 9.2 Classification of Integrity Constraints

A conceptual schema includes two kinds of constraints: *inherent* and *explicit*. The former are implicitly assumed by the corresponding conceptual modeling language. A typical example is the referential integrity constraint: many languages assume that a relationship may exist only if the entities that it relates also exist. The latter are those defined by the conceptual modelers. For example, the (also) typical constraint that "the salaries of employees cannot decrease" is explicit because it is not implicitly assumed by any (known) language. In this chapter, we deal only with explicit constraints.

Integrity constraints may be classified from several points of view. In the following, we describe three classifications, according to:

- the reason why the constraint must hold (the source);
- the facts involved by the constraint (the scope);
- the cause of the violation of the constraint.

### 9.2.1 Classification According to Source

Integrity constraints may be classified according to their source into analytical, deontic, and empirical constraints.

A constraint is *analytical* if its truth follows from the definition or meaning of the facts involved in it. Violations of analytical constraints are due to errors in the representation of facts. For example, the constraint "a door cannot be both open and closed at the same time" is analytical.

A constraint is *deontic* if it expresses a condition that holds in the domain because of imposition by some authorized agent. This agent is the source of the constraint. Violations of deontic constraints may be caused by errors in the representation of facts or because the behavior of the domain deviates from the stated condition. For example, the constraint "an employee's salary may not decrease" is deontic.

A constraint is *empirical* if it expresses a condition that holds empirically in the domain. Nobody has stated that the condition must be satisfied, but the domain behaves in a way that satisfies it. Violations of empirical constraints may be caused by errors in the representation of facts or because some exception has arisen in the domain. For example, in the case of a supermarket the constraint "A customer does not buy more than 999 units of any item" would be empirical.

The following are examples of constraints with their classification:

1. A person's age cannot be negative (analytical)
2. A person cannot be fired unless he is an employee (analytical).
3. A person cannot be married to himself (analytical).
4. A customer cannot open two or more accounts on the same day (deontic).
5. All employees report on their activities at least once a month (deontic).

6. All new employees are assigned to some department within one month (deontic).
7. A person may not be over 150 years old (empirical).
8. A book has at least five pages (empirical).
9. A person has at most 30 children (empirical).

## 9.2.2 Classification According to Scope

Constraints are conditions that must be satisfied by the information base and the events. Usually, a constraint involves only a limited set of facts in the information base and/or a limited set of events, and this allows us to classify it according to the facts involved or *scope*. We distinguish six kinds, which are:

- A *static* constraint involves the facts of a single state of the information base, and it must be satisfied in every state. All (complete) conceptual modeling languages allow static constraints to be defined.
- A *transition* constraint involves the facts of two or more states of the information base. Usually, such a constraint involves facts of only two consecutive states, constraining the transition between them, but in general the constraint may refer to any number of states. By extension, we also use the term "transition constraints" for those constraints that must be satisfied only in *some* states of the information base.
- An *event* constraint involves only one event.
- An *event history* constraint involves two or more events that occur at the same or different times. Constraints of this kind are often used to define allowed temporal orderings of event occurrences.
- A *global* constraint involves the facts of one or more states of the information base and one or more events.
- A particular kind of global constraint, called an *event precondition* constraint, involves only an event and the state of the information base when the event occurs. There are many event precondition constraints, and most conceptual modeling languages allow their definition.

The following are examples of constraints, with their classification according to their scope:

1. All employees are always assigned to some project (static).
2. A customer may not be the holder of more than three accounts at any time (static).
3. An employee's salary may not decrease (transition).

4. An employee cannot be assigned to the same project for more than one year (transition).
5. The initial deposit of a new bank account must be at least one euro (event).
6. A customer may not open two accounts on the same day (event history).
7. A customer may not open a new account if he is a holder of some account that has been overdrawn for more than 30 days during the last year (global).
8. A customer may not open a new account if the total balance of the accounts he already has is negative (event precondition).
9. A library member may not reserve an item for a future loan period if he already has that item on loan (event precondition).

Note that the above classification is based on *where* the facts involved in the constraint are located. The five kinds are exclusive (the event precondition constraint is a particular kind of global constraint). However, sometimes the same constraint may be defined in several equivalent ways, involving different facts, and then the constraint may be classified into different kinds.

For example, consider the constraint "There may be at most one director". If we define it in terms of the entity type *Director*, then it is a static constraint: in each state of the information base, the population of *Director* may have at most one instance. However, if directors can be created only with the event *NewDirector*, we can define the constraint in terms of this event type, and then it is a precondition constraint: a *NewDirector* event may happen only if the population of *Director* is empty.

### 9.2.3 Classification According to Cause of Violation

We have already mentioned that a constraint may be violated by the arrival of an input message or by the absence of one or more messages during a time interval. In the first case, we say that the cause of the violation is the event reported by the message, and that the constraint is *event-violable*. In the second case, we say that the cause of the violation is the passing of time, and then the constraint is *time-violable*.

A few examples of each class are:

1. The salary of an employee may not decrease (event-violable).
2. The initial deposit in an account must be at least one euro (event-violable).

3. An account may not be overdrawn for more than 30 days (time-violable).
4. All employees must report on their activities at least once per month (time-violable).

## 9.3 Representation in an Information System

In this section, we study how to represent static constraints in current-state conceptual models, in the logic and the UML languages. Throughout this section, we use examples from a hypothetical meeting management system. The system deals with committees that organize meetings, which take place in rooms.

### 9.3.1 Logical Representation

In logic, integrity constraints can be defined by formulas that the information base must satisfy (they must be true) or, equivalently, such constraints can be defined by predicates, called inconsistency predicates, which cannot have any corresponding fact in the information base. We say that a *condition* constraint is a constraint defined by a formula, and an *inconsistency* constraint is a constraint defined by an inconsistency predicate. We study condition constraints first, and then inconsistency constraints.

#### 9.3.1.1 Condition Constraints

In logic, a static condition constraint is defined by a closed first-order formula $\phi$ that the information base is required to satisfy at any time. The formula $\phi$ can involve only facts of the current state of the information base.

For example, consider the following relationship types (see Fig. 9.1):

> *HoldsMeeting (organizer:Committee, Meeting)*
> *TakesPlace (Meeting, location:Room)*
> *Date (Meeting, Date)*
> *MayUse (Committee, Room)*

The static constraint

> *IC*1: "The location of an unfinished or future meeting must be one of the rooms that the meeting organizer may use"

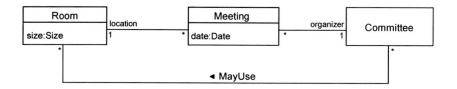

**Fig. 9.1.** Fragment of the schema of a meeting management system

can then be defined by the formula[1]

$HoldsMeeting(c,m) \wedge Date(m,d) \wedge CurrentDate(cd) \wedge$
$d \geq cd \wedge TakesPlace(m,r) \rightarrow MayUse(c,r)$

where *CurrentDate(cd)* holds if *cd* is the current date.

It is useful to distinguish between targeted and untargeted condition constraints. If *E* is an entity type defined in the conceptual schema, a condition constraint $\phi$ is *targeted* at *E* when it can be rewritten as:

$E(e) \rightarrow \varphi(e)$

That is, subformula $\varphi(e)$ must be true in the information base for any *e* that is an instance of *E* at any time. The variable *e* must occur and be free in $\varphi(e)$. A condition constraint is *untargeted* if it cannot be targeted at any entity type defined in the conceptual schema.

For example, *IC*1 is targeted at *Meeting*:

$Meeting(m) \rightarrow \forall c,d,cd,r$
$(HoldsMeeting(c,m) \wedge Date(m,d) \wedge CurrentDate(cd) \wedge$
$d \geq cd \wedge TakesPlace(m,r) \rightarrow MayUse(c,r))$

As another example, the static constraint

*IC*2: "A committee cannot hold two meetings on the same day"

is targeted at *Committee*:

$Committee\ (c) \rightarrow \forall m1,m2,d1,d2$
$(HoldsMeeting(c,m1) \wedge HoldsMeeting(c,m2) \wedge$
$m1 \neq m2 \wedge Date(m1,d1) \wedge Date(m2,d2) \rightarrow d1 \neq d2)$

---

[1] Recall that variables without quantifiers are assumed to be universally quantified in front of the formula.

Most condition constraints are targeted, and often they can be targeted at several entity types. *IC2*, for example, can also be expressed as targeted at *Meeting*:

$$Meeting\ (m1) \rightarrow \forall c, m2, d1, d2$$
$$(HoldsMeeting(c, m1) \wedge HoldsMeeting(c, m2) \wedge$$
$$m1 \neq m2 \wedge Date(m1, d1) \wedge Date(m2, d2) \rightarrow d1 \neq d2)$$

An example of an untargeted condition constraint might be

*IC3*: "There must be at least one large room"

which is defined by the formula

$$\exists r\ (Room(r) \wedge Size(r, Large))$$

### 9.3.1.2 Inconsistency Constraints

The idea of inconsistency constraints consists in defining an inconsistency predicate for each constraint, and requiring that no facts of this predicate may hold in the information base at any time. The general form of an inconsistency predicate *Inc* is

$$Inc(x_1, \ldots, x_m) \leftrightarrow \phi'(x_1, \ldots, x_m)$$

In general, an inconsistency predicate may have any number $m$ of arguments, with $m \geq 0$. A fact of an inconsistency predicate corresponds to a violation of the corresponding constraint. The $m$ arguments give the values for which such a violation exists. This is an advantage over condition constraints, whose evaluation returns only "true" or "false".

For example, the definition of the constraint *IC2* by an inconsistency predicate *OverlappingMeetings* could be

$$OverlappingMeetings(c, m1, m2) \leftrightarrow$$
$$HoldsMeeting(c, m1) \wedge HoldsMeeting(c, m2) \wedge$$
$$m1 \neq m2 \wedge Date(m1, d) \wedge Date(m2, d)$$

The meaning of a fact *OverlappingMeetings(c,m1,m2)* is that committee $c$ holds meetings $m1$ and $m2$ on the same day. Note that $c$, $m1$ and $m2$ are the values for which the constraint is violated.

The distinction between targeted and untargeted constraints applies also to inconsistency constraints. An inconsistency constraint is *targeted* at an entity type $E$ if it can be expressed in the form

$$Inc(e, x_1, \ldots, x_m) \leftrightarrow E(e) \wedge \varphi'(e, x_1, \ldots, x_m)$$

An inconsistency constraint is *untargeted* if it cannot be targeted at any existing entity type.

For example, *IC*2 can be expressed as targeted at *Committee*:

$$OverlappingMeetings(c,m1,m2) \leftrightarrow$$
$$Committee(c) \land$$
$$HoldsMeeting(c,m1) \land HoldsMeeting(c,m2) \land m1 \neq m2 \land$$
$$Date(m1,d) \land Date(m2,d)$$

Finally, an example of an untargeted inconsistency constraint might be *IC*3:

$$NoLargeRoom \leftrightarrow \neg \exists r \, (Room(r) \land Size(r,Large))$$

## 9.3.2 Representation in UML

UML has a few predefined static constraints, normally with an associated graphical symbol. The most important is the cardinality constraint, which we studied in Chap. 4. Some other examples are the aggregation and the composition constraints, which we saw in Chap. 7. Other predefined constraints will be presented later on in this book.

More general static constraints must be specified as invariants. An *invariant* is a constraint that is linked to an entity type. An invariant constraint consists of an OCL expression of type *Boolean*, which must be true for each instance of an entity type at any time. The specification of an invariant has the general form

```
context EntityType inv constraintName:
   an OCL expression of type Boolean
```

The name of the constraint is optional.

Only condition constraints can be specified by invariants. Inconsistency constraints cannot be defined using the standard constructs of UML.

Targeted condition constraints can be expressed naturally by invariants. A condition constraint targeted at an entity type *E* is expressed by an invariant in the context of *E*. For example, the invariant corresponding to *IC*1 targeted at *Meeting* is (see Fig. 9.1)

```
context Meeting inv usesAuthorizedRoom:
   date ≥ CurrentDate implies
      organizer.room->includes(location)
```

where *CurrentDate* is a variable that holds the current date. The expression must be true for each instance of *Meeting* at any time.

As another example, the constraint *IC*2 targeted at *Committee* is defined by the invariant

```
context Committee inv meetingsOnDistinctDays:
  meeting -> isUnique(date)
```

Now the expression must be true for each instance of *Committee* at any time.

Untargeted condition constraints can be expressed by invariants too, although not as naturally as in the case of targeted constraints. In principle, the invariant corresponding to an untargeted condition constraint could be linked to any entity type. In particular, all of them could be grouped in a special-purpose entity type, if so desired. However, in practice, it may be sensible to link untargeted condition constraints to the entity types that are semantically more natural.

For example, the invariant corresponding to *IC3* can be linked to *Room*:

```
context Room inv atLeastOneLargeRoom:
  Room.allInstances()-> exists(size = Size::Large)
```

In this form, the invariant states that for each instance of *Room*, there must be at least one large room. This is an overspecification because, in this constraint, the invariant needs to be true only once. On the other hand, the invariant alone does not express *IC3* completely because the invariant is true when the population of *Room* is empty. The invariant needs to be complemented by another constraint requiring that there is at least one room. This new constraint cannot be expressed as a UML invariant. A better context for the invariant would be a singleton entity type, if there is one in the schema.

## 9.3.3 Representation of Constraints by Operations

In object-oriented languages such as UML, an alternative (although not standard) representation of constraints is by means of operations. One of the advantages of this form of representation is that it can be used for condition and inconsistency constraints. In general, in this book we shall use operations only when the standard representation is not possible or when the use of operations provides a better representation of integrity constraints.

In what follows, we shall explain how to define static constraints in this way. We deal first with condition constraints. The idea consists in associating each constraint with a query operation, called a *constraint* operation. The only purpose of a constraint operation is to specify the corresponding constraint. Constraint operations are purely conceptual; they may or may not be part of the implementation. We indicate that an operation is a constraint operation by means of the stereotype «*IC*». All operations stereotyped by «*IC*» represent constraints. In this book, we shall show constraint

**Fig. 9.2.** Four examples of constraint operations in UML

operations in the class diagrams, but in practice a conceptual modeler might prefer not to show them.

The constraint operation corresponding to a condition constraint targeted at $E$,

$$E(e) \rightarrow \varphi(e)$$

is defined as an *instance* operation of $E$, and its specification has the general form:

```
context E::conditionName():Boolean
  body: an OCL expression of type Boolean
```

where *conditionName* is a name that identifies the constraint. The semantics is that the result of the body expression at any time, for any instance $e$ of $E$, must be the same as the result of the evaluation of $\varphi(e)$ in the information base. Furthermore, this result must be *true*. Note that it is implicit that the result of the operation must be true at all times during the lifespan, and for all instances of the hosting entity type ($E$) at any time.

Consider, as an example, the condition constraint $IC1$ targeted at *Meeting*. Figure 9.2 shows the corresponding operation in the entity type *Meeting*. The formal specification in OCL is

```
context Meeting::usesAuthorizedRoom():Boolean
  body: date ≥ CurrentDate implies
        organizer.room->includes(location)
```

Targeting a constraint at an entity type $E$ does not imply the semantics that it can be violated only when there are "local" changes to instances of $E$. In the above example, the constraint is targeted at *Meeting*, but it may be violated if there is a change in the rooms that a committee may use. The intended semantics is only that the evaluation of the operation *usesAuthorizedRoom* must give the value *true* for each instance of *Meeting* and at all times.

If a condition constraint can be targeted at two or more entity types, we then have the choice of where to host the constraint operation. From a conceptual point of view, all alternatives are valid. The conceptual modeler may choose the place he thinks is more natural or easier to specify.

As another example, the constraint operation corresponding to *IC2* targeted at *Committee* would be

```
context Committee::meetingsOnDistinctDays():Boolean
  body: meeting -> isUnique(date)
```

The constraint operation corresponding to an untargeted condition constraint $\phi$ is defined as a *class* operation of some entity type, and its specification has the same general form as before:

```
context E::conditionName():Boolean
  body: an OCL expression of type Boolean
```

Now the semantics is that the result of the evaluation of this operation at any time must be the same as the result of the evaluation of $\phi$ in the information base. Moreover, this result must be *true*. Note that, in this method, it is implicit that the result of the operation must be true at all times during the lifespan.

For example, the untargeted constraint *IC3* could be defined by the constraint operation (shown underlined in Fig. 9.2)

```
context Room::atLeastOneLargeRoom():Boolean
  body: Room.allInstances() -> exists(size = Size::Large)
```

Inconsistency constraints can be defined similarly. The main difference is that now the result of the constraint operation must give the values for which the corresponding constraint is violated.

For example, if *IC2* is defined as an inconsistency constraint targeted at *Committee*, the constraint operation is then an instance operation of *Committee*, with signature

```
context Committee::overlappingMeetings():Set(Meeting)
```

The constraint will be satisfied if the operation returns the empty set for all committees. If for some committee the result is not the empty set, the meaning is that the constraint is violated for that committee. In this case, the result gives the set of (two or more) meetings of that committee that would be held on the same day.

As a new example of an inconsistency constraint, consider

> *IC4*: "Two meetings cannot share the same room on the same day"

This constraint can be targeted at *Meeting*. Figure 9.2 also shows the corresponding constraint operation in *Meeting*, with stereotype «*IC*». The formal specification in OCL would be

```
context Meeting::hasRoomConflictWith():Set(Meeting)
  body: location.meeting->select
          (m|m <> self and m.date = self.date)
```

For any given meeting (*self*), the result of the operation is the set of meetings that have the same location as *self* and have the same date. The constraint is satisfied when the operation gives the empty set for all meetings.

## 9.4 Particular Kinds of Static Constraint

Most constraints defined in an information system are static. Some of them appear so often that they have a particular construct in some conceptual modeling languages. A prominent example is the cardinality constraint of relationship types, which we studied in Chap. 4. Other important particular kinds of constraint related to taxonomies will be studied in the next chapter. A few more particular kinds are presented below.

### 9.4.1 Key Constraints

One of the best-known constraints is the key constraint. A *key* of entity type $E$ is a set of one or more attributes of $E$ such that the mapping from the population of $E$ to the corresponding group of attribute values is one-to-one. A key is *simple* if it consists of a single attribute; otherwise it is *composite*. Two different instances of $E$ cannot have identical values for all attributes in the key. An entity type may have any number of keys.

UML does not provide a specific construct for defining key constraints and therefore they must be defined by invariants or constraint operations.

There are two examples of keys in Fig. 9.3. One is the attribute *name* of *Country*. If there may not be two countries with the same name, then *name* is a key of *Country*. Formally

```
context Country inv uniqueName:
  Country.allInstances()->isUnique(name)
```

According to the standard interpretation of invariants, the above OCL expression must be true for each instance of *Country*. In this case, the invariant is an overspecification because the expression is exactly the same for each instance. A finer specification could be given by an untargeted condition constraint, such as

```
context Country::uniqueName():Boolean
  body: Country.allInstances()->isUnique(name)
```

where *uniqueName* is now a class operation of *Country*.

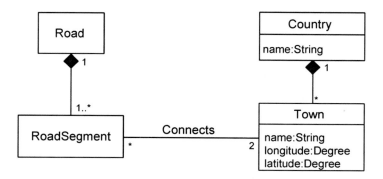

**Fig. 9.3.** Examples of reference constraints

The second example of a key in Fig. 9.3 is the set of the two attributes *longitude* and *latitude* of *Town*. The formal specification in UML is

```
context Town inv longitudeAndLatitudeAreKey:
  Town.allInstances()->
    isUnique(Tuple{lo=longitude,la=latitude})
```

## 9.4.2 Reference Constraints

As we saw in Chap. 5, there are three kinds of references: simple, compound, and set. Here we shall ignore the difference between mutable and immutable references. References are built from one or more relationship types that satisfy a given constraint. UML does not provide a specific construct for defining them, and therefore they must be defined by invariants or constraint operations.

Simple keys are simple references. Therefore, the attribute *name* of *Country* in Fig. 9.3 is also a simple reference for *Country*.

Another example of a simple reference is the association *road–roadSegment*. Each road segment references a road, and all roads can be referenced in this way. Note that the two cardinalities of the association suffice to define it as a simple reference, without any further specification.

Composite keys are compound references. Therefore the key {*longitude*, *latitude*} of *Town* is a compound reference for *Town*.

If we assume that a town name is unique within a country, but that two towns in different countries may have the same name, then another example of a compound reference for *Town* in Fig. 9.3 is the attribute *name* of *Town* and the association *town–country*. The formal specification is

```
context Town inv uniqueNameAndCountry:
  Town.allInstances()->isUnique(Tuple{n=name,c=country})
```

Finally, if we assume that there is at most one road segment between any two towns, then the association *Connects* is a set reference for *RoadSegment*. The formal specification is

```
context RoadSegment inv roadSegmentReferencedByTwoTowns:
  RoadSegment.allInstances()->isUnique(Tuple{twoTowns=town})
```

### 9.4.3 Inclusion Constraints

In general, an *inclusion* constraint defines that a set $A$ must be included in another set $B$. The sets may be populations of entity types or of relationship types. An *equality* constraint between sets $A$ and $B$ is equivalent to two inclusion constraints, one of $A$ in $B$, and another of $B$ in $A$.

The commonest inclusion constraints are between two entity types. They state that, at any time, the population of an entity type $E_1$ is a subset of the population of another entity type $E_2$. We shall denote by $E_1$ *IsA* $E_2$ the inclusion constraint of $E_1$ in $E_2$. Normally, if $E_1$ *IsA* $E_2$, then $E_1$ is a specialization of $E_2$, as we shall study in the next chapter. For example, *Student IsA Person*. However, there may be an inclusion constraint between two types such that one cannot be seen as a specialization of the other. For example, if a library allows borrowing of videotapes, we may have *Videotape IsA LoanableObject*. Other libraries may have a different borrowing policy, and for them the inclusion constraint would not hold.

In UML, an inclusion constraint $E_1$ *IsA* $E_2$ is represented graphically by means of a solid-line path from $E_1$ to $E_2$ with a large hollow triangle at the end of the path where it meets $E_2$. We shall see many examples in the next chapter.

Inclusion constraints between relationship types are similar, but they occur less frequently. They state that, at any time, the population of a relationship type $R_1$ is a subset of the population of another relationship type $R_2$. We shall denote the inclusion constraint of $R_1$ in $R_2$ by $R_1$ *IsA* $R_2$. $R_1$ and $R_2$ must have the same degree. Normally, as in the previous case, if $R_1$ *IsA* $R_2$ then $R_1$ is a specialization of $R_2$, as we will study in the next chapter. For example, *Manages IsA Works*.

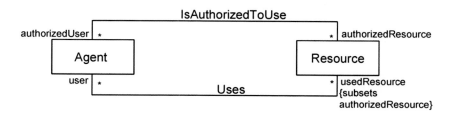

**Fig. 9.4.** *Uses* is included in, but is not a specialization of, *IsAuthorizedToUse*

UML represents the inclusion constraints of entity and relationship types in the same way. However, for inclusion constraints $R_1$ *IsA* $R_2$ such that $R_1$ is not seen as a specialization of $R_2$, UML offers an alternative representation. Figure 9.4 shows an example. Here, some agents are authorized to use some resources and some agents use some resources. Assume that in a given domain, there is a rule that an agent may use a resource only if it is authorized to use it. For some conceptual modelers, *Uses* is not a specialization of *IsAuthorizedToUse*, even if the population of *Uses* is included in that of *IsAuthorizedToUse*. In cases such as this one, we may define the constraint as indicated in Fig. 9.4, by adorning the participant *usedResource* with the property string

> *{subsets <authorizedResource>}*

The meaning is that the set of resources that an agent uses is a subset of those it is authorized to use. The adornment can be defined in any of the association ends. In this example, an alternative equivalent definition would be to adorn the association end *user* with the property string

> *{subsets <authorizedUser>}*

The meaning now is that the set of agents that use a resource is a subset of those that are authorized to use it.

### 9.4.4 Disjunction Constraints

In general, a *disjunction* (or exclusion) constraint defines that two sets cannot have any element in common. The sets may be populations of entity types or of relationship types.

The commonest disjunction constraints are between two entity types. They state that, at any time, the populations of the two types must be disjoint. We shall denote the disjunction constraint of $E_1$ and $E_2$ by $E_1$

*Disjoint* $E_2$, for example *Man Disjoint Woman*. Of course, if $E_1$ is disjoint with $E_2$, then $E_2$ is disjoint with $E_1$, and no type can be disjoint with itself.

UML has a construct for graphically defining disjunction constraints, but it can be used only in the context of taxonomies, as will be explained in the next chapter. In the general case, we have to rely on OCL. For example, if we want to state that *Employee* is disjoint with *Retiree*, we can write

```
context Employee inv EmployeeIsDisjointWithRetiree:
  Employee.allInstances()->
    intersection(Retiree.allInstances())->isEmpty()
```

Disjunction constraints between relationship types are similar, but they occur less frequently. They state that, at any time, the population of the two types must be disjoint. We shall denote the disjunction constraint of $R_1$ with $R_2$ by $R_1$ *Disjoint* $R_2$. $R_1$ and $R_2$ must have the same degree. In UML, these constraints can be represented as in the previous case, which means that in general we have to rely on OCL. For example, if we have the following relationship types:

> *IsAuthorOf* (*author:Person, Paper*)
> *Reviews* (*reviewer:Person, Paper*)

and we want to define that the author of a paper cannot be one of its reviewers (that is, *IsAuthorOf Disjoint Reviews*), we can write

```
context Paper inv authorsDoNotReviewTheirPapers:
  author->intersection(reviewer)->isEmpty()
```

### 9.4.4.1 Inference Rules for Inclusion and Disjunction Constraints

Given a set of inclusion and disjunction constraints, new ones can be inferred by means of the following inference rules:

- (Reflexivity.) For every entity or relationship type $X$, $X$ *IsA* $X$ holds.
- (Transitivity.) If $X$ *IsA* $Y$ and $Y$ *IsA* $Z$ hold, then $X$ *IsA* $Z$ also holds.
- (Joint Transitivity.) If $X$ *Disjoint* $Y$ and $Z$ *IsA* $X$ hold, then $Z$ *Disjoint* $Y$ also holds.

A set $S$ of inclusion and disjunction constraints is not strongly satisfiable if $X$ *Disjoint* $X$ is derivable from $S$ by means of the above inference rules. For example, the following set of constraints is not strongly satisfiable (why?):

> *TeachingAssistant IsA Teacher*
> *TeachingAssistant IsA Student*
> *Teacher Disjoint Student*

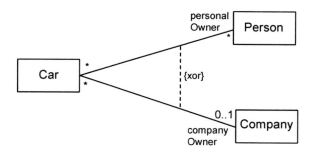

**Fig. 9.5.** An example of *xor* constraint

### 9.4.4.2 Xor Constraints

One kind of disjunction constraint that is predefined in UML is the constraint named *xor*. It may be applied to a set of associations that share a participant entity type, and it specifies that any instance of the shared entity type may have links from only one of the associations. Figure 9.5 shows an example. The constraint states that cars may be owned by persons or by a company, but not by persons and a company. The equivalent invariant is

```
context Car inv:
  personalOwner->notEmpty() implies companyOwner->isEmpty()
  and
  companyOwner->notEmpty() implies personalOwner->isEmpty()
```

An *xor* constraint is not satisfiable if, in some of its associations, the shared entity type has a mandatory participation. In the example of Fig. 9.5, if we had *Cmin(car;personalOwner)* = 1 then the satisfaction of the constraint would require an empty population of the *car–companyOwner* association.

Likewise, an *xor* constraint is not satisfiable if there is an inclusion constraint between any pair of its associations.

### 9.4.5 Covering Constraints

A *covering* constraint between a set $A$ and sets $B_1$, ..., $B_n$ defines that $A$ must be a subset of the union of $B_1$, ..., $B_n$. The sets may be populations of entity types or of relationship types. Formally,

$$A \subseteq B_1 \cup ... \cup B_n$$

Note that when $n = 1$, a covering constraint is an inclusion constraint of $A$ in $B_1$. Even so, inclusion constraints are dealt with separately because they have wider consequences.

The commonest covering constraints are between entity types. We shall denote by

$$E \text{ Covered } E_1, \ldots, E_n$$

the covering constraint between $E$ and $E_1, \ldots, E_n$. For example,

*Gift Covered Book, Album, Flower*

UML has a construct for graphically defining covering constraints, but it can be used only in the context of taxonomies, as will be explained in the next chapter. In the general case, we have to rely on OCL. For example, if we want to state the above constraint, we can write

```
context Gift inv isABookAlbumOrFlower:
    self.oclIsTypeOf(Book) or
    self.oclIsTypeOf(Album) or
    self.oclIsTypeOf(Flower)
```

Covering constraints between relationship types are similar, but they occur less frequently. The relationship types must have the same degree.

Given a set of covering constraints, new ones can be inferred by means of the following inference rules ($X$ and $Y$ are entity or relationship types, and $S$ and $S_j$ are sets of these types):

- (Augmentation.) If $X \in S$ then $X$ *Covered* $S$ holds.
- (Transitivity.) If $X$ *Covered* $S_1$ and $Y$ *Covered* $S_2$ hold and $Y \in S_1$, then $X$ *Covered* $S_3$ holds, where $S_3 = (S_1 - \{Y\}) \cup S_2$.

If considered alone, any set of covering constraints is strongly satisfiable. An information base in which all entity types have the same instances, all binary relationship types have the same instances, and so on, satisfies any set of covering constraints. Of course, when we take into account other constraints that may exist in the schema, the covering constraints may become unsatisfiable.

### 9.4.6 Constraints of Recursive Binary Relationship Types

Many recursive binary relationship types have particular properties that may be defined as constraints. In conceptual modeling, the most important properties are symmetry, transitivity, and reflexivity. In what follows, we give their formal definition in logic and in UML. The examples refer to the schema shown in Fig. 9.6, which deals with a domain of sets and their relationships.

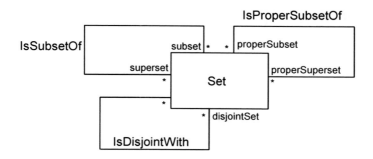

**Fig. 9.6.** Examples of recursive associations

A relationship type $R(p_1:E, p_2:E)$ is *symmetric* if

$$R(x,y) \rightarrow R(y,x)$$

*asymmetric* if

$$R(x,y) \rightarrow \neg R(y,x)$$

and *antisymmetric* if

$$R(x,y) \land R(y,x) \rightarrow x = y$$

In Fig. 9.6, the association *IsDisjointWith* is symmetric, *IsProperSubsetOf* is asymmetric, and *IsSubsetOf* is antisymmetric. The formal definition of these properties as invariants is

```
context Set inv IsDisjointWithIsSymmetric:
  disjointSet.disjointSet->includes(self)
context Set inv IsProperSubsetOfIsAsymmetric:
  properSuperset.properSuperset->excludes(self)
context Set inv IsSubsetOfIsAntisymmetric:
  superset->excluding(self).superset->excludes(self)
```

$R$ is *transitive* if

$$R(x,y) \land R(y,z) \rightarrow R(x,z)$$

and *intransitive* if

$$R(x,y) \land R(y,z) \rightarrow \neg R(x,z)$$

In Fig. 9.6, the associations *IsProperSubsetOf* and *IsSubsetOf* are transitive. The formal definition of this property as an invariant is:

```
context Set inv IsProperSubsetOfIsTransitive:
  properSuperset->includesAll(properSuperset.properSuperset)
context Set inv IsSubsetOfIsTransitive:
  superset->includesAll(superset.superset)
```

$R$ is *reflexive* if

$$E(x) \rightarrow R(x,x)$$

and *irreflexive* if

$$E(x) \rightarrow \neg R(x,x)$$

In Fig. 9.6, the association *IsProperSubsetOf* is reflexive and *IsDisjointWith* is irreflexive. The formal definition of these properties as invariants is

```
context Set inv IsProperSubsetOfIsReflexive:
  properSuperset->includes(self)
context Set inv IsDisjointWithIsIrreflexive:
  disjointSet->excludes(self)
```

There are some relationships between the above constraints:

- An asymmetric relationship type is antisymmetric and irreflexive.
- An intransitive relationship type is irreflexive.

### 9.4.7 Entity Type Cardinality Constraints

An *entity type cardinality constraint* specifies a minimum and maximum (*min*, *max*) number of instances for the population of a given entity type. In UML, this constraint can be defined by an invariant with the general form

```
context E inv cardinalityConstraint:
  let numberOfInstances:integer = E.allInstances()->size() in
  numberOfInstances >= min and numberOfInstances <= max
```

## 9.5 Creation-Time Constraints

A creation-time constraint is a particular kind of transition constraint that appears several times in most conceptual schemas. A *creation-time constraint* of an entity type $E$ is a constraint that its instances must satisfy only at the time when they become an instance of it. The distinction between condition and inconsistency constraints that we made for static constraints applies also to creation-time constraints. In the following, we first introduce this constraint by means of an example, and then show how to define it in UML.

Assume a domain in which there are salespeople who sell products in stores; see Fig. 9.7. In this domain, consider the constraint

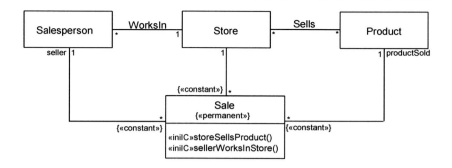

**Fig. 9.7.** Two examples of creation-time constraints

"The store in which the sale is made sells the product sold"

The invariant

```
context Sale inv theStoreSellsTheProduct:
  store.product->includes(productSold)
```

would define the constraint incorrectly, because it requires that the store sells the product at any time at which the sale exists. A sale becomes an instance of *Sale* at some time, and then remains in this situation forever. The invariant need not hold at every time that the sale is an instance of *Sale*, but only when it becomes an instance of *Sale*. The store must sell the product at that time only. Later, the store may cease to sell a product, but such changes must not affect the previous sales.

Creation-time constraints cannot be defined in standard UML. The only possibility is to extend the language. Several options exist. In what follows we shall describe one of them, which is a variant of the constraint operations described above.

A creation-time condition constraint of an entity type *E* can be represented by an operation stereotyped «*iniIC*», with the general form

```
context E::conditionName():Boolean
  body: an OCL expression of type Boolean
```

Now the semantics is that the operation must be evaluated at the time when an entity becomes an instance of the entity type *E*, and the result of the evaluation must be *true*.

Figure 9.7 shows an example corresponding to the above constraint. The name of the operation is *storeSellsProduct*. Its formal specification in OCL is

```
context Sale::storeSellsProduct():Boolean
  body: store.product->includes(productSold)
```

As another example, consider the creation-time constraint

"The seller of the sale works in the store that made the sale"

The specification of the corresponding constraint operation is

```
context Sale::sellerWorksInStore():Boolean
  body: store = seller.store
```

It is interesting to observe that the association *sale–store* is constant and that it could be defined as a derived association. In this case, the above constraint would not be necessary. The derivation rule would be

```
context Sale::store:Store
  derive: seller.store
```

## 9.6 Bibliographical Notes

Motro (1989) introduced the distinction between the two components of integrity, namely validity and completeness. The distinction was made for relational databases, but it is also relevant for information bases and events. Reiter (1992) argued clearly that integrity constraints are statements not about the domain but about the contents of the information base. That publication also discussed the subtleties of the concept of integrity constraint satisfaction. A modern view on these topics was presented by Godfrey et al. (1998).

When a constraint is violated, the system must produce some response. There are several possible response actions. Nicolas and Yazdanian (1978) suggested either rejecting the update that produces the violation, or executing a compensating action. Furtado et al. (1987) discussed both of these responses for some constraints in the ER model. Borgida (1985b) described other responses, like marking the update as an exception or modifying the violated constraint.

Wieringa et al. (1989) presented the classification of constraints into analytical, empirical, and deontic constraints. A similar classification was given by Boman et al. (1997).

The distinction between static and transition constraints is classical. It has been described in (Nicolas and Yazdanian 1978), in the report (Griethuysen 1982), and in many other places. A more complete classification was given in (Dubois et al. 1986). Dignum et al. (1987) provided a different classification, based on an analysis of natural-language sentences.

Static constraints have been studied since the beginning of databases. The initial work focused on particular kinds of constraints. Nicolas (1982) was a pioneer in extending constraints to any closed formula in first-order logic. Godfrey et al. (1998) and Thalheim (2000) provided a modern treatment of constraints in a logical framework. The inconsistency predicates were introduced by Kowalski (1978). They were used by DAPLEX (Shipman 1981) with a slight change in meaning.

There has been a great deal of work on particular kinds of constraints. Tsichritzis and Lochovsky (1982) presented several constraints and the constructs provided by seven modeling languages. Ram and Khatri (2005) described a comprehensive list of set-based constraints. Most of the work has been done in the context of specific modeling languages. Of particular historical interest is SDM, described in (Hammer and McLeod 1981). Bracchi et al. (1979), Bodart and Pigneur (1993) and Thalheim (2000) described constraints in the ER model. Dey et al. (1999) described particular constraints involving relationship types. The language that provides the most specific constructs for defining particular kinds of constraints is probably ORM (Halpin 2001) and its ancestors. In UML/OCL, Ackermann and Turowski (2006) identified a collection of constraint patterns, which can be specified by means of constraint stereotypes as suggested by Costal et al. (2006).

There are several methods for the analysis of the satisfiability of particular constraints. Atzeni and Parker (1988) presented the inference rules for inclusion and disjunction constraints, and algorithms for checking their satisfiability. Lenzerini (1987) extended that work to covering constraints. Formica (2002) presented a method for checking the satisfiability of a specific class of constraint. Jarrar and Heymans (2006) analyzed the satisfiability of some of the ORM constraints. In the context of UML constraints, a similar work was presented by Berardi et al. (2005). A satisfactory solution for the general class of OCL constraints has not been found yet. Queralt and Teniente (2006b) suggested an approach based on the use of methods that test query containment in deductive database systems.

An alternative to satisfiability analysis suggested by Lundberg (1983) is the use of tools that check whether a particular information base (object diagram) satisfies a set of constraints. So far, the most complete of these tools is USE, presented by Richters and Gogolla (2000) and Gogolla et al. (2005).

Nicolas and Yazdanian (1978) formalized creation-time constraints for the first time (and also deletion-time constraints, which we have not studied here) in the logical representation. The TaxisDL software description language (Borgida et al. 1993) allowed the definition of initial (and final) assertions, which must hold when an object becomes (or ceases to be) an instance of a class.

The use of operations for the specification of integrity constraints was presented in (Olivé 2003b).

## 9.7 Exercises

**9.1** Consider a schema with an entity type *Person* and the relationship type

*IsParentOf (parent:Person, child:Person)*

Assume a particular state of the domain, and describe an information base that is:

1. Invalid.
2. Incomplete.
3. Invalid and incomplete.

**9.2** Assuming the schema given in the previous exercise:

1. Define informally some constraints that the information base must satisfy to have integrity.
2. Do these constraints ensure the integrity of the information base?

**9.3** Consider a schema with the base entity type *Person*, the following base relationship types

*Sex (Person, Sex)*
*IsMotherOf (mother:Person, child:Person)*
*IsFatherOf (father:Person, child:Person)*

the derived entity types *Man* and *Woman*, and the derived relationship types

*IsParentOf (parent:Person, child:Person)*
*IsSiblingOf (Person, sibling:Person)*

Assuming that there is only one event type, *Birth*, which communicates the person born, his or her sex, his father and mother, determine which of the following statements are constraints and, for those which are, explain how they can be violated:

1. A person's sex is either male or female.
2. A person may be an only child.
3. A person cannot be a parent of himself.

4. Two persons are siblings if they have a common parent.
5. A person cannot be sibling of himself.
6. A person can have at most one father and one mother.
7. A person can be a parent of at most 20 children.
8. A mother is a female person.

**9.4** Classify, according to the source, scope and cause of violation, each of the following constraints found in a hotel room management system. Assume that the only events are *Reservation, Cancellation,* and *Registration.*

1. The departure date of a reservation cannot be before the arrival date.
2. A reservation must be guaranteed with a credit card.
3. On the day of arrival of a noncancelled reservation, there must be either a cancellation or an arrival of that reservation.
4. A person cannot occupy two different rooms on the same day.
5. For maintenance purposes, a room cannot be occupied for more than 90 consecutive days.
6. A person cannot make a reservation if he has cancelled two or more reservations during the last year.
7. A single room cannot be occupied by two or more persons.

**9.5** Consider the schema shown in Fig. 9.8 and define in OCL the following constraints:

1. The chapters of a book have different titles.
2. The chapters of a book have different numbers.
3. In a book, chapter numbers are consecutive, starting at number 1.
4. The initial page number of a chapter is less than that of its final page.
5. The initial page number of each chapter of a book (except the first) is greater than that of the final page of the previous chapter.

**Fig. 9.8.** Example of schema dealing with books and their chapters

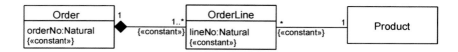

**Fig. 9.9.** Example of schema dealing with orders, their lines and the products ordered

**9.6** Consider the schema shown in Fig. 9.9 and define the following constraints:

1. *OrderNo* is a key of *Order*.
2. The association *orderLine–order* and the attribute *lineNo* are an immutable compound reference for *OrderLine*.
3. The associations *orderLine–order* and *orderLine–product* are an immutable compound reference for *OrderLine*.

**9.7** Modify Fig. 9.3 and the constraints given in Sects. 9.4.1 and 9.4.2 to indicate that the simple, compound and set references given for *Country*, *Town*, and *RoadSegment* are immutable.

**9.8** Some of the constraint examples given in the seminal paper (Nicolas 1982) have become popular. The constraints of this exercise are based on them. Assume the schema shown in Fig. 9.10. Define in OCL the following constraints:

1. If a department $d$ sells a product $p$, then there is a company $c$ that supplies $p$ to $d$.
2. The products of the family "*Aspirin*" are supplied only by the company "*Bayer*".
3. If a company supplies the product "*Hydrogen*", then it also supplies the product "*Oxygen*".
4. If a company supplies some product of the family "*Liquid*", then it also supplies some product of the family "*Gas*".
5. No company can supply two different departments with the product "*Hydrogen*".
6. There is at least one family which is supplied by every company.

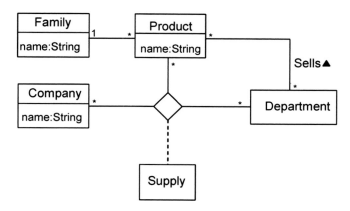

**Fig. 9.10.** Example of schema dealing with supplies of products to departments

# 10 Taxonomies

It is often the case that the instances of an entity type must also necessarily be an instance of another entity type. This can be understood as a special relationship, an *IsA* relationship, between entity types (and, in general, between concepts). *IsA* relationships are constraints. Entity types and their *IsA* relationships form a network structure called a taxonomy. Taxonomies are a very important part of conceptual schemas, and the objective of this chapter is to study them.

We begin by studying the concept of specialization in Sect. 10.1. The inverse concept, generalization, is presented in Sect. 10.2. Taxonomies are described in Sect. 10.3. We shall see that a taxonomy determines the entity types of which an entity can be an instance. We shall also see that derivability has a significant influence on how the *IsA* and other similar constraints of a taxonomy can be satisfied. When an entity type has subtypes, some relationship types or constraints may be refined. This is studied in Sects. 10.4 and 10.5, respectively. Taxonomies can be extended to relationship types. Section 10.6 introduces the concepts of specialization and generalization of relationship types.

## 10.1 Specialization

An entity type $E'$ is a *specialization* of an entity type $E$ if $E'$ has the defining properties of $E$ and some others. $E'$ is more specialized, because it contains more defining properties than does $E$. Many commonly used concepts are specializations. For example, a definition of *bicycle* is[1]

> A *bicycle* is a pedal-driven land vehicle with two wheels attached to a frame, one behind the other.

Therefore, *bicycle* is a specialization of *vehicle*. A bicycle has the defining properties of a vehicle, to which are added "travels on land", "is pedal-driven", and "has two wheels attached to a frame, one behind the other."

---

[1] Wikipedia.

The specialization operation consists in defining one entity type as a specialization of another. Specialization establishes a relationship between two entity types, usually called an *IsA* relationship, which we study in the following section.

### 10.1.1 The *IsA* Relationship

Let $E$ and $E'$ be entity types. We write $E'$ *IsA* $E$ to indicate textually that $E'$ is a specialization of $E$. For example, *Bicycle IsA Vehicle*. In terms of the populations, $E'$ *IsA* $E$ is an inclusion constraint of $E'$ in $E$: at any time, the instances of $E'$ are also instances of $E$. Naturally, there may be instances of $E$ which are not instances of $E'$. Formally, if $E'$ *IsA* $E$, then in logic we have

$$E'(e) \rightarrow E(e)$$

If $E'$ *IsA* $E$, then we say that $E'$ is a *subtype* of $E$, and that $E$ is a *supertype* of $E'$. For example, *Bicycle* is a subtype of *Vehicle*, and *Vehicle* is a supertype of *Bicycle*. Sometimes we say that $E'$ is subsumed by $E$, or that $E$ subsumes $E'$, and also that $E'$ is a *hyponym* of $E$, and that $E$ is a *hypernym* of $E'$.

In Chap. 7, we saw that a role is a set of properties that characterize the situation of the instances of an entity type $E$ at a given time. Normally, the instances of $E$ are in a given situation only temporarily, and not all instances of $E$ need to be in the same situation. For example, "is a student" is a role of *Person*. When an instance of $E$ can play only one role of a role type, then that role type can be represented as a subtype of $E$. For example, if a person can be at most one student, then the student role type can be represented by the entity type *Student*, defined as a subtype of *Person*.

It is easy to see that the relationship *IsA* is transitive. If we have $E''$ *IsA* $E'$ and $E'$ *IsA* $E$, then we also have $E''$ *IsA* $E$. On the other hand, in many formalizations, the *IsA* relationship is considered to be reflexive.

A relationship $E'$ *IsA* $E$ is *direct* if there are not two other relationships such that $E'$ *IsA* $E''$ and $E''$ *IsA* $E$. Otherwise, it is *indirect*. Subtypes and supertypes of direct (or indirect) *IsA* relationships are also called direct (or indirect). An entity type cannot be an indirect subtype of itself. Apart from particular cases, a schema should not include indirect or reflexive *IsA* relationships.

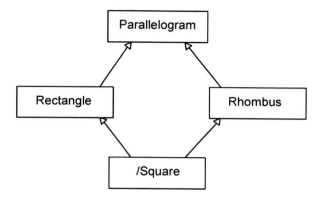

**Fig. 10.1.** Examples of specializations. *Rectangle* and *Rhombus* are of single specialization. *Square* is of multiple specialization

An entity type is of *single* specialization if it is a direct subtype of one and only one entity type. An entity type is of *multiple* specialization if it is a direct subtype of two or more entity types. For example, if we define

> *Square IsA Rectangle* and
> *Square IsA Rhombus*

then *Square* is of multiple specialization.

The most widely used graphical representation of specialization is a solid-line path from the subtype to the supertype, with a large hollow triangle at the end of the path where it meets the supertype. UML also uses this form of representation. Figure 10.1 shows an example: *Rectangle* and *Rhombus* are single specializations of *Parallelogram*; *Square* is a multiple specialization of *Rectangle* and *Rhombus*; and *Parallelogram* is an indirect supertype of *Square*.

### 10.1.2 Entity Types Derived by Intersection and Multiple Classification

One particular kind of multiple-specialization entity type is the entity type derived by intersection, which we studied in Sect. 8.3. An entity type $E$ is derived by intersection of entity types $E_1, \ldots, E_n$ if $E$ is a direct subtype of $E_1, \ldots, E_n$ and the instances of $E$ are exactly those which are at the same time an instance of $E_1, \ldots, E_n$. In Fig. 10.1, *Square* is an entity type derived by intersection of *Rectangle* and *Rhombus*.

In conceptual models that allow multiple classification, an entity may be an instance of several types not related by specializations. This means that it is not always necessary to define entity types derived by intersection. As we saw in Sect. 8.6, there must be a justification for defining derived types.

For example, in Fig. 10.1, an entity *e* may be an instance of both *Rectangle* and *Rhombus*. It is not necessary to define a new type derived by intersection, such as *Square*, and to indicate that *e* is a direct instance of it, and thus an indirect instance of *Rectangle* and *Rhombus*. *Square* must be defined in a schema only if there is a justification for it. In this example, a possible justification could be that we wish to explicitly define that an entity that is both a rectangle and a rhombus is called a "square".

### 10.1.3 The Entity Type *Entity*

Many conceptual models require an auxiliary entity type called *Entity* or similar (*Object*, *Thing*, etc.) such that it is a direct or indirect supertype of all entity types defined in a schema. The existence of this type is handy for methodological purposes and for the analysis of schemas. In this book, we shall assume that *Entity* is defined in all schemas,[2] although for reasons of space it is not generally shown in the diagrams.

All entities that are an instance of some type *E* are also an instance of *Entity*. Therefore, for any entity type *E* defined in a schema, we have *E IsA Entity*.

On the other hand, if an entity *e* is an instance of *Entity* at some time, it must also be an instance of some other type at that time. That is, no entity may be solely an instance of *Entity*.

## 10.2 Generalization

An entity type *E* is a *generalization* of entity types $E_1, \ldots, E_n$ (with $n \geq 1$) if the set of defining properties of each of the $E_1, \ldots, E_n$ includes the defining properties of *E*. The entity type *E* is more general than $E_1, \ldots, E_n$ because it has fewer defining properties. For example, *Person* is a generalization of *Man* and *Woman*, because the concepts of *man* and *woman* include the properties of *person*.

---

[2] *Entity* could be omitted in those rare schemas in which it would be a direct supertype of only one type.

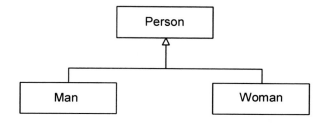

**Fig. 10.2.** *Person* generalizes *Man* and *Woman*

The generalization operation consists in defining an entity type as a generalization of others. The generalization establishes a relationship between several entity types called *Gens*, which we study in the following.

### 10.2.1 The *Gens* Relationship

Generalization and specialization are two different views of the *IsA* relationship, one from the supertype and the other from the subtypes. However, the term "specialization" refers to a single *IsA* relationship, while "generalization" refers to a set of *IsA* relationships that have the same supertype. We shall adopt this meaning and we shall denote textually the generalization of $E_1, \ldots, E_n$ into $E$ by $E$ Gens $E_1, \ldots, E_n$. Gens is an abbreviation for *Generalizes*. For example, *Person Gens Man, Woman*. There is an obvious relationship between *IsA* and *Gens*: if $E$ Gens $E_1, \ldots, E_n$, then $E_1$ IsA $E, \ldots$, and $E_n$ IsA $E$.

Formally, in logic, if $E$ Gens $E_1, \ldots, E_n$, then

$$E_i(e) \rightarrow E(e) \quad i = 1, \ldots, n$$

In UML, a generalization is represented graphically by combining its *IsA* relationships into a single tree with a hollow triangle used as an arrowhead. Figure 10.2 shows an example.

A given entity type may be the supertype of several generalizations. For example, *Person* is the supertype of the following two generalizations:

> *Person Gens Man, Woman*
> *Person Gens Child, Young, Adult.*

In addition, an entity type may be a subtype of several generalizations. For example, *Employee* is a subtype of the following two generalizations (see Figure 10.3):

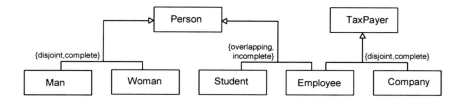

**Fig. 10.3.** Examples of generalizations. *Person* is a common supertype of two generalizations. *Employee* is a common subtype of two generalizations

> *Person Gens Student, Employee*
> *TaxPayer Gens Employee, Company*

## 10.2.2 Constraints on Generalizations

Two important static constraints related to generalizations are the *covering* (or completeness) and *disjointness* constraints. We shall discuss them in the following paragraphs.

A generalization $E$ Gens $E_1, \ldots, E_n$ satisfies the covering constraint if the instances of $E$ must be an instance of at least one $E_i$ ($i = 1, \ldots, n$). Formally,

$$E(e) \rightarrow E_1(e) \vee \ldots \vee E_n(e)$$

The generalizations that must satisfy the covering constraint are called *complete*; otherwise, they are called *incomplete*. For example,

> *Person Gens Man, Woman*

is complete while

> *Vehicle Gens Bicycle, Car*

is incomplete (there are other kinds of vehicles).

The covering constraint of generalizations is exactly the same as the one that we studied in the preceding chapter. However, there is a subtle point that is worth mentioning. If a generalization $E$ Gens $E_1, \ldots, E_n$ must satisfy the covering constraint, then given that

$$E_i(e) \rightarrow E(e) \quad i = 1, \ldots, n$$

we have not only

$$E(e) \rightarrow E_1(e) \vee \ldots \vee E_n(e)$$

but also

$$E(e) \leftarrow E_1(e) \vee \ldots \vee E_n(e)$$

which is not required by the covering constraint alone.

A generalization $E$ *Gens* $E_1, \ldots, E_n$ satisfies the disjointness constraint if each instance of $E$ is an instance of at most one $E_i$. Formally, for each $E_i$ ($i = 1, \ldots, n$),

$$E_i(e) \rightarrow \neg E_1(e) \wedge \ldots \wedge \neg E_{i-1}(e) \wedge \neg E_{i+1}(e) \wedge \ldots \wedge \neg E_n(e)$$

The generalizations that must satisfy the disjointness constraint are called *disjoint*; otherwise, they are called *overlapping*. In the particular case of $n = 1$, the generalization is disjoint. For example,

*Person Gens Man, Woman*

is disjoint while

*Person Gens SinglePerson, Student*

is overlapping.

The disjointness constraint is equivalent to a set of disjunction constraints between two entity types, which we studied in the preceding chapter. A generalization $E$ *Gens* $E_1, \ldots, E_n$ is disjoint if $E_i$ is disjoint with $E_j$ for $i,j = 1, \ldots, n$, with $j > i$. In total, there are $n(n - 1)/2$ disjunction constraints.

A generalization is overlapping if it need not satisfy some of these disjunction constraints. For example, the generalization

*Person Gens SinglePerson, MarriedPerson, Student*

is overlapping, because students may be single or married. Note that *SinglePerson* is disjoint with *MarriedPerson*.

Covering and disjointness are orthogonal constraints; therefore, we have four kinds of generalizations

- complete/disjoint;
- complete/overlapping;
- incomplete/disjoint;
- incomplete/overlapping.

Incomplete and overlapping generalizations are not subjected to the covering and disjointness constraints. In this respect, they are unconstrained.

In UML, covering and disjointness constraints are defined graphically by placing the keywords *complete* or *incomplete* and *disjoint* or *overlapping* near the common part of the tree or the arrowhead; see Fig. 10.3.

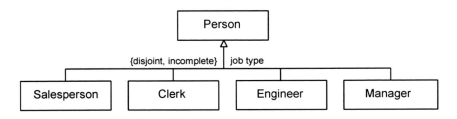

**Fig. 10.4.** Generalization of *Person* according to the *job type* dimension

### 10.2.3 Generalization/Specialization Dimension

In principle, a generalization may be any set of *IsA* relationships with the same supertype. In practice, however, it makes sense to group into a generalization the *IsA* relationships that belong to the same dimension. A *dimension* can be seen as a kind of attribute of $E$ that may take $n$ values $V_1$, ..., $V_n$ (with $n \geq 2$). There is one subtype $E_i$ for each possible value $V_i$ of this attribute. An instance $e$ of $E$ is also an instance of the subtype $E_i$ if $e$ has the value $V_i$ in the dimension attribute.

For example, consider the dimension "job type" of persons (Fig. 10.4). According to this dimension, a person may be a salesperson, clerk, engineer or manager. In this case we have *Person Gens Salesperson, Clerk, Engineer, Manager.*

Often, the dimension is a condition that may take two values: *true* or *false*. For instance, according to the "right angles" dimension, *Parallelograms* may be *Rectangle* or *NonRectangle*, and according to the "equal sides" dimension, *Parallelograms* may be *Rhombus* or *NonRhombus*.

In UML, the set of *IsA* relationships that belong to the same dimension is called a *generalization set*. Graphically, the *IsA* relationships that belong to the same generalization set may be combined into a single tree with an arrowhead (see Fig. 10.4). The name of the dimension may be placed near the arrowhead. The completeness and disjointness constraints that apply to the generalization set are also placed near the arrowhead.

There is a relationship between the characteristics of the dimension attribute and the taxonomic constraints of the generalization:

- If the attribute is single-valued, the generalization is disjoint; otherwise, it is overlapping.
- If the attribute is total, the generalization is complete; otherwise, it is incomplete.

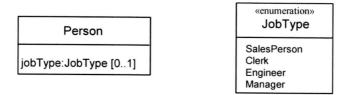

**Fig. 10.5.** Representation by an explicit dimension attribute of the schema shown in Fig. 10.4

In the example of Fig. 10.4 we have assumed that every person has at most one job type and that there are persons without a job.

## 10.2.4 Explicit Subtypes versus Explicit Dimension Attributes

The schema in Fig. 10.4 is equivalent to that in Fig. 10.5. In the former, the subtypes are explicit and the dimension attribute is implicit, while in the latter, the dimension attribute is explicit and the subtypes are implicit. Sometimes the dimension attribute is in fact represented by a binary association.

The knowledge represented in the two schemas is the same. The explicit dimension attribute gives smaller schemas, but explicit subtypes are to be preferred when the subtypes participate (or may participate in the future) in one or more relationship types. In the above example, if we need to represent the sales made by a salesperson or the department managed by a manager, then the schema in Fig. 10.4 is better.

If we want to explicitly represent both the subtypes and the dimension attribute, then we must define one of them as derived.

Though the dimension attribute may be an explicit attribute of the supertype, we may not wish to define a subtype for each possible value, but rather for only some of them. For example, there may be the association *LivesIn (Person, placeOfResidence:Town)*. Instances of *Town* might be *New York, Paris*, or many others. A dimension of *Person* could be the person's place of residence, but in a particular application we might be interested only in people from certain places, such as *New York* or *Paris*. In this case we would define only the subtypes of interest (*NewYorker, Parisian*), and the generalization would be incomplete.

### 10.2.5 Partitions

A *partition* is a generalization that satisfies both the covering and the disjointsness constraint. A given entity type may be the supertype of several partitions. Each partition has a different dimension. In UML, partitions are generalization sets for which the constraints are disjoint and complete.

We write $E$ *Partd* $E_1, ..., E_n$ to denote the partition of $E$ into $E_1, ..., E_n$. *Partd* is an abbreviation for *Partitioned*. For example,

> *Person Partd Man, Woman*

## 10.3 The Taxonomy of a Conceptual Schema

In conceptual modeling, a *taxonomy* is a set of concepts and a set of taxonomic constraints. A taxonomy usually refers to the set of entity types in a schema and their taxonomic constraints. However, given that relationship types are concepts too, there might be taxonomies of relationship types, but they are of lesser practical interest. The taxonomy of the entity types is the core of a schema. The taxonomy defines the relevant entity types in the domain and determines the possible participants in relationship types.

Every taxonomy includes the entity type *Entity*, which is the only one that has no supertype. All the other types have one or more supertypes. The types that are not supertypes are called *leaf* types. In Fig. 10.6, $C$ and $D$ are leaf entity types.

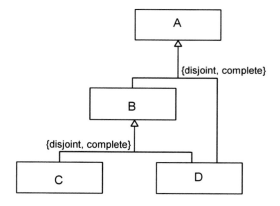

**Fig. 10.6.** Example of a taxonomy that is not satisfiable: there is an inclusion and a disjunction constraint between $D$ and $B$

The set of *taxonomic* constraints consists of the inclusion, disjunction, and covering constraints involving the entity types in the taxonomy. The taxonomic constraints include not only those that are explicitly defined in the schema, but also those that can be deduced from them, using the inference rules described in the preceding chapter.

The set of taxonomic constraints is strongly satisfiable if there are no inclusion and disjunction constraints between the same pair of entity types. In Fig. 10.6, the taxonomic constraints are not satisfiable.

### 10.3.1 Valid Type Configurations

In single-classification conceptual models, an entity may be an instance of only one leaf type, while in multiple-classification models an entity may be an instance of two or more leaf types. The concept of a valid type configuration, described below, allows us to check whether these conditions are satisfied.

A *valid type configuration VTC* is a nonempty set of entity types $E_1$, ..., $E_n$ that satisfies the following conditions:

- There may be an entity that is an instance of $E_1$, ..., $E_n$ at a given time. An entity may be an instance of $E_1$, ..., $E_n$ at a given time if there is no disjunction constraint between a pair of types of $E_1$, ..., $E_n$.
- *VTC* includes at least one leaf type.
- If $E_{i,j} \in VTC$ and there is an inclusion constraint of $E_{i,j}$ in $E_i$ then we must have $E_i \in VTC$.
- If $E_i \in VTC$ and there is a covering constraint of $E_i$ in $E_{i,1}$, ..., $E_{i,m}$, then for some (one or more) $j = 1$, ..., $m$ we must have $E_{i,j} \in VTC$.

For example, consider the taxonomy shown in Fig. 10.7. The following are valid type configurations:

$VTC_1 = \{Entity, Person, Man\}$
$VTC_2 = \{Entity, Person, Man, Student\}$
$VTC_3 = \{Entity, Person, Man, Employee, TaxPayer\}$
$VTC_4 = \{Entity, Person, Man, Student, Employee, TaxPayer\}$
$VTC_5 = \{Entity, Person, Woman\}$
$VTC_6 = \{Entity, Person, Woman, Student\}$
$VTC_7 = \{Entity, Person, Woman, Employee, TaxPayer\}$
$VTC_8 = \{Entity, Person, Woman, Student, Employee, TaxPayer\}$
$VTC_9 = \{Entity, Company, TaxPayer\}$

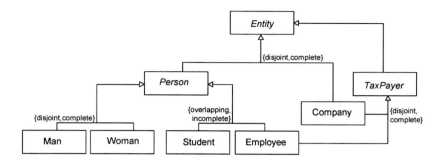

**Fig. 10.7.** Example of taxonomy

According to this schema, there may be entities that are an instance of more than one leaf entity type, such as an instance of *Woman*, *Student*, and *Employee*. If such entities cannot exist in the domain, then we must change the taxonomy.

The set of taxonomic constraints defined in a taxonomy is satisfiable if each entity type defined in that taxonomy appears in one or more valid type configurations. The example in Fig. 10.6 is not satisfiable, because the only valid type configuration is

$$VTC = \{A, B, C\}.$$

## 10.3.2 Taxonomic Constraints and Derivability

As we know from the preceding chapter, a constraint is a condition that may in some situations be violated, although it is assumed that the information system will enforce them. Naturally, this also applies to taxonomic constraints.

However, there is a relationship between taxonomic constraints and the derivability of entity types, such that some taxonomic constraints are satisfied by a schema. That is, in some cases the derivation rules and other constraints defined in a schema entail a taxonomic constraint. When this occurs, the constraint is general domain knowledge rather than a constraint in the strictest sense.

In what follows, we study the commonest constraints entailed by a schema. The examples are based on the taxonomy shown in Fig. 10.8. *Person* is derived by union of *Man* and *Woman*. *Child* and *Young* are derived by specialization of *Person*. *Adult* is derived by specialization of *Person* and exclusion of *Child* and *Young*.

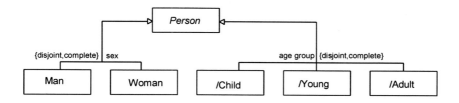

**Fig. 10.8.** Example of taxonomy. *Person* is derived by union. *Child, Young* and *Adult* are derived by specialization of *Person*

### 10.3.2.1 Inclusion Constraints

If we have

- the inclusion constraint of $E'$ in $E$, and
- $E'$ is derived by specialization of $E$,

then the inclusion constraint is entailed by the derivation rule of $E'$.

There are three examples in Fig. 10.8. *Child, Young*, and *Adult* are derived by specialization of *Person*. The three inclusion constraints of *Child* in *Person, Young* in *Person*, and *Adult* in *Person* are then entailed by the derivation rules. They are not constraints in the strict sense, because they cannot be violated.

If we have

- the inclusion constraint of $E'$ in $E$, and
- $E$ is derived by union of a set of types that includes $E'$,

then the inclusion constraint is entailed by the derivation rule of $E$.

In Fig. 10.8, there are two examples. *Person* is derived by union of *Man* and *Woman*. The two inclusion constraints of *Man* in *Person* and *Woman* in *Person* are implied by the derivation rule of *Person*.

If we have

- the inclusion constraint of $E'$ in $E$,
- $E'$ is derived, and
- $E$ is base,

then the inclusion constraint must be implied by the derivation rule of $E'$. If it is not, then the rule can be transformed into an equivalent one that entails the constraint.

The idea is that if the derivation rule of $E'$,

$$E'(e) \leftrightarrow \phi(e)$$

does not entail the constraint

$$E'(e) \rightarrow E(e)$$

then we can transform it into

$$E'(e) \leftrightarrow \phi(e) \wedge E(e)$$

which now entails the constraint.

### 10.3.2.2 Disjunction Constraints

If we have

- the disjunction constraint of $E_1$ and $E_2$, and
- $E_1$ is derived by specialization of another type $E$ and by exclusion of a set of entity types that includes $E_2$,

then the disjunction constraint is entailed by the derivation rule of $E_1$.

In the example in Fig. 10.8, *Adult* is derived by specialization of *Person* and exclusion of *Child* and *Young*. Therefore, the disjunctions

*Adult Disjoint Child*
*Adult Disjoint Young*

are entailed by the schema.

If we have

- the disjunction constraint of $E_1$ and $E_2$,
- $E_1$ is derived, and
- $E_2$ is base,

then the disjunction constraint must be entailed by the derivation rule of $E_1$. If it is not, then the rule can be transformed into another one that entails the constraint.

### 10.3.2.3 Covering Constraints

If we have

- the covering constraint of $E$ on $E_1$, ..., $E_n$, and
- $E$ is derived by union of $E_1$, ..., $E_n$,

then the covering constraint is entailed by the derivation rule of $E$.

An example is given in Fig. 10.8. *Person* is derived by union of *Man* and *Woman*. Therefore, the covering constraint of *Person* on *Man* and *Woman* is entailed by the derivation rule of *Person*.

If we have

- The covering constraint of $E$ on $E_1$, ..., $E_n$, and
- $E_j \in \{E_1, ..., E_n\}$ is derived by specialization of $E$ and exclusion of $\{E_1, ..., E_n\} - \{E_j\}$,

then the covering constraint is entailed by the derivation rule of $E_j$.

In the example of Fig. 10.8, *Adult* is derived by specialization of *Person* and exclusion of *Child* and *Young*. Therefore, the covering constraint of *Person* on *Child*, *Young* and *Adult* is entailed by the derivation rule of *Adult*.

## 10.3.3 Partitions and Derivability

Let us apply the previous analysis to the particular case of partitions.

### 10.3.3.1 Inclusion Constraints

A partition $P = E$ *Partd* $E_1$, ..., $E_n$ includes $n$ inclusion constraints of $E_i$ in $E$. In some particular cases, some or all of these constraints are entailed by the schema. The most frequent cases are:

- When $E$ is derived by union of the subtypes of $P$. It is clear that in this case the derivation rule of $E$ entails the above $n$ inclusion constraints, and these are entailed by the schema.
- When $E_i$ is derived by specialization of $E$. In this case, the derivation rule of $E_i$ entails the inclusion constraint of $E_i$ in $E$, and this is entailed by the schema.

### 10.3.3.2 Disjunction Constraints

A partition $P = E$ *Partd* $E_1$, ..., $E_n$ includes $n(n - 1)/2$ disjunction constraints between pairs $E_i$ and $E_j$, with $i, j = 1, ..., n, j > i$. In some particular cases, a disjunction constraint of $E_i$ and $E_j$ is entailed by the schema. The most frequent particular case is:

- When $E_i$ (or $E_j$) is derived by specialization of $E$ and by exclusion of the other subtypes of $P$. In this case, $E_i$ is disjoint with all other subtypes of $P$.

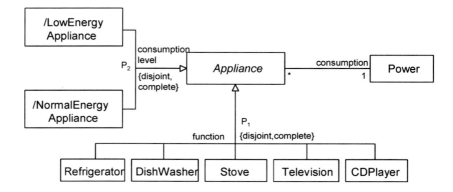

**Fig. 10.9.** Fragment of a schema with two partitions

### 10.3.3.3 Covering Constraints

A partition $P = E$ *Partd* $E_1$, ..., $E_n$ includes a covering constraint of $E$ on $E_1$, ..., $E_n$. In some particular cases, this covering constraint is entailed by the schema. The most frequent particular cases are:

- When $E$ is derived by union of the subtypes of $P$. It is clear that in this case the derivation rule of $E$ entails the covering constraint.
- There is a subtype $E_i$ derived by specialization of $E$ and exclusion of the other subtypes of $P$.

As an example, consider the schema fragment shown in Fig. 10.9, with two partitions ($P_1$ and $P_2$). If we assume also that

- *Appliance* is derived by union of the subtypes of $P_1$
- *LowEnergyAppliance* is derived by specialization of *Appliance* with the rule

```
context LowEnergyAppliance::
        allInstances():Set(LowEnergyAppliance)
   body: Appliance.allInstances()->
        select(consumption ≤ Limit)
```

- *NormalEnergyAppliance* is derived by exclusion of the other subtypes of $P_2$,

then the only taxonomic constraints not entailed by the schema are the ten disjunction constraints between the five subtypes of $P_1$.

## 10.4 Relationship Type Refinement

We know that a relationship type $R(p_1{:}E_1, ..., p_n{:}E_n)$ consists of a set of participants, and that a participant is an entity type that plays a role in $R$. But what happens to $R$ if $E_i$ is one of its participants, and the taxonomy includes a specialization $E_{i,k}$ *IsA* $E_i$? The generic answer is: nothing special. The instances of $E_{i,k}$ are also instances of $E_i$ and can therefore participate in relationships of type $R$. This is sometimes seen as if the subtypes *inherit* the relationship types defined in their supertypes.

However, it often happens that when an instance $e$ of $E_i$ is also an instance of one or more subtypes $E_{i,k}$ of $E_i$, the instances of $R$ in which $e$ participates must satisfy additional constraints. The same may happen when an instance of $E_i$ is also an instance of other entity types, even if they are not a subtype of $E_i$. In general, we give the name *refinement of a relationship type* to the definition of additional integrity constraints when the participants are also of other types. The most important refinements are participant refinement and cardinality constraint strengthening. By extension, redefining a derivation rule in a subtype of a participant is also considered a refinement. In what follows, we study each of these refinements.

### 10.4.1 Participant Refinement

A participant refinement of a relationship type constrains the types of its participants. For instance, assume the domain of the Olympic Games and consider the following relationship type and partitions:

> *WinsGoldMedal* (*winner:Athlete, Event*)
> *Athlete Partd MaleAthlete, FemaleAthlete*
> *Event Partd ManEvent, WomanEvent*

If we want to state that male athletes can only win gold medals in men's events, and that female athletes can only win gold medals in women's events, then we refine the participants of *WinsGoldMedal* twice, as follows:

- If the winner is an instance of *MaleAthlete*, then the event must be an instance of *ManEvent*.
- If the winner is an instance of *FemaleAthlete*, then the event must be an instance of *WomanEvent*.

For presentation purposes, we shall first formalize this kind of refinement for a simple yet frequent case, and then we shall extend it to the gen-

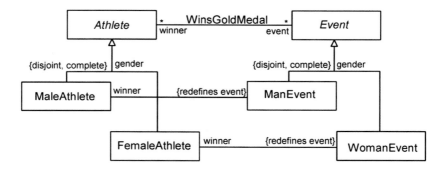

**Fig. 10.10.** Two participant refinements of *WinsGoldMedal*

eral case. We shall deal only with binary relationship types. The generalization to *n*-ary ones is easy.

We textually denote by

$$R(p_i:E_{i,j} \rightarrow p_k:E_{k,l})$$

with $i, k = 1...2$, a participant refinement of $R(p_1:E_1,p_2:E_2)$. The first argument, $p_i:E_{i,j}$, is the antecedent and the second argument, $p_k:E_{k,l}$, is the consequent. The meaning is that when the participant $p_i$ is an instance of $E_{i,j}$, the participant $p_k$ must be an instance of $E_{k,l}$. Using this notation, the participant refinements of the example would be represented by

*WinsGoldMedal (winner:MaleAthlete → event:ManEvent)*
*WinsGoldMedal (winner:FemaleAthlete → event:WomanEvent)*

In logic, a participant refinement $R(p_i:E_{i,j} \rightarrow p_k:E_{k,l})$ is represented by the constraint

$$R(e_1,e_2) \wedge E_{i,j}(e_i) \rightarrow E_{k,l}(e_k)$$

Note that this constraint is additional to the referential constraints of $R(p_1:E_1,p_2:E_2)$:

$$R(e_1,e_2) \rightarrow E_1(e_1)$$
$$R(e_1,e_2) \rightarrow E_2(e_2)$$

It is important to see that a participant refinement of $R$ does not introduce a new relationship type in the schema: it only adds a new constraint on $R$.

UML allows an attribute in an entity type that is defined in one of its supertypes to be redefined. Similarly, it allows an association in an entity type in which one of its supertypes participates to be redefined. The attribute type and the type of an association participant are two of the characteristics that may be redefined. We shall see later that multiplicities and derivability are other characteristics that can be redefined.

Participant refinements can be expressed as redefinitions. Figure 10.10 shows the above example in UML. The association *WinsGoldMedal* is redefined twice. One redefinition expresses that if the winner is a *MaleAthlete* then the event must be a *ManEvent,* and the other that if the winner is a *FemaleAthlete* the event must be a *WomanEvent.*

The general case of participant refinement of $R(p_1{:}E_1,p_2{:}E_2)$ is textually denoted by

$$R(p_i{:}\{E_{i,1}, \ldots, E_{i,n}\} \rightarrow p_k{:}\{E_{k,1}, \ldots, E_{k,m}\})$$

with $i$, $k = 1\ldots2$. Now, the antecedent and the consequent are a set of entity types. The meaning is that when a participant $p_i$ of $R$ is an instance of *all* the types $E_{i,1}, \ldots, E_{i,n}$, a participant $p_k$ must be an instance of *some* of the types $E_{k,1}, \ldots, E_{k,m}$. In logic, the constraint to be added to the schema is

$$R(e_1,e_2) \wedge E_{i,1}(e_i) \wedge \ldots \wedge E_{i,n}(e_i) \rightarrow E_{k,1}(e_k) \vee \ldots \vee E_{k,m}(e_k)$$

Normally, the types $E_{i,1}, \ldots, E_{i,n}$ are subtypes of $E_i$, and $E_{k,1}, \ldots, E_{k,m}$ are subtypes of $E_k$, but this is not mandatory.

A participant refinement

$$R(p_i{:}\{E_{i,1}, \ldots, E_{i,n}\} \rightarrow p_k{:}\{E_{k,1}, \ldots, E_{k,m}\})$$

makes sense if:

- There may be an entity that is simultaneously an instance of $E_i$, $E_{i,1}$, $\ldots$, and $E_{i,n}$, that is, if there is a valid type configuration *VTC* such that $\{E_i, E_{i,1}, \ldots, E_{i,n}\} \subseteq VTC$.
- There may be an entity that is simultaneously an instance of $E_k$, $E_{k,j}$, with $j = 1, \ldots, m$, that is, if there is a valid type configuration *VTC'* such that $\{E_k, E_{k,j}\} \subseteq VTC'$.

If these conditions are not satisfied, the participant refinement does not have any effect. For example,

$$WinsGoldMedal\ (winner{:}\{FemaleAthlete, MaleAthlete\} \rightarrow$$
$$event{:}WomanEvent)$$

makes no sense because a winner cannot be an instance of *FemaleAthlete* and *MaleAthlete* at the same time.

## 10.4.2 Particular Kinds of Participant Refinement

There are three particular kinds of participant refinement that are worth mentioning. The first is when the antecedent and/or the consequent are entities rather than entity types. We use the same textual notation as before, although we are now referring to entities rather than entity types.

For example, consider the relationship type and specialization

> *MayPay* (*Customer, PaymentMethod*)
> *TroublesomeCustomer IsA Customer*

and assume that there is a rule that troublesome customers can pay only in cash. The rule can be represented by the participant refinement

> *MayPay* (*customer: TroublesomeCustomer →*
> *paymentMethod:Cash*)

This refinement cannot be expressed graphically in UML. We must rely on OCL for the formal definition:

```
context TroublesomeCustomer inv mustPayInCash:
  paymentMethod = PaymentMethod::InCash
```

where we have assumed that *PaymentMethod* is an enumeration.

The second particular kind is when the antecedent is missing:

$$R(\to p_k:\{E_{k,1}, \ldots, E_{k,m}\})$$

The obvious meaning is that the participant $p_k$ must necessarily be an instance of some of the entity types $E_{k,1}, \ldots, E_{k,m}$, independently of the types of the other participants. Formally,

$$R(e_i, e_k) \to E_{k,1}(e_k) \lor \ldots \lor E_{k,m}(e_k)$$

The last particular kind is when the consequent is missing:

$$R(p_i:\{E_{i,1}, \ldots, E_{i,n}\} \to)$$

Here, the meaning is that a participant $p_i$ cannot simultaneously be an instance of all the entity types $E_{i,1}, \ldots, E_{i,n}$. Formally,

$$R(e_i, e_k) \land E_{i,1}(e_i) \land \ldots \land E_{i,n}(e_i) \to false$$

or equivalently,

$$R(e_i, e_k) \to \neg (E_{i,1}(e_i) \land \ldots \land E_{i,n}(e_i))$$

For example, suppose that we have the relationship type

> *Drives* (*driver:Person, Car*)

with

$$Card(driver;\ car;\ Drives) = Card(car;\ driver;\ Drives) = (0,\infty)$$

and the partition

*Person Gens Child, Young, Adult*

If, as seems likely, children cannot drive cars, then we must define the participant refinement as

*Drives(driver:Child →)*

or, equivalently,

*Drives(→ driver:{Young, Adult})*

Neither of the latter two kinds of participant refinement can be represented graphically in UML. Again, we have to rely on OCL for the formal definition. One possibility is

```
context Child inv mayNotDriveCars:
  car->isEmpty()
```

and another is

```
context Person inv onlyYoungsAndAdultsMayDriveCars:
  car->notEmpty() implies
          self.oclIsTypeOf(Young) or self.oclIsTypeOf(Adult)
```

In this example, an alternative that follows the maximal-participation guideline described in Sect. 4.3, would be to define an entity type that generalizes *Young* and *Adult* and to define it as the driver participant in *Drives*, instead of *Person*. In this way, there is no need to state that children cannot drive cars. Naturally, in this example, some conceptual modelers may prefer to refine participants rather than adding new entity types.

### 10.4.3 Cardinality Constraint Strengthening

Sometimes a cardinality constraint $Card(p_i;p_j;R) = (min,max)$ of a relationship type $R(p_1:E_1,p_2:E_2)$ is strengthened when an entity playing the role $p_k$ ($k = 1, 2$) is also an instance of the entity types $E_{k,1}, \ldots, E_{k,n}$. That is, in this case the cardinality is $Card(p_i;p_j;R) = (min_1,max_1)$ with $min_1 > min$ or $max_1 < max$. As in the general case, $max_1$ must be greater than zero.

For example, consider the relationship type *IsPartOf* (*part:Wheel, whole:Vehicle*), with

$$Card(whole;\ part) = (0,\infty)$$
$$Card(part;\ whole) = (0,1)$$

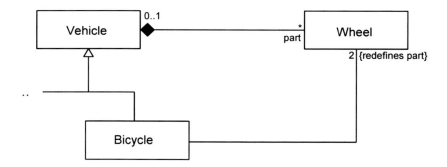

**Fig. 10.11.** Example of cardinality strengthening

Assume also that we have the specialization *Bicycle IsA Vehicle*. If we want to define that, when the vehicle is a bicycle, the number of wheels must be 2, we strengthen the cardinality *Card(whole; part)* to (2,2).

Textually, we represent this kind of refinement by the expression

$$Card(p_i:\{E_{i,1}, \ldots, E_{i,n}\}; p_j:\{E_{j,1}\}; R) = (min,max)$$

Using this notation, the above refinement would be

$$Card(whole:\{Bicycle\}; part; IsPartOf) = (2,2).$$

In logic, the meaning of $Card(p_1:\{E_{1,1}, \ldots, E_{1,n}\}; p_2:\{E_{2,1}\}; R) = (min,max)$ is the constraint

$$E_1(e_1) \wedge E_{1,1}(e_1) \wedge \ldots \wedge E_{1,n}(e_1) \rightarrow$$
$$min \leq |\{e_2 \mid R(e_1,e_2) \wedge E_{2,1}(e_2) \}| \leq max$$

and similarly for the other values of $i, j$.

In UML, cardinality constraint strengthening can be expressed as redefinitions. Figure 10.11 shows the above example in UML. The association *vehicle–part* is redefined to express that if the whole is a *Bicycle*, then the multiplicity of the part role must be 2.

As a more complex example, consider the following partitions of *Person*:

> *Person Partd Man, Woman*
> *Person Partd UnmarriedPerson, MarriedPerson*

Let us assume that we have the following relationship type:

> *IsMarriedTo(husband:MarriedPerson, wife:MarriedPerson)*
> *Card(husband; wife) = Card(wife; husband) = (1,1)*

To indicate that the *husband* must be a *Man* and that the *wife* must be a *Woman*, we could define the refinements as

$PRef_1 = IsMarriedTo(\rightarrow husband\colon Man)$
$PRef_2 = IsMarriedTo(\rightarrow wife\colon Woman)$

Alternatively, we could define the relationship type with different participants:

*IsMarriedTo'(husband:Man, wife:Woman)*
$Card(husband;\ wife) = Card(wife;\ husband) = (0,1)$

Now we must define the refinements

$PRef_3 = IsMarriedTo'(\rightarrow husband\colon MarriedPerson)$
$PRef_4 = IsMarriedTo'(\rightarrow wife\colon MarriedPerson)$

and strengthen the cardinalities

$CRef_1 = Card(husband\colon\{MarriedPerson\};\ wife) = (1,1)$
$CRef_2 = Card(wife\colon\{MarriedPerson\};\ husband) = (1,1)$

We would be worse off if we were to define the relationship type with the participant *Person* (see Fig. 10.12):

*IsMarriedTo'' (husband:Person, wife:Person)*
$Card(husband;\ wife) = Card(wife;\ husband) = (0,1)$

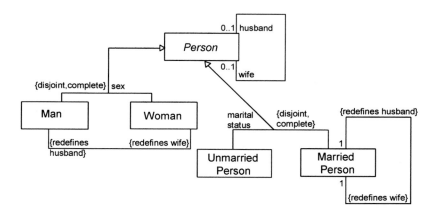

**Fig. 10.12.** Example of refinements. The association *husband-wife* is refined in the subtypes of *Person*

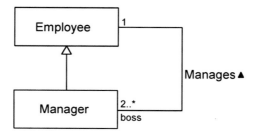

**Fig. 10.13.** Example of cardinality and inclusion constraints that cannot be strongly satisfied

In this case, we would need to define the above as *PRef*₁, *PRef*₂, *PRef*₃, *PRef*₄, *CRef*₁ and *CRef*₂. In UML, only this alternative may be represented graphically, as shown in Fig. 10.12.

### 10.4.4 Interaction of *IsA* and Cardinality Constraints

A set of cardinality constraints may be strongly satisfiable when it is considered in isolation but cease to be so when we take into account the strengthening of these constraints or take inclusion constraints into accounts.

Figure 10.13 shows an example of this. The cardinalities of *Manages* are strongly satisfiable if we do not take into account that *Manager IsA Employee*. However, if we take this inclusion constraint into account then the cardinalities cannot be strongly satisfied. The reader is invited to check that a nonempty finite population of *Employee*, *Manager*, and *Manages* that satisfies the two cardinalities and the inclusion constraint does not exist.

Fortunately, there are methods, similar to those presented in Chap. 4, that check the strong satisfiability of cardinalities, taking into account their strengthening and inclusion constraints. Readers who are interested in this topic should consult the references provided at the end of this chapter.

### 10.4.5 Derivation Rule Redefinition

The population of a derived relationship type is defined by a derivation rule. Sometimes, the rule may be long or complex because the subtype of a given participant must be taken into account. When this happens, it may be

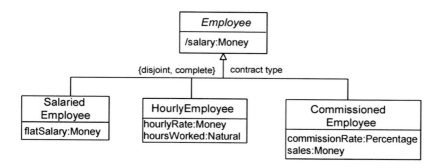

**Fig. 10.14.** The derivation rule of salary depends on the contract type of the employee

practical to define a generic rule for *R* and to redefine it in a participant subtype.

Consider the schema shown in Fig. 10.14. Every employee has a salary, which depends on his contract type. Salaried employees are paid a flat salary. Hourly employees are paid on the basis of the number of hours they work. Commissioned employees are paid a commission based on their sales.

The complete derivation rule of the attribute *salary* at the level of *Employee* might be:

- If the employee is salaried, the salary is his flat salary.
- If the employee is hourly, the salary is the hourly rate multiplied by the number of hours worked.
- If the employee is commissioned, the salary is the commission rate multiplied by the amount of the sales.

It is not difficult to see that, in some cases, rules like this one may be very long or complex. A better alternative might be to provide a generic rule, if any were needed, at the level of *Employee*, and to redefine it in *SalariedEmployee*, *HourlyEmployee*, and *CommissionedEmployee*. We would then have four short rules instead of a single long one.

In standard UML, derivation rules cannot be redefined. A handy alternative is to define the derivation rule by means of defining operations, as explained in Chap. 8. Defining operations (like any other operation) can be redefined in the subtypes. In the above example, the four operations would be

```
context Employee::salary():Money
   body: (abstract)
context SalariedEmployee::salary():Money
   body: flatSalary
context HourlyEmployee::salary():Money
   body: hourlyRate * hoursWorked
context CommissionedEmployee::salary():Money
   body: commissionRate * sales
```

It is enlightening to compare these four rules with a single rule defined in *Employee*:

```
context Employee::salary():Money
   body: if self.oclIsTypeOf(SalariedEmployee) then
              self.oclAsType(SalariedEmployee).flatSalary
         else
           if self.oclIsTypeOf(HourlyEmployee) then
               self.oclAsType(HourlyEmployee).hourlyRate *
                  self.oclAsType(HourlyEmployee).hoursWorked
           else
             self.oclAsType(CommissionedEmployee).
               commissionRate *
                  self.oclAsType(CommissionedEmployee).sales
           endif
         endif
```

### 10.4.6 Redefining a Base Relationship Type as Derived

UML allows a base relationship type $R(p_1:E_1, ..., p_n:E_n)$ to be redefined as a derived type in a subtype of a participant. Figure 10.15 shows two examples of this. In general, the association *CanTeach* and the attribute *salary* of teachers are base. However, for specialist teachers, both are derived. A specialist teacher can teach any course of his specialty, and his salary is

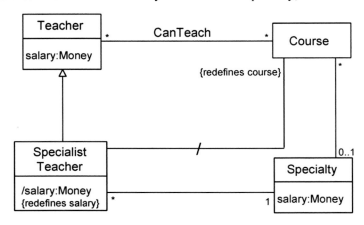

**Fig. 10.15.** *CanTeach* and *salary* of *Teacher* are redefined as derived types

given by the attribute *salary* of *Specialty*. We express these redefinitions by redefining the association and the attribute and marking them as derived. The derivation rules are

```
context SpecialistTeacher::course:Course
  derive specialty.course
context SpecialistTeacher::salary:Money
  derive specialty.salary
```

It is worth noting that a base relationship type redefined in a subtype as derived becomes hybrid. In the above example, the association *CanTeach* and the attribute *salary* of teachers are now hybrid. Their population is given by the above derivation rules and the explicit assignments of courses and salaries for the nonspecialist teachers.

## 10.5 Constraint Specialization

Sometimes, a constraint defined in an entity type is strengthened in some subtype. This is called *constraint specialization*. The idea is to replace a constraint $\phi$ of the parent type with a stronger one $\phi'$ such that $\phi'$ implies $\phi$.

Constraint specialization can be formalized in logic as follows. Let $E$ and $E'$ be entity types such that $E'$ *IsA* $E$. Let *IC* and *IC'* be condition constraints targeted at $E$ and $E'$, respectively:

$$IC: E(e) \rightarrow \varphi(e)$$
$$IC': E'(e) \rightarrow \varphi'(e)$$

If

$$\varphi'(e) \rightarrow \varphi(e)$$

then we say that *IC'* is a refinement of constraint *IC* in $E'$.

In UML, constraints cannot be specialized. The instances of a subtype *inherit* the constraints that must be satisfied by the instances of the supertype. Of course, a subtype may add new constraints, but it is not possible to specialize or redefine a constraint defined in a supertype.

Constraint specialization is possible when constraints are represented by operations. According to one of the basic principles of object orientation, when a constraint operation defined in a supertype $E$ is redefined in a subtype $E'$, the instances of subtype $E'$ must satisfy the constraint as specified in $E'$, and not as specified in $E$. The instances of $E$ which are not instances of $E'$ must satisfy the constraint as specified in $E$.

Consider the schema shown in Fig. 10.16. *Committee* has an attribute *maxNumberOfMembers*, which indicates the maximum number of mem-

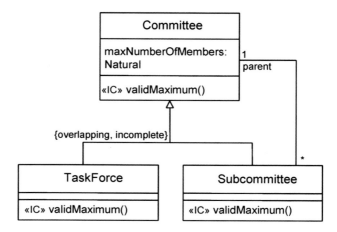

**Fig. 10.16.** Examples of constraint specialization

bers that a committee is allowed to have at any time. This number is defined when a committee is created, although it may be changed later. In general, the value of this attribute must be less than 100, but for *Task-Force*, a subtype of *Committee*, the value of that attribute must be less than 10. Similarly, for a *Subcommittee*, a subtype of *Committee*, the value of this attribute must not be greater than that of its parent committee. Figure 10.16 shows the condition constraint operation *validMaximum*, defined in *Committee* and redefined in *TaskForce* and in *Subcommittee*. The formal specification of these operations in OCL might be

```
context Committee::validMaximum():Boolean
  body: maxNumberOfMembers < 100
context TaskForce::validMaximum():Boolean
  body: maxNumberOfMembers < 10
context Subcommittee::validMaximum():Boolean
  body: maxNumberOfMembers • parent.maxNumberOfMembers
```

A potential ambiguity arises in the particular case of a constraint operation defined in a supertype $E$ that is redefined in $n$ overlapping subtypes $E_1, ..., E_n$. The natural and declarative interpretation is: when an entity $e$ is an instance of two or more subtypes $E_1, ..., E_n$ that redefine the same constraint defined in a supertype $E$, the entity $e$ must satisfy the constraint specified in all subtypes of which $e$ is an instance. Figure 10.16 shows an example of this. A particular committee *com* may be both a task force and a subcommittee. In this case, the semantics is that *com* must satisfy the constraint *validMaximum* as specified in *TaskForce* and in *Subcommittee*.

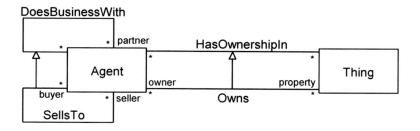

**Fig. 10.17.** Two examples of relationship type specialization

## 10.6 Specialization/Generalization of Relationship Types

### 10.6.1 *IsA* and *Gens* Between Relationship Types

*IsA* and *Gens* relationships between relationship types are similar to those between entity types. Here, we comment on the *IsA* relationship; the extension to the *Gens* relationships is easy.

A relationship type $R'$ is a *specialization* of a relationship type $R$ if $R'$ has the defining properties of $R$ and others. $R'$ is more specialized because it contains more defining properties than does $R$. The two relationship types $R$ and $R'$ must have the same degree.

Figure 10.17 shows two examples of relationship type specialization, taken from the Cyc ontology. An agent has ownership in a thing if it owns part of it or the whole thing. An agent owns a thing if it has full ownership of the thing. Therefore, *Owns IsA HasOwnershipIn*.

Similarly, two agents do business with each other if they at least occasionally negotiate to buy or sell products or services from one other. One agent sells to another if it sells goods or services to it. Therefore, *SellsTo IsA DoesBusinessWith*.

In terms of the populations, $R'$ *IsA* $R$ is an inclusion constraint of $R'$ in $R$: at any time, the instances of $R'$ are also instances of $R$. Naturally, there may be instances of $R$ which are not instances of $R'$. Formally, if $R(p_1:E_1, ..., p_n:E_n)$ and $R'(p'_1:E'_1, ..., p'_n:E'_n)$ are relationships types such that $R'$ *IsA* $R$, then in logic we have

$$R'(e_1, ..., e_n) \rightarrow R(e_1, ..., e_n)$$

When a relationship type $R'$ specializes another $R$, every participant $p'_1$ of $R'$ corresponds to a participant $p_i$ of $R$, and for each participant there must be a specialization $E'_i$ *IsA* $E_i$.

In UML, associations can be specialized, but attributes cannot. Association specialization is represented graphically in the same way as entity type specialization (see Fig. 10.17).

### 10.6.2 Reification and Specialization

We know that a relationship type $R$ can be reified into an entity type $E$. Assume that we have another relationship type $R'$ reified into $E'$ and such that $R'$ *IsA* $R$. Then, the question is: Does $R'$ *IsA* $R$ imply that $E'$ *IsA* $E$? Or, similarly, does $E'$ *IsA* $E$ imply that $R'$ *IsA* $R$?

The answer is affirmative. The entity type $E$ and the relationship type $R$ reified by it are the same concept seen from two different perspectives. Therefore, a specialization of $R$ induces a specialization of $E$, and vice versa.

Figure 10.18 shows an example in UML. There are several groups in a company, and employees may be members of them. Each membership has a starting date. Committees are groups, and employees may chair them. Every chairmanship has an appointment date. "To chair" is a specialization of "To be a member"; therefore, *Chairmanship* is a specialization of *Membership*. The two specializations are the same, and only one must be shown in the diagrams. In general, it seems preferable to show the specialization of the entity types (association classes), as is done in Fig. 10.18.

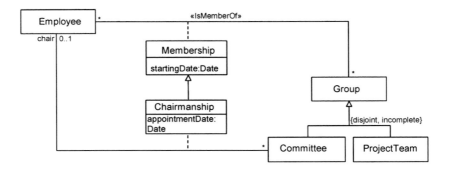

**Fig. 10.18.** Example of specialization of association classes in UML

## 10.7 Bibliographical Notes

The concepts of specialization, generalization, and taxonomy have a long tradition in philosophy and the natural sciences. Meyer (1997, Appendix 24.15) gave a short account of the history of these concepts.

Taxonomies have been thoroughly studied and used in artificial intelligence. (Quillian 1968) is considered to be a seminal, pioneering work. Since then all knowledge representation languages have included, to some extent, the concepts of specialization, generalization, and taxonomy. As is often the case, not everybody has attributed the same meaning to the *IsA* relationship. (Brachman 1983) is a classic text that surveys the many meanings ascribed to *IsA*.

Two workshops held in 1989, one in Europe and the other in the USA, were centered on taxonomies. (Lenzerini et al. 1991) and (Sowa 1991) are the proceedings. These proceedings reflect the state of the art at that time.

A problem that has received a lot of attention is, in our terms, the automatic placement of a derived entity type in a taxonomy on the basis of an analysis of its derivation rule. Woods (1991) provided an overview of this problem and its possible solutions. In the field of conceptual modeling of information systems, the problem has received less attention, because it is assumed that the conceptual modeler manually places the entity type in the taxonomy.

Smith and Smith (1977) were probably the first to study generalization in the context of database modeling. All the conceptual models and languages that have appeared after that time include the concepts of specialization, generalization, partition, and taxonomy, to varying degrees. We would like to mention particularly

- Taxis (Mylopoulos et al. 1980, Borgida et al. 1984);
- IFO (Abiteboul and Hull 1987);
- ERT (Theodoulidis et al. 1992);
- NIAM (Nijssen and Halpin 1989) and its variants (Halpin and Proper 1995a);
- the work of Martin and Odell (1995);
- the family of languages called Description Logics (Borgida 1995).

The equivalence between explicit subtypes and explicit dimension attributes was discussed by Batini et al. (1992), Assenova and Johannesson (1996), Poulovassilis and McBrien (1998), and Halpin (2001).

Smith and Smith (1977), Champeaux et al. (1993), Wieringa et al. (1995), and Martin and Odell (1995) recommended the use of partitions in conceptual schemas.

Valid type configurations were presented in Olivé et al. (1999). A related topic, valid type configuration transitions, will be studied in Chap. 14; for a general treatment see (Wieringa et al. 1995, Norrie et al. 1996, Olivé et al. 1999). The relationship between taxonomic constraints and derivability was presented by Olivé and Teniente (2002).

Participant refinement and cardinality constraints strengthening have been studied in many publications. We mention especially the works by Mylopoulos et al. (1980), Brachman and Schmolze (1985), Champeaux et al. (1993, Chap. 7), Cook and Daniels (1994, Chap. 3), Martin and Odell (1995, Chap. 10), and Analyti et al. (1997). The presentation in this chapter is based on Costal et al. (2001). For an analysis of the relationship between taxonomic constraints and association redefinition see (Costal and Gómez 2006). Derivability redefinition was mentioned by Ceri and Fraternali (1997, Chap. 11).

Calvanese and Lenzerini (1994) formulated the problem of the interaction between *IsA* and cardinality constraints and provided a method for checking the satisfiability of a schema.

Constraint specialization and exceptions have not yet attracted much attention in conceptual modeling. A general framework was presented in (Wieringa et al. 1991). The presentation in this chapter is based in (Olive 2003b).

## 10.8 Exercises

**10.1** Browse your favorite dictionary and select three concepts that could be entity types and are a specialization of other concepts. List the properties added in each case.

**10.2** Give ten subtypes of *Person* and show the specialization relationships between them. At least one of these subtypes must be of multiple specialization, and at least one must be derived by intersection.

**10.3** Give your own example of each of the four kinds of generalization.

**10.4** WordNet is an online lexical database that contains a very large number of English words, organized in synsets. Among the information provided by WordNet for each noun (concept), there are its supertypes (hypernyms) and subtypes (hyponyms). Browse WordNet (http://www.cogsci.princeton.edu/~wn/) and try to find a noun and its direct and indirect supertypes and subtypes. Can you imagine some application of WordNet in conceptual modeling?

**10.5** Consider the following schema:

$P_1$ = *Magnitude Partd Power, Speed, Volume*
$P_2$ = *Unit Partd PowerUnit, SpeedUnit, VolumeUnit*
$R_1$ = *ExpressedIn(Magnitude, Unit)*
$R_2$ = *HasValue(Magnitude, value:Decimal)*

Define the refinements of $R_1$ that are necessary in order to require that a power, speed, or volume magnitude be expressed in a power, speed, or volume unit, respectively.

**10.6** Consider a system that stores many crosswords and their clues (or definitions) and solutions. Each crossword is identified by a number. A crossword is a rectangular grid of black and white squares; the aim is to fill in the white squares with letters, forming words reading across and down, by solving clues which yield the words. Each white square is part of a horizontal and/or a vertical word. There may be grids of different size. The black squares are used to separate words. See the entry in Wikipedia for more details and the variants. Assume that the squares in which answers begin are numbered; the clues and their solutions are then referred to by these numbers and a direction, for example "1 Across" or "17 Down".

Define the structural schema corresponding to this system. It must be possible to display a crossword from the information stored in the information base. The schema must include the entity types *Row*, *Column*, *Square*, *BlackSquare*, and *WhiteSquare*. Show the instantiation of your schema corresponding to an example of a small crossword, including the clues and the solution. You must define all the integrity constraints and derivation rules that are necessary. Ensure that there is a clue for each word, and that the number of letters in the solution of each clue is the same as the number of white squares in the sequence (or entry) where they are placed.

# 11 Domain Events

In the preceding chapters of this book, we studied the structural part of a conceptual schema, that is, the structural schema. In this chapter, we start the study of the behavioral part, called the behavioral schema.

The structural schema defines the types of the facts contained in the information base. These facts change over time, but they cannot change in any arbitrary way. Only some changes of the information base are permissible. These changes are called domain events. The definition of the domain event types is the most important part of the behavioral schema.

In the first section of this chapter we analyze the concept of domain event. There are other kinds of event, but they will be studied in the next chapter. In Sect. 11.2, we explain that domain events can be seen as entities, and we study how to represent them in the conceptual schema and in the information base. An important part of a behavioral schema is dedicated to defining the constraints and effects of events. In Sect. 11.3, we explain how to define domain event constraints. The effects of domain events can be defined using either of two approaches: the postcondition and procedural approaches. These are explained in Sects. 11.4 and 11.5, respectively. In Sect. 11.6, we explain that the structural schema must be consistent with the domain event types.

As we have done in most of the preceding chapters, we sketch here the representation of the behavioral schema in the logic language, and give much more detail of its representation in the UML.

Our main examples in this chapter (and the next one) will be about a material requirements planning (MRP) system. Such systems serve to manage material requirements in a manufacturing process. However, we shall consider only an elementary version, one that is not representative of a full-fledged MRP system. The details will be introduced where they arise.

## 11.1 Domain Events as Sets of Structural Events

As we already know, an information system maintains a representation of the state of a domain in its information base. The state of a domain at any given point in time is the set of instances of the relevant entity and relationship types that exist in the domain at that time. The relevant entity and relationship types are those defined in the conceptual schema.

The representation of the state of the domain in the information base is not static. Most domains change over time, and therefore their state changes too. When the state of a domain changes, the information base must change accordingly. Of course, a domain cannot change in an arbitrary way. Only some changes are acceptable. The acceptable changes are called domain events. This concept (of a domain event) can be defined precisely in terms of a more basic concept, called a structural event, which we define in the following.

### 11.1.1 Structural Events

We say that there is a change in the domain state between times $t_1$ and $t_2$ if the domain state at $t_1$ is different from that at $t_2$. However, in conceptual modeling we are mostly interested in changes between consecutive time points. We say that the state of the domain at time $t$ changes if the domain state at that time, $t$, is different from the domain state at the previous time, $t$ - 1. Both states must satisfy all static constraints.

A state change is a set of one or more structural events. A *structural event* is an elementary change in the population of an entity or relationship type[1]. The precise number and meaning of structural events depend on the conceptual modeling language used. To give an intuitive idea of the meaning, let us assume for the moment a language that has only the concepts of entity and relationship types. In this language, there are four kinds of structural event:

- *Entity insertion.* An entity insertion structural event occurs at time $t$ if an entity $e$ is an instance of some type $E$ at $t$, and $e$ was not an instance of $E$ at time $t$ - 1.

---

[1] At the information base level, structural events are elementary actions that insert a fact to the information base or remove a fact from it. In a relational database, structural events correspond roughly to the operations of insertion into, deletion from, and updating of a relation.

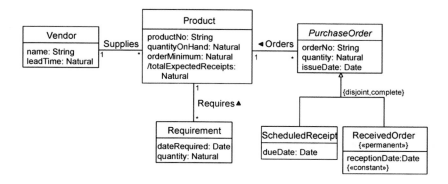

**Fig. 11.1.** Fragment of the schema for an MRP application

- *Entity deletion.* An entity deletion structural event occurs at time *t* if an entity *e* was an instance of some type *E* at time *t* - 1, and *e* is not an instance of *E* at *t*.
- *Relationship insertion.* A relationship insertion structural event occurs at time *t* if there is a relationship instance of some type *R* at *t*, and that relationship was not an instance of *R* at time *t* - 1.
- *Relationship deletion.* A relationship deletion structural event occurs at time *t* if there is a relationship that was an instance of some type *R* at time *t* - 1, and is not an instance of *R* at *t*.

As an example, consider the first schema fragment for our MRP system, shown in Fig. 11.1. As can be seen, the information base includes, among many other things, the instances of the existing products and, for each of them, relationships[2] with:

- The vendor that supplies the product. We shall assume that all products are purchased (i.e. there are no manufactured products).
- The purchase orders issued to replenish the stock for the product. A purchase order may be a scheduled receipt (not yet received) or a received order.
- The requirements (customer orders) for the product. We are not interested in which customers require the product.
- The product number that identifies the product.
- The current quantity on hand of the product.
- The minimum quantity of the product that can be ordered from its vendor.

---

[2] Recall that in UML relationship types may be attributes or associations.

- The total expected receipts of the product (a derived attribute, defined as the sum of the quantities of the scheduled receipts).

When the company starts dealing with a new product, the domain state changes. This change consists of the following six structural events:

- The insertion of the corresponding entity into *Product*.
- The insertion of the corresponding relationship into the *Supplies* association.
- The insertion of the corresponding values into the three base attributes *productNo*, *quantityOnHand*, and *orderMinimum*.
- The insertion of the corresponding value (zero) into the derived attribute *totalExpectedReceipts*.

Another change in our domain state occurs when the material ordered by a scheduled receipt is received. A scheduled receipt is an order for material to replenish the stock. When a scheduled receipt is received, the change in the domain state consists of the following eight structural events:

- The insertion of the received order into *ReceivedOrder*.
- The insertion of the corresponding value into the attribute *receptionDate* of *ReceivedOrder*.
- The deletion of the received order from *ScheduledReceipt*.
- The deletion of the corresponding value from the attribute *dueDate* of *ScheduledReceipt*.
- The update (deletion followed by insertion) of the attribute *quantityOnHand* of *Product* (the quantity on hand of the received product is increased).
- The update of the derived attribute *totalExpectedReceipts* of *Product*.

The number and semantics of the structural events depend on the language used. In many languages, an update of a single-valued attribute is considered as a single structural event, and not two as above. Some languages assume that a structural event of entity deletion includes the deletion of all its attributes. The structural events of UML will be presented in Sect. 11.5.

Continuing with our simple language, for each entity or relationship type, there are two *structural event types*: insertion and deletion. These event types are called structural because they are completely determined by the structural part of a conceptual schema. Structural event types are not explicitly defined by the conceptual modeler. Their definition is implicit.

The concept of derivability (base, derived, or hybrid) applies also to structural event types. The derivability of a structural event type is the same as that of the corresponding entity or relationship type.

Base structural events must be communicated by the users, in the way that will be explained in the next sections and chapter. A system has no other means of knowing the base structural events that happen at any time point. An example is an insertion into the *Vendor* entity type.

In contrast, derived structural events can be inferred when needed by the system from the base structural events, using the derivation rules of the corresponding entity or relationship type. For example, the insertion and deletion of values for the attribute *totalExpectedReceipts* of *Product* can be inferred by the system from the insertions into and deletions from *ScheduledReceipt*, using the derivation rule of that attribute.

#### 11.1.1.1 Structural Events for Permanent and Constant Types

The instances of a permanent entity type $E$ never cease to be instances of it. Therefore, no state change can include instances of the structural event type corresponding to deletions from $E$. In our example, *ReceivedOrder* is a permanent entity type. Once an order has been received, it remains as such forever. No state change can include instances of structural events that delete orders from *ReceivedOrder*.

The instances of a constant entity type $E$ are the same at all times. Neither new instances can be added to $E$ nor can instances be removed from it. Therefore, no state change can include instances of the structural event types corresponding to insertions into and deletions from $E$.

There are no structural events related to data types, because data types are constant and immutable.

A similar reasoning applies for permanent and constant relationship types. In our example, the reception date of *ReceivedOrder* is constant. When an order is received (becomes an instance of *ReceivedOrder*), its reception date is given and cannot be changed later. Therefore, no state change can include instances of structural events that add, delete, or update reception dates of existing received orders.

### 11.1.2 Domain Events

A state change may be simple or composite. A state change is *simple* when it consists of only one structural event. A *composite* state change consists of two or more structural events. Most state changes are composite. The state change corresponding to a new product is composite, because it consists of six structural events.

A *domain event* is a state change that consists of a nonempty set of structural events that are perceived or considered a single change in the domain. A domain event is a state change such that the states before and after the change satisfy all static constraints, and the change is permissible. The time at which the change occurs is the *occurrence time* of the event.

A simple state change can be only one domain event. In general, a composite state change may be one or more domain events.

A "new product" is an example of a domain event, because the set of six structural events it consists of is seen as a single change. If we remove any one of the six structural events, the resulting set cannot be perceived as a domain event, because there is something "missing" and, on the other hand, the resulting state of the domain would not satisfy all integrity constraints.

Some conceptual models consider that at any time point there may occur at most one domain event. In general, however, two or more domain events may occur at the same time. When this happens, the state change is composite and consists of more than one domain event. For example, a company can start dealing with two products at the same time. In this case, the two corresponding domain events will have the same occurrence time.

## 11.2 Representation in an Information System

Domain events may be represented in several ways in an information system. In this book, we represent domain events as entities. In the next chapter, we shall see that other kinds of event can be represented by entities too. This allows one to define relationships between events and other entities, integrity constraints, derivation rules, etc. in a way very similar to that for ordinary entities. In what follows, we explain first how to define domain events as entities, and then study their representation in logic and in UML. We assume current-state (nontemporal) information bases.

### 11.2.1 Domain Events as Entities

A domain event is a set of one or more structural events that occur at some time point. Most domain events are caused by actions performed outside the information system, and they must be communicated to the system by the users. We might then conclude that, in order to communicate a domain event, users need to give its corresponding set of base structural events.[3]

---

[3] Derived structural events can be inferred by the system and, therefore, they need not be communicated by the users.

Such a conclusion would be acceptable in some cases, but it is impractical in many others.

In general, as we explain below, it is much more practical to view a domain event as an entity, and to define a mapping that gives, for each domain event, its set of base structural events. In this book, we view domain events as entities, called *event entities*.

For example, consider the domain event corresponding to the reception of a scheduled receipt. If users have to communicate the event by giving all its base structural events, then they need to know which entity and relationship types are changed by the reception (scheduled receipts, received orders, reception and due dates, and quantity on hand of products), and they have to give the corresponding insertions and deletions. In this particular example, the users would have to tell the system about:

- The insertion of the received order into *ReceivedOrder*.
- The insertion of the corresponding value into the attribute *receptionDate* of *ReceivedOrder*.
- The deletion of the received order from *ScheduledReceipt*.
- The deletion of the corresponding value from the attribute *dueDate* of *ScheduledReceipt*.
- The update (deletion followed by insertion) of the attribute *quantityOnHand* of *Product* (the quantity on hand of the received product is increased).

Clearly, if the number of types affected is large, or is not obvious, or is likely to change, users will find such communication awkward.

Event entities are instances of domain event types. A *domain event type* is a concept whose instances, at a given time, are identifiable domain events that occur at that time.

Like any other entity, event entities may participate in relationships. The *characteristics* of an event entity are the relationships in which it participates. In particular, there is one relationship between each event entity and a time point, representing the event occurrence time. We assume that the characteristics of an event entity are determined when the event occurs, and are immutable.

For example, we could define the domain event type *OrderReception*. Each instance corresponds to a particular reception of a scheduled receipt, which occurs at some time. In this example, the characteristic of the event is simply the order received. It is much easier for a user to tell the system that "an *OrderReception* event of scheduled receipt *SR* has occurred" than to explicitly tell it about the above-mentioned structural events.

In general, the characteristics of a domain event must include relationships with the entities involved in the event. For example, an instance of *OrderReception* has an association with the scheduled receipt being received. We have two options here:

1. The characteristics include also the external identifiers of the entities involved, from which the relationships with them can be derived.
2. The characteristics include only the relationships with the entities involved, without the external identifiers.

For domain events, the latter is preferred because it is simpler and more general.

Each event entity denotes a set of structural events, called the *event effect*. Event entities may be seen as labels for event effects. The correspondence between an event entity and its effect is given by a mapping expression, which maps each instance of a given domain event type to the corresponding event effect, taking into account the characteristics of the event and the information base. We study how to define these expressions in Sects. 11.4 and 11.5.

In the above example, an informal mapping expression could be "An *OrderReception* event of a scheduled receipt *SR* maps to the following structural events:

- The insertion of *SR* into *ReceivedOrder*.
- The insertion of the current date as the value for the attribute *receptionDate*.
- The deletion of *SR* from *ScheduledReceipt*.
- The removal of the value for the attribute *dueDate* of *SR*.
- If the product corresponding to *SR* is *P* and the quantity of *SR* is *Q*, and the current quantity on hand of product *P* is *QOH*, then replace it (deletion followed by insertion) by $QOH + Q$."

This expression is defined only once in the behavioral schema. It is assumed that the system will apply it every time an *OrderReception* event occurs. Note that with the use of mapping expressions, users do not need to know about the event effect. If, for some reason, the mapping expression has to change, the users need not be aware of it.

Domain event types have a name, which must be unique in a schema. The importance of choosing good names cannot be overstated. Naturally, the name should be agreed on and be well understood by the people involved. A useful rule is that the name should be a singular noun, possibly with adjectives. When this rule is followed, if *Ev* is the name of a domain event type, then the following sentence has meaning:

An instance of this domain event type is an *Ev* event

The application of the rule to *OrderReception* gives

An instance of this domain event type is an *OrderReception* event

which has a clear meaning.

## 11.2.2 Logical Representation

In the logical representation, domain event types are represented by unary predicates, where the argument is a symbol that denotes an event entity. The schema will also include relationship types representing the characteristics of events. Recall that, in logic, relationship types are represented by predicates of arity two or more. We shall assume the existence of a predefined binary predicate *OccurrenceTime*, which gives the occurrence time of each event.

At every time point, the information base contains an arbitrary symbol for each domain event entity that has occurred at that time. We say that the event entity is represented by that symbol in the information base, or that the symbol denotes the event entity. The type of an event entity is given by an atomic formula of the corresponding predicate. Thus, if $A$ is an event entity instance of event type *Ev*, the information base will contain the formula *Ev(A)*.

For example, the logical representation of the domain event type *OrderReception* is

- a unary predicate *OrderReception*;
- a predicate *OrderReceived (OrderReception, ScheduledReceipt)*.

A particular order reception will be represented in the information base as an instance of each of the above two predicates, and of *OccurrenceTime*.

In nontemporal information bases, event entities exist in the information base only during the period of time in which they occur. It is assumed that events are instantaneous, that the response of the system to them is also instantaneous, and that after the response (and before the next time tick), events are removed from the information base. Current-state information bases do not remember past events.

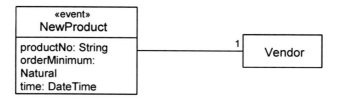

**Fig. 11.2.** Draft definition of domain event type *NewProduct*

### 11.2.3 UML Representation

In UML, domain event types can be represented by a special kind of entity type[4]. We shall use the stereotype «*event*» for them. An entity type with this stereotype will define an event type. Event characteristics may be defined as attributes or associations.

Figure 11.2 shows a draft definition of *NewProduct*, which we shall refine later on. The attribute *productNo* gives the number of the new product. The association with *Vendor* gives the vendor of the new product. The attribute *orderMinimum* gives the minimum quantity of this product that can be ordered from its vendor. The attribute *time* gives the occurrence time. It is assumed that the occurrence time is the time at which the system knows of the event.

Event characteristics are immutable. This means that they are constant with respect to the event. For presentation reasons, the constant-constraint stereotype will not be shown in the diagrams in this chapter.

Like any other entity type, domain event types may be specialized and/or generalized. This allows us to build a taxonomy of domain event types, where common elements are defined only once.

In particular, it is convenient to define a root entity type named *Event*. All event types are direct or indirect subtypes of *Event*. In fact, *Event* is defined as being derived by union of their subtypes. We define for this event type the attribute *time*, which gives the occurrence time of each event. We define also the operation *effect*, whose purpose will be made clear later. This operation has no parameters or result type. For simplicity, we assume that all subtypes of *Event* are event types and, therefore, it is not necessary to stereotype them as «*event*».

In medium-to-large taxonomies, with many domain event types and other kinds of event type, it is convenient to generalize all domain event

---

[4] UML includes a concept of an event, but it is not adequate when events are seen as entities, which is the view we take here.

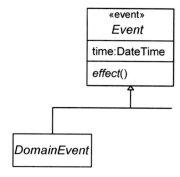

**Fig. 11.3.** Top level taxonomy of event types

types into a common type. To this end, we define an event type *DomainEvent* as shown in Fig. 11.3. *DomainEvent* is the direct or indirect supertype of all domain event types. Each particular domain event type must be defined as a subtype of *DomainEvent*.

## 11.3 Domain Event Constraints

As we have seen, a domain event is a set of one or more structural events that occur at a time point. However, not all sets of structural events are domain events. A set *StrEv* of structural events is a domain event if it is an acceptable change in the domain. This means that, in general, the set *StrEv* has to satisfy a number of conditions involving its elements and/or the state of the information base before the occurrence of the event. It is assumed that the states of the information base before and after the occurrence of the domain event satisfy all defined static constraints.

Let *DomEv* be a domain event represented by an entity *EvEnt*, with a mapping expression which maps *EvEnt* to its effect (the set of structural events) *StrEv*. A *domain event constraint* of *EvEnt* is a condition that the characteristics of *EvEnt* and/or the state of the information base before the occurrence of *DomEv* must satisfy in order to guarantee that *StrEv* is an acceptable change. For example, an event constraint for *NewProduct* (Fig. 11.2) is that there does not exist in the information base a product with the same *productNo*.

A domain event entity that violates one of its constraints represents an event that cannot (or is not allowed to) occur in the domain. The likely cause of the violation is that the characteristics are incorrect. For example, if an instance of *NewProduct* violates the above constraint, it is probably because its *productNo* is incorrect.

The set of event constraints must guarantee that if *EvEnt* satisfies all of them, then the mapping expression will map *EvEnt* to a nonempty set of structural events *StrEv* that is an acceptable change in the state of the domain.

In this book, we deal only with current-state information bases. This means that an event constraint involves only the state of the information base before the occurrence of the event. In the case of temporal information bases, event constraints may involve any previous state of the information base.

### 11.3.1 Logical Representation

In the logical representation of a schema, an event constraint is a closed formula involving facts about an event and other facts in the information base in the state before the occurrence of the event. Like any other constraint, event constraints can be expressed by inconsistency predicates.

For example, consider the event type *NewProduct*, and the constraint that there does not exist a product with the same *productNo*. Assume that the existing products, before the occurrence of the event, are given by a predicate *Product*, and that their product numbers are represented by the binary predicate *ProductWithPNo(Product, ProductNo)*. If we represent the constraint by means of the inconsistency predicate *ProductExists*, its definition is

$$
\begin{aligned}
&ProductExists(prNo) \leftrightarrow \\
&\qquad NewProduct(newPr), \\
&\qquad ProductNo(newPr, prNo), \\
&\qquad Product(prod), \\
&\qquad ProductWithPNo(prod, prNo)
\end{aligned}
$$

That is, there is a *ProductExists* inconsistency if an instance *newPr* of the event type *NewProduct* has a product number *prNo* equal to that of an existing instance *prod* of the entity type *Product*.

### 11.3.2 UML Representation

Domain event constraints are always creation-time constraints because they must be evaluated when the events occur. In UML, these constraints are best expressed by constraint operations and formalized in OCL.

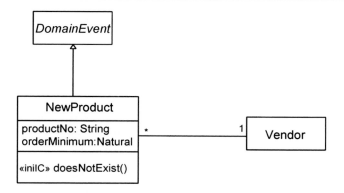

**Fig. 11.4.** Extension of Fig. 11.2 showing the event constraint *doesNotExist*

As an example, consider a *NewProduct* event and the constraint that there does not exist a product with the same *productNo*. This is an event constraint that we define by the constraint operation *doesNotExist* in *New-Product*, as shown in Fig. 11.4. The specification in OCL is

```
context NewProduct::doesNotExist():Boolean
   body: not Product.allInstances()->
                    exists(productNo = self.productNo)
```

Recall that the constraints that must be satisfied by the characteristics of an event are also event constraints. According to Fig. 11.4, the constraints that must be satisfied by an instance of *NewProduct* are:

- It has a value for the *productNo* attribute, and this value is a string.
- It has a value for the *orderMinimum* attribute, and this value is a natural number.
- It is associated with an existing vendor.
- The constraint defined by the operation *doesNotExist*.

If an instance of *NewProduct* satisfies these four constraints, then the mapping expression (see below) will map it to a nonempty set of structural events that is an acceptable change in the state of the information base.

Note that in Fig. 11.4 we have the unconstrained cardinality

$$Card(vendor; newProduct) = (0, \infty)$$

This means that several *NewProduct* events of the same vendor may occur at the same time.

## 11.4 Event Effects: The Postcondition Approach

In this section, we start our study of the specification of the effects of domain events. As we already know, the effect of an event is a set of structural events, that is, a set of changes in the population of entity and relationship types defined in the structural schema. There are two main approaches to the definition of that set: the postcondition and the procedural (or structural-events) approach. In the former, the definition is a condition that satisfies the information base after the application of the event effect. In the latter, the definition is a procedure whose evaluation gives the corresponding structural events. The postcondition approach is the most widely used in conceptual modeling. We study the postcondition approach in this section, and the procedural approach in the next.

In the postcondition approach, the effect of an event entity *EvEnt* is defined by a condition *C* on the information base. The idea is that *EvEnt* leaves the information base in a state that satisfies *C*. The condition *C* is called the postcondition of *EvEnt* because it defines the state of the information base *after* the change. Given that *EvEnt* is a domain event, the state after the occurrence of the event must be different from the state before the occurrence. It is assumed also that the state after the occurrence of the event satisfies all static constraints. Therefore, the effect of the event *EvEnt* is a state of the information base that satisfies the condition *C* and all static constraints.

In general, the condition *C* involves:

- facts of the state of the information base after the occurrence of the event;
- the characteristics of the event; and
- facts of the state of the information base before the occurrence of the event.

Note that the postcondition approach does not require an explicit definition of the set of structural events corresponding to the event effect. Instead, it requires the definition of the condition *C* that the information base must satisfy after the occurrence of the event.

The postcondition approach leaves to the designer the task of determining the set of structural events that achieve the desired state in the information base. More precisely, the designer will have to determine a set of structural events at the database level that leave the database in the state corresponding to the desired state of the information base.

In many cases, there is only one reasonable nonempty set of structural events that achieve this result. In other cases, however, there are several

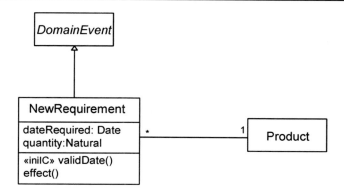

**Fig. 11.5.** Definition of the domain event type *NewRequirement*

such sets, and then the designer has the freedom to choose the one he prefers. Note that satisfaction of the domain event constraints must guarantee that there will be at least one possible set.

## 11.4.1 Logical Representation

In the logical representation of the schema and the information base, the postcondition is a closed formula that the information base must satisfy. For example, consider the event *NewRequirement*, shown in Fig. 11.5. The effect of this event is that a new instance of the entity type *Requirement* (see Fig. 11.1) has been created, with the appropriate values for its attributes and association. Using an ad hoc notation, we can define this effect as follows:

> *Event*:
> > *NewRequirement(nr)*
> *Characteristics*:
> > *RequiredOn(nr,d)*
> > *RequiredQty(nr,qty)*
> > *RequiredProduct(nr,p)*
> *Post*:
> > $\exists r(Requirement'(r),$
> > > not *Requirement(r),*
> > > *DateRequired'(r,d),*
> > > *QuantityRequired'(r,q),*
> > > *ProductRequired'(r,p))*

In the above definition, we refer to the facts holding immediately before and after the event effect by unprimed and primed predicates, respectively. The postcondition states that after the event effect, the information base includes:

- an instance (*r*) of *Requirement*,
- such that *r* was not an instance of *Requirement* prior to the occurrence of the event, and
- with the appropriate facts of the predicates *DateRequired*, *QuantityRequired*, and *ProductRequired*.

### 11.4.2 UML Representation

In UML, we can represent the effect of a domain event in several ways. We shall describe one way here, which can be used as is, or as a basis for the development of alternative ways.

We define a particular operation in each domain event type, whose purpose is to specify the effect. To this end, we use the operation *effect* that we have defined in *Event* (see Fig. 11.3). This operation will have a different specification in each event type. The postcondition of this operation will be exactly the postcondition of the corresponding event. We use OCL to specify these postconditions.

Let us illustrate the use and the consequences of this approach by means of examples from our MRP system. The first example is the domain event type *NewRequirement*, shown in Fig. 11.5. The constraint *validDate()* states that a requirement must be required on a date greater than the date of the event's occurrence time. The formal specification is

```
context NewRequirement::validDate():Boolean
  body: dateRequired > time.date
```

The effect of one instance of *NewRequirement* is the addition of one instance to the entity type *Requirement* (see Fig. 11.1). Therefore, in this case the specification of the *effect* operation is as simple as

```
context NewRequirement::effect()
  post: --There exists a new instance of Requirement
    r.oclIsNew() and
    r.oclIsTypeOf(Requirement) and
    r.dateRequired = dateRequired and
    r.quantity = quantity and
    r.product = product
```

We do not define preconditions in the specification of *effect* operations. The reason is that we *implicitly* assume that the events satisfy their constraints *before* the application of their effect. In our example, we assume implicitly that the required date is valid. On the other hand, remember that the information base satisfies all static constraints before the occurrence of the event.

In our example, the postcondition states simply that a new instance *r* of *Requirement* has been created in the information base, with the corresponding values for its attributes and association. It is assumed also that, after the application of the effect, the information base will satisfy all constraints. Any implementation of the *effect* operation that changes the information base to a state that satisfies the postcondition and the static constraints is valid.

An alternative specification of the effect could be

```
context NewRequirement::effect()
  post: --There exists a new instance of Requirement
    Requirement.allInstances() -> one
      (r:Requirement|
        Requirement.allInstances@pre()->excludes(r) and
        r.dateRequired = dateRequired and
        r.quantity = quantity and
        r.product = product)
```

This specification illustrates that, in general, the postcondition involves

- facts of the state of the information base after the occurrence of the event, such as *Requirement.allInstances()*;
- the characteristics of the event, such as *dateRequired*; and
- facts of the state of the information base before the occurrence of the event, such as *Requirement.allInstances@pre()*.

Note that, in the above postconditions, the expressions

```
        r.oclIsNew() and r.oclIsTypeOf(Requirement)
```
and
```
        Requirement.allInstances () -> one
          (r:Requirement|
                Requirement.allInstances@pre()->excludes(r))
```

require that, in the new state of the information base, there is a new instance (*r*) of the entity type *Requirement*. The reader may wonder whether it would be enough to require that there exists an instance of *Requirement* with the appropriate attributes. Such a postcondition could be

```
context NewRequirement::effect()
  post: --There exists a Requirement with the
        --appropriate attributes
    Requirement.allInstances()->exists
      (dateRequired = self.dateRequired and
       quantity = self.quantity and
       product = self.product)
```

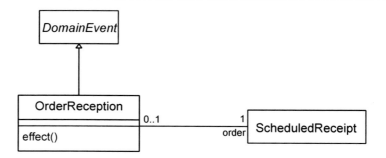

**Fig. 11.6.** Definition of the domain event type *OrderReception*

This postcondition is not satisfactory. The reason is that if the information base already contains a different requirement $r'$, then a set of structural events that changes the product, date required, and/or quantity of $r'$ to those for the event would be a valid implementation of the operation, but it does not correspond to the semantics of the event.

The specification of the external event type *NewProduct* is similar (see Fig. 11.4), but raises a subtle point. We assume that there is a static constraint stating that the instances of *Product* are identified by the attribute *productNo*. The specification of the effect of *NewProduct* could be

```
context NewProduct :: effect ()
  post: --There exists a new instance of Product
    p.oclIsNew() and
    p.oclIsTypeOf(Product) and
    p.productNo = productNo and
    p.quantityOnHand = 0 and
    p.orderMinimum = orderMinimum and
    p.vendor = vendor
```

The subtlety lies in the event constraint *doesNotExist*(), which requires that there is not a product in the information base with the same *productNo*. When this constraint is in place, the newly created product ($p$) cannot conflict with any other existing product.

The reader may wonder what would happen if the event constraint *doesNotExist*() had not been defined. The answer is that if there already exists a product $p_1$ with the same *productNo*, then one option for the designer could be to delete $p_1$ and to replace the associations involving $p_1$ by new ones involving $p$. In this way both the postcondition and the information base constraint would be satisfied after the occurrence of the event. It is likely that this set of structural events would not be an acceptable change, and therefore we must keep the event constraint.

Another external event type that raises an issue that is worth considering is *OrderReception* (see Fig. 11.6). An instance of *OrderReception* occurs when a scheduled receipt is received. The event effect is that the scheduled receipt now becomes a *ReceivedOrder* (see Fig. 11.1), and that the quantity on hand of the corresponding product is increased by the quantity received. Therefore, the specification of *effect*() for *OrderReception* is

```
context OrderReception::effect()
  post:
    --The order has been received
    order.oclIsTypeOf(ReceivedOrder) and
      order.oclAsType(ReceivedOrder).receptionDate =
        time.date and
    --The quantity on hand is increased
    order.product.quantityOnHand =
      order.product.quantityOnHand@pre + order.quantity
```

The postcondition states that the purchase order *order* must be an instance of *ReceivedOrder*. However, according to the referential constraint of Fig. 11.6, *order* was an instance of *ScheduledReceipt* before the effect of the event, and the postcondition does not state its removal. It seems that it might be acceptable to leave that purchase order as an instance of both *ScheduledReceipt* and *ReceivedOrder*. But this is not acceptable, because *ScheduledReceipt* and *ReceivedOrder* are disjoint, as indicated in Fig. 11.1. Therefore, the only way left to the designer to satisfy both the postcondition and the disjointness constraint is to remove the purchase order from *ScheduledReceipt*, which is what was intended.

## 11.4.3 The Frame Problem

It is not always easy to characterize an event effect by means of a condition. It may happen that several domain states satisfy a given condition, and that not all of them are valid characterizations of that effect.

As a simple example, consider again the event type *NewProduct*, shown in Fig. 11.4. We reproduce its postcondition below:

```
context NewProduct::effect()
  post: --There exists a new instance of Product
    p.oclIsNew() and
    p.oclIsTypeOf(Product) and
    p.productNo = productNo and
    p.quantityOnHand = 0 and
    p.orderMinimum = orderMinimum and
    p.vendor = vendor
```

This postcondition states clearly that, in the new state of the information base, there must be one new product (*p*), with the given attributes and associations. The designer/programmer has to write an implementation (a method) of the *effect* operation that ensures satisfaction of the postcondition. One possible implementation, which seems sensible, consists in just inserting a new instance into *Product*, with the corresponding attributes and associations.

But there are other implementations of *effect* that also satisfy the postcondition, but do not seem acceptable: for example, one that proceeds as before (inserting a new instance into *Product*, with the corresponding attributes and associations) but also deletes all instances of *ScheduledReceipt*. Clearly, this implementation satisfies the postcondition, but does other things that are not necessary. The change in the population of *ScheduledReceipt* is not necessary in this case.

Therefore we need a means to specify what cannot change. At first glance, it seems that such specification is easy, but it is not. The problem is known as the *frame problem*. The frame problem is the problem of stating succinctly those parts of the information base that are not affected by an event, and that therefore they must remain unchanged. It is an old problem of the postcondition approach, for which there does not exist a satisfactory solution in the general case.

In practice, the frame problem is greatly mitigated by the assumption of minimal set. It is assumed that the set of structural events is minimal in the sense that if any of them is removed from the set, then the resulting set does not achieve the desired state in the information base. In the above example, this assumption rules out the possibility of an implementation that deletes the instances of *ScheduledReceipt*.

## 11.5 Event Effects: The Procedural Approach

We know that the effect of a domain event is a set of one or more structural events. The effect may be defined by an expression (procedure or method) whose execution produces that set. This way of defining an event effect is called the procedural or the structural-events approach. This approach is in contrast to the previous one, which defines a condition that characterizes the state of the information base after the event. In the procedural approach, the new state of the information base is the previous state plus the entities or relationships inserted, and minus the entities or relationships deleted.

In the procedural approach, the effect of an event entity *EvEnt* is defined by an expression written in some language. The idea is that the execution of a procedure yields the set *StrEv* of structural events defined by *EvEnt*.

The application of *StrEv* to the previous state of the information base produces the new state.

It is assumed that the set *StrEv* is such that it leaves the information base in a new state that satisfies all the static constraints. Therefore, when defining the expression, one must take the existing constraints into account, and to ensure that the new state of the information base will satisfy all of them. This fact is seen as a disadvantage of the procedural approach with respect to the postcondition one.

On the other hand, any implementation of the expression must be such that it produces exactly the set *StrEv* (or, more precisely, the implementation, seen at the conceptual level, must behave as if it produced *StrEv*). The designers/programmers do not have the freedom that they have with the postcondition approach. Their job is to implement the structural events given in *StrEv* in terms of creation, deletion, or modification operations of the implementation database. In this respect, some authors say that the procedural approach is less declarative (or more procedural) than the postcondition one.

The procedural approach does not suffer from the frame problem. The only changes allowed are those indicated in *StrEv*. This is an important advantage of the approach. In this section we sketch the representation of this approach in logic, and then we comment on its use in UML.

## 11.5.1 Logical Representation

We shall explain the logical representation of the procedural approach by means of a simple example. Consider the domain event type *OrderReception* (see Fig. 11.6). It has only one characteristic (besides the occurrence time):

*ScheduledReceiptReceived (OrderReception, ScheduledReceipt)*

Using an ad hoc notation, a simple expression that defines the effect of an instance of *OrderReception* might be

> *Event*:
> > *OrderReception(oRec)*:
> *Characteristics*:
> > *ScheduledReceiptReceived(oRec,sr)*
> *Locals*:
> > *ProductOrdered(sr,p)*,
> > *QuantityOrdered(sr,q)*,
> > *DueDate(sr,dD)*,
> > *HasQOH(p,qoh)*

*Insertions*:
   *ReceivedOrder*(*sr*),
   *HasQOH*(*p,qoh* + *q*),
   *ReceptionDate*(*sr,CurrentDate*)
*Deletions*:
   *ScheduledReceipt*(sr),
   *DueDate*(*sr,dD*),
   *HasQOH*(*p,qoh*)

In this expression, the first lines give names to the instance of *OrderReception* (*oRec*) and to its characteristic (*sr*, the scheduled receipt just received). The *Locals* part is used to give names to the entities related to the event or to its characteristics. Thus, *p* is the product ordered, *q* is the quantity ordered, and *qoh* is the quantity on hand that we have of product *p* before the occurrence of the event.

The structural events corresponding to the effect of *oRec* are given in the *Insertions* and *Deletions* parts. There are three insertions: the entity *sr* must be inserted into *ReceivedOrder*, the relationship (*p,qoh* + *q*) must be inserted into *HasQOH*, and relationship (*sr,CurrentDate*) must be inserted into *ReceptionDate*. There are also three deletions: the entity *sr* must be removed from *ScheduledReceipt*, the relationship (*p,qoh*) must be deleted from *HasQOH*, and the relationship (*sr,dD*) must be deleted from *DueDate*.

Note that *ScheduledReceipt* and *ReceivedOrder* are disjoint (Fig. 11.1). Given that the effect of *oRec* includes the insertion of *sr* into *ReceivedOrder*, we need to specify also the deletion of *sr* from *ScheduledReceipt*.

## 11.5.2 UML Representation

In UML, the procedural approach means that we provide a method for the *effect* operations. The method is an expression whose execution yields the structural events. The method is written in some language, which may be informal, semiformal, or formal. If it is informal or semiformal, then the formal analysis of and reasoning about the resulting conceptual schemas is hindered.

UML does not prescribe or provide any particular language yet. OCL cannot be used for writing methods. In practice, most people use human languages for writing methods at the conceptual level. Graphically, the method may be shown (if needed) by means of a note attached to the corresponding *effect* operation. Figure 11.7 shows again the UML representation of *OrderReception*. The note attached to the *effect* operation describes the method in natural language.

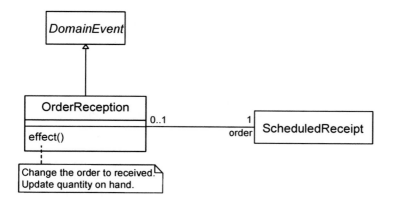

**Fig. 11.7.** Extension of Fig. 11.6, now showing the method of *effect* by means of a note

However, UML defines the abstract syntax of a set of primitive actions, which may serve as a basis for the design of particular surface languages. We summarize below the primitive actions that correspond to our structural events. For each of them, we give a brief description of their intent and their main constraints.[5]

There are three structural events related to entities and their types:

- *CreateObjectAction* is an action that creates (a new symbol that represents) an entity and classifies it as an instance of the given entity type. The new object has no attribute values and participates in no links.
- *ReclassifyObjectAction* adds a set $N$ ("new") of entity types to a given entity $e$, and removes a set $O$ ("old") of entity types from that entity. After the action is completed, $e$ is an instance of its existing entity types and the entity types $N$ given to the action; however, $E$ is not an instance of the entity types $O$ given to the action. Neither adding an entity type that duplicates an already existing one, nor removing an entity type that does not classify the input entity $e$, has any effect.
- *DestroyObjectAction* is an action that destroys an entity. This action has no other effect.

There are also three structural events related to attributes:

- *AddStructuralFeatureValueAction* adds a value to an attribute. The semantics of this action depends on the value of a boolean parameter (*isReplaceAll*). If *isReplaceAll* is true, then the existing values of the at-

---

[5] For the complete details of these actions, see the official UML documents.

tribute are removed before the new value is added, except that if the new value already exists, then it is not removed under this option. If *isReplaceAll* is false, then adding an existing value has no effect. The semantics is undefined for adding a value that violates the upper multiplicity of the attribute. Note that the semantics of this action is that of an update when *isReplaceAll* is true.

- *RemoveStructuralFeatureValueAction* removes a value from an attribute. Removing a value succeeds even when it violates the minimum multiplicity. Removing a value that does not exist has no effect.
- *ClearStructuralFeatureAction* removes all values of an attribute. This action removes all values from an attribute in a single action, with no intermediate states where only some of the existing values are present.

Associations have also three structural events:

- *CreateLinkAction* creates a new link for an association. Recreating an existing link has no effect. The semantics is undefined for creating a link that violates the upper multiplicity of one of its association ends. When the association is reified, the action creates an instance of the reification type (association class), called a *link object*. There is a similar operation, *CreateLinkObjectAction*, which can be used to create link objects.
- *DestroyLinkAction* destroys a link. Destroying a link that does not exist has no effect. When the association is reified the action destroys the link object.
- *ClearAssociationAction* is an action that destroys all links of an association in which a particular entity participates. This action is introduced to remove all links from an association in which an entity participates in a single action, with no intermediate states where only some of the existing links are present.

For example, the structural events corresponding to the effect operation of *OrderReception* (Fig. 11.7) are:

- *ReclassifyObjectAction* is applied to the scheduled receipt received *sr*. The entity *sr* is classified as an instance of *ReceivedOrder* and removed from *ScheduledReceipt*.
- *AddStructuralFeatureValueAction* is applied to *sr*. The current date is added to the *receptionDate* attribute of *sr*.
- *AddStructuralFeatureValueAction* is applied to *p*, the product corresponding to *sr*. The attribute *quantityOnHand* of *p* is updated.

As stated in the UML specification document, a surface action language would encompass both primitive actions and control mechanisms. In addition, a surface language may map higher-level constructs to actions. For example, in a composition association where the deletion of an instance implies the deletion of all its components, the above actions require a *DestroyObjectAction* for the composite and another such action for each of the component instances. A surface language could choose to define a delete-composition operation as a single unit as a shorthand for several deletions that cascade across other associations. A particular surface language could implement each semantic construct one-to-one, or it could define higher-level, composite constructs to offer the modeler both power and convenience.

## 11.6 Consistency with the Structural Schema

The set of domain event types defined in the behavioral schema must be consistent with the structural schema. This consistency comprises three properties:

- satisfiability of event constraints;
- correctness of domain event types;
- completeness of domain event types.

In what follows we describe each property in turn.

For each domain event type, there must be at least one consistent state of the information base and one set of values of the event characteristics such that the event constraints are satisfied. Otherwise, the instances of the event type could never occur.

As an example of nonsatisfiable event constraint, assume that the domain event type *OrderReception* (Fig. 11.7) also includes the constraint

```
context OrderReception::orderReceivedAlready():Boolean
  body: order.oclIsTypeOf(ReceivedOrder)
```

There is a contradiction between this constraint, the referential constraint that the order must be an instance of *ScheduledReceipt* and the disjoint constraint between *ScheduledReceipt* and *ReceivedOrder* (Fig. 11.1).

The criteria for correctness of domain event types depend on the approach used in the specification of their effect. A domain event type specified using the postcondition approach is correct if, for each pair consisting of an event instance and a consistent state of the information base that satisfy the event constraints, there exists at least one nonempty set of structural events that satisfies the postcondition and the static constraints.

An example of an incorrect specification of the postcondition of *OrderReception* is

```
context OrderReception::effect()
  post:
    order.oclIsTypeOf(ReceivedOrder) and
    order.oclAsType(ReceivedOrder).receptionDate =
      time.date and
    order.oclIsTypeOf(ScheduledReceipt)
```

Given that *ReceivedOrder* and *ScheduledReceipt* are disjoint, this postcondition cannot be satisfied.

A domain event type specified using the procedural approach is correct if, for each pair consisting of an event instance and a consistent state of the information base that satisfy the event constraints, the resulting effect consists of a nonempty set of structural events that leave the information base consistent.

A set of domain event types $\{D_1, ..., D_n\}$ is complete with respect to a structural schema if, for each structural event type $S_j$ determined by that schema, there are one or more domain event types $D_i$ such that the effect of their instances includes instances of $S_j$.

For example, the set of the three domain event types *NewProduct*, *New Requirement*, and *OrderReception* (Figs. 11.4, 11.5, and 11.6, respectively) specified in this chapter is incomplete with respect to the structural schema shown in Fig. 11.1. There are several structural event types determined by the schema without instances in the effects of the domain event types, for example, insertion into and deletion from *Vendor*, and changes (deletion and insertion) to *Supplies*.

In general, the consistency between a structural schema and a set of domain event types cannot be formally verified. It is part of the task of schema validation to ensure it.

## 11.7 Bibliographical Notes

Wand and Weber (1988) defined the necessary conditions an information system must satisfy if it has to provide a good representation of the state of a changing domain, taking events into account. The important role of events in conceptual modeling had already been recognized by the early 1980s. The concept of an event was one of the concepts defined in an influential ISO report (Griethuysen 1982). Some of the early methods in which events played an important part were

- DREAM (Riddle et al. 1978);
- Structured analysis (McMenamim and Palmer 1984);
- JSD (Jackson 1983);
- CIAM (Gustaffsson et al. 1982); and

- REMORA (Rolland and Richard 1982).

Currently, (almost) all complete conceptual modeling languages take events and their effects into account. Most object-oriented conceptual modeling languages and methods model the behavior of information systems with state transition diagrams, a topic that we shall study in Chaps. 13 and 14. A different approach (not described in this book) is the use of high-level Petri nets (Sølvberg and Kung 1985, Kung and Sølvberg 1986, Oberweis and Sander 1996). Olivé (2000b) characterized the main approaches that have been studied in conceptual modeling and reviewed some of the research works that contributed to them.

Most current languages and methods represent events as invocations of actions or operations, or as the reception of signals or messages. Among them there are Syntropy (Cook and Daniels 1994), Object-oriented SSADM (Robinson and Berrisford 1994), ROOM (Selic et al. 1994), IDEA (Ceri and Fraternali 1997), Catalysis (D'Souza and Wills 1999), IDEFIX (IEEE 1999), and Larman's method (Larman 2002).

The idea of modeling events as entities, and event types as entity types, dates back to at least 1980. Three papers appeared during that year describing the idea: (Borgida and Greenspan 1980, Bubenko 1980 and Mylopoulos et al. 1980). Among the object-oriented methods that allowed a (reasonably complete) specification of a behavioral schema based on that idea there were

- CIAM (Gustaffsson et al. 1982);
- OSA (Embley et al. 1992);
- TaxisDL (Jarke et al. 1992);
- KAOS (Dardenne et al. 1993);
- IFO$_2$ (Teisseire et al. 1994);
- Martin and Odell's method (Martin and Odell 1995).

Structural events, domain events and action request events correspond to the elementary actions, permissible actions and commands, respectively, defined by Griethuysen (1982). Engels et al. (1992) described (with different names) structural and domain events.

Many publications have been dedicated to developing logical theories in which an information base can evolve with time. In this chapter, we have only sketched the issues of updating logical information bases. The presentation was based on the simple framework presented by, among others, Kung (1984), Veloso and Furtado (1985), Lipeck (1986) and Johannesson (1995). See (Bonner and Kifer 1998) for a survey of representative logical methods and formalisms. The book by Chomicki and Saake (1998) contains several chapters dealing with the updating of logical information bases.

The frame problem was first mentioned by McCarthy and Hayes (1969). Since then, the frame problem has attracted a lot of attention in the artificial-intelligence community. Borgida et al. (1995) discussed the problem in the context of the software engineering field, and showed that there was not an adequate solution in the postcondition approach to behavior specification.

In this chapter we have described a particular semantics concerning the preconditions and postconditions of events and static constraints. Bicarregui and Ritchie (1995) and Queralt and Teniente (2006) described another kind of semantics and compared it with the one described here.

A topic that requires more research is the automatic synthesis of procedures (methods) from their postconditions and the constraints, in the line of (Qian 1993, Pastor and Olivé 1995).

Veloso and Furtado (1985) presented the basic concepts of consistency between a structural schema and domain event types. Kung (1984) analyzed the satisfiability and correctness of domain event types with respect to the structural schema. Snoeck and Dedene (1998) presented a less formal method for consistency analysis.

Parts of this chapter are based on (Olivé and Raventós 2006).

There are many good textbooks on MRP systems. The examples in this chapter were inspired by (Lunn and Neff 1992).

## 11.8 Exercises

**11.1** Assuming the structural schema shown in Fig. 11.1 define the structural events corresponding to a domain event that cancels a given scheduled receipt. Such a cancellation removes the scheduled receipt from the domain.

**11.2** Design and specify in UML a domain event type whose instances cancel scheduled receipts (see the previous exercise).

**11.3** Design in UML/OCL the structural schema and the domain event types (with their characteristics, constraints and effects) of a system that keeps tracks of the state of a Tower of Hanoi game. This game consists of three or more pegs and four or more disks of different sizes that can slide onto any peg. The goal is to move all disks from an initial peg to another one, obeying the rules: (1) Only one disk may be moved at a time; (2)

Each move takes the upper disk from one of the pegs and slides it onto another peg; (3) A disk can be moved either to an empty peg or on top of a larger disk. Assume that there are only two domain event types: Initialization and Move. The characteristics of the Initialization event are the number of pegs and the number of disks.

**11.4** Design the structural schema of a system that represents the name, sex, marital status (single, married, divorced, or widowed) and marriage relationships of the persons existing in some community. Assume that the relevant domain events are birth, marriage, divorce, and death. Define these events, with their constraints and effects (in the postcondition approach). Check that the events are consistent with the structural schema.

**11.5** Consider a software system that supports on-line playing of one-person card games such as solitaire/patience. Select a simple variant of the game that you may learn easily. Then do the following (in UML):

    1. Create the structural schema.
    2. Determine the main domain events.
    3. Define the event constraints.
    4. Define the event effects using the postcondition approach.

Use the terminology defined in Wikipedia (solitaire terminology), and assume that the cards in the stock are turned over one by one.

# 12 Action Request Events

In the preceding chapter we studied the concept of a domain event and how to specify domain event types. We now study the events that request the information system to perform an action. The nature of these events is quite distinct from that of domain events, but they are modeled in a similar way.

In the first section, we analyze the concept of an action request event. We shall see that there are several kinds of them. In Sect. 12.2, we explain how to define action request event types, their characteristics, and their constraints in UML. Sections 12.3 and 12.4 explain how to define the effect of action request events. We deal first with a particular case (query events) and then with the general case. Section 12.5 explains that events may be specialized. Section 12.6 deals with generating conditions, a topic that is to be followed up in the next chapter.

In this chapter, we give the details of the representation of the behavioral schema only in UML. The representation in logic would be similar to that described in the previous chapter.

The main examples in this chapter are a continuation of those of the previous chapter, which were about a material requirements planning (MRP) system. The new details will be introduced where they arise. For ease of reference, Fig. 12.1 reproduces a part of the structural schema of the example.

## 12.1 Actions and Action Request Events

An information system performs actions. The net effect of an action may be a change to the information base and/or the communication of some information or command to one or more recipients. An *action request event* (or, for short, request) is a request to the information system to perform an action.

In conceptual modeling, we assume that the system performs the requested actions instantly. This assumption is called the *perfect-technology*

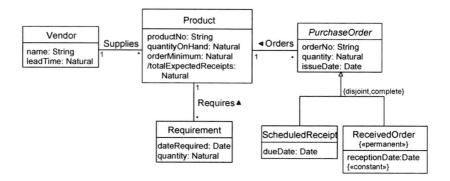

**Fig. 12.1.** Fragment of the schema for an MRP application

assumption, by which one assumes that the system has processors able to do anything and everything instantly.

Depending on how they are initiated, requests may be explicit, temporal or generated. An *explicit* request is initiated explicitly by users or by other actions. Such requests are called *external* or *induced*, respectively. An external request is initiated by a user. Most requests are external. An induced request is initiated by another action, as part of its effect.

An example of an external request is "order reschedule". Users issue this request when they want to change (delay) the due date of a scheduled receipt. When the system receives this request, it has to make the desired change and send an email that notifies the change to the corresponding vendor.

An example of an induced request is "send an email message to a vendor", whose (obvious) effect is to send an email to a vendor. This request may be initiated by, among others, the external request "order reschedule".

A *temporal* request is initiated by the passing of time. The request occurs independently of the system. In our MRP system, the schema includes the entity type *OverdueOrder*, as shown in Fig. 12.2. An overdue order is a scheduled receipt not received before or on its due date. Assume that we have a scheduled receipt *SR* due on September, 1st 2004. On the arrival of the day September 2nd 2004, if *SR* has not been received yet, then *SR* becomes an overdue order; in this case the system must perform the action of classifying *SR* as an instance of *OverdueOrder* and sending a reminder to the corresponding vendor.

An example of temporal request of a different sort occurs in the (hopefully frequent) situation in which an employee receives a letter from his employer stating that, effective from some future day, that employee will

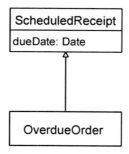

**Fig. 12.2.** Overdue orders are scheduled receipts not received before or on their due date

have a salary increase. For example, assume that on July 1st 2004 employee Maria receives a letter stating that she will have a salary increase of € 1000 effective from October 1st 2006. On the arrival of this day, the system must change Maria's salary.

A *generated* request is initiated when some generating condition $C$ is satisfied. The system detects when $C$ is satisfied and generates the corresponding request. In principle, the generating condition might take any form, but the most widely used particular forms are the following:

- *State-based.* A change in the truth value of a boolean condition over the information base in two consecutive states.
- *Event-based.* The occurrence of a domain event when the information base satisfies a given condition.

An example of a state-based generating condition is the automatic issue of scheduled receipts. The condition is

> "The quantity on hand plus the total expected receipts of a product is equal to or greater than the sum of the required quantities of that product."

When the truth value of the condition changes between two consecutive states (from true to false), the system must issue a scheduled receipt for the corresponding product.

An example of an event-based generating condition is the automatic issue of a scheduled receipt when a "new product" event occurs. In this case, the condition is

*Event* = NewProduct
*Condition* = True

When a *NewProduct* domain event occurs and the information base satisfies the *True* condition (i.e. always) the system must generate a scheduled receipt for the corresponding product.

Another example of an event-based generated request occurs in the subscription services provided by some news sources. Customers may subscribe to news about particular topics. The news is entered into the system (domain events), and for those items whose topics match the ones selected by a subscriber, the system sends him an email message. In this case the generating condition, is

$E$ = News
$C$ = One of its topics in the event instance matches one of the topics selected by a subscriber

Two important kinds of external request are domain event notifications and queries. A *domain event notification* is an external request whose only effect is a change to the information base that corresponds to exactly a single domain event. By means of domain event notifications, users tell the system that a domain event has occurred. The system must change the information base to reflect the change in the domain. For example, when a *NewProduct* domain event occurs, a user issues a domain event notification *NewProductNotification*, by which the system knows that the event has happened in the domain.

In conceptual modeling, we assume that if the domain changes at time $t$, then such an event will be communicated to the system at $t$. This assumption is called *instantaneous communication*. Therefore, we assume that the system knows about the events at the earliest possible time, without any delay between their occurrence and their communication to the system.

The basic idea of domain event notifications is that a domain event has occurred in the domain, that the event has not been produced directly by the system, and that the system must know that it has occurred. If, for some practical reason, the instantaneous-communication assumption did not hold, and there were a time lapse between the occurrence of the event and its communication to the system, the information base would not represent accurately the domain state during that time.

The ways in which domain events become known by the system may be diverse. It is not mandatory that they are communicated by users. For example, consider a system that controls the movement of the elevators in a building. The system may be connected to devices (hardware and/or software) that sense the arrival of cages at floors and send a signal to the system. In this case, domain events are communicated by automatic means, instead of manual ones.

A *query* is an external request that provides some information to the initiator of the request. Queries do not change the information base. The perfect-technology assumption also applies to queries, and therefore query events are assumed to be processed instantly. A query event occurs at some time point and it is assumed that the system answers it instantly.

### 12.1.1 Scope of this Chapter

This chapter deals only with requests that are explicit or are generated by an event-based generating condition. The reason for leaving out requests that are generated by a state-based generating condition, and temporal requests, is that their definition in most object-oriented languages (including UML) is best done with state transition diagrams, which are studied in the next two chapters.

## 12.2 Action Request Event Types

Requests can be modeled as entities, exactly as we did for domain events. Requests are instances of *action event request types* (or, for short, request types). A *request type* is a concept whose instances, at a given time, are identifiable requests that occur at that time. It is assumed that action requests are instantaneous, that the response of the system to them is also instantaneous (that is, the perfect-technology assumption), and that after the response (and before the next time tick), action requests are removed from the information base.

Request types have a name, which must be unique in a schema. The importance of choosing good names cannot be overstated. Naturally, the name should be agreed on and be well understood by the people involved. A useful rule is that the name should be a singular noun, possibly with adjectives. When this rule is followed, if *Ev* is the name of a request type, then the following sentence has meaning:

> An instance of this request type is an *Ev* event

The application of the rule to *OrderReschedule* gives

> An instance of this request type is an *OrderReschedule* event

which has a clear meaning.

In medium-to-large taxonomies, it is convenient to generalize all request and query types into common types. To this end, we define the event types *ActionRequest* and *Query*. These types are the direct or indirect supertypes

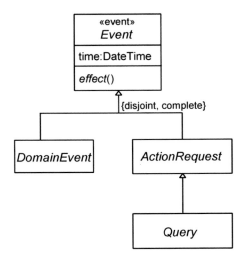

**Fig. 12.3.** Top level taxonomy of event types

of all request and query types, respectively. These types are defined as abstract (derived by union of their subtypes). Figure 12.3 shows the integration of these types with the top-level taxonomy introduced in the preceding chapter (see Fig. 11.3). The taxonomy shown in Fig. 12.3 could be predefined, and be part of all conceptual schemas.

On the other hand, we can include additional event types that define common parts of two or more request types. In the example of Fig. 12.4, we have generalized *OrderReschedule* and *OrderDetails* into *ExistingScheduledReceiptEvent*, an ad hoc request type, and we have defined in it the common *orderNo* attribute. We shall see other advantages of these types in the following sections.

Domain event notification types need not be explicitly defined by the conceptual modeler. For practical purposes, we may assume that for each domain event type there is a domain event notification type whose effect is the generation of the corresponding domain event, as we shall explain in Sect. 12.4. The convention that we will follow here is that the name of such an event type is the same as that of its domain event type with the suffix "*Notification*". For example, the domain event notification type corresponding to the domain event type *OrderReception* will be *OrderReceptionNotification*. For simplicity, we shall omit the suffix when it is clear from the context.

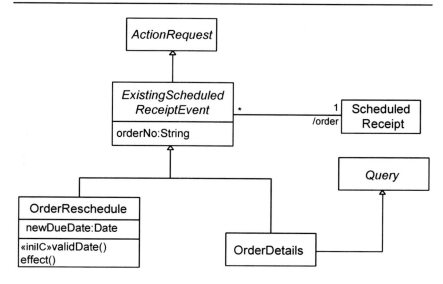

**Fig. 12.4.** Definition of *OrderReschedule* and *OrderDetails* event types as subtypes of general event types

### 12.2.1 Characteristics of Action Request Events

The characteristics of a request are the set of relationships in which it participates. There is at least one relationship between each request and a time point, representing the occurrence time of the request. We assume that the characteristics of a request are determined when the event occurs, and remain fixed.

The characteristics of a request may be derived. The value for a derived characteristic is computed from other characteristics and/or the state of the information base when the request occurs, as specified by the corresponding derivation rule.

In the example of Fig. 12.4, the attribute *orderNo* identifies a scheduled receipt. The association between *existingScheduledReceiptEvent* and *order* may be derived from *orderNo*. The derivation rule is

```
context ExistingScheduledReceiptEvent::
         order:ScheduledReceipt
  derive: ScheduledReceipt.allInstances()->
          any(orderNo = self.orderNo)
```

The characteristics of a domain event notification type are exactly the same as those of its corresponding domain event type.

## 12.2.2 Constraints of Action Request Events

A request constraint is a condition that a request must satisfy to occur. A request constraint involves the characteristics of the request and the state of the information base before the occurrence of the request. For example, a constraint of *OrderReschedule* is that the rescheduled order exists. The system must check that each request satisfies its constraints.

It is assumed that the state of the information base before the occurrence of the request satisfies all defined constraints. Therefore, a request *E* can occur (or is allowed to occur) when the domain is in a state *S* if

- the state *S* satisfies all constraints, and
- the request *E* satisfies its event constraints.

An information system checks the constraints of a request when it is received and before it has any effect in the information base or produces any answer. Requests that do not satisfy their constraints are not allowed to occur and, therefore, they must be rejected. According to the perfect-technology assumption, constraint checking is done instantaneously.

Request constraints are always creation-time constraints, because they must be evaluated when the request occurs. In UML, these constraints are best expressed by constraint operations. In this chapter we shall define constraints by operations and we will specify them in OCL.

Figure 12.4 shows the event constraint *validDate*() of *OrderReschedule*, which states that the new due date must be greater than the current due date of the rescheduled order. The formal specification is

```
context OrderReschedule::validDate():Boolean
  body: newDueDate > order.dueDate
```

On the other hand, the order must exist. This is also an event constraint. However, in this case the constraint can be expressed as a cardinality constraint. The multiplicity 1 of the *order* role requires that each instance of *ExistingScheduledReceiptEvent* must be linked to exactly one scheduled receipt. The constraint is violated if the derivation rule of *order* does not give an instance of *ScheduledReceipt*.

An event constraint defined in a supertype applies to all its direct and indirect instances. This is one of the advantages of defining event taxonomies: common constraints can be defined in a single event type. Figure 12.4 shows an example. The constraint that the order must exist is defined in the event type *ExistingScheduledReceiptEvent*. This constraint applies to the instances of both *OrderReschedule* and *OrderDetails*. Note that the constraint has been defined by a cardinality constraint, as explained above.

## 12.3 Effects of Queries

Queries are a particular kind of request. For presentation purposes, it is appropriate to study first how to specify the effects of queries, before dealing with the specification in the general case. We shall describe the specification only in the postcondition approach, in UML.

A query is an external request whose effect is to provide some information to the initiator of the request. In conceptual modeling, we define the informational content of answers, but we abstract from the details concerning the format and characteristics of output devices (screen, printer, or voice). The effect is specified by an expression whose evaluation in the information base gives the requested information. The query expression is written in some language, which depends on the conceptual modeling language used.

In UML, we can represent the answer to a query event, and the query expression, in several ways. We shall describe one of them here, which can be used as is, or as a basis for the development of alternative ways.

The answer to a query is modeled as one or more attributes and/or associations that have some predefined name. In the examples given here, we shall use names starting with *answer*. An alternative could be the use of a stereotype to indicate that an attribute or association is the answer.

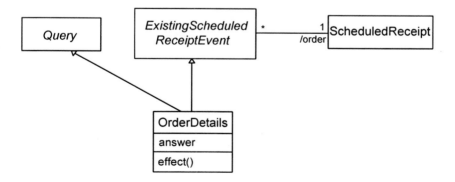

**Fig. 12.5.** Definition of query event type *OrderDetails*. The answer is given by the attribute *answer*

Plan 2003-09-04

Product ABC

| | Now | 1 | 2 | 3 | 4 | 5 | 6 | 7 |
|---|---|---|---|---|---|---|---|---|
| | | | | Day | | | | |
| Requirements | | 20 | | 20 | 20 | | 5 | 40 |
| Scheduled Receipts | | | 25 | | | | | |
| Planned Order Receipts | | | | | 25 | | | 30 |
| Projected On Hand | 25 | 5 | 30 | 10 | 15 | 15 | 10 | 0 |
| Planned Order Release | | 25 | | | 30 | | | |

**Fig. 12.6.** Example of an MRP worksheet

We need a way to define the values of the attributes and associations of the answer. To this end, we use the operation *effect()* that we have hosted in *Event* (see Fig. 12.3). This operation will have a different specification in each event type. For queries, its purpose is to specify the values of the attributes and associations of the answer. The specification of the operation can be done by means of postconditions, using OCL.

Figure 12.5 shows the representation of query type *OrderDetails*. An instance of this query requests the details of a given scheduled receipt (product number, quantity ordered, and vendor's name). The answer is given by the following attribute:

```
answer: TupleType(pNo:String,
                  quantity:natural,
                  vendorName:String)
```

The specification of the *effect* operation might be

```
context OrderDetails::effect()
  post:
    answer =
      Tuple{pNo = order.product.productNo,
            quantity = order.quantity,
            vendorName = order.product.vendor.name}
```

In the context of an MRP system, a much more challenging example of a query event is that of a *worksheet*. We need to describe the contents of a worksheet a little before we study how to define it formally. A worksheet shows, in condensed form, a plan for a specific product. Figure 12.6 shows the worksheet for a product ABC in a plan produced on 2003-09-04. We

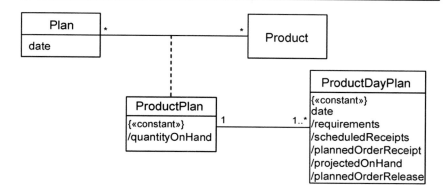

**Fig. 12.7.** Fragment of the schema of an MRP system showing the entity types, attributes and associations related to plans

assume that the planning horizon is seven days, which correspond to the seven columns in the Worksheet.

The first row shows the requirements for the product on the corresponding day, obtained from the instances of the entity type *Requirement* (see Fig. 12.1). These are the quantities required by the customers on each day.

The second row shows the scheduled receipts for the product due on the corresponding day, obtained from the instances of the entity type *ScheduledReceipt* (see Fig. 12.1). In the worksheet, we see that 25 units of product ABC are due to be received on day 2.

The third row shows the quantities that we need to receive on each day to satisfy the requirements. The planned order receipts have not yet been released to the vendor. In the worksheet we see that we need to receive 25 units on day 4, and 30 units on day 7. The minimum quantity we may receive is given by the attribute *orderMinimum* of *Product*, shown in Fig. 12.1. In this case, we assume that the minimum is 25 units.

The fourth row shows the quantities on hand that we shall have at the end of each day, assuming that the planned order receipts arrive as planned. Those quantities are defined as the "projected on hand" for the previous day, plus the scheduled receipts, minus the requirements and plus the planned order receipts.

The last row shows the dates on which the planned orders should be released to the vendors and the quantities to be ordered. It takes into account the purchasing lead time, which is the same for all products from the same vendor, and defined in the attribute *leadTime* of *Vendor* (see Fig. 12.1). In this case, we assume that the lead time is 3 days. Given this lead time, if we need 25 units on day 4, we should release an order for them on day 1.

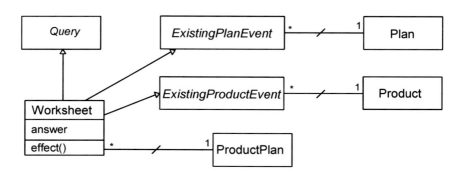

**Fig. 12.8.** Definition of the query event type *Worksheet*. The characteristics are the *date* of the plan and the *productNo* of the product. The answer is the attribute *answer*

Figure 12.7 shows a fragment of the schema corresponding to the MRP plans. In principle, there is an instance of *Plan* for each working day; that is, plans are regenerated every day. For each product existing on the day of the plan, there is a link of the association *plan–product*, reified into *ProductPlan*. The derived attribute *quantityOnHand* gives the quantity on hand of the corresponding product when the plan is created. The values of this attribute appear in the column labeled "Now" in the worksheet (Fig. 12.6).

For each instance of *ProductPlan* there are *ph* instances of *ProductDayPlan*, where *ph* is the planning horizon (we assume *ph* = *7* days in our example). Each instance of *ProductDayPlan* corresponds to a particular day. The attributes of *ProductDayPlan* correspond to the values shown in the worksheet.

We now have all we need to specify formally the contents of a worksheet. We shall consider *Worksheet* to be a query event type, as shown in Fig. 12.8. An instance of *Worksheet* is a query of the worksheet data corresponding to a given plan and product. The derived association with *ProductPlan* gives the requested product plan. Moreover, the association allows us to state that an instance of *Worksheet* must refer to an existing product plan.

The attribute *answer* gives the data needed to show the worksheet. The type of this attribute is

```
answer:
  TupleType(
    qohNow: Natural,
    periods:Set(
      TupleType(
        date:Date,
        requirements:Natural,
        scheduledReceipts:Natural,
        plannedOrderReceipt:Natural,
        onHand:Integer,
        plannedOrderRelease:Natural)))
```

The specification of the *effect* operation might be

```
context Worksheet::effect()
  post:
    answer =
      Tuple(qohNow = productPlan.quantityOnHand,
            periods = productPlan.productDayPlan ->
              collect (pdp|
                Tuple(date = pdp.date,
                  requirements = pdp.requirements,
                  scheduledReceipts = pdp.scheduledReceipts,
                  plannedOrderReceipt =
                    pdp.plannedOrderReceipt,
                  onHand = pdp.projectedOnHand,
                  plannedOrderRelease =
                    pdp.plannedOrderRelease))->asSet())
```

## 12.4 Effects of Action Request Events

An action request event is a request to an information system to perform an action. The effect of the request is the result of the execution of the action. In the postcondition approach, the effect of a request is defined by a condition that, in the general case, may involve four kinds of assertion:

- *Domain events*. One or more domain events have occurred. The action must induce these events, which, in turn, will change the information base as specified in their respective effect. The characteristics of the induced domain events are determined by the request. The induced events must satisfy their constraints; otherwise, the request will be rejected.
- *Assertions about the information base*. The action leaves the information base in a state that satisfies a given condition. Instead of stating that one or more domain events have occurred, this kind of assertion specifies a condition that the information base must satisfy after the execution of the action. The implementation will achieve this effect by means of domain events.
- *Communications*. The action has communicated some information or command to one or more recipients.

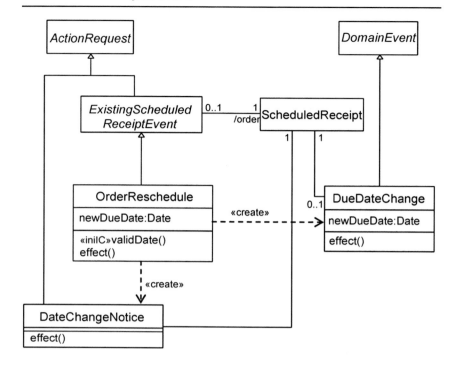

**Fig. 12.9.** Definition of the effects of *OrderReschedule* events

- *Requests.* One or more requests have occurred. The action must induce these requests, which, in turn, will execute their respective actions.

In UML, we can represent the effect of a request by means of the *effect* operation, similarly to what we did for domain events. We can assert that a domain or action request event has occurred by asserting that an instance of the corresponding event type has been created. An assertion that the information base is in some state can be defined as we did for domain events.

As an example, consider the request type *OrderReschedule*, shown in Fig. 12.9. An instance of this type requests the system to delay an order. The system must change the due date of the order, and tell the corresponding vendor that the due date has been delayed. The effect of the request may be specified with two postconditions as follows:

```
context OrderReschedule::effect()
  post Create domain event DueDateChange:
    ddc.oclIsNew() and
    ddc.oclIsTypeOf(DueDateChange) and
    ddc.scheduledReceipt = order and
    ddc.newDueDate = newDueDate
  post Inform the vendor:
    dcn.oclIsNew() and
    dcn.oclIsTypeOf(DateChangeNotice) and
    dcn.scheduledReceipt = order
```

The first postcondition requires the creation of an instance of the domain event type *DueDateChange*, whose definition is shown in Fig. 12.9 (right). The effect of a *DueDateChange* domain event is

```
context DueDateChange::effect()
  post: scheduledReceipt.dueDate = newDueDate
```

Note that in Fig. 12.9 we have shown a usage dependency between *OrderReschedule* and *DueDateChange*, with the standard stereotype «create», to indicate graphically that the effect of an *OrderReschedule* includes the generation of instances of *DueDateChange*. There is a similar dependency with *DateChangeNotice*. The use of these dependencies is optional, but they help one understand the effects of events.

We can encapsulate in an operation all the details needed to communicate a piece of information or a command to a recipient. We define an entity type (if it does not exist already) whose instances are the recipients, with an operation that performs the actions needed for the recipient to receive the information or command. In UML, the operation must be defined as a query (*isQuery = true*). Then, the assertion that some piece of information or command has been communicated to one or more recipients is the assertion that the corresponding operations have been invoked.

As an example, consider the request *DateChangeNotice*, induced by an *OrderReschedule*. The action must send an appropriate email to the vendor:

```
context DateChangeNotice::effect()
  post: let subject:String = …
        let body:String =   …
        in
          scheduledReceipt.product.vendor ^
            sendEMail(subject,body)
```

In this expression, we assume that the entity type *Vendor* hosts an operation with signature *sendEMail(subject:String,body:String)*. Note that in OCL the expression

```
scheduledReceipt.product.vendor ^ sendEMail(subject,body)
```

is true if a *sendEMail* message has been sent to the vendor with the arguments shown.

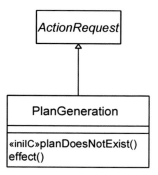

**Fig. 12.10.** An instance of *PlanGeneration* requests the generation of a plan for the next day

As another example, consider now the most important request in an MRP system: the generation of a plan. This is the event with which users request the system to generate a plan. We assume that in our system the plan is regenerated on a daily basis (there are never two plans with the same date). Every day (for example, at night), users request the system to generate the plan for the following day, with a planning horizon of seven days.

Figure 12.10 shows the event type *PlanGeneration*. Its instances have no characteristics (besides the occurrence time, defined at the *Event* level). There is only one event constraint, *planDoesNotExist*, which prevents a plan being generated twice for the same day. The formal definition is

```
context PlanGeneration::planDoesNotExist():Boolean
   body: not Plan.allInstances() ->
            exists(p:Plan|p.date = self.time.date + 1)
```

In this example, the event effect will be defined as conditions that the information base must satisfy after the execution of the action. We have to create an instance of *Plan*, a link in the association *plan–product* for each existing product at the time the plan is generated, and for each *Product-Plan* thus created, an instance of *ProductDayPlan* for each day of the seven days in the planning horizon (see Fig. 12.7). The formal definition of the event effect is

```
context PlanGeneration :: effect()
  post: --An instance of Plan is created
    pl.oclIsNew() and
    pl.oclIsTypeOf(Plan) and
    pl.date = self.time.date + 1 and
    --For each product, there is a link Plan-Product
    pl.product = Product.allInstances() and
    --An instance of ProductDayPlan is created
    --for each of the next seven days
    pl.productPlan -> forAll
        (pp: ProductPlan |
          Sequence {1..7} -> forAll(i:Integer|
            pdp.oclIsNew() and
            pdp.oclIsTypeOf(ProductDayPlan) and
            pdp.productPlan = pp and
            pdp.date = self.time.date + i))
```

Note that the attribute *quantityOnHand* of *ProductPlan* and almost all attributes of *ProductDayPlan* are derived. Their values are defined by derivation rules and, therefore, their values must not be set in the above postcondition, thus making the specifications simpler. These attributes are constant, which means that they have a creation-time derivation rule. We illustrate two of these attributes in the following.

The attribute *quantityOnHand* of *ProductPlan* gives the quantity on hand of the corresponding product when the plan is created. Its creation-time rule is very simple:

```
context ProductPlan::quantityOnHand:Natural
  derive: product.quantityOnHand
```

The attribute *projectedOnHand* of *ProductDayPlan* gives the quantity on hand that we shall have at the end of the day, assuming that the planned order receipts arrive as planned. Its creation-time rule is

```
context ProductDayPlan::projectedOnHand:Natural
  derive:
    let projectedAvailablePreviousDay:Natural =
          if date = productPlan.plan.date then
            productPlan.quantityOnHand
          else
            ProductDayPlan.allInstances() ->
              any(productPlan = self.productPlan and
                  date = self.date - 1).projectedOnHand
          endif
    in
      projectedAvailablePreviousDay +
      scheduledReceipts +
      plannedOrderReceipt +
      requirements
```

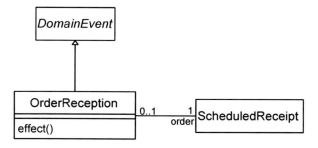

**Fig. 12.11.** Definition of the domain event type *OrderReception*

## 12.4.1 Effects of Domain Event Notifications

As we know, a domain event notification is an external action request whose only effect is a change to the information base that corresponds to exactly a single domain event. For each domain event type, there is a domain event notification type, whose only effect is generation of the corresponding domain event.

For example, consider the domain event type *OrderReception*, shown in Fig. 12.11. The event effect is that the scheduled receipt now becomes a *ReceivedOrder* (see Fig. 12.1), and that the quantity on hand of the corresponding product is increased by the quantity received. Therefore, the specification of *effect*() for *OrderReception* is

```
context OrderReception::effect()
  post: --The order is now received
    order.oclIsTypeOf(ReceivedOrder) and
    order.oclAsType(ReceivedOrder).receptionDate =
      self.time.date
  post: --The quantity on hand is increased
    order.product.quantityOnHand =
      order.product.quantityOnHand@pre +
      order.quantity
```

Corresponding to *OrderReception*, there would implicitly be a domain event notification type, named *OrderReceptionNotification*, and whose predefined effect would be the generation of an instance of *OrderReception*. Formally, the effect could be defined by

```
context OrderReceptionNotification::effect()
  post:
    oRec.oclIsNew() and
    oRec.oclIsTypeOf(OrderReception) and
    oRec.order = order
```

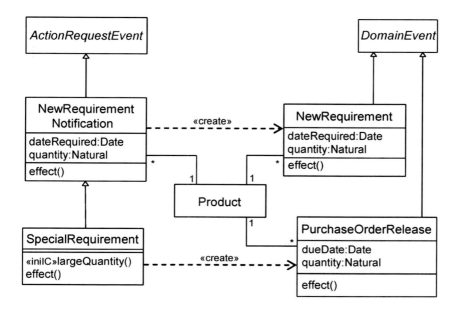

**Fig. 12.12.** *SpecialRequirement* is a specialization of *NewRequirementNotification*

## 12.5 Event Specialization

Like any other entity type, domain and action request event types may be specialized. We may use these specializations when we want to define an event type whose characteristics, constraints, and/or effect are extensions and/or specializations of another event type.

For example, assume that some instances of the domain event notification *NewRequirementNotification* are special because they require a large quantity of their product and, in this case, there is a rule that the quantity required must be ordered immediately from the corresponding vendor. This special behavior can be defined in a new event type, *SpecialRequirement*, defined as a specialization of *NewRequirementNotification*, as shown in Fig. 12.12.

Note that *SpecialRequirement* adds a new constraint called *largeQuantity*. The quantity required must be at least ten times the quantity of the product that can be ordered. The new constraint *largeQuantity* can be defined as

```
context SpecialRequirement::largeQuantity():Boolean
  body: quantity > product.orderMinimum * 10
```

The effect of a *SpecialRequirement* is the same as that of a *NewRequirementNotification*, but we want the system to create an instance of *PurchaseOrderRelease*. We define this extension as an additional postcondition of the *effect* operation:[1]

```
context SpecialRequirement::effect()
  post:
    -- Create an instance of event PurchaseOrderRelease
    pOR.oclIsNew() and
    pOR.oclIsTypeOf(PurchaseOrderRelease)and
    pOR.product = self.product and
    pOR.quantity = self.quantity and
    pOR.dueDate = self.dateRequired
```

## 12.6 Generating Conditions

Generated requests are initiated when a generating condition is satisfied. As we saw in Sect. 12.1, generating conditions may be state-based or event-based. State-based generating conditions cannot be defined with the constructs presented in this chapter. In the following chapters we shall study state transition diagrams, which allow an easy definition of those conditions.

Event-based generating conditions can be defined with the constructs studied in this chapter. Recall that the general form of these conditions is

> "When an instance of the domain event type *E* occurs and the state of the information base prior to the event occurrence satisfies the condition *C*"

where *E* can be any domain event type. Given that domain events are induced by requests, we can extend the definition of the inducing requests by checking whether or not *C* is satisfied and, if so, generating the appropriate event.

For example, assume that, in the MRP system, when an order is received (i.e. an instance of *OrderReception* occurs; see Fig. 12.11), we want to send an acknowledgment email message to the corresponding vendor. The generating condition is

---

[1] Recall that in UML, when an operation is redefined, new postconditions can be added.

"When an instance of the event type *OrderReception* occurs and the state of the information base prior occurrence of the event satisfies the condition *True*"

The checking of the generating condition (not needed in this case) and, if it is satisfied, the generation of the event can be part of the effect of *OrderReceptionNotification*. The complete effect is now

```
context OrderReceptionNotification::effect()
  post:
    oRec.oclIsNew() and
    oRec.oclIsTypeOf(OrderReception) and
    oRec.order = order
  post  Sending an acknowledgement message:
    let subject:String = …
    let body:String =   … in
      order.product.vendor ^ sendEMail(subject,body)
```

## 12.7 Bibliographical Notes

Many of the bibliographical notes given in Chap. 11 are applicable here, and we shall not repeat them.

Wieringa (2003, Chap. 3) gave a detailed description and classification of what we have called domain and action request events.

## 12.8 Exercises

**12.1** Consider a Web-based online shopping system that is familiar to you. Give a list of five or more requests (seen by the customers) that the system deals with. For each of them, give a short description (in natural language) of its effect. Classify each request in terms of its kind (general action request, or query) and source (external, generated, or temporal).

**12.2** In the context of an MRP system, define the characteristics, constraints, and effect of the domain event type *VendorChange* and the request type *VendorChangeRequest*. An instance of *VendorChange* corresponds to the change of the vendor of a product. Its characteristics are the product whose vendor changes and the new vendor of the product, which is an existing vendor. An instance of *VendorChangeRequest* requests the system to change the vendor of a product. Its characteristics are also the product whose vendor changes (identified by its *productNo*) and the new vendor of the product (identified by its *name*). The effect of an instance of *VendorChangeRequest* is to induce the corresponding instance of *Vendor-*

*Change*. Note that *VendorChangeRequest* is not the domain event notification of *VendorChange*, because its characteristics are the identifiers of the product and vendor, instead of the associations with the changed product and the new vendor.

**12.3** One of the main outputs of an MRP system is a listing of the planned order releases. The listing includes all products for which there is a planned order release on the first day of the current plan. The listing is used by the planner, who has to release purchase orders to the corresponding vendors. Assume that the listing is the answer to a query *PlannedOrderReleasesListing*. This answer gives the set of product numbers that must be ordered and the quantity that must be ordered, according to the current plan (i.e. the plan with a date equal to the current day). In the example of Fig. 12.6, if there were only one product, the answer would be the set {<ABC,25>}. Define the effect of this query.

**12.4** Another main output of an MRP system is reschedule notices, used to suggest adjustments (delays) to the due date of scheduled receipts. For an example, see Fig. 12.6, where the product ABC is shown with a scheduled receipt due on day 2. However, it can be seen that the scheduled receipt is not needed at that time, and that we could delay it to day 3. Assume that there exists a query *SuggestedReschedules*. In order to keep the exercise simple, assume that the answer gives only the set of product numbers that have scheduled receipts that can be rescheduled, according to the current plan (i.e. the plan with a date equal to the current day). In the example of Fig. 12.6, if there were only one product, the answer would be the set {ABC}. Define the effect of this query.

**12.5** Consider the Olympic medal winner database compiled by the International Olympic Committee (http://www.olympic.org/uk/index_uk.asp). The database can be searched by filling in the form given on the Web page (http://www.olympic.org/uk/athletes/results/search_r_uk.asp).

1. Design the structural schema corresponding to the domain represented in this database. Define all relevant integrity constraints.
2. Design the search form as a query. Define in OCL the constraints and the effect of this query. Check that the query can be instantiated as indicated in the three examples shown on the Web page. Check also that the answer that would be returned by each example query matches the one given on the website.

# 13 State Transition Diagrams

In the two preceding chapters, we studied how to define the effect of events by means of *effect*() operations. An alternative, or complementary, way is the use of state transition diagrams. This is the main topic of this chapter. We start in Sect. 13.1 with a brief review of finite state machines and their associated state transition diagrams. We then explain, in Sect. 13.2, how entities can be modeled as state machines, and that in this case state transition diagrams are part of the behavioral schema. Sections 13.3 to 13.5 describe how state transition diagrams can be defined in UML.

Statecharts are an extension of state transition diagrams, introducing nested states, orthogonality, and broadcasting. Statecharts can be defined in UML. We shall study statecharts in the next chapter.

Our main examples in this chapter (and the next one) will be based on the popular EU-Rent case study. EU-Rent is a fictitious car rental company with branches in several countries which provides typical car rental services. The details of the examples will be introduced where they arise. A complete description of the case study can be found in the references given in the bibliographical notes at the end of this chapter.

## 13.1 Finite State Machines

A *finite state machine* (or, for short, state machine) is a machine that at any time is in one and only one of a finite number of states. In any state, the machine may receive inputs. When the machine receives an input it performs a transition from its current state (called the source state) to a target state. The target state depends on the source state and the input received. The source state and the target state in a transition may be the same, and then the transition is called a self-transition. Transitions are assumed to be instantaneous.

State machines are abstract models of real-world systems. The concrete meaning of "state" and "input" depends on the system being modeled.

There are several types of state machine. In the following we review only three of them: finite automata, Moore machines, and Mealy machines.

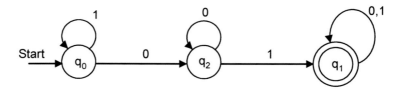

Fig. 13.1. The state transition diagram of a finite automaton

### 13.1.1 Finite Automata

The simplest state machines are the finite automata. A *finite automaton* consists of a finite set of states and a set of transitions from state to state that occur on input of symbols chosen from a given alphabet. For each input symbol, there is exactly one transition out of each state (possibly back to that state itself). One state is the initial state, in which the automaton starts. Some states may be designated as final states.

A directed graph, called a *state transition diagram* (or, for short, transition diagram), is associated with a finite automaton as follows. The vertices of the graph correspond to the states of the finite automaton. If there is a transition from state $q$ to state $p$ on input $a$, then there is an arc labeled $a$ from state $q$ to state $p$ in the transition diagram.

Figure 13.1 shows a transition diagram of a finite automaton. The initial state is $q_0$, indicated by the arrow labeled *Start*. For each state there are two outgoing transitions, labeled 0 and 1. The final state is $q_1$, shown by the double circle. Once a final state is reached, the finite automaton remains in it forever.

### 13.1.2 Moore and Mealy Machines

The finite automata described above do not produce any output. They change their state in response to the input symbol received, but do nothing else. The Moore and Mealy machines are extensions to finite automata that produce an output.

A Moore machine extends a finite automaton by associating an output with each state. Each state has exactly one output. In a state transition diagram, the outputs are shown as labels of the corresponding state. Every time the machine reaches a state, it produces the output associated with that state.

A Mealy machine is like a Moore machine except that the output is associated not with a state, but with a transition. Thus, the output produced depends on the source state and input symbol received.

It can be shown that for each Moore machine there exists a Mealy machine that produces the same outputs for all inputs. Conversely, it can be shown that for each Mealy machine there exists a Moore machine that produces the same outputs for all inputs. The Moore and Mealy machines are said to be equivalent.

## 13.2 Entities as State Machines

In general, entities can be modeled as state machines. Each entity modeled in this way is a different machine, but the associated transition diagram is the same for all instances of the same entity type. Transition diagrams are part of the behavioral schema.

For example, in the EU-Rent case study, cars can be modeled as machines. Each car will have its own machine, but the transition diagram will be common to all instances of the entity type *Car*. Likewise, car rentals can be modeled as machines too. Each car rental will have its own machine, but the transition diagram will be common to all instances of the entity type *Rental*.

In principle, not all entities need to be modeled as machines. Transition diagrams are an effective mechanism for defining the behavior of the instances of some entity types. However, they are not intended to be the best mechanism in all cases. This is one reason why some conceptual modeling languages offer several ways to model behavior. In the present example, transition diagrams are well suited to modeling the behavior of cars and rentals, but it is doubtful that they are the best way for modeling the behavior of all entity types.

The states of the machine corresponding to an entity *e* are the situations in which *e* may be during its existence. The set of states is described in the corresponding transition diagram. At any time, each entity is in one and only one state.

In our example, we could define the following set of states of a car:

- *Available*. A car is available when it is physically located in the parking area of the branch that owns it.
- *InUse*. A car is in this state when it has been picked up by a customer and has not been returned yet.

- *InTransfer*. The company may request a transfer of a car from one branch, where it is not being used, to another branch that needs it. A car is in transfer while it is being transferred between two branches.
- *InChecking&Preparation*. A car is in this state when it is being checked for damage or is being serviced for maintenance or repair.

For some entity types, one can define situations according to two or more different perspectives, which give rise to two or more sets of states. A typical example is *Person*. One perspective may be the marital status, and then the set of states of a person is *single, married, divorced* and *widowed*. However, when the perspective is the period of life, then the set of states may be *child, young* and *adult*. We shall study how to define two or more sets of states for a given entity type later on in this chapter.

In some perspectives, an entity could be in an unlimited number of states. For example, assume that cars have an attribute *mileage*, which gives the distance traveled by a car. If each possible value of this attribute is a different state of the car, then the number of states may be very large or even infinite. In practice, we model only those states that help in defining event constraints or effects. In the EU-Rent case, cars with a mileage greater than 40,000 km must be sold. From the point of view of saleability, we may then distinguish two states of cars: *Not for sale* (mileage ≤ 40,000 km) and *To be sold* (mileage > 40,000 km).

The set of states of a car rental could be:

- *Pending*. A rental is pending from the time it has been created until it has a car allocated to it or it is canceled.
- *Allocated*. The rental has a car allocated to it.
- *Opened*. A rental is opened when the allocated car has been picked up and it has yet not been returned.
- *Closed*. A rental is closed when the rented car has been returned by the customer.
- *Canceled*. A rental is canceled if it has been explicitly canceled by the customer or the car has not been picked up by the due time.

In the most usual (and interesting) case, a machine has two or more states. However, a machine could have only one state. This is indeed a degenerate case, but acceptable.

States have a name, which must be unique to the state machine. A practical rule is that the name $N$ of a state of an entity type $E$ should be such that one of the following sentences is meaningful:

> The $E$ is $N$
> The $E$ is in the state of $N$

According to this rule, *Available* would be a good state name of *Car*, because the sentence

> The car is *Available*

has a clear meaning.

Conceptually, the state of an entity could be modeled by means of an attribute. The attribute would be total and single-valued. The instances of the attribute type would be the set of possible states. For example, the states of a car could be represented by an attribute *availability*. The possible values of this attribute are the states defined above (*Available*, *InUse*, etc.). Each car would have a single value for this attribute.

The main inputs of a state machine associated with an entity *e* are the domain events that change the state of the entity and/or the relationships (attributes or associations in UML) in which *e* participates. In general, however, the inputs of a state machine may be any domain or request event.

In the case study, the inputs to the state machine of a car are the following domain events:

- *Purchase*. The company receives a new car.
- *Pick-Up*. The car is picked up by the customer who reserved it.
- *Return*. The customer returns the car to the company.
- *Transfer*. The car starts to be transferred to another branch.
- *Reception*. A transferred car is received by its destination branch.
- *TakenForService*. The car is sent to a garage or service depot where it will be serviced.
- *CarReady*. The car becomes available after being checked and prepared for use.
- *Sale*. The car is sold.

In the state machine of a rental, the inputs are domain and temporal request events. The domain events are:

- *Reservation*. A customer reserves a car of a specific model for a particular date interval.
- *Allocation*. A car is allocated to the rental.
- *Pick-Up*. The car is picked up by the customer who reserved it.
- *Extension*. The customer extends the time period of the rental.
- *Return*. The customer returns the car to the company.
- *Cancellation*. The customer cancels the rental.

The temporal request events are:

- *End of the scheduled pickup day.* As its name implies, this event happens at the end of the scheduled pickup day of the rental.
- *Ninety minutes after the scheduled pickup time.* Similarly, this event happens 90 minutes after the scheduled pickup time of the rental.

When, as is often the case, the same event changes the relationships of several entities, the event may be input to the finite state machines of all of them. In the above examples, the domain event *Pick-Up* is input to the state machines of a car and of its current rental.

A transition involves a source state $s$, an event $d$, and a target state $t$. The event $d$ is called the *trigger* of the transition. When the state machine is in state $s$ and it receives an event $d$ for which there is a transition to state $t$, it performs that transition to $t$. We say that $d$ *fires* the transition. If the machine receives an event which is not the trigger of any transition, then the machine is unaffected by the event.

In the case study, an example of a transition of a car is:

- Source state: *Available*.
- Trigger: domain event *Pick-Up*.
- Target state: *InUse*.

The meaning is that when a car is in the state *Available* and the domain event *Pick-Up* of that car occurs, the new state of the car is *InUse*.

However, most conceptual modeling languages extend the concept of transition by including guards. A *guard* is a condition over the information base and/or the parameters of the trigger. Guards are defined by boolean expressions. In this case, a transition involves a source state $s$, a guard $g$, an event $d$, and a target state $t$. There may be two or more transitions with the same source state and event, but with different guards. When the state machine is in state $s$ and it receives an event $d$ for which there is a transition to state $t$ and the guard $g$ is true, that transition is *enabled*. If there is only one enabled transition, then it is fired. If there are several enabled transitions only one of them is fired. In principle, the choice of which transition is fired is nondeterministic. If an event does not enable any transition, then the machine is unaffected by the event.

In the case study, an example of a transition of a car with a guard is:

- Source state: *Available*.
- Guard: the car is not assigned to a rental.
- Trigger: domain event *Transfer*.
- Target state: *InTransfer*.

The meaning is that when a car is in the state *Available* and the domain event *Transfer* occurs, if the car is not assigned then the new state of the car is *InTransfer*.

When a transition fires, the state of the machine changes to the target state. Additionally, the machine may perform some action. In general, one can distinguish four kinds of action:

- Transition. The action is performed when the transition is fired.
- State entry. The action is performed when the machine enters a state.
- State exit. The action is performed when the machine exits a state.
- In state. The action is performed while the machine is in a state.

A conceptual modeling language may allow all of the above kinds of actions to be defined, or only a subset of them. When two or more kinds are possible, the semantics of the language specifies the order in which these actions are performed.

## 13.2.1 Entity Life Cycle

The *life cycle* of an entity *e* at a time point *t* is the sequence of states in which *e* has been since its creation until *t*. For example, the life cycle of a car rental *cr* at *t* could be

> *Pending, Allocated, Opened.*

A life cycle is *complete* if its last state is a final state. The above life cycle is not complete, because *Opened* is not a final state.

Transition diagrams define two kinds of constraint on entity life cycles:

- The set of allowed states. This is a static constraint.
- The set of legal sequences of these states. This is a transition constraint because it involves two or more states of the information base.

For example, the transition diagram of *Rental* defines that the above life cycle is valid, but

> *Pending, Opened, Allocated*

is not valid because there does not exist a transition from *Pending* to *Opened*.

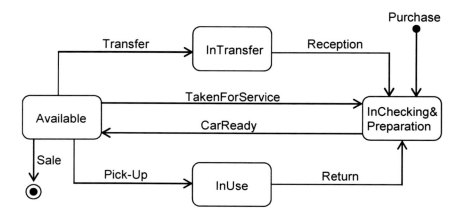

**Fig. 13.2.** State transition diagram of *Car*

## 13.3 State Transition Diagrams in UML

UML includes many features for specifying state machines, but only a subset of them is needed for the behavioral conceptual modeling of most systems. In particular, UML defines two kinds of state machine: behavioral and protocol state machines. Both could be used for conceptual modeling. However, in this chapter we shall use only protocol state machines, because they are simpler than the behavioral ones, and because they can be integrated more easily with the behavioral schemas that we have studied in previous chapters.

A *protocol state machine* is associated with an entity type, and it is described by a transition diagram. The actions performed by a protocol state machine are associated with transitions. Therefore, in this respect it is a Mealy machine. These machines have no actions to be performed when they enter or exit a state, or while they are in a state.

An entity type may have several protocol state machines. Each protocol state machine has a unique name. By default, the name of the protocol state machine is that of its associated entity type.

A transition diagram consists of states and transitions. Figures 13.2 and 13.3 show the transition diagrams of *Car* and *Rental*, respectively, in our case study. Graphically, states are shown as rectangles with rounded corners, with the state name shown inside the rectangle.

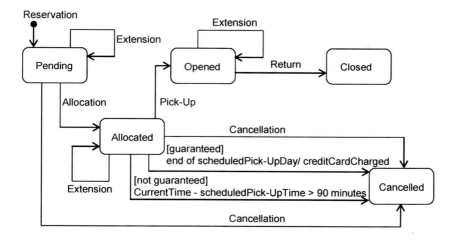

**Fig. 13.3.** State transition diagram of *Rental*

Transitions are shown by solid arrows from the source state to the target state, labeled with a transition string. For protocol state machines, the general form of a transition string is:

[guard] event/postcondition

where both the guard and the postcondition are boolean expressions. Each transition must have an event, and may or may not have a guard and a postcondition. The semantics of a transition depends on the kind of event, as explained below.

UML distinguishes four kinds of event that can trigger transitions:

- *Call* event. An occurrence of this kind of event happens when there is an invocation of an operation defined in the entity type which the transition diagram is associated with.
- *Change* event. An occurrence of this kind of event occurs when the value of a boolean condition changes from *false* to *true*.
- *Time* event. Events of this kind occur when a time expression is satisfied. The expression may refer to an absolute time or to the passage of a given amount of time after an entity enters a state.
- *Signal* event. Events of this kind occur when an entity receives a signal. We shall not use these events in this chapter.

For call events, the semantics of a transition involves the transition string and the preconditions and postconditions of the corresponding op-

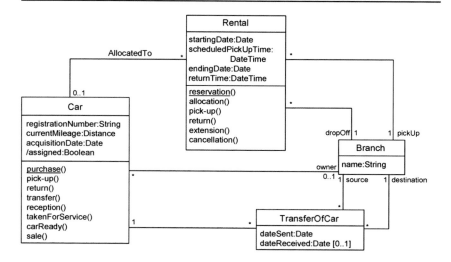

**Fig. 13.4.** Fragment of the schema of the EU-Rent case study

eration. Assume an operation *Op* with a precondition *Pre_Op* and post-condition *Post_Op*. The semantics of a transition with a string

[guard] event / postcondition

between a source *s* and a target *t* state is the following. When

- an entity *e* is in the source state *s*, and
- there is an invocation of the operation *Op* to the entity *e* (call event), and
- the precondition *Pre_Op* is satisfied, and
- the guard is satisfied,

then

- the entity *e* changes to the target state *t*, and
- the information base satisfies the postcondition *Post_Op*, and
- the information base also satisfies the postcondition specified in the transition string.

In addition, it is assumed that the static integrity constraints are satisfied both before and after the invocation of the operation.

All the events shown in the example in Fig. 13.2 are call events. Therefore, the entity type *Car* will include one operation for each of them. In general, if there is an operation that is not referred to by any transition of a

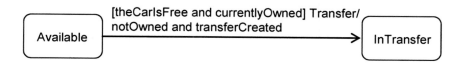

**Fig. 13.5.** Alternative specification of the *Transfer* transition

protocol state machine, then the operation can be called in any state of the protocol state machine, and does not change the current state.

Figure 13.4 shows a fragment of a structural schema, including the call event operations in *Car*. The preconditions and postconditions of these operations must be specified in some way. Consider, for example, the operation *Transfer*. Its specification in OCL might be

```
context Car::transfer(transferredTo:Branch)
  pre theCarIsFree: not assigned
  pre currentlyOwned: owner->notEmpty()
  post notOwned: owner->isEmpty()
  post transferCreated:
    t.oclIsNew() and
    t.oclIsTypeOf(TransferOfCar) and
    t.dateSent = CurrentDate and
    t.car = self and
    t.source = self.owner@pre and
    t.destination = transferredTo
```

A *Transfer* event can occur only when the car is in the state *Available*, it is not assigned to any rental, and it is owned by some branch. The effect of the event is that the car is now in the state *InTransfer*, that it is not owned by any branch, and that an instance of the entity type *TransferOfCar* has been created, with the corresponding values for its attributes and links.

Note that, in the example of the call event *Transfer*, the transition has neither a guard nor a postcondition, but the operation has a precondition and a postcondition. An alternative could have been the transition shown in Fig. 13.5 with a guard and a postcondition, and then the specification of the operation would just be

```
context Car::transfer(transferredTo:Branch)
  post: True
```

In Fig. 13.5 we have shown only the names of the guard and of the postcondition. The corresponding specification would need to be given elsewhere.

As another example, consider the call event *Reception*. The specification of its operation in OCL might be:

```
context Car::reception(receivingBranch:Branch)
  post theBranchOwnsTheCar: owner = receivingBranch
  post transferCompleted:
    let pendingTransfer:TransferOfCar = transferOfCar
        ->select(dateReceived@pre->isEmpty())->any(true)
    in pendingTransfer.dateReceived = CurrentDate
```

A *Reception* event can occur only when the car is in the state *InTransfer*. The effect of the event is that the car is now in the state *InChecking&Preparation*, that it is owned by the receiving branch, and that the pending transfer is now complete.

When an event appears in only one transition (as happens in all events shown in Fig. 13.2), it is practical to define only the preconditions and postcondition of the corresponding operation, thus making unnecessary the use of the guard and the postcondition of the transition.

When the same event appears in two or more transitions, it is practical to define the common part of the guard in the precondition of the operation, and the common part of the postconditions in the operation postcondition. In Fig. 13.3, the event *Extension* may trigger three transitions, but its precondition and effect are the same in the three cases and therefore they are defined in the corresponding operation:

```
context Rental::extension(newEndDate:Date)
  post: endingDate = newEndDate
```

## 13.3.1 Transitions Triggered by Change and Time Events

When the event that triggers a transition

[guard] event/postcondition

is a change or time event, the semantics of the transition is simpler, because it does not involve any operation. The semantics is the following. When

- an entity *e* is in the source state, and
- the event occurs, and
- the guard is satisfied,

then

- the entity *e* changes to the target state, and
- the information base satisfies the postcondition.

In addition, it is assumed that the static integrity constraints are satisfied both before and after the invocation of the operation.

In the Fig. 13.3, we have an example of a time event in the transition *[guaranteed] end of scheduledPick-UpDay/creditCardCharged*

The meaning is that if a rental has been guaranteed by credit card and the car has not been picked up by the end of the scheduled pickup day, one day's rental is charged to the credit card and the rental is canceled.

Transitions triggered by change and time events are important in many conceptual modeling languages because they are the only means by which we can define some functions of the information system. When we must specify that something needs to be done when a condition over the information base becomes true, or when a time expression is satisfied, then we need to use transition diagrams, and to define the corresponding transitions triggered by a change or time event.

This is illustrated in the above example. If one of the functions of the information system is to do something when "a car has not been picked up by the end of the scheduled pickup day", we must attach this condition to a transition, in some transition diagram. The postcondition of the transition has to specify the effect of the time event.

### 13.3.2 Unexpected-Event Reception

In UML, the interpretation of the reception of an event in an unexpected situation (current state and guard) is a semantic variation point: the event can be ignored, rejected, or deferred, an exception can be raised, or the application can stop on an error.

### 13.3.3 Initial State

We know that, at any time, an entity is in one and only one state. This implies that when an entity *e* begins to be an instance of the corresponding entity type, *e* must be in some state. The question, then, is how do we specify the first or initial state of *e*?

In UML the initial state is specified by a special kind of state, called – not surprisingly – the initial state. Graphically, an initial state is shown as a small filled black circle with an outgoing transition. The meaning is that when an entity is created it is placed in the initial state, and its outgoing transition is automatically fired, moving the entity to another state. Figure 13.2 shows an example. When a car is created, it is in the state *InChecking&Preparation*. Similarly, Figure 13.3 shows that when a rental is created, it is in the state *Pending*.

Note that the initial state does not behave like an ordinary state, because entities do not remain in it during a period of time. Instead, once they enter that state, its outgoing transition is immediately fired, and thus the state is left.

The initial state has an outgoing transition. The implicit trigger of this transition is the invocation of a creation operation. In the example of Fig. 13.2, the creation operation is *Purchase*. This is a class operation because it creates new instances of *Car*. Its specification might be

```
context
  Car::purchase(carRegistrationNumber:String,
                initialMileage:Distance, buyer:Branch)
  post:
    c.oclIsNew() and
    c.oclIsTypeOf(Car) and
    c.registrationNumber = carRegistrationNumber and
    c.currentMileage = initialMileage and
    c.acquisitionDate = CurrentDate and
    c.owner = buyer
```

The transition diagrams of constant entity types do not have initial states, because, by definition, instances of these types are never created.

### 13.3.4 Final State

When an entity ceases to be an instance of an entity type that has a transition diagram, it then, of course, ceases to be in any of its states. We can say that there is a transition from the last state which the instance was in to "nowhere". Given that in UML the transitions involve two states, we need a state that means "nowhere". This special state is called the final state. Graphically, it is shown as a circle surrounding a small solid filled circle (see Fig. 13.2).

The transitions to the final state define the valid states in which an entity can cease to exist. In the example of Fig. 13.2, a car can cease to exist only if it is in the state *Available*. The effect of the event *Sale* is that the car ceases to exist in the company.

The transition diagrams of permanent entity types do not have final states, because, by definition, instances of these types never cease to exist. In the present example, *Rental* is a permanent entity type. The state transition diagram of Fig. 13.3 does not have final states.

### 13.3.5 Junction

A *junction* is a pseudostate with at least one incoming and one outgoing transition. In general, the incoming transitions have a trigger, and both the

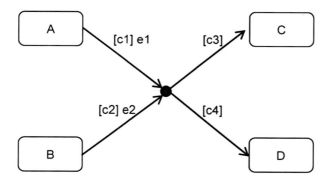

**Fig. 13.6.** Example of use of a junction pseudostate

incoming and the outgoing transitions have a guard. A junction is represented by a small black circle.

A junction provides a means to simplify two or more transitions by factoring out their common parts. For example, a junction can be used to converge multiple incoming transitions into a single outgoing transition representing a shared transition path. Conversely, a junction can be used to split an incoming transition into multiple outgoing transition segments with different guard conditions.

Figure 13.6 shows the use of a junction to simplify four transitions:

- The transition from $A$ to $C$ triggered by $e1$ and guarded by the condition [$c1$ and $c3$].
- The transition from $A$ to $D$ triggered by e1 and guarded by the condition [$c1$ and $c4$].
- The transition from $B$ to $C$ triggered by $e2$ and guarded by the condition [$c2$ and $c3$].
- The transition from $B$ to $D$ triggered by $e2$ and guarded by the condition [$c2$ and $c4$].

In this example the common part is that the target state is $C$ or $D$ depending on whether condition $c3$ or $c4$ is true.

When an incoming transition fires, an outgoing transition whose guard evaluates to true also fires immediately. An incoming transition may fire only if there is an outgoing transition that also fires. If multiple outgoing transitions have guards that are true, an arbitrary one is selected. A predefined guard denoted "else" may be defined for at most one outgoing transition. This transition fires if all the guards labeling the other transitions evaluate to false.

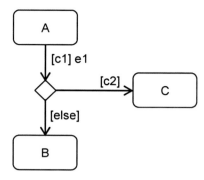

**Fig. 13.7.** Example of use of a choice pseudostate

Junctions are considered as static conditional branches because the guards of both the incoming and outgoing transitions are evaluated before the transitions fire. In the example of Fig. 13.6, the conditions $c3$ and $c4$ are evaluated at the same time as $c1$ and $c2$, that is, before the firing of the transitions.

## 13.3.6 Choice

A *choice* is a pseudostate similar to a junction, but the guards of the outgoing transitions are evaluated once the incoming transitions have produced their effect. Choices are considered as dynamic conditional branches because the target state is not known until the operations associated with the incoming transitions have been completed. A choice pseudostate is shown by a diamond-shaped symbol.

Another important difference from junctions is that the guard of at least one outgoing transition must evaluate to true. If more than one of the guards evaluates to true, an arbitrary one is selected. If none of the guards evaluates to true, then the state machine is considered ill-formed: we may avoid this by defining one outgoing transition with the predefined "else" guard.

Figure 13.7 shows an example. The target state of the transition leaving from $A$ is not determined until the operation corresponding to the trigger $e1$ has been completed. Then, if the guard $c2$ evaluates to true, the target state is $C$; otherwise, it is $B$.

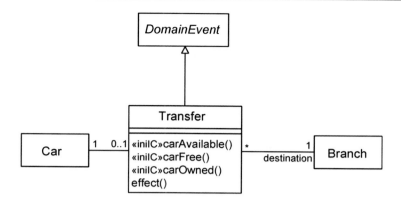

**Fig. 13.8.** Definition of the domain event *Transfer*

## 13.4 From Domain and Action Request Events to Call Events

None of the four kinds of UML event correspond directly to the domain
and action request events that we studied in the two preceding chapters.
However, we can establish a clear mapping between these events and call
events. The mapping is through the invocation of operations. If an event
*Event* maps to a call event *CallEvent* that appears in the transition diagram
of an entity type *E*, then the effect of *Event* includes an invocation of the
operation corresponding to *CallEvent* to the appropriate instance of *E*.

The idea is to define events as we did in the preceding chapters, but to
change the definition of an effect. Now an effect is an invocation of the
operations of the entity types associated with the state machines that must
receive an event. The global effect of the event will be the union of the effects in the state machines invoked. The effect in each state machine is as
described before.

Consider, for example, the *Transfer* domain event, shown in Fig. 13.8.
Its characteristics are the car being transferred and the destination branch.
The event constraints are that the car must be available, free, and currently
owned by a branch. If the effect of the event were defined as we described
in the previous chapters, its specification would be

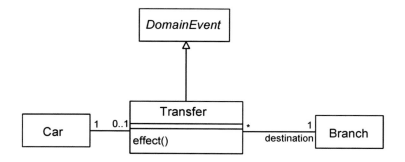

**Fig. 13.9.** Revised definition of the domain event *Transfer*

```
context Transfer::effect()
  post notOwned: car.owner->isEmpty()
  post transferCreated:
    t.oclIsNew() and
    t.oclIsTypeOf(TransferOfCar) and
    t.dateSent = CurrentDate and
    t.car = self.car and
    t.source = self.car.owner@pre and
    t.destination = self.destination and
    t.car.state = CarState::InTransfer
```

where we have assumed that cars have a new attribute, *state*, which gives the current state of each car (*InTransfer* after a transfer event).

When cars are modeled by state machines, parts of the constraints and effect of an event move to the state transition diagram and the operations. A revised definition of *Transfer* is shown in Fig. 13.9. The constraints that the car must available, free, and currently owned by a branch have been moved from Fig. 13.8 to the state machine of *Car*. Now, the postcondition of the *effect()* operation is just the invocation of the corresponding operation in *Car*:

```
context Transfer::effect()
  post: car^transfer(destination)
```

The parameters of the operations invoked are the characteristics of the event that are relevant to the receiving state machine. In general, however, it may be better to define only one parameter in these operations: the event that has happened. In this way, the invocations are simple, uniform and flexible. For these reasons, from now on we shall define the call event operations with a single parameter. Thus, the specification of the above operation would be:

```
context Transfer::effect()
  post: car^transfer(self)
```

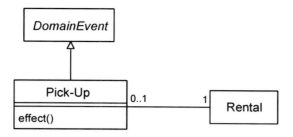

**Fig. 13.10.** Definition of the domain event *Pick-Up*

and the signature and specification of the operation in *Car* would now be

```
context Car::transfer(event:Transfer)
  pre theCarIsFree: not assigned
  pre currentlyOwned: owner->notEmpty()
  post notOwned: owner->isEmpty()
  post transferCreated:
    t.oclIsNew() and
    t.oclIsTypeOf(TransferOfCar) and
    t.dateSent = event.time.date and
    t.car = self and
    t.source = self.owner@pre and
    t.destination = event.destination
```

When the same event is input to two or more state machines, the effect of the event includes an invocation of each of them. We have an example in the event *Pick-Up* (see Fig. 13.10), which is input to both the rental given as characteristic and the allocated car:

```
context Pick-Up::effect()
  post: rental^pick-Up(self) and rental.car^pick-Up(self)
```

## 13.4.1 Localization of Event Constraints and Effects

The mapping between domain and call events described above allows the constraints and the effect of an event to be defined in three different places:

- the event type;
- the preconditions and postconditions of the call event operations;
- the guards and postconditions of the state transition diagrams.

The complete set of constraints that an event must satisfy is the union of the set of constraints defined in each of these three places. Similarly, the global effect of an event is the union of the effects defined in these three

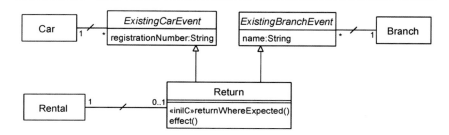

**Fig. 13.11.** Definition of the action request event *Return* in the event-type-based style

places. It is not difficult to obtain automatically the complete set of constraints and the whole effect of an event. A supporting tool for conceptual modeling should be able to obtain it when requested.

The mapping allows the behavioral schema to be defined in three different styles:

- *Event-type-centered.* All constraints are defined in the event type, except those that define the valid state transitions (which are defined in the transition diagrams). The effect of an event is defined in the *effect*() operation of the event type, except for the change of state (which is defined in the transition diagrams).

- *Operation-centered.* Now, the purpose of the *effect*() operation of the event type is just to invoke the call event operations of the affected entities. The only constraints defined in the event type are those that check the existence of these entities. The other constraints are defined in the operations, except those that define the valid state transitions (which are defined in the transition diagrams). The effects of events are defined in the operations invoked, except for the change of state (which is defined in the transition diagrams).

- *Transition-centered.* As before, the only constraints defined in the event type are those that check the existence of the entities affected by an event, and the purpose of the *effect*() operation of the event type is to invoke the corresponding operations of the affected entities. The operations invoked do nothing, except to provide a link between event types and transition diagrams. The other constraints are defined in the transitions included in the transition diagrams. The effects of events are defined in the transitions also.

The above are pure styles. The definition of the constraints and effect of a given event does not need to follow any one of them strictly. A hybrid style is also possible. For example, it may be sensible to localize most of the constraints and most of the effect in the preconditions and postconditions of the operations invoked. At the event type level, we may define the constraints that ensure that the affected entities do exist, and the effect that invokes the corresponding operations. In the transition diagram, we may define the changes of state and those constraints and effects which are specific to the transitions.

By way of illustration, consider the request type *Return*. Using the event-type-centered style, the complete definition of the constraints and effect would be as follows:

1. In the event type, we define the characteristics and constraints shown in Fig. 13.11. The constraints are that the car, the rental, and the receiving branch must exist. There is also the constraint that the car must be returned to the expected drop off branch:

```
context Return::returnWhereExpected():Boolean
   body: branch = rental.dropOff
```

The effect of the event is

```
context Return::effect()
   post notifyTheCarStateMachine: car ^ return(self)
   post notifyTheRentalStateMachine: rental ^ return(self)
   post recordReceivingTime: rental.returnTime = time
```

2. The specification of the *return*() operation in the two entity types is trivial:

```
context Car::return(event:Return)
   post: True
context Rental::return(event:Return)
   post: True
```

3. In the state transition diagrams, the transitions triggered by a *Return* event are defined as shown in Figs. 13.2 and 13.3.

In the operation-centered style, the complete definition of the constraints and effect would be as follows:

1. In the event type we define the characteristics and constraints shown in Fig. 13.12. Note that there are only two constraints: the car and the rental must exist. The effect of the event is:

```
context Return::effect()
   post notifyTheCarStateMachine: car ^ return(self)
   post notifyTheRentalStateMachine: rental ^ return(self)
```

2. The specification of the *return*() operation is now

```
context Car::return(event:Return)
   post: True
```

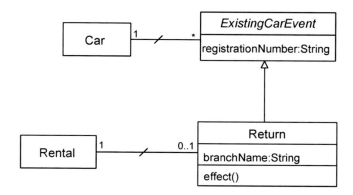

**Fig. 13.12.** Definition of the action request event *Return* in the operation-centered and transition-centered styles

```
context Rental::return(event:Return)
  pre returnWhereExpected:
        self.dropOff.name = event.branchName
  post recordReceivingTime: self.returnTime = time
```

3. In the state transition diagrams, the transitions triggered by a *Return* event are defined as shown in Figs. 13.2 and 13.3.

In the transition-based style, the complete definition of the constraints and effect would be as follows:

1. The definition in the event type is the same as in the previous case (see Fig. 13.12).
2. The specification of the *return()* operation in the two entity types is trivial:

```
context Car::return(event:Return)
  post: True
context Rental::return(event:Return)
  post: True
```

3. In the transition diagram of *Car*, the transition triggered by a *Return* event is defined as in the previous styles (and is shown in Fig. 13.2). The transition string of the transition triggered by *Return* in the transition diagram of *Rental* is different from that shown in Fig. 13.3. Now it is

[dropOff.name = event.branchName] Return/returnTime = event.time

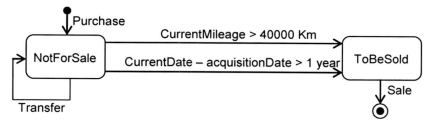

**Fig. 13.13.** Another transition diagram of *Car*

## 13.5 Entity Types with Multiple State Transition Diagrams

An entity may have several state machines, each one described by a different transition diagram. An entity is at any time in one (and only one) state in each machine. This means that an entity type may have several transition diagrams. Each diagram defines the set of states which an entity may be in from some point of view.

For example, from the point of view of availability, a car may be in the states shown in Fig. 13.2. Independently of availability, from the point of view of saleability, a car may be in the two states (*NotForSale, ToBeSold*) shown in Fig. 13.13. Cars are to be sold when they reach one year old or 40,000 km, whichever occurs first. At any time, a car is in one state of availability and in one state of saleability.

The transition diagrams of an entity type do not have common states. Each transition diagram must have its own set of states, and a state belongs to only one transition diagram.

The transition diagrams of an entity type may or may not have events in common. Assume that an entity type has two transition diagrams, *A* and *B*. When an event type *Ev* appears in *A* but does not appear in *B*, the meaning is that occurrences of *Ev* are ignored in the state machines defined by *B*. In other words, *B* does not define any additional constraint or effect for the occurrences of *Ev*. For example, consider the transition diagrams shown in Figs. 13.2 and 13.13. The event type *Pick-Up* appears only in Fig. 13.2. This means that the transition diagram of Fig. 13.13 does not define any additional constraint for it, nor any additional effect.

When an event type *Ev* appears in two transition diagrams *A* and *B*, an occurrence of *Ev* may trigger a transition in the state machines defined by both *A* and *B*. In this case, *B* defines additional constraints and effects for the occurrences of *Ev*. In particular, an event may satisfy the constraints defined in *A* but not satisfy those defined in B. Similarly, the effects of the occurrence of an event are defined partly in *A* and partly in *B*.

The diagram shown in Fig. 13.13 has three events in common with that in Fig. 13.2: *Purchase, Transfer*, and *Sale*. The additional constraints and effects of these events that are defined in Fig. 13.13 are:

- *Purchase*. The additional effect is that when a car is created, it is in the state *NotForSale*.
- *Transfer*. The additional constraint is that *Transfer* events can occur only when cars are in the state *NotForSale*. It is not permissible to transfer a car that is to be sold.
- *Sale*. The additional constraint is that *Sale* events can occur only when cars are in the state *ToBeSold*. It is not permissible to sell a car that is in the *NotForSale* state.

## 13.6 Bibliographical Notes

There are many good textbooks on the theory of automata. (Hopcroft et al. 2001) is the second edition of a classical textbook on this topic.

The use of state machines for behavioral schemas has a long tradition in conceptual modeling. Ferrentino and Mills (1977) noted that "state machines provide a convenient and indispensable mathematical framework for defining precise specifications of complex software systems". Davis (1988) gave one of the first analyses of the use of state transition diagrams for behavioral modeling, including a comparison with alternative approaches.

Many conceptual modeling languages approach behavioral modeling by using state transition diagrams (and their extensions). Among the first languages that took that approach, there are OOA (Shlaer and Mellor 1992), OMT (Rumbaugh et al. 1991), and OSA (Embley et al. 1992). Other languages, such as OO–Method (Pastor et al. 2001) use state transition diagrams only for entity life cycle modeling.

EU-Rent is a widely known case study of business rules. The initial report was published in 1995. Business Rules Group (2000) is the third edition of that report.

## 13.7 Exercises

**13.1** Consider the transition diagram of *Car* shown in Fig. 13.2. Give an example of a complete and legal life cycle and an example of a complete and illegal life cycle.

**13.2** In a junction pseudostate, an incoming transition may fire only if there is an outgoing transition that also fires. Justify this rule. Give an example that would violate this rule.

**13.3** Define the domain event type *Extension* of the EU-Rent case study using the transition-centered style.

**13.4** Consider an information system that records information about a community of people, their marital status, and their marriage relationships. A person may be alive or dead. A living person's marital status may be single, married, divorced or widowed. Assume that the relevant domain events (and characteristics) are:

- *Birth* (*name*:*String*, *sex*:*Sex*)
- *Death* (*dead*:*Person*). The death of a married person implies that his or her spouse becomes widowed.
- *Marriage* (*husband*:*Man*, *wife*:*Woman*)
- *Divorce* (*spouse*: *Person*). The person given is any of the two spouses.

Define:

1. The structural schema.
2. The state transition diagram for the entity type *Person*, with at least one state for each possible marital status.
3. The above domain events, with the corresponding characteristics and event constraints. If you wish, you may change the indicated types of the characteristics.
4. The domain event effects. Use whichever mapping style that you prefer for this case.

# 14 Statecharts

In this chapter, we study statecharts. Statecharts are an extension of the state transition diagrams that we studied in the previous chapter. Statecharts can be defined in UML. The main extensions provided by statecharts are state hierarchies and parallelism. These are presented in Sects. 14.1 and 14.2, respectively.

Our main examples in this chapter continue the EU-Rent case study introduced in the previous chapter. The details of the examples will be introduced where they arise.

## 14.1 The State Hierarchy

As we have seen in the previous chapter, a state transition diagram (or, for short, transition diagram) defines a set of states which entities of a given type may be in during their existence, and the allowed state transitions. An entity type may be associated with zero, one, or more transition diagrams. Each diagram defines the states of some entities according to a given perspective. For example, Figure 14.1 (reproduced from the previous chapter) shows a transition diagram of the entity type *Car* according to its availability. The diagram defines that a car may be *Available*, *InTransfer*, *InChecking&Preparation*, or *InUse*, and the allowed transitions between these states.

One of the drawbacks of transition diagrams is that they are "flat", in the sense that they do not provide a means to easily represent substates of a state. For example, assume that we need to distinguish three substates of the state *InUse* (see Fig. 14.1):

- *NormalUse*. A car is in this state if it is *InUse*, it has not been reported as broken, and it is not overdue.
- *Broken*. A car is in this state if it is *InUse*, and the customer has reported that it is broken.
- *Overdue*. A car is in this state if it is still *InUse*, but it has not been returned by the scheduled ending date and is not broken.

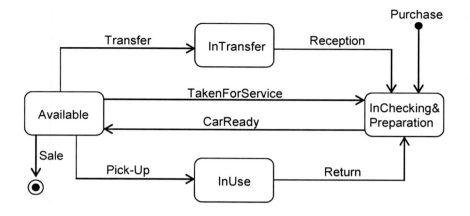

**Fig. 14.1.** State transition diagram of *Car*

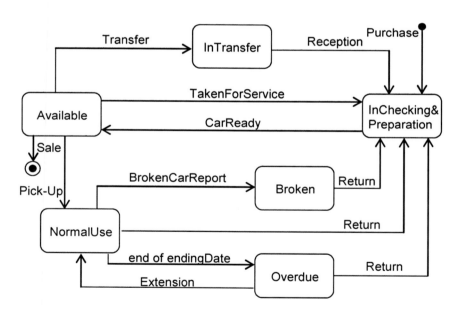

**Fig. 14.2.** Transition diagram of *Car* with the substates of *InUse*

In transition diagrams, we cannot depict both a state (such as *InUse*) and its substates. We might forget about the state and show directly the substates, as we have done in Fig. 14.2, but it is easy to see that this solution does not scale well for systems that have many substates, where it would result in unstructured and chaotic transition diagrams. In particular, in Fig. 14.2 we have had to define three transitions triggered by *Return*, one for each substate of *InUse*.

Statecharts allow us to explicitly represent the hierarchical relation between states and substates. Statecharts can be defined in UML. We shall follow the UML interpretations and notational conventions for statecharts in this chapter.

### 14.1.1 Simple Composite States

The states of a statechart can be simple or simple composite states. A *simple state* is a state that does not have substates. The transition diagrams that we studied in the preceding chapter consist of only simple states. A *simple composite state* is a state that can be decomposed into a set of mutually exclusive disjoint substates and a set of transitions. Transitions are allowed to originate and terminate at any level. Figure 14.3 shows the statechart of the previous example in UML.[1] *InUse* is a simple composite state; all the other states are simple.

### 14.1.2 State Configuration and Entity Life Cycle

If an entity is in a simple composite state, then it must also be in one of the substates of that state. If a car is in the state *InUse*, then it must also be in one of the three substates of *InUse*. Therefore, when a statechart has one or more simple composite states, an entity may be in several states at the same time. We call a set of states in which an entity may be at a given time a *state configuration*. The *active state configuration* of an entity is the state configuration that the entity has at a given time. In the example of Fig. 14.3, when a car is overdue, its active state configuration is $\sigma = \{Overdue, InUse\}$. In transition diagrams, where all states are simple states, the state configurations are singletons.

---

[1] In some cases, it is convenient to hide the decomposition of a composite state. The composite state may then be represented by a simple-state graphic with a special icon, and the content of the composite state may be shown in a separate diagram.

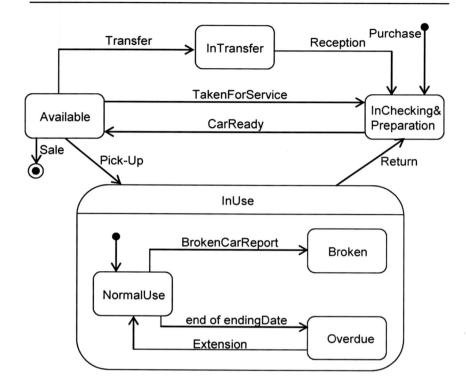

**Fig. 14.3.** Statechart of *Car* with the state *InUse* and its three substates

In a statechart, the life cycle $\gamma$ of an entity $e$ at a time point $t$ is the sequence of state configurations $\sigma_1,\ldots,\sigma_n$ which $e$ has been in since its creation until $t$. Statecharts define the set of legal life cycles. For example, a legal life cycle of car, according to the statechart of Fig. 14.3, could be

$$\gamma = \{\{\textit{InChecking\&Preparation}\}, \{\textit{Available}\},$$
$$\{\textit{InUse, NormalUse}\}, \{\textit{InUse, Broken}\}\}$$

### 14.1.3 Initial Pseudostate

A simple composite state $s$ may have at most one initial pseudostate, which is the source for a single transition to a substate of $s$, called the default state of $s$. A transition to the enclosing state represents a transition to its default state. In Fig. 14.3, *InUse* has an initial pseudostate with a transition

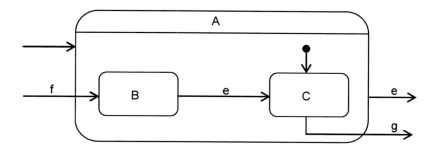

**Fig. 14.4.** *A* is a simple composite state, with substates *B* and *C*

to *NormalUse*. Transitions to *InUse* (such as that triggered by *Pick-Up*) represent a transition to the default state *NormalUse*.

A transition may go directly to a substate of a simple composite state. Figure 14.4 shows an example: the event *f* triggers a transition that goes directly to *B*, a substate of *A*.

### 14.1.4 Conflicting Transitions

Figure 14.3 shows a transition whose source is a simple composite state. The transition is enabled when an event *Return* occurs and a car is in the state *InUse*, independently of the substate that the car is in.

A conflict may occur when two transitions are enabled at the same time, one originating in a particular state and the other in one of its containing states. Figure 14.4 shows an example. When the active state configuration is {*B*, *A*} and event *e* occurs, two transitions are enabled: one originating in *B* and one in *A*. Only one of the transitions may fire. In UML, the conflict is solved by the rule that a transition originating from a substate has a higher priority than a conflicting transition originating from any of its containing states. By application of this rule to the above example, the transition that will fire is that emanating from *B*.

## 14.2 Parallelism

Up to now, we have seen two kinds of state in statecharts: simple states and simple composite states. A third kind is *orthogonal* states. An orthogonal state can be decomposed into two or more orthogonal regions. Each region has a set of mutually exclusive disjoint states and a set of tran-

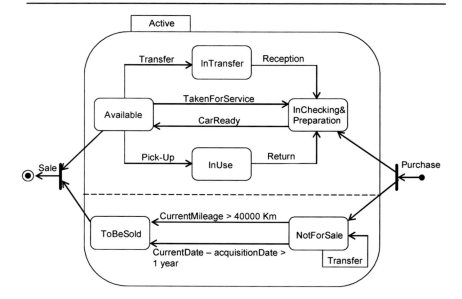

**Fig. 14.5.** Statechart of *Car*

sitions. A simple composite state has only one region. Orthogonal states and simple composite states are called *composite* states. Therefore, the states of a statechart may be simple or composite, and a composite state may be simple composite or orthogonal. The whole statechart may be considered as a composite state. Graphically, regions are separated by dashed lines.

When an entity is in an orthogonal state, it must be in *all* of its regions. When the state configuration of an entity includes an orthogonal state, it must also include a state from each of its regions.

Figure 14.5 shows an example. The whole statechart consists of an initial pseudostate, an orthogonal state (named *Active*), and a final state. *Active* consists of two regions. The first region defines the states of a car according to its availability, as we saw earlier in Fig. 14.1. The second region defines EU-Rent's policy concerning the sale of cars: cars are to be sold when they reach one year old or 40,000 km, whichever occurs first. Initially, a car is in the state *NotForSale*. When the condition "currentMileage > 40,000 km" changes from false to true (a change event), the car enters the state *ToBeSold*. The same happens when the time condition "Current-Date - acquisitionDate > 1 year" becomes true.

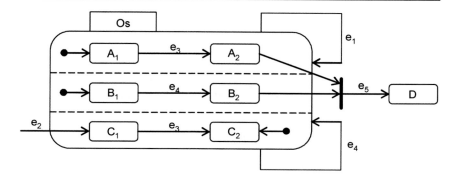

**Fig. 14.6.** Example of orthogonal state $O_S$ with three regions

When an entity is in the state *Active*, it must also be in the two regions. An example of a state configuration could be

$$\sigma = \{Active, InUse, ToBeSold\}$$

Orthogonal states are sometimes called "AND decompositions" because they require the entity to be in *each* of the components (regions) of the state. Simple composite states are called "OR decompositions" because they require the entity to be in *one* (and only one) of the components (states).

### 14.2.1 Initial Pseudostate

Each region $r$ of an orthogonal state $s$ may have at most one initial pseudostate, which is the source of a single transition to a substate of $r$, called the *default* state of $r$. A transition to the enclosing state $s$ represents a transition to the default state in each of its regions.

If a transition explicitly enters one region of an orthogonal state, this region is entered explicitly and the default states of the other regions are entered implicitly.

In the example of Fig. 14.6, each of the three regions has an initial pseudostate. When the transition triggered by $e_1$ is fired, the entity enters states $A_1$, $B_1$ and $C_2$. When the transition triggered by $e_2$ is fired, the entity enters states $C_1$, $A_1$, and $B_1$.

An orthogonal state $s$ must have an initial pseudostate in each of its regions if there are one or more transitions whose target is $s$. In the example of Fig. 14.5 the two regions of *Active* do not have initial pseudostates, because there are no transitions whose target is the state *Active*.

## 14.2.2 Firing Multiple Transitions

In the presence of orthogonal states, it is possible to fire multiple transitions as a result of the same event occurrence, as many as one transition in each region of such a state. When two or more transitions in different regions of an orthogonal state are enabled, all of them will be fired simultaneously.

In Fig. 14.5, if the active state configuration of a car is {*Active, Available, NotForSale*}, and an event *Transfer* occurs for that car, two transitions become enabled, one in each region. Both of them will be fired simultaneously.

A conflict may occur when two transitions are enabled at the same time, one originating in a region and the other in the enclosing state. Figure 14.6 shows an example. When the active state configuration includes the state $B_1$ and event $e_4$ occurs, two transitions are enabled: one originating in $B_1$ and one in the enclosing state. Only one of the transitions may fire. In UML, the conflict is solved by the rule that a transition originating from a substate has higher priority than a conflicting transition originating from any of its containing states. By application of this rule to the above example, the transition that will fire is that emanating from $B_1$.

## 14.2.3 Fork

A *fork* is a pseudostate with only one incoming transition, and two or more outgoing transitions terminating on states in different regions of an orthogonal state. The transitions outgoing from a fork must not have guards or triggers. The notation for a fork is a short, heavy bar.

A fork is used to specify a transition to an orthogonal state when we do not want to enter the default states of each region of that state. The combined semantics of a fork, its incoming transition, and its outgoing transitions is essentially the same as that of its incoming transition. The only difference is that the target is a state in each of the (two or more) regions of an orthogonal state. The target states are those of the outgoing transitions and, if there are more regions, the default states of the remaining regions.

There is an example in Fig. 14.5 on the right. The source of the incoming transition is an initial pseudostate. The targets of the two outgoing transitions are the states *InChecking&Preparation* and *NotForSale*. The trigger of the transition is the event *Purchase*. The semantics is that an occurrence of the event *Purchase* creates a car with the state configuration {*Active, InChecking&Preparation, NotForSale*}.

Note that forks are pseudostates. A fork does not behave like an ordinary state, because entities do not remain in it during a period of time. Instead, once they enter a fork, its outgoing transitions are immediately fired, and thus the pseudostate is left.

### 14.2.4 Join

A *join* is a pseudostate with two or more incoming transitions originating in different regions of an orthogonal state, and exactly one outgoing transition. The incoming transitions must not have guards or triggers. The notation for a join is again a short, heavy bar.

A join is used to specify a transition from two or more regions of an orthogonal state. The combined semantics of a join, its incoming transitions, and its outgoing transition is essentially the same as that of its outgoing transition. The only difference is that the transition is enabled when the entity is in two or more states of an orthogonal state. The source states are those of the incoming transitions.

There is an example in Fig. 14.5 on the left. The sources of the incoming transitions are the states *Available* and *ToBeSold*. The target of the outgoing transition is the final state. The trigger of the transition is the event *Sale*. The semantics is that an occurrence of the event *Sale* finishes the life cycle of a car if its active state configuration is {*Active*, *Available*, *ToBeSold*}.

Figure 14.6 also contains a join. The transition will be enabled when the active configuration state includes the states $A_2$ and $B_2$ and event $e_5$ occurs. If the transition fires, the entity will leave the state $O_S$ and enter the state $D$.

## 14.3 Bibliographical Notes

(Harel 1987) was the first (and the classical) paper on statecharts. Harel and Naamad (1996) described the precise semantics of statecharts as implemented in a commercial system. Crane and Dingel (2005) surveyed the existing formalisms for statechart modeling and presented a classification of their differences. Wieringa (2003) discussed possible choices in the execution semantics of statecharts. Eshuis et al. (2002) distinguished between requirements-level and implementation-level semantics of statecharts, and defined an execution semantics for requirements-level statecharts.

(Coleman et al. 1992) was one of the first attempts to integrate of statecharts and object-oriented design. Harel and Gery (1997) presented what can be considered the currently accepted integration.

Analysis of the consistency of statecharts with the structural schema was studied by Formica and Frank (2002), but this is a topic that needs more research.

Statechart specialization is another research topic for which a satisfactory solution has not been reached yet, at least at the conceptual level. The main references are (Schrefl and Stumptner 2000, 2002). See also (Harel and Kupferman 2002, Van Der Straeten et al. 2004) for alternative approaches.

## 14.4 Exercises

**14.1** Consider the statechart of *Car* shown in Fig. 14.5. Give an example of a complete and legal life cycle and an example of a complete and illegal life cycle.

**14.2** Consider an information system for supporting the activities of a library. A book may be available, on hold, or on loan, and may be reserved or nonreserved. When a user borrows a book that is available or on hold, that book becomes on loan. When a nonreserved book is returned, it becomes available. A book can be reserved by at most one user. A reserved book cannot be reserved by another user.

When a book is returned, if it is reserved by another user it becomes on hold, and the system sends an email to that user requesting him to collect the book. If the book is not collected within one week, the reservation is automatically canceled and the book becomes available.

Assume that the relevant domain events (and characteristics) of this system are:

- *Purchase (isbn:ISBN, title:String)*. The library has only one copy of each book.
- *Loan (book:Book, user:User)*
- *Return (book:Book)*
- *Reservation (book:Book, user:User)*
- *Renewal (book:Book)*. A user renews the loan of a book. A book can be renewed only if there is no reservation for the book.
- *Loss (book:Book)*. The book ceases to exist in the library.

Define:

1. The structural schema.
2. The statechart for the entity type *Book*, with an orthogonal state.
3. The above domain events, with the corresponding characteristics and event constraints. If you wish, you may change the indicated types of the characteristics.
4. The domain event effects. Use whichever mapping style that you prefer for this case.

# 15 Use Cases

We know that a conceptual schema defines the general knowledge required by an information system to perform its functions. But what are the functions of the information system, and what is the knowledge required to perform them? Currently, the answer to these questions is based on the use cases. Use cases define the functionality provided by an information system. The use cases of an information system are determined during requirements elicitation, one of the most important phases of requirements engineering.

A detailed study of use cases is beyond the scope of this book. The interested reader may find a few key bibliographical references at the end of this chapter. The purpose of this chapter is to briefly review the concept of a use case and explain its relationship to the conceptual schema. We begin in Sect. 15.1 by identifying the kinds of actor that interact with an information system. Then, in Sect. 15.2, we deal with use cases and their specification. Finally, in Sect. 15.3, we explain the mapping of use cases to requests.

Our main examples in this chapter continue the EU-Rent case study introduced earlier. The necessary details of the examples will be given where they arise.

## 15.1 Actors

In general usage, an actor is someone who plays a role in a play or film. In the field of information systems, an *actor* is a role played by a physical entity that interacts with an information system. The physical entity may be a person, an organization, or another system. A single physical entity may play any number of different roles in the same system and, conversely, a given actor can be played by several different entities. In some instances, a user role is a subtype of another, more general role, and represents a more specialized version of that role. The set of actors of a system is the external environment of that system.

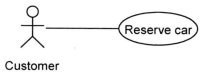

Customer

**Fig. 15.1.** Example of actor–use case association in UML

There are several kinds of actor. A *stakeholder* is an actor who has a vested interest in the system. Stakeholders are people who use, build, or manage the system, or are affected in some way by its use. A *primary actor* is a stakeholder who has goals fulfilled through using services of the system. Typically, but not always, a primary actor initiates the interaction with the system. A *supporting* or *secondary* actor provides a service to the system. An *offstage*, or *tertiary*, actor is a stakeholder who is not a primary actor. The system itself is considered an *internal* actor.

Some examples of actors in the EU-Rent system are:

- *Customer*, a primary actor who uses the system to fulfill goals such as to reserve a car, cancel a reservation, or extend a rental.
- *Payment Authorization Service*, a supporting actor that provides authorizations of customer payments to the EU-Rent system.
- *Police*, an offstage actor that must be informed by the system when a car is several days overdue.

In UML, an actor is represented by a "stick man" icon with the name of the actor in the vicinity of (usually above or below) the icon; see Fig. 15.1 for an example. In UML, the specialization/generalization relationship between actors is represented in the same way as for that between entity types.

Actor names should follow the guidelines used for entity types, namely common nouns in the singular form, possibly with an adjective.

## 15.2 Use Cases

### 15.2.1 Definition

An information system usually serves many actors, to whom it provides many different services. The functionality provided by an information system is too large to be analyzed as a single unit. We need a means of partitioning that functionality into smaller, more manageable pieces. The concept of a use case is very useful for this purpose.

A *use case* is a set of actions performed by a system which yields an observable result that is typically of value for one or more actors of the system. Usually, the value is the achievement of a single business goal or task. The entire set of use cases of a system partitions it into pieces meaningful to actors.

An important use case for EU-Rent is *Reserve car*. In order to reserve a car, the system must perform a set of actions, which achieve the goal of making a car rental reservation. This goal is of value for the customer, the managers and the entire company.

Each use case has a name, which should capture its essence. A suggested guideline is to name a use case with an active-verb phrase that represents the goal or task.

A *scenario* is an execution of a use case with particular actors and in a particular state of the information base. A use case may be seen as a type whose instances are scenarios. A scenario is one path through the set of actions of its use case. In general, a scenario does not include all the actions of its use case.

In UML, a use case is shown as an ellipse, either containing the name of the use case or with the name of the use case placed below the ellipse; see Fig. 15.1.

## 15.2.2 Use Case Actors

The actors of a use case are the actors of the system who participate in the use case. With respect to a use case, actors may be classified as stakeholders, or as primary, supporting, or offstage actors in the same way as we did for the actors of the system.

The primary actor has a goal that can be satisfied by the execution of the use case. The primary actor is often, but not always, the actor who initiates the interaction with the system. Sometimes the primary actor may have an intermediary initiate the interaction. In other cases, a primary actor may request the system to trigger a use case when some event occurs.

The primary actor of the example use case *Reserve car* is *Customer*. Alternatively, the primary actor could be *Clerk* if we are sure that customers will not interact directly with the system, and then *Customer* would be an offstage actor.

In UML, the participation of actors in use cases is shown by binary associations. Generally, the names of the association and of its two roles are not shown, as the actor and the use case define the association uniquely. Figure 15.1 shows the *Reserve car* use case and its primary actor.

Associations between actors and use cases may have multiplicities. When an actor has an association with a use case with a multiplicity that is greater than one at the use case end, it means that a given actor can be involved in multiple use cases of that type. The specific nature of this multiple involvement is not specified. Thus, an actor may initiate multiple use cases in parallel, or they may be mutually exclusive in time. On the other hand, a use case might require simultaneous action by several separate actors.

### 15.2.3 Use Case Specification

The specification of a use case describes the system's behavior as a response to a request from the primary actor. Use cases can be specified in several degrees of detail. In conceptual modeling, we are mostly interested in detailed specifications. On the other hand, there are two kinds of use case: essential and real. *Essential* use cases are technology-free and implementation-independent, keeping the interface out and focusing on the actor's intent. *Real* use cases include the details of the user interface and the actions performed by the users with it. Real use cases are refinements of essential use cases. Both kinds of use case are useful for the development of the conceptual schema.

There is no standard template for specifying use cases. There is, however, some agreement about the core sections. Two of these sections are the name and the primary actor of the use case. The others, which we describe below, are the scope, the stakeholders and interests, the preconditions, the success guarantees, the trigger, the main success scenario, and the extensions. The following example of the *Reserve car* use case illustrates the sections of a specification:

**Use case:** Reserve car
**Scope:** EU-Rent system
**Primary Actor:** Customer
**Stakeholders and interests**:
Customer: Wants to make a car rental reservation.
Branch manager: Wants to ensure that the reservation can be honored.
Company: Rentals requested by blacklisted customers must be refused.
Company: Wants to ensure that customers receive the best price for their rental.
**Precondition:** None.
**Success Guarantees:** Reservation is saved. Reservation can be honored. Price is correctly calculated.

**Trigger:** The customer wants to make a rental reservation for a car.
**Main Success Scenario:**
1. The customer identifies himself.
2. The system verifies that the customer has not been blacklisted.
3. The customer describes the rental reservation he wants to make by specifying the rental period, the pickup branch, the drop-off branch, and the car group.
4. The system verifies that the customer is allowed to make the reservation.
5. The system verifies that there may be cars available in the desired car group for the duration of the rental.
6. The system presents the price of the rental.
7. The customer accepts the rental proposal.
8. The system saves the reservation.
9. The system confirms the rental reservation to the customer.
**Extensions:**
1a. The customer is new:
      1a1. <u>Create customer</u>.
2a. The customer has been blacklisted:
      2a1. The system notifies customer. Use case ends.
4a. The customer is not allowed to make the reservation:
      4a1. The system notifies the customer.
      4a2. The customer changes the rental period.
            4a2a. The customer decides to exit:
                  4a2a1. Use case ends.
5a. There are no cars available:
      5a1. The system notifies the customer.
      5a2. The customer changes the car group or the rental period.
            5a2a. The customer decides to exit:
                  5a2a1. Use case ends.
7a. The customer refuses the proposal:
      7a1. The customer changes the car group or the rental period.
            7a1a. The customer decides to exit:
                  7a1a1. Use case ends.
7b. The customer wants to guarantee the rental:
      7b1. The customer gives his credit card information.

Typically, the *scope* of a use case is the system under design. However, it could be also the whole business, a business unit, or a system component.

The *stakeholders and interests* section lists the actors that have an interest in the behavior of the use case, and the specific interests that they have in it. In the present example, we describe three actors and their respective interests.

The *preconditions* section states the conditions that must be true when an actor initiates a scenario.

The *success guarantees* section defines what must be true either at the end of successful completion of the main success scenario or at the end of a successful alternative path. The guarantee should satisfy the interests of all stakeholders. In the example, we define that at the end of a successful scenario the reservation made will be saved, the reservation can be honored by the pickup branch, and the customer gets the best price.

The *trigger* section describes the starting condition that causes the initiation of the use case. A *Reserve car* scenario starts when a customer wants to make a rental reservation for a car.

The *main success scenario* describes the basic flow of a successful scenario. It is written as a sequence of action steps, but the steps can be executed in parallel or in a different order or can even be repeated. It is recommended that the steps should be numbered. An action step may be an interaction between two actors; a validation, performed usually by the system; or an internal state change.

In the example, the first step is an interaction between the customer and the system (identification), the second is a validation, the third is an interaction between the customer and the system (describing the reservation), the fourth and the fifth are system validations, the sixth is an interaction between the system and the customer, the seventh is an interaction between the customer and the system, the eighth is an internal change (the system records the reservation), and the last is an interaction between the system and the customer.

The *extensions* section defines alternate flows when some condition is satisfied. An extension is related to an action step of the main success scenario, and has two parts: a condition and a sequence of action steps. An extension can be seen as a miniature use case that may be triggered when the main success scenario is at the step indicated and the condition is satisfied. At the end of the extension, by default the scenario merges back with the main scenario, but it can end with the failure of the whole use case.

In the example there are six extensions to the main success scenario (1a to 7b). In what follows, we shall make some comments on the first three. The code of the extension (such as 1a) gives the number of the step where the condition could be detected (1) and a letter (a) that identifies the condition in the step. Several extensions can be attached to the same action step. If it is necessary to define an extension that can be detected during any step, then we use a code starting with an asterisk, such as *a.

Extension 1a states that if, in the first step, the customer is new then it is necessary to create a new customer. In this case, the only action step (1a1) is the execution of another use case (*Create customer*), as we shall explain in the next subsection.

Extension 2a defines what happens if the customer has been blacklisted. In this case, the system notifies the customer (2a1) and the use case fails.

In extension 4a the system detects that the customer is not allowed to make the reservation, because a customer may have only one car at any time or for some similar reason. There are two action steps in this extension: the system notifies the customer of the problem (4a1) and the customer changes the rental period (4a2). Here we see an extension within an extension. If, in action step 4a2, the customer, instead of changing the rental period, decides to exit (condition 4a2a), then the use case fails.

Sometimes an extension is defined as an explicit use case, as we shall see in the next subsection.

## 15.2.4 Relationships Between Use Cases

There are three main kinds of relationship between use cases: include, extend and specialization/generalization relationships. We study them in the following.

An *include* relationship from a base use case to an inclusion use case means that the behavior defined in the inclusion use case is included in the behavior of the base use case. This is useful for extracting common behaviors from several use cases into a single description. The inclusion use case is not necessarily a separate instantiable use case. It may be a fragment. The common part is included by all the base use cases that have that inclusion use case in common. Execution of an inclusion use case is analogous to a subroutine call.

We have found an example of an include relationship in the above *Reserve car* use case: step 1a1 includes the use case *Create customer* in the extension 1a. The specification of this use case is as follows:

**Use case:** Create customer
**Scope:** EU-Rent system
**Primary Actor:** Customer
**Stakeholders and interests**:
**Precondition:** The customer does not exist.
**Trigger:** A new customer wants to make a rental car reservation.
**Main Success Scenario:**
1. The customer provides his personal information (name, address, date of birth).
2. The customer provides the details of his driving license.
3. The system records the information about the new customer.
**Extensions:**
1a. The customer is below 25:
      1a1. The system notifies the customer. Use case ends.
2a. The driving license is not valid or the customer does not have the required experience:
      2a1. The system notifies the customer. Use case ends.

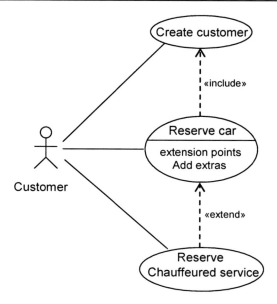

**Fig. 15.2.** Examples of relationships between use cases

In UML, an include relationship between use cases is shown by a dashed arrow with an open arrowhead from the base use case to the inclusion use case. The arrow is labeled with the keyword *«include»*; see Fig. 15.2 for an example.

An *extend* relationship from an extending use case to a base use case means that the behavior defined in the extending use case can be inserted into the behavior defined in the base use case. The extension takes place at one or more specific *extension points* defined in the base use case. The extension may be conditional: in this case, the extension takes place only if a condition holds when the first extension point is reached.

The base use case is defined independently of the extending use case and is meaningful independently of the extending use case. An important difference between include and extend relationships is that in the former, the base use case is aware of ("sees") the inclusion use case, while in the latter, the base use case is unaware of the possible extending use cases.

One possible extension point in the *Reserve car* use case example could be *Add extras*, placed between action steps 6 and 7. The idea is that one or more use cases could extend the behavior of *Reserve car* by offering extras to the customer, such as a chauffeured service or additional equipment. For example, the following use case could extend *Reserve car*:

**Use case:** Reserve chauffeured service
**Scope:** EU-Rent system
**Primary Actor:**
**Stakeholders and interests**:
**Precondition:** The customer is reserving a car.
**Success Guarantees:**
**Trigger:** The customer requests a chauffeured service.
**Main Success Scenario:**
1.  The customer selects a chauffeured service.
2.  The system shows the price and other conditions of the service.
3.  The customer accepts the conditions.

In UML, extension points are indicated by a text string in a compartment of the use case ellipse named "extension points". An extend relationship between use cases is shown by a dashed arrow with an open arrowhead from the extending use case to the base use case. The arrow is labeled with the keyword «*extend*»; see Fig. 15.2 for an example. The condition of the relationship and the references to the extension points may, optionally, be shown in a note attached to the corresponding extend relationship (not shown in Fig. 15.2).

A *specialization/generalization* relationship between a child use case and a parent use case means that the child has the same behavior as the parent but may insert additional behavior into it.

In UML, a specialization/generalization relationship between use cases is represented in the same way as between entity types.

### 15.2.5 Use Case Model

A *use case model* is a model that describes the use cases of a system. In UML, a use case model is described by a use case diagram, which shows the relationships between the actors and use cases, the generalizations between the actors, and the relationships between the use cases. Figure 15.2 is a miniature use case diagram. UML does not provide further support for the specification of use cases.

## 15.3 Mapping Use Cases to Requests

Use cases describe how actors interact with an information system. During this interaction, an actor generates action request events to the system, requesting the execution of some system action. The complete set of requests generated by a use case and their detailed characteristics can be determined only for real use cases.

The set of use cases should be consistent with the set of requests defined in the behavioral schema. This consistency comprises two properties:

- Each request generated by a use case should be defined in the behavioral schema.
- Each request defined in the behavioral schema should be generated by one or more use cases.

For essential use cases, we can determine only some requests that change the information base (including the domain event notifications), and a few queries. Some action steps in essential use cases are very abstract, and their mapping to particular requests cannot be determined at this level. For example, step 1 of the *Reserve car* use case, "The customer identifies himself", may be implemented in real use cases in several ways, each generating different requests.

Most of the queries and the details of the communication between actors are not shown in essential use cases. For example, in a real *Reserve car* use case, the user interface could show lists of available car groups and of branches where to pick up and drop off the rented cars. Such lists make it easy for users to define the characteristics of a reservation. These lists are obtained by querying the information base.

The mapping of use cases to the requests that may be generated during their execution can be documented in several ways. In the following, we describe three possibilities: textual references, creation dependencies, and sequence diagrams.

As an illustration, we consider the *Reserve car* use case. The action request events that may be generated are the following domain event notifications[1] and queries (Fig. 15.3 shows two domain events and a query):

- *NewReservation*. A customer defines a new rental reservation.
- *PeriodChange*. A customer changes the starting and/or ending date of a reservation.
- *CarGroupChange*. A customer changes the car group of a reservation.

---

[1] We shall omit the suffix *Notification* when it is clear from the context that we are referring to domain event notifications.

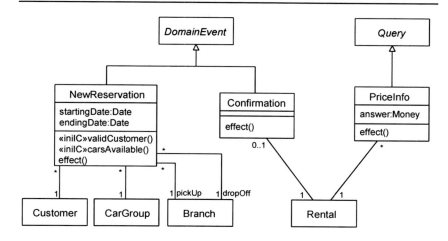

**Fig. 15.3.** Examples of requests generated in the *Reserve car* use case

- *Guarantee.* A customer guarantees the reservation by means of a credit card.
- *Confirmation.* A customer confirms the reservation made in the use case.
- *BlackListCheck.* A query whose answer gives whether or not a customer is currently blacklisted.
- *PriceInfo.* A query whose answer is the best price of a given rental.

The *Create customer* use case generates a notification of the domain event *NewCustomer*.

### 15.3.1 Textual References

The simplest way of documenting the mapping of use cases to requests is by including textual references to requests near the places in the use case specification where they are generated. The exact form of the references may depend on the tools used.

As an example, we reproduce below some parts of the specification of the *Reserve car* use case, including references to the action requests in the form [→ *actionRequest*]:

**Use case:** Reserve car
**Main Success Scenario:**
1. The customer identifies himself.
2. The system verifies that the customer has not been blacklisted [→ *BlackList-Check*].
3. The customer describes the rental reservation he wants to make by specifying the rental period, the pickup branch, the drop-off branch, and the car group [→ *NewReservation*].
4. The system verifies that the customer is allowed to make the reservation.
5. The system verifies that there may be cars available in the desired car group for the duration of the rental.
6. The system presents the price of the rental [→ *PriceInfo*].
7. The customer accepts the rental proposal [→ *Confirmation*].
8. The system saves the reservation.
9. The system confirms the rental reservation to the customer.
**Extensions:**
4a. The customer is not allowed to make the reservation:
    4a1. The system notifies the customer.
    4a2. The customer changes the rental period [→*PeriodChange*].
5a. There are no cars available:
    5a1. The system notifies the customer.
    5a2. The customer changes the car group or the rental period
            [→ *CarGroupChange*], [→*PeriodChange*].
7a. The customer refuses the proposal:
    7a1. The customer changes the car group or the rental period
            [→ *CarGroupChange*], [→*PeriodChange*]
7b. The customer wants to guarantee the rental:
    7b1. The customer gives his credit card information [→*Guarantee*].

## 15.3.2 Creation Dependencies

In UML, the simplest graphical way to represent the mapping of use cases to requests is by means of a usage dependency with the standard stereotype *«create»*. The meaning is that the instances of a use case create instances of the action request type.

Figure 15.4 illustrates this representation for the example of the *Reserve car* use case.

## 15.3.3 Sequence Diagrams

In UML, another graphical way to represent the mapping of use cases to requests is by means of sequence diagrams. A sequence diagram shows,

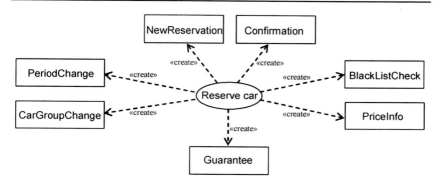

**Fig. 15.4.** Example of graphical mapping of a use case to the requests generated

for one particular scenario of a use case, the action requests that the actors generate and their temporal order.

Figure 15.5 illustrates this representation for the example of the *Reserve car* use case and its main success scenario.

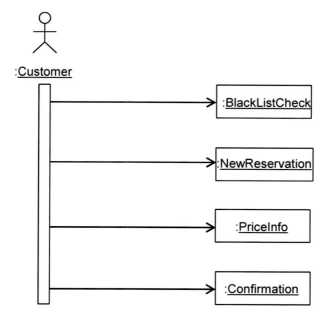

**Fig. 15.5.** The system sequence diagram for the main success scenario of the *Reserve car* use case

## 15.4 Bibliographical Notes

The origin of the concept of a use case can be traced back at least to the idea of event partitioning put forward by McMenamim and Palmer (1984). The modern view of use cases originated in the work of Ivar Jacobson in 1986. Jacobson (2004) explained the origin and evolution of use cases. Use cases are sometimes confused with scenarios and related concepts. Rolland et al. (1998) provided a framework to classify the existing concepts and approaches.

Cockburn (2001) was influential in defining what use cases are and how to write them effectively. Adolph and Bramble (2003) gave several useful patterns related to use cases.

Currently, use cases are integrated into most development methodologies of information systems. Use cases are part of UML. Use cases may be used in several phases of the development life cycle. Alexander and Maiden (2004) described in detail the role of use cases and scenarios through the system development life cycle. Essential use cases were described by Constantine and Lockwood (1999).

The mapping of use cases to requests using textual references is very similar to that of use cases to operations defined by Sendall and Strohmeier (2000). Glinz (2000) described the use of textual references and dependencies for the mapping of use cases to the structural schema. He also discussed the consistency of use cases with respect to the structural schema.

Larman (2005) described the mapping of use cases to system events or operations. He proposed the use of system sequence diagrams for particular scenarios of a use case, and the use of preconditions and postconditions in the system operations as a precise specification of use cases. A somewhat similar approach was taken by Catalysis (D'Souza and Wills 1999) and OO-Method (Insfrán et al. 2002).

## 15.5 Exercises

**15.1** Consider the use case *Compose and send an email* for your favorite webmail client. Write the main success scenario for it in two versions: essential and real.

**15.2** Visit the website of a car rental company that allows on-line reservations. Analyze the real use case that customers must execute to reserve a car in it. Take into account all the alternate flows.

1. Specify the real use case, including its extensions.
2. Specify the essential use case, again including its extensions.
3. Determine the requests generated by the real use case.
4. Document the mapping of the real use case to the requests using textual references.

**15.3** Visit a website that allows free on-line playing of Sudoku puzzles and consider the real use case corresponding to the solution of a new puzzle.

1. Specify the use case, including its extensions.
2. Determine the requests generated by the use case.
3. Document the mapping of the use case to the requests using creation dependencies.

# 16 Case Study

In the preceding chapters, we studied the elements from which schemas are made up. We followed a bottom-up approach, starting with the basic elements of entity and relationship types, and then proceeding to more complex elements until we reached the state transition diagrams and statecharts.

However, schemas are not defined in this way. In most projects, conceptual modeling comprises two main kinds of activity: domain analysis and use case analysis. In domain analysis, we study and define the existing or designed domain concepts and their properties. In use case analysis, we elicit and define the knowledge the system has to know to carry out the functions required by the use cases.

This chapter illustrates the activities of conceptual modeling by means of a case study. We define a fragment of the schema of a well-known real-world information system. The system chosen is osCommerce (for "Open Source Commerce"), an e-commerce and online-store management software program. It is available[1] as free software under the GNU General Public License. osCommerce was started in March 2000 in Germany, and since then it has been adopted by thousands of stores around the world.

In Sect. 16.1, we show the main concepts of the osCommerce domain, extracted from the (limited and sometimes imprecise) public documentation of the system.[2] Sections 16.2 to 16.5 focus on a few key use cases in the four main areas of the system: configuration, administration, customers and the catalog area. The use cases and the required knowledge have been extracted from the documentation, experimentation (as a user) with the standard version of the system and an analysis of its relational database schema. The interested reader can find the complete up-to-date schema of the system on the companion website to the book.

---

[1] www.oscommerce.com
[2] www.oscommerce.com/solutions/documentation

## 16.1 Main Domain Concepts

Figure 16.1 shows the main concepts in the osCommerce domain. More details will be given later on.

The products in the store are manufactured by manufacturers, are grouped into categories, and belong to tax classes.

Products may have attributes. An attribute is an option/value pair, such as *Size/Small*, *Size/Large*, or *Color/Yellow*. The price of a product varies depending on the attributes it has.

A customer has one or more addresses. Each address is located in a country. Moreover, if the country has zones (states or provinces), then the address must be located in a zone.

A shopping cart contains one or more items (not shown in the figure), each of which is a quantity of a product with a set of attributes. When a customer confirms that he wants to buy the contents of his shopping cart, the system generates an order. An order contains one or more order lines, each of which is a quantity of a product with a set of attributes.

In the following sections, we refine the above concepts and develop several fragments of the structural and behavioral schemas of osCommerce.

## 16.2 Store Configuration

When osCommerce is installed, the system assigns initial values to a set of parameters. In most cases, these values must be changed. There are a few use cases that can be applied to make these changes. In what follows, we only describe two parts of the initial configuration of the system: the store data and the minimum values.

### 16.2.1 Store Data

Figure 16.2 shows the store data used by osCommerce. *Store* is a constant entity type that has only one instance, which is created and initialized on installation. We can ensure that there will be only one instance of *Store* with the constraint defined by the following class operation:[3]

```
context Store::alwaysOneInstance():Boolean
  body: Store.allInstances()->size() = 1
```

---

[3] For the sake of uniformity, we define all constraints and derivation rules by operations in this chapter.

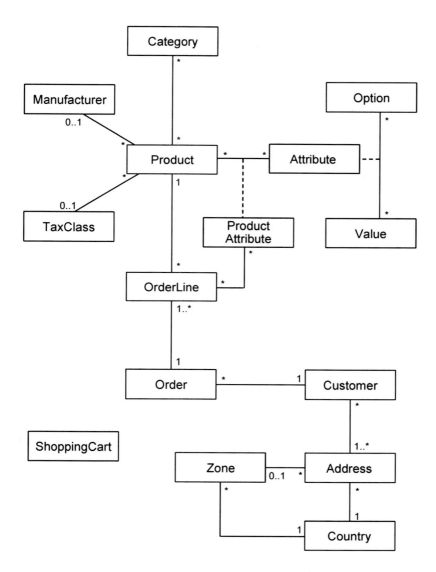

**Fig. 16.1.** Main entity and relationship types in the osCommerce domain

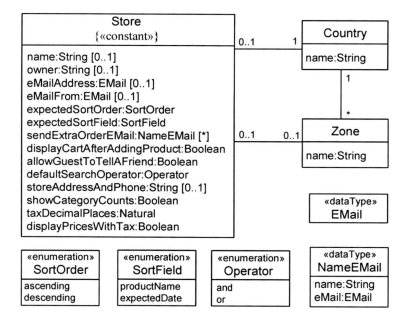

**Fig. 16.2.** Fragment of the structural schema dealing with a store and its localization

To change the initial values, the system administrator starts the use case *Change store data:*[4]

**Use case:** Change store data
**Primary Actor:** System administrator
**Trigger:** The system administrator wants to change the initial values of the store data.
**Main Success Scenario:**
1. The system displays the current values of the store data.
2. The system administrator provides a new value for one of the store attributes:

        [→ *NameChange*]
        [→ *OwnerChange*]
        [→ *ZoneChange*]
        [→ *EMailAddressChange*]
        [→ *EMailFromChange*]

---

[4] In this chapter, we document the mapping of use cases to requests by means of textual references. If not indicated otherwise, the requests are domain event notifications, which we name omitting the suffix *Notification*.

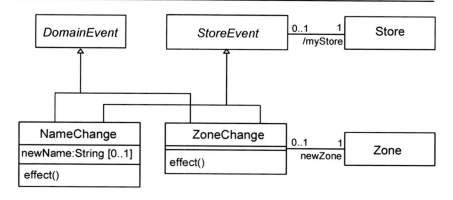

**Fig. 16.3.** Definition of domain event types *NameChange* and *ZoneChange*

  [→ *ExpectedSortOrderChange*]
  [→ *ExpectedSortFieldChange*]
  [→ *SendExtraOrderEMailChange*]
  [→ *DisplayCartAfterAddingProductChange*]
  [→ *AllowGuestToTellAFriendChange*]
  [→ *DefaultSearchOperatorChange*]
  [→ *AddressAndPhoneChange*]
  [→ *ShowCategoryCountsChange*]
  [→ *TaxDecimalPlacesChange*]
  [→ *DisplayPricesWithTaxChange*]
3. The system validates that the value is correct.
4. The system saves the new value.
5. The system displays the new values of the store data.
The system administrator repeats steps 2–5 until he is done.

We show only the definitions of the first and third domain events (Fig.
16.3); the others are quite similar. Since these event types change attributes
or associations of the store, it is practical to define the association with
*Store* in a single place (*StoreEvent*). In this case, the association is derived.
Given that *Store* has only one instance, the derivation rule is

```
context StoreEvent::myStore():Store
  body: Store.allInstances()->any(true)
```

The event effects are

```
context NameChange::effect()
  post: myStore.name = self.newName
```

```
context ZoneChange::effect()
  post: myStore.zone = self.newZone
```

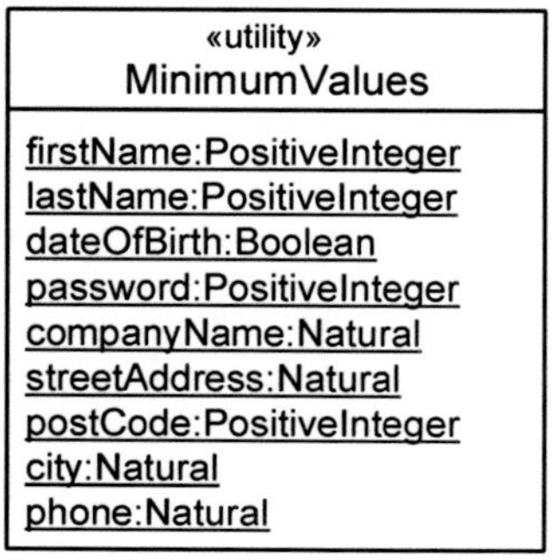

```
              «utility»
            MinimumValues

        firstName:PositiveInteger
        lastName:PositiveInteger
        dateOfBirth:Boolean
        password:PositiveInteger
        companyName:Natural
        streetAddress:Natural
        postCode:PositiveInteger
        city:Natural
        phone:Natural
```

**Fig. 16.4.** Fragment of the structural schema dealing with the minimum values of some attributes

## 16.2.2 Minimum Values

osCommerce allows defining a minimum length to be defined for the string values of some attributes and allows one to specify that some attributes or associations are either mandatory or optional. Figure 16.4 shows a few of the minimum values. On installation, the system assumes some initial values, but they can be changed with the use case *Assign minimum values*:

**Use case:** Assign minimum values
**Primary Actor:** System administrator
**Trigger:** The system administrator wants to change the minimum values of some attributes.
**Main Success Scenario:**
1. The system displays the current minimum values.
2. The system administrator provides a new value for one of the minimum values:
        [→ *FirstNameMinimumChange*]
        [→ *LastNameMinimumChange*]
        [→ *DateOfBirthOptionalChange*]
        [→ *PasswordMinimumChange*]
        [→ *CompanyNameMinimumChange*]
        [→ *StreetAddressMinimumChange*]
        [→ *PostCodeMinimumChange*]
        [→ *CityMinimumChange*]
        [→ *PhoneMinimumChange*]
3. The system validates that the value is correct.
4. The system saves the new value.

5. The system displays the new current minimum values.

The system administrator repeats steps 2–5 until he is done.

We show only the definition of the first domain event (Fig. 16.5); the others are quite similar. The event effect is

```
context FirstNameMinimumChange::effect()
  post: MinimumValues.firstName = self.newMinimum
```

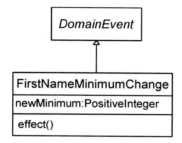

**Fig. 16.5.** Definition of *FirstNameMinimumChange* domain event type

## 16.3 Store Administration

In osCommerce, the products in the store are manufactured by manufacturers and are grouped into categories. In the following, we study a few use cases that are used by the store administrator to define manufacturers, categories, and products.

### 16.3.1 Manufacturers

Figure 16.6 shows the schema fragment corresponding to manufacturers. osCommerce is a multilingual system able to deal with any number of languages. Languages can be added or deleted as desired by the store. In Fig. 16.6, the association class *ManufacturerInLanguage* defines that a manufacturer may have a different URL in each language, and that the system

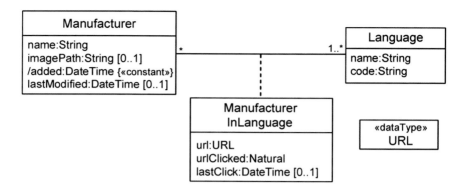

**Fig. 16.6.** Fragment of the structural schema dealing with manufacturers

records the number of times a URL in a language has been clicked and the last time that it was clicked.[5]

There are five constraints related to the fragment shown in Fig. 16.6. The first three are that a *Manufacturer* is identified by its *name*, and that a *Language* is identified by its *name* and by its *code*. Using class operations, these constraints can be formally defined as follows:

```
context Manufacturer::nameIsUnique():Boolean
  body: Manufacturer.allInstances()->isUnique(name)
context Language::nameIsUnique():Boolean
  body: Language.allInstances()->isUnique(name)
context Language::codeIsUnique():Boolean
  body: Language.allInstances()->isUnique(code)
```

osCommerce can only work properly if there is at least one language. We can define this constraint with the following class operation:

```
context Language::atLeastOneLanguage():Boolean
  body: Language.allInstances()->size() > 0
```

The last constraint is the rule that each manufacturer must have a URL in each language. This can be defined with the operation

```
context Manufacturer::aURLinEachLanguage():Boolean
  body:
    self.language->size() = Language.allInstances()->size()
```

The attribute *Manufacturer::added* is constant and derived. Its derivation rule is

---

[5] *ManufacturerInLanguage* is the partial reification of the two common participants in the three relationship types *manufacturer–language–url*, *manufacturer–language–urlClicked*, and *manufacturer–language–lastClick*.

```
context Manufacturer::added():DateTime
  body: Now()
```

where Now() is assumed to be a system operation that gives the current time.

In the following, we define the three main use cases related to manufacturers that can be started by the store administrator: *Add/Edit/Delete a manufacturer*:

**Use case:** Add a manufacturer
**Primary Actor:** Store administrator
**Trigger:** The store administrator wants to add a manufacturer.
**Main Success Scenario:**
1. The store administrator provides the details of the new manufacturer:
        [→ *NewManufacturer*].
2. The system validates that the data is correct.
3. The system saves the new manufacturer.

**Use case:** Edit a manufacturer
**Primary Actor:** Store administrator
**Trigger:** The store administrator wants to edit a manufacturer.
**Main Success Scenario:**
1. The store administrator selects the manufacturer to be edited.
2. The store administrator provides the new details of the selected manufacturer:
        [→ *EditManufacturer*].
3. The system validates that the data is correct.
4. The system saves the changes.

**Use case:** Delete a manufacturer
**Primary Actor:** Store administrator
**Trigger:** The store administrator wants to delete a manufacturer.
**Main Success Scenario:**
1. The store administrator selects the manufacturer to be deleted.
2. The system warns the store administrator of the number of products linked to the manufacturer to be deleted.
3. The store administrator confirms that he wants to delete the manufacturer:
        [→ *DeleteManufacturer*].
4. The system deletes the manufacturer and, if requested, changes the status of the products manufactured by it to "out of stock".

Figure 16.7 shows the definition of the three domain event types. *ExistingManufacturerEvent* groups the event types dealing with an existing manufacturer. *ManufacturerURLEvent* groups the event types that define or change the URLs of a manufacturer. Note that the cardinalities of the ternary association *HasURL* ensure that the characteristics of the instances

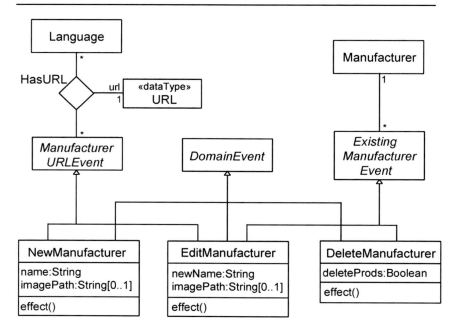

**Fig. 16.7.** Definition of domain event types related to manufacturers

of *NewManufacturer* and *EditManufacturer* include the URL of the manufacturer in each existing language.

The name of a new manufacturer must be different from that of any of the existing manufacturers. This is captured by the event constraint defined by the following operation:

```
context NewManufacturer::nameDoesNotExist():Boolean
  body: not Manufacturer.allInstances()->
              exists(name = self.name)
```

Likewise, the new name of an existing manufacturer must be different from that of any of the other manufacturers. This is captured by the following event constraint:

```
context EditManufacturer::newNameDoesNotExist():Boolean
  body:
    newName <> self.manufacturer.name implies
      not Manufacturer.allInstances()->
              exists(name = self.newName)
```

The effect of a new-manufacturer event is[6]

```
context NewManufacturer::effect()
  post:
    m.oclIsNew() and
    m.oclIsTypeOf(Manufacturer) and
    m.name = self.name and
    m.imagePath = self.imagePath and
    Language.allInstances()->
      forAll(l|
        self.hasURL->select(language=l).url =
        m.manufacturerInLanguage->select(language=l).url)
```

The effect of an edit-manufacturer event is similar:

```
context EditManufacturer::effect()
  post:
    manufacturer.name = self.name and
    manufacturer.imagePath = self.imagePath and
    Language.allInstances()->
      forAll(l|
        self.hasURL->select(language=l).url =
        manufacturer.manufacturerInLanguage->
          select(language=l).url)
```

An instance of *DeleteManufacturer* deletes the corresponding manufacturer and, if *deleteProds* is true, it also changes the status of the products of the manufacturer to "out of stock" (see Fig. 16.10). Formally,

```
context DeleteManufacturer::effect()
  post deleteManufacturer:
    not manufacturer@pre.oclIsKindOf(OclAny)
  post changeProductsToOutOfStock:
    deleteProds implies
      manufacturer@pre.product@pre->
        forAll(status = ProductStatus::outOfStock)
```

## 16.3.2 Categories

Figure 16.8 shows the schema fragment corresponding to categories. An instance of the ternary association *HasName* represents the name of a category in a language. The figure shows the three cardinalities of *HasName* that can be defined in UML; in this case, the other nine cardinalities are unconstrained.

An interesting issue here is the identification of categories. None of the main identification methods studied in Chap. 5 can be used for identifying the instances of *Category*. In this case, however, they can be identified by

---

[6] The navigation of *n*-ary associations assumes that they have been reified. In the example of Fig. 16.7, it is assumed that there exists an association class named *HasURL*.

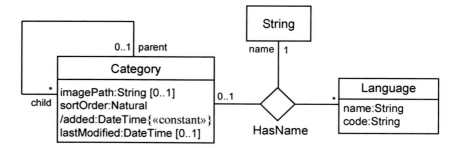

**Fig. 16.8.** Fragment of the structural schema dealing with product categories

means of the instances of *HasName*. In each language, each category has a unique name. Therefore, a category may be identified by a language and a string (a name).

In osCommerce the categories are arranged hierarchically. This constraint can be expressed as follows:

```
context Category::isAHierarchy():Boolean
  body: not self.allParents->includes(self)
```

where *allParents*() is a helper operation defined as

```
context Category
  def: allParents():Set(Category) =
         self.parent->union(self.parent.allParents())
```

Categories in the same hierarchical level are displayed as indicated by their sort order.

In the following, we define the main use cases related to categories that can be started by the store administrator:

**Use case:** Add a product category
**Primary Actor:** Store administrator
**Trigger:** The store administrator wants to add a category.
**Main Success Scenario:**
1. The store administrator provides the details of the new product category, including its parent category, if any:
      [→ *NewCategory*].
2. The system validates that the data is correct.
3. The system saves the new category.

**Use case:** Edit a product category
**Primary Actor:** Store administrator
**Trigger:** The store administrator wants to edit a category.

**Main Success Scenario:**
1. The store administrator selects the category to be edited.
2. The store administrator provides the new details of the selected category:
     [→ *EditCategory*].
3. The system validates that the data is correct.
4. The system saves the changes.

**Use case:** Move a product category
**Primary Actor:** Store administrator
**Trigger:** The store administrator wants to change the placement of a category in the category hierarchy.
**Main Success Scenario:**
1. The store administrator selects the category to be moved.
2. The store administrator indicates the new parent category, if any:
     [→ *MoveCategory*].
3. The system validates that the data is correct.
4. The system saves the new placement.

**Use case:** Delete a product category
**Primary Actor:** Store administrator
**Trigger:** The store administrator wants to delete a category.
**Main Success Scenario:**
1. The store administrator selects the category to be deleted.
2. The system warns the store administrator about the number of subcategories and products linked to the category to be deleted.
3. The store administrator confirms that he wants to delete the category:
     [→ *DeleteCategory*].
4. The system deletes the category, its subcategories, and the products linked to it.

The definitions of the domain event types *NewCategory*, *EditCategory*, *MoveCategory*, and *DeleteCategory* are similar to these of the corresponding types for manufacturers. In what follows, we describe only the definition of *NewCategory* (see Fig. 16.9).

The name of a new category in a given language must be different from that of any of the existing categories in that language. This is captured by the event constraint

```
context NewCategory::namesDoNotExist():Boolean
  body:
    Language.allInstances()->forAll(l|
      l.hasName.name->
        excludes(self.hasNewName->
          select(language=l)->any(true).name))
```

The event effect is

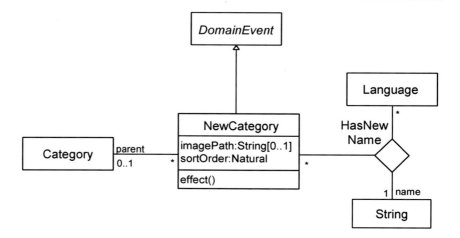

**Fig. 16.9.** Definition of the domain event type *NewCategory*

```
context NewCategory::effect()
  post:
    c.oclIsNew() and
    c.oclIsTypeOf(Category) and
    c.imagePath = self.imagePath and
    c.sortOrder = self.sortOrder and
    c.parent = self.parent and
    Language.allInstances()->
      forAll(l|
        self.hasNewName->select(language=l).name =
          c.hasName->select(language=l).name)
```

### 16.3.3 Products

Figure 16.10 shows the schema fragment corresponding to products. A product is identified by a name in a language. In each language, product names are unique. This can be captured by the constraint

```
context Language::nameUnique():Boolean
  body: self.productInLanguage->isUnique(name)
```

Figure 16.11 shows the schema fragment corresponding to product attributes. An option has a set of values. An attribute is an option/value pair, such as *Size/Small* or *Color/Yellow*. A product attribute is the reification of the relationship between a product and an attribute. For example, the option *Size* may have the values *Large*, *Medium*, and *Small* (i.e. there are three instances of *Attribute*), and the product *FashionT-Shirt* may exist in a

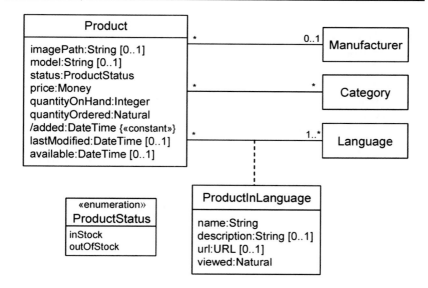

**Fig. 16.10.** Fragment of the structural schema dealing with products

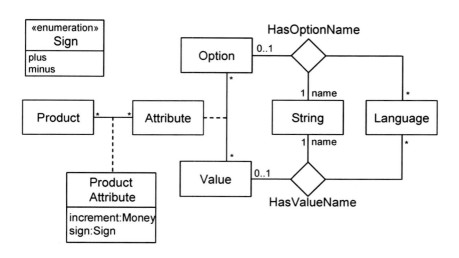

**Fig. 16.11.** Fragment of the structural schema dealing with product attributes

store with the sizes *Large* and *Small* (i.e. there are two instances of *ProductAttibute*, one between *FashionT-Shirt* and the attribute *Size/Large*, and the other between *FashionT-Shirt* and the attribute *Size/Small*).

The identification of *Option* and *Value* is similar to that of *Product* and *Category*: in a given language, names are unique. The cardinalities of the association *HasOptionName* ensure that each option has a unique name in a language. Taken together with the rule that there is at least one language, this guarantees the identifiability of options. Similar considerations apply to values.

The entity types *Attribute* and *ProductAttribute* are identifiable by means of a compound reference consisting of the two intrinsic relationship types of their reification.

There are several use cases related to products. In what follows, we describe only the use case *Add a product*, which includes the use cases *Add product option* and *Add product option value*.

**Use case:** Add a product
**Primary Actor:** Store administrator
**Trigger:** The store administrator wants to add a product to the store catalog.
**Main Success Scenario:**
1. The store administrator selects the product category.
2. The store administrator provides the product data:
         [→ *NewProduct*].
3. The system validates that the data is correct.
4. The system saves the new product.
5. The store administrator provides a product attribute:
         [→ *NewProductAttribute*].
6. The system validates that the product attribute is correct.
7. The system saves the new product attribute.
The store administrator repeats steps 5–7 until he is done.
**Extensions:**
5a. The product does not have product attributes:
         5a1. The use case ends.
5b. The product option is new:
         5b1. Add product option.
5c. The product option value is new:
         5c1. Add product option value.

**Use case:** Add product option
**Primary Actor:** Store administrator
**Trigger:** The store administrator wants to add a product option to the store catalog.

**Main Success Scenario:**
1. The store administrator provides the product option data:
        [→ *NewProductOption*].
2. The system validates that the data is correct.
3. The system saves the new product option.

**Use case:** Add product option value
**Primary Actor:** Store administrator
**Trigger:** The store administrator wants to add a value to a product option.
**Main Success Scenario:**
1. The store administrator selects the product option.
2. The store administrator provides the product option value data:
        [→ *NewProductOptionValue*].
3. The system validates that the data is correct.
4. The system saves the new product option value.

In the following we describe only the domain event type *NewProductAttribute* (see Fig. 16.12). An instance of *NewProductAttribute* cannot add a product attribute that already exists. This event constraint can be represented by the constraint operation

```
context NewProductAttribute::attributeDoesNoExist():Boolean
  body:
    not self.product.productAttribute->
         exists(attribute.value=self.value and
           attribute.option = self.option)
```

Moreover, the option/value pair of the new attribute must be valid. This is ensured by the event constraint

```
context NewProductAttribute::optionValueIsValid():Boolean
  body: self.option.value->includes(self.value)
```

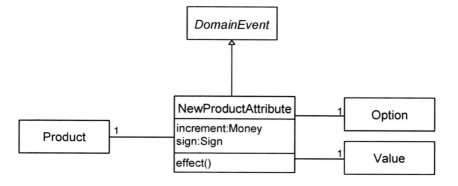

**Fig. 16.12.** Definition of the domain event type *NewProductAttribute*

The effect of the event is

```
context NewProductAttribute::effect()
  post:
    pa.oclIsNew() and
    pa.oclIsTypeOf(ProductAttribute) and
    pa.increment = self.increment and
    pa.sign = self.sign and
    pa.product = self.product and
    pa.attribute.option = self.option and
    pa.attribute.value = self.value
```

## 16.4 Customers

Figure 16.13 shows the fragment of the structural schema corresponding to customers and addresses. A customer has one or more addresses, one of which is the primary address. The primary address is the default shipping and delivery address for the orders placed in the store, and the basis for tax calculations. Note that *Address* is a data type. The first and last names in an address may be different from those of its customer. Each address is located in a country. Moreover, if the country has zones, then the address must be located in a zone whose name is the same as the name of the state, and the country of the zone must be the same as the country of the address. This rule is captured by the constraint

```
context Country::addressesHaveZoneIfNeeded():Boolean
  body:
    self.zone->notEmpty() implies self.address-> forAll
      (a|a.state ->notEmpty() and a.state = a.zone.name and
         self = a.zone.country)
```

Customers are identified by their *eMailAddress*:

```
context Customer::eMailIsUnique():Boolean
  body: Customer.allInstances()->isUnique(eMailAddress)
```

There are several use cases related to customers. In what follows, we describe only the use case *Create customer*; this is included in the use case *Place order*, which we shall discuss in the next section.

**Use case:** Create customer
**Primary Actor:** Customer
**Trigger:** The customer wants to open an account in the store.
**Main Success Scenario:**
1. The customer provides the required customer data:
    [→ *NewCustomer*].
2. The system validates the customer data.
3. The system saves the customer data.

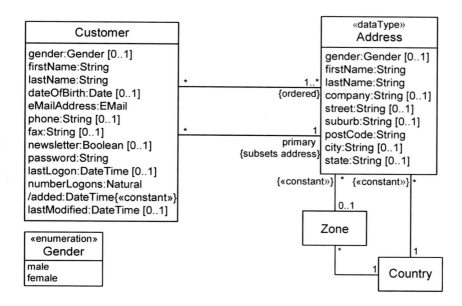

**Fig. 16.13.** Fragment of the structural schema dealing with customers and addresses

Figure 16.14 shows the definition of *NewCustomer*. The instances of this domain event type must satisfy several constraints. The first constraint is similar to some others that we have seen before: there cannot exist a customer with the same email address:

```
context NewCustomer::eMailDoesNotExist():Boolean
  body: not Customer.allInstances()->
              exists(eMailAddress = self.eMailAddress)
```

The second constraint ensures that the password is the same as the password confirmation:

```
context NewCustomer::passwordCorrect():Boolean
  body: password = pwConfirmation
```

The other constraints guarantee that the attributes of *NewCustomer* satisfy the minimum requirements stated by the system administrator; see Fig. 16.4 again. These are the following:

```
context NewCustomer::firstNameRight():Boolean
  body: primary.firstName.size() >=  MinimumValues.firstName
context NewCustomer::lastNameRight():Boolean
  body: primary.lastName.size() >= MinimumValues.lastName
```

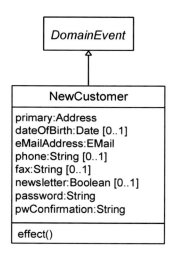

**Fig. 16.14.** Definition of the domain event type *NewCustomer*

```
context NewCustomer::dobRight():Boolean
   body:
     MinimumValues.dateOfBirth implies dateOfBirth->notEmpty()
context NewCustomer::companyRight():Boolean
   body:
     MinimumValues.companyName > 0 implies
        primary.company->notEmpty() and
        primary.company.size()>= MinimumValues.companyName
context NewCustomer::streetRight():Boolean
   body:
     MinimumValues.streetAddress > 0 implies
        primary.street->notEmpty() and
        primary.street.size()  >= MinimumValues.streetAddress
context NewCustomer::postCodeRight():Boolean
   body: primary.postCode.size()>= MinimumValues.postCode
context NewCustomer::cityRight():Boolean
   body:
     MinimumValues.city > 0 implies
        primary.city->notEmpty() and
        primary.city.size() >= MinimumValues.city
context NewCustomer::phoneRight():Boolean
   body:
     MinimumValues.phone > 0 implies
        phone->notEmpty() and
        phone.size() >= MinimumValues.phone
```

The effect of an instance of *NewCustomer* is

```
context NewCustomer::effect()
  post:
    c.oclIsNew() and
    c.oclIsTypeOf(Customer) and
    c.gender = primary.gender and
    c.firstName = primary.firstName and
    c.lastName = primary.lastName and
    c.dateOfBirth = dateOfBirth and
    c.eMailAddress = eMailAddress and
    c.phone = phone and
    c.fax = fax and
    c.newsletter = newsletter and
    c.password = password and
    c.numberLogons = 0 and
    c.primary = primary and
    c.address = Set{primary}
```

## 16.5 Online Catalog

The online catalog includes the use cases that may be started by the customers of the store. In the following, we describe the most important use case (*Place an order*) and a query.

### 16.5.1 Shopping Carts

Figure 16.15 shows the fragment of the schema corresponding to shopping carts. A shopping cart is anonymous until the customer logs in: at this moment it becomes a customer shopping cart. If a customer leaves a session with a nonempty shopping cart, then the cart will be automatically restored in his next session. Anonymous shopping carts can exist only in the context of a session, and they are automatically removed when the session expires. If a customer shopping cart exists in the context of a session then its customer is the same as the customer of the session. This is captured by the constraint

```
context CustomerShoppingCart::sameCustomer():Boolean
  body: self.session.customer = self.customer
```

A shopping cart contains a sequence of one or more items, each of which is a quantity of a product. If the product has attributes (Fig. 16.11), then the shopping-cart item specifies one attribute for each option that the product has. For example, if the product has one or more values for the option *Size*, then each shopping-cart item of that product specifies one and only one value for *Size* (for example, *Small*). These constraints can be represented by the following two operations:

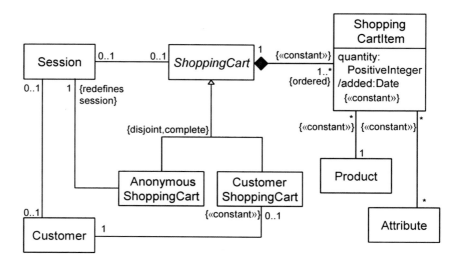

**Fig. 16.15.** Fragment of the structural schema dealing with shopping carts

```
context ShoppingCartItem::productHasTheAttributes():Boolean
   body: product.attribute->includesAll(attribute)
```

```
context ShoppingCartItem::onlyOneAttributePerOption():Boolean
   body: self.attribute->isUnique(option)
```

The creation and updating of a shopping cart are part of the use case *Place an order*, which we shall describe in the next section. However, we shall define here two main domain event types and one action request type, shown in Fig. 16.16.

The domain event type *RemoveProduct* removes a shopping-cart item from its shopping cart. Its effect is

```
context RemoveProduct::effect()
   post: not shoppingCartItem@pre.oclIsKindOf(OclAny)
```

This postcondition ensures that the removed shopping-cart item will not exist in the new state of the information base (i.e. after the execution of the *effect* operation). Moreover, if the shopping cart has only one item, the shopping cart will be removed as well (why?).

The domain event type *ChangeQuantity* changes the quantity of a shopping-cart item. Formally, its effect is

```
context ChangeQuantity::effect()
   post: shoppingCartItem.quantity = self.quantity
```

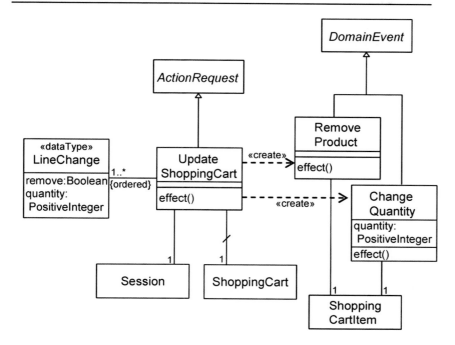

**Fig. 16.16.** Definition of the action request type *UpdateShoppingCart* and the domain event types *RemoveProduct* and *ChangeQuantity*

osCommerce allows customers to remove and/or change the quantity of several items in a single use case step. We could define this change as a single domain event type, but if we already have (or will need) *RemoveProduct* and *ChangeQuantity* then it is better to define that change as an action request type. This is what we have done in Fig. 16.16.

An instance of *UpdateShoppingCart* creates several instances of *RemoveProduct* and *ChangeQuantity*, as specified by its *LineChange*. In the request, there must be a line change for each shopping-cart item. Formally, this is an event constraint defined as

```
context UpdateShoppingCart::complete():Boolean
  body: lineChange->size() =
        shoppingCart.shoppingCartItem->size()
```

The effect is

```
context UpdateShoppingCart::effect()
  post:
    lineChange->forAll
      (lc|let cartItem:ShoppingCartItem =
              shoppingCart.shoppingCartItem->
                at(lineChange->indexOf(lc))
          in
            (lc.remove or lc.quantity <> cartItem.quantity)
              implies
                if lc.remove then
                   rp.oclIsNew() and
                   rp.oclIsTypeOf(RemoveProduct) and
                   rp.shoppingCartItem = cartItem
                else
                   cq.oclIsNew() and
                   cq.oclIsTypeOf(ChangeQuantity) and
                   cq.shoppingCartItem = cartItem and
                   cq.quantity = quantity
                endif))
```

## 16.5.2 Orders

When the customer confirms that he wants to buy the contents of his shopping cart, the system generates an order. Figure 16.17 shows the schema fragment corresponding to orders.

Orders are identified by their attribute *id*, which is assigned automatically when the order is created. The derivation rule is

```
context Order::id():PositiveInteger
  body:
    if Order.allInstances()->size() = 0 then 0
    else
      Order.allInstances()->
        sortedBy(id)->last().id + 1
    endif
```

Each order has a status. Initially the status is *pending*, but it may change later on. Each change is represented by an instance of *OrderStatusChange*. The derived attribute *Order::status* gives the current status of the order. The derivation rule is

```
context Order::status():OrderStatus
  body: orderStatusChange->sortedBy(added)->last()
```

The primary address of an order is that of its customer when the order is created. This is captured by a creation-time derivation rule with the defining operation

```
context Order::primary():Address
  body: customer.primary
```

The attributes *eMailAddress* and *phone* are defined similarly.

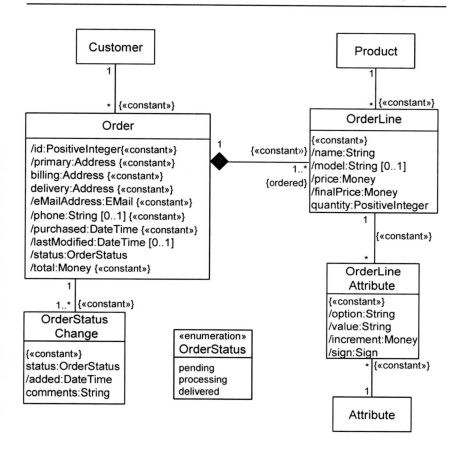

**Fig. 16.17.** Fragment of the structural schema dealing with orders

The derived attribute *Order::total* gives the total amount of an order. We shall ignore the shipping costs and taxes here. The derivation rule is then

```
context Order::total():Money
  body: orderLine->collect(finalPrice*quantity)->sum()
```

The final price of an order line is the price of the product plus or minus the increments of its attributes. The derivation rule is

```
context OrderLine::finalPrice():Money
  body:
    if orderLineAttribute->isEmpty() then price
    else
      orderLineAttribute->collect
        (if sign = Sign::plus then increment
        else -increment
        endif)->sum() + price
    endif
```

Note that all attributes of *OrderLine*, *OrderLineAttribute*, and *Order-StatusChange*, as well as most of *Order*, are constant.

There are a few use cases that deal with shopping carts and orders. We describe the most important of them, *Place an order*, below:

**Use case:** Place an order
**Primary Actor:** Customer
**Precondition:** None.
**Trigger:** The customer wants to place an order.
**Main Success Scenario:**
1. At any time before step 10 the customer logs in:
    [→*LogIn*].
The system adds the contents of the anonymous shopping cart to the customer shopping cart.
2. The system displays the contents of the shopping cart.
3. The customer browses the product catalog.
4. The customer selects a product to buy:
    [→*AddProductToShoppingCart*].
5. The system adds the product to the shopping cart.
6. The system displays the contents of the shopping cart.
7. The customer changes the contents of the shopping cart:
    [→*UpdateShoppingCart*].
8. The system updates the shopping cart.
9. The system displays the contents of the updated shopping cart.
The customer repeats steps 3, 4 and 7 as necessary to build his order.
10. The customer checks out the order.
11. The system shows the shipping address and the shipping methods available.
12. The customer selects the preferred shipping method.
13. The system shows the billing address and the payment methods available.
14. The customer selects the preferred payment method.
15. The system displays a summary of the order.
16. The customer confirms the order:
    [→*OrderConfirmation*].
17. The system saves the order.
**Extensions:**
1a. The customer is new:
    1a1. <u>Create customer</u>.
16a. The customer wants to change the contents of the shopping cart:

16a1. The customer changes the contents of the shopping cart:
[→*UpdateShoppingCart*].
16a2. The customer continues with the checkout procedure at step 11.
11a, 16a. The customer wants to change the shipping address:
11a1. The system shows the known addresses of the customer.
11a2. The customer selects a different shipping address.
11a3. The customer continues with the checkout procedure at step 11.
13a, 16b. The customer wants to change the billing address:
13a1. The system shows the known addresses of the customer.
13a2. The customer selects a different billing address.
13a3. The customer continues with the checkout procedure at step 13.
16c. The customer wants to change the shipping method:
16c1. The customer selects the new shipping method.
16c2. The customer continues with the checkout procedure at step 13.
16d. The customer wants to change the payment method:
16d1. The customer selects the new payment method.
16d2. The customer continues with the checkout procedure at step 15.
11a2a,16a2a. The customer wants to define a new shipping address:
11a2a1. The customer gives the new address:
[→*NewAddress*].
11a2a2. The system saves the new address.
11a2a3. The customer continues with the checkout procedure at step 11.
13a2a,16b2a. The customer wants to define a new billing address:
13a2a1. The customer gives the new address:
[→*NewAddress*].
13a2a2. The system saves the new address.
13a2a3. The customer continues with the checkout procedure at step 13.

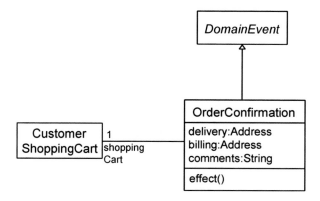

**Fig. 16.18.** Definition of the domain event type *OrderConfirmation*

In this use case, the most important domain event is *OrderConfirmation*, shown in Fig. 16.18. We omit here the shipping and payment methods. The intended effect is as follows:

```
context OrderConfirmation::effect()
  post theOrderIsCreated:
    o.oclIsNew() and
    o.oclIsTypeOf(Order) and
    o.customer = shoppingCart@pre.customer@pre and
    o.billing = billing and
    o.delivery = delivery and
    osc.oclIsNew() and
    osc.oclIsTypeOf(OrderStatusChange) and
    --The initial status of the order is pending
    osc.status = OrderStatus::pending and
    osc.comments = comments and
    o.orderStatusChange = Set{osc} and
    --There is an order line for each shopping cart item
    shoppingCart@pre.shoppingCartItem@pre->forAll
      (i|OrderLine.allInstances()->one
        (ol|ol.order = o and
          ol.product = i.product@pre and
          ol.quantity = i.quantity@pre and
          i.attribute@pre->forAll
            (iAtt|OrderLineAttribute.allInstances()->one
              (olAtt|olAtt.orderLine = ol and
                olAtt.attribute = iAtt))))
  post theShoppingCartIsRemoved:
    not shoppingCart@pre.oclIsKindOf(OclAny)
  post updateProductQuantities:
    let productsBought:Set(Product) =
        shoppingCart@pre.shoppingCartItem@pre.product@pre
        ->asSet()
  in productsBought->forAll(p|
      let quantityBought:PositiveInteger =
          shoppingCart@pre.shoppingCartItem@pre->select
          (product = p).quantity->sum()
    in p.quantityOnHand =
        p.quantityOnHand@pre-quantityBought and
      p.quantityOrdered =
        p.quantityOrdered@pre + quantityBought)
```

### 16.5.3 Show Previous Orders

osCommerce includes many predefined queries that can be requested by users in several use case steps and as a standalone use case. As an example, we describe here the query *ShowPreviousOrders*, shown in Fig. 16.19. The answer to an instance of *ShowPreviousOrders* is given in attribute *answer*, whose type is the complex type:

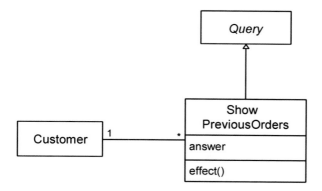

**Fig. 16.19.** Definition of the query *ShowPreviousOrders*

```
Set(TupleType(date:Date,
              id:Natural,
              name:String,
              country:String,
              status:OrderStatus,
              total:Money))
```

The answer is given by the effect operation

```
context ShowPreviousOrders::effect()
  post:
    answer =
      customer.order->collect(o|
        Tuple{date = o.purchased.date,
              id = o.id,
              name = o.delivery.firstName.
                        concat(o.delivery.lastName),
              country = o.delivery.country.name,
              status = o.status,
              total = o.total})->asSet()
```

# 17 Metamodeling

One principle of conceptual modeling is that domain objects are instances of entity types. Entity types, however, can also be seen as objects, and so they are also instances of types known as meta entity types. This is the basis of metamodeling, which we discuss in this chapter. Metamodeling is very important in the field of information systems, particularly in conceptual modeling.

This chapter begins with a discussion of meta entity types in Sect. 17.1. Powertypes have received special attention in conceptual modeling. This kind of meta entity type is described in Sect. 17.2. Section 17.3 shows that the participants in some relationships are not entities, but rather entity types. Section 17.4 discusses the concept of meta relationship types. Equipped with this battery of concepts, we then deal with metaschemas, the fundamental objects of metamodeling, in Sect. 17.5. Finally, Sect. 17.6 shows how a UML metaschema can be extended using stereotypes.

## 17.1 Meta Entity Types

### 17.1.1 Definition

In Chap. 2 we defined an entity type as "a concept whose instances at a given time are identifiable individual objects that are considered to exist in the domain at that time". We also saw that classification consists in determining the entity types which an object is an instance of at a given time. A classification defines an *InstanceOf* relationship between an object and an entity type.

Now the question is: can an entity type also be an entity? Or the inverse: can an entity also be an entity type? The answer to these questions is yes. An entity type defined in the schema of a system may also be an entity in the information base of the same system or of another system.

For example, consider a system that supports an ornithologist's research on the behavior and evolution of a few specific bee-eaters and turtledoves. Figure 17.1 shows a fragment of the schema and information base of that system. The figure uses a dashed arrow to represent an *InstanceOf*

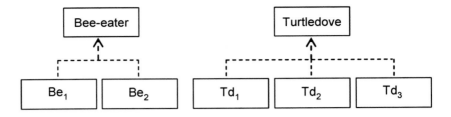

**Fig. 17.1.** Fragment of the schema and information base of a system that records bee-eaters and turtledoves

relationship between an entity and a type. In the figure, *Bee-eater* and *Turtledove* are entity types, of which there are two and three instances, respectively.

Now let us consider another system that records the bird species that exist in a certain range, including their characteristics, habitats, distribution and sounds. Figure 17.2 shows a fragment of the schema and information base of this system. The entity type *BirdSpecies* has four entities: *Bee-eater*, *Turtledove*, *RockPigeon*, and *Goshawk*. Thus, *Bee-eater* and *Turtledove* are entity types in the system shown in Fig. 17.1, whereas they are entities in the system shown in Fig. 17.2.

If needed, any entity type (that is, any concept) can be seen as an entity. This duality manifests itself clearly in the definition of a concept, especially in definitional theory. As we saw in Chap. 2, in definitional theory, a concept is a set of properties. If we view this set of properties as an object, then a concept may also be an object.

We often view sets of things as single objects. For example, a *team* is defined as

A group of people who play a game or sport together against another group.[1]

Therefore, just as a team, which is a set of people, is viewed as an object, a concept, which is a set of properties, may be viewed as an object.

However, an entity cannot generally be seen as an entity type. For example, the soccer team called *Barcelona* is not a set of properties, and it cannot therefore be seen as an entity type (matches are played by teams, not by sets of properties). To be an entity type, namely a concept, an entity must be a set of properties that can be observed in the objects in the domain.

A *meta entity type* is an entity type whose instances are entity types. The instances of a meta entity type are both entities and entity types. In the

---

[1] Longman Dictionary of Contemporary English Online.

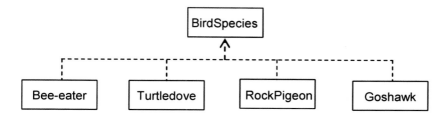

**Fig. 17.2.** Fragment of the schema and information base of a system that records bird species

system shown in Fig. 17.2, *BirdSpecies* is a meta entity type because its instances are also entity types. A given entity type may be an instance of several meta entity types.

Biology provides many examples of meta entity types, but they can be found anywhere. Many organizations use the meta entity type *EmployeeType*, which has instances such as *Engineer*, *Clerk*, *Salesperson* and *Manager*. At home we use the entity type *ApplianceType*, which has instances such as *Refrigerator*, *Dishwasher*, and *CDPlayer*. Banks have *AccountType*, instances of which are *SavingsAccount* and *CheckingAccount*. In conceptual modeling, we use *DataType*, which has instances such as *String*, *Decimal*, *Integer*, *Float*, and *Boolean*.

### 17.1.2 Classification Level

The *InstanceOf* relationship defines a hierarchy between entities, entity types, meta entity types, etc. From this hierarchy we can determine the classification level, which is defined as follows. The *classification level* of an entity or entity type is a natural number that indicates its level in the hierarchy of *InstanceOf* relationships. By definition, the classification level of entities that are not entity types is 0. In the example shown in Fig. 17.1, the classification level of $Be_1$, $Be_2$, $Td_1$, $Td_2$ and $Td_3$ is 0. These are specific birds that do not correspond to entity types (entity types do not fly, whereas birds do). None of the entities shown in Fig. 17.2 has a level of 0.

The classification level of entity types whose instances are not entity types is 1. In Fig. 17.1, the classification level of *Bee-eater* and *Turtledove* is 1. In Fig. 17.2, the classification level of *Bee-eater*, *Goshawk*, *RockPigeon* and *Turtledove* is also 1. The characteristic shared by these entity types is that their instances are specific birds and not entity types. The instances of level-1 entity types must be level-0 entities. The entity type called *Entity* also has a level of 1, because its instances are all of the

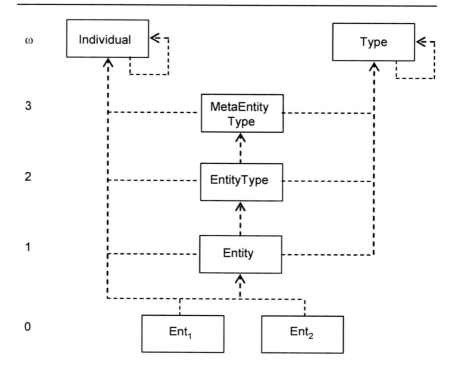

**Fig. 17.3.** *InstanceOf* relationships between special entity types. The classification levels are shown on the left

entities in an information base. All level-1 entity types are direct or indirect subtypes of *Entity*.

The classification level of meta entity types whose instances are not meta entity types is 2. In Fig. 17.2, the level of *BirdSpecies* is 2. There are no examples in Fig. 17.1. The instances of level-2 meta entity types must be level-1 entity types. By analogy with the entity type *Entity*, we also define a special level-2 meta entity type called *EntityType*, whose instances are all level-1 entity types. Therefore,

> *Entity InstanceOf EntityType*
> *BirdSpecies IsA EntityType*

In the general case, we may have meta entity types that are also entities and thus instances of a *meta meta entity type*, whose classification level will be 3. The instances of level-3 meta meta entity types must be level-2 meta entity types. By analogy with the previous cases, we also define a special level-3 meta meta entity type called *MetaEntityType*, whose instances are all level-2 meta entity types. Therefore,

   *EntityType InstanceOf MetaEntityType*
   *BirdSpecies InstanceOf MetaEntityType*

The number of classification levels may increase indefinitely, and so it is convenient to assume that the hierarchy ends at some point. We therefore define a special entity type, called *Individual*, whose instances are all entities, entity types, meta entity types, meta meta entity types, etc., including itself. The concept of classification levels does not apply to *Individual*.

Sometimes it is useful to have an entity type akin to *Individual* that does not include level-0 entities. We call this entity type *Type* because its instances, including itself, are entity types. The concept of classification levels does not apply to *Type*.

We can define other types akin to *Individual* and *Type*. These types are called *ω-types*. Their common characteristic is that their instances have several classification levels. Figure 17.3 shows the above special entity types and their *InstanceOf* relationships. The figure also includes two specific entities (*Ent*₁ and *Ent*₂) to show that they are *InstanceOf Individual*, but not *InstanceOf Type*.

### 17.1.3 *InstanceOf* versus *IsA*

It is easy to confuse *InstanceOf* and *IsA* relationships, because many natural languages use the same expression to denote them. For example, in English we say "3 is an integer" and "an integer is a rational number". In both cases, we use the expression "is a" despite the fact that in the former case we mean

   3 *InstanceOf Integer*

while in the latter case we mean

   *Integer IsA Rational*

The confusion is even greater in metamodeling, as the entities related by *InstanceOf* and *IsA* are entity types, meta entity types, meta meta entity types, and so on. In these cases, we need criteria to determine which relationship is appropriate.

One such criterion is that *IsA* is transitive, whereas *InstanceOf* is not. Thus, if we have

   *Integer IsA Rational*

*Rational IsA Number*

we easily infer that

*Integer IsA Number*

However, when we have

3 *InstanceOf Integer*
*Integer InstanceOf EntityType*

we cannot infer that

3 *InstanceOf EntityType*

Another criterion is that in an $E_1$ *IsA* $E_2$ relationship, both $E_1$ and $E_2$ must have the same classification level, which must be greater than 0. However, in $E_1$ *InstanceOf* $E_2$, the classification level of $E_1$ must be one less than that of $E_2$, unless $E_2$ is an $\omega$-type. By applying this criterion, we see that

*Integer InstanceOf Rational*

is invalid because their classification level is 1. Nor can we say that

3 *IsA Integer*

because the classification level of 3 is 0, while that of *Integer* is 1.

Let us now analyze the interaction between *InstanceOf* and *IsA*. We distinguish four cases:

- From *C InstanceOf A* and *A IsA B*, we can infer *C InstanceOf B*. This is a well-known property, by which *C* is an indirect instance of *B*.
- From *C InstanceOf B* and *A IsA B*, we cannot infer anything new. *C* may or may not also be an instance of *A*.
- From *A IsA B* and *B InstanceOf C*, we cannot infer anything new. *A* may or may not be an instance of *C*. For example, from

  *YoungBee-eater IsA Bee-eater*
  *Bee-eater InstanceOf BirdSpecies*

  we cannot infer that *YoungBee-eater InstanceOf BirdSpecies*.
- From *A IsA B* and *A InstanceOf C*, we cannot infer *B InstanceOf C*. For example, from

  *YoungBee-eater IsA Bee-eater*
  *YoungBee-eater InstanceOf YoungBirdType*

  we cannot infer that *Bee-eater InstanceOf YoungBirdType*.

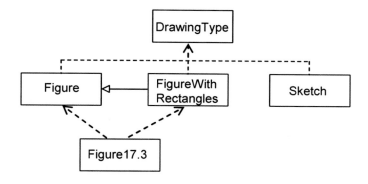

**Fig. 17.4.** Examples of *InstanceOf* and *IsA*.

As an additional example, consider the domain of figures and assume the following entities and entity types (see Fig. 17.4):

- the entity *Figure*17.3, shown in the previous subsection;
- the entity type *FigureWithRectangles*, whose instances are all figures that contain at least one rectangle;
- the entity type *Figure*, whose instances are all possible figures;
- the meta entity type *DrawingType*, whose instances are *Figure*, *Sketch*, etc.

The *InstanceOf* and *IsA* relationships here are

      *Figure*17.3 *InstanceOf FigureWithRectangles*
      *FigureWithRectangles IsA Figure*
      *Figure InstanceOf DrawingType*
      *FigureWithRectangles InstanceOf DrawingType*
      *Sketch InstanceOf DrawingType*

from which we can infer only that

      *Figure*17.3 *InstanceOf Figure*

## 17.1.4 Monolevel and Multilevel Information Bases

In Chap. 2, we saw that an information base contains a symbol for each object represented in the system, as well as the classification of these objects into the entity types defined in the schema. If, in a given domain, we have the classification *A InstanceOf B*, then:

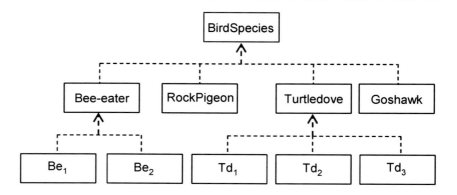

**Fig. 17.5.** Integration of the schemas and information bases of Figs. 17.1 and 17.2

- *A* will be represented by a symbol in the information base.
- *B* will be represented by a symbol in the schema.
- The information base will represent the classification of *A* as an object of type *B*.

An information base is *multilevel* if it can contain one or more sequences of classifications of the form

> *A InstanceOf B*
> *B InstanceOf C*

A multilevel information base may contain a classification of an entity as an object of type *B* and a classification of *B* as an object of another type *C*. An information base is *monolevel* if, when it contains the classification *A InstanceOf B*, it cannot contain a classification of *B* as belonging to another type *C*. The classifications into the special entity types shown in Fig. 17.3 are implicitly present in all information bases, and they are not taken into account in determining whether an information base is monolevel or multilevel.

Most information bases are monolevel. The information base shown in Fig. 17.1 is monolevel: each of the five entities that it contains is a direct *InstanceOf* one of the two entity types defined in the schema. The information base shown in Fig. 17.2 is also monolevel: each of the four entities is a direct *InstanceOf BirdSpecies*, which is defined in the schema.

Usually, all of the entities represented in a monolevel information base have the same classification level. In Fig. 17.1, this level is 0. In Fig. 17.2, it is 1. However, as explained below, the entities of a monolevel information base may have different classification levels.

If we integrate the systems shown in Figs. 17.1 and 17.2, we obtain the system shown in Fig. 17.5, whose information base is multilevel. It contains the following classifications, among others:

> $Be_1$ *InstanceOf Bee-eater*
> *Bee-eater InstanceOf BirdSpecies*

In multilevel information bases, there are entity types that appear in both the information base and the schema, as in the case of the entity types *Bee-eater* and *Turtledove* in Fig. 17.5, for instance. This means that the clear distinction between the information base and the schema that exists in the case of monolevel information bases is blurred for multilevel ones. If so desired, the problem can be avoided by ignoring the distinction between the information base and the schema and dealing only with knowledge bases, which include both. We tend to keep the distinction, however, because it is very common in the information systems field.

## 17.1.5 Logical Representation

Chapter 2 discussed the logical representation of *A InstanceOf E* classifications in monolevel information bases. In essence, the information base contains a symbol denoting *A*, the schema contains a symbol denoting *E* and the information base contains the formula $E(A)$, which means that *A* is an instance of *E*.

If we use this logical representation with the system shown in Fig. 17.2, the schema will contain the predicate *BirdSpecies* and the information base will contain the following formulas:

> *BirdSpecies(Bee-eater)*
> *BirdSpecies(Turtledove)*
> *BirdSpecies(RockPigeon)*
> *BirdSpecies(Goshawk)*

This form of representation ignores the fact that *Bee-eater*, etc., are entity types, because it is irrelevant to this system.

This logical representation cannot be used for multilevel information bases (at least in first-order logic), because we cannot represent the classifications shown in Fig. 17.5 as

> *Bee-eater($Be_1$)*
> *BirdSpecies(Bee-eater)*

because then the symbol *Bee-eater* would be both a predicate and a term, which is not permissible in first-order logic.

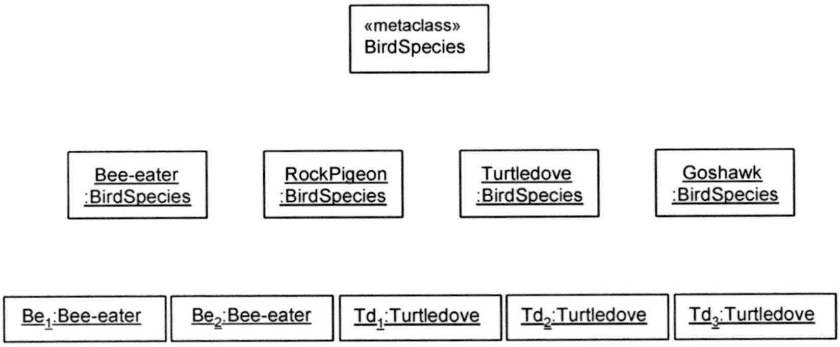

**Fig. 17.6.** UML representation of the entities, entity types, and meta entity type shown in Fig. 17.5

In first-order logic, the solution is to represent all classifications using a single binary predicate, which we shall call *In*. Thus,

$$In(A,B)$$

means *A InstanceOf B*. Using this predicate, the classifications shown in Fig. 17.5 are represented by the following formulas:

> *In(Bee-eater,BirdSpecies)*
> *In(Turtledove,BirdSpecies)*
> *In(RockPigeon,BirdSpecies)*
> *In(Goshawk,BirdSpecies)*
> *In(Be$_i$,Bee-eater)*
> *In(To$_i$,TurtleDove)*

The main drawback of this form of representation is that entity types do not have an associated predicate. If we need them, they must be defined as derived. For example, if we need a predicate that corresponds to the entity type *Bee-eater*, we must define a new derived predicate such as *P_Bee-eater* using the derivation rule

$$P\_Bee\text{-}eater(e) \leftrightarrow In(e,Bee\text{-}eater)$$

where *Bee-eater* is a constant that denotes the entity type called *Bee-eater*.

When classifications are expressed with the *In* predicate, the logical representation of an *A IsA B* relationship is the following formula:

$$In(e,A) \rightarrow In(e,B)$$

### 17.1.6 Representation in UML

UML does not allow a uniform, coherent representation of types, meta entity types, etc., in multilevel information bases. UML is essentially geared towards monolevel information bases, but it does include constructs that provide some expressiveness, as explained below.

In UML, it is easy to represent the classification of an entity into one or more entity types. The graphical notation is a rectangle containing the name of the entity, a colon, and the names of the entity types, all underlined. At the bottom of Fig. 17.6, this notation is used to represent the two bee-eaters and three turtledoves shown in Fig. 17.1.

A meta entity type can be represented as an entity type using the stereotype *metaclass*. The instances of entity types in this stereotype are entity types. Figure 17.6 shows an example: the instances of *BirdSpecies* are entity types.

To show the classification of an entity type into a meta entity type, we can use the same notation as for the classification of an entity in an entity type. Figure 17.6 uses this notation to indicate that *Bee-eater*, *Turtledove*, *RockPigeon*, and *Goshawk* are instances of *BirdSpecies*. However, this kind of classification is not usually shown in UML.

## 17.2 Powertypes

Powertypes are a particular kind of meta entity type; they occur frequently and receive special attention in conceptual modeling. UML provides a special notation for them. A *powertype P* of an entity type $E$ is a meta entity type whose instances are subtypes of $E$. Normally, $P$ is a level-2 meta entity type and its instances are level-1 entity types. The entity type $E$ is not an instance of $P$.

For example, the meta entity type *BirdSpecies* described in the previous section is a powertype of *Bird*. The instances of *BirdSpecies* (*Bee-eater*, etc.) are subtypes of *Bird*.

In logic, the representation of a powertype $P$ of $E$ consists of a formula for each instance $E_i$ of $P$. The formula is as follows:

$$In(E_i,P) \rightarrow \forall e \ (In(e,E_i) \rightarrow In(e,E))$$

That is, if $E_i$ is an instance of $P$, then each instance of $E_i$ must also be an instance of E.

In UML, a powertype $P$ of $E$ is represented as an ordinary entity type. Each entity type that is an instance of $P$ must have an *IsA* relationship (arrow) with $E$. To indicate instances of $P$, the string ": $P$" is placed next to

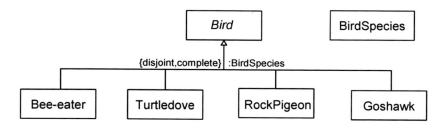

**Fig. 17.7.** *BirdSpecies* is a powertype of *Bird*

the set of *IsA* arrows from those instances to *E*. Figure 17.7 shows an example of this.

Another example of a powertype is *ApplianceType*, whose instances (such as *WashingMachine*, *Fridge*, and *Stove*) are subtypes of *Appliance*. Figure 17.8 shows its representation in UML. The association *appliance–applianceType* could be defined as derived because an appliance's type is the subtype of which it is an instance. If, for example, an appliance is a fridge, then the appliance must be associated with the instance of *ApplianceType* that corresponds to *Fridge*.

Powertypes may have attributes and participate in associations. The next section shows that these attributes and associations have a particular set of characteristics. In Fig. 17.8, *ApplianceType* has the attribute *averagePrice* and participates in the following relationship type:

> *Produces* (*Company*, *ApplianceType*)

which indicates the types of appliances produced by a company. Note how this differs from

> *ProducedBy* (*Appliance*, *Company*)

which indicates the company that manufactured a particular appliance.

## 17.3 Class Relationship Types

We know that an information base contains a representation of the entities that exist in a domain and their relationships. We have just seen that an entity type may be an entity. This leads us to the question of whether there may be relationships between entity types.

The answer is yes. There are relationships in which all or some of the participants are entity types. In other words, there are relationships in

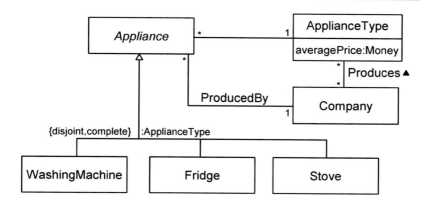

**Fig. 17.8.** *ApplianceType* is a powertype of *Appliance*

which all or some of the participants have a classification level greater than 0. These relationships, like any other, must be instances of a relationship type called a *class relationship type*. The instances of a class relationship type are relationships in which some of the participants are entity types. Apart from this, class relationship types are the same as ordinary relationship types, and their logical representation is identical.

Let us suppose that we are interested in the average length of each species of bird. The relationship type would be

*AverageLength (BirdSpecies, Length)*

which is a class relationship type because its instances include relationships such as

*AverageLength (Bee-eater, Length28cms)*
*AverageLength (TurtleDove, Length30cms)*

in which the first participant is an entity type. The second participant is a specific length, which is a characteristic not of a particular bird, but of the whole species.

Most class relationship types are binary and their instances relate a level-1 entity to a level-0 entity. As shown above, this is the case for *AverageLength*. However, all cases are possible. An example in which both participants have a level of 1 is

*IsLarger (large:BirdSpecies, small:BirdSpecies)*

in which the relationship is between two bird species. An instance might be

*IsLarger* (*TurtleDove, Bee-eater*)

which represents the fact that turtledoves are typically larger than bee-eaters.

UML does not allow a coherent representation of class relationship types, but it does include a construct that provides limited expressiveness, as explained below.

In UML, attributes may be static or nonstatic. Let $A(E_1, E_2)$ be an attribute. Attribute $A$ is *nonstatic* (which is the default) if each instance of $E_1$ has a value for the attribute. It is *static* if the attribute has a value that applies to the entity type $E_1$. In both cases, the value of the attribute is an instance of $E_2$. In graphical representations, static attributes are underlined.

Figure 17.9 (left) shows four examples of static attributes. The entity type is *Account*, and the four attributes are

- *minimumBalance*: *Money*. Indicates the minimum balance that must be maintained by all accounts.
- *interestRate*: *Percentage*. Gives the interest rate earned by accounts. All accounts earn the same interest rate.
- *numberOfAccounts*: *Natural*. Indicates the total number of existing instances of *Account*. This is a derived attribute.
- *totalBalance*: *Money*. Gives the sum of the balances of all existing accounts. This is also a derived attribute.

Sometimes it is useful to group a set of static attributes into a single entity type. UML provides a stereotype for this purpose, called *utility*. An entity type with the stereotype *utility* has no instances and can have only static attributes (and operations). Figure 17.9 (right) shows an example.

The attributes of powertypes and the associations in which they participate are class relationship types. Figure 17.8 shows three examples: the attribute *averagePrice*, the association *appliance–applianceType* and the association *Produces*.

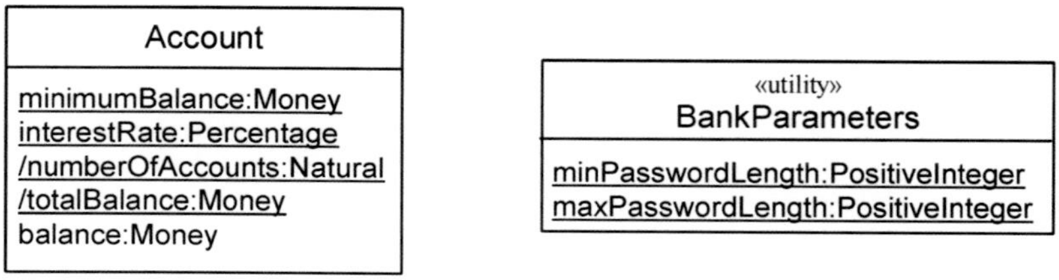

| Account |
| --- |
| minimumBalance:Money<br>interestRate:Percentage<br>/numberOfAccounts:Natural<br>/totalBalance:Money<br>balance:Money |

| «utility»<br>BankParameters |
| --- |
| minPasswordLength:PositiveInteger<br>maxPasswordLength:PositiveInteger |

**Fig. 17.9.** Examples of static attributes

## 17.4 Meta Relationship Types

### 17.4.1 Definition

Meta relationship types have not yet been studied enough, and unfortunately there does not exist a commonly accepted definition of them. By analogy with meta entity types, a meta relationship type should be a relationship type whose instances are both relationships and relationship types. This definition, however, is not widely accepted. In fact, most of the literature on metamodeling implicitly assumes otherwise.

If a meta entity type is something whose instances are entity types, then a consistent use of language requires that a meta relationship type be something whose instances are relationship types.

However, entity and relationship types are concepts, and definitional theory states that concepts are sets of properties. An entity type is a set of properties that specific objects must satisfy in order to be instances of that type. A relationship type is a set of properties that specific relationships must satisfy in order to be instances of that type.

If both entity and relationship types are concepts and the former are considered as instances of entity types, then the latter should also be considered as instances of entity types. This leads us to the most widely accepted definition: a *meta relationship type* is an entity type whose instances are both relationship types and entities.

We shall consider an example schema in which relationship types are instances of entity types. We shall then explain a problem that would arise if meta relationship types were relationship types.

Cyc is one of the largest ontologies currently in existence. What we call a relationship type is a function or a predicate in Cyc. Functions and predicates are direct instances of one or more meta entity types. In Cyc, these meta entity types are neither functions nor predicates; they are what we call entity types.

For example, consider the ternary relationship type

*HasPositionIn* (*Person, Organization, PositionType*)

which indicates that a person works in an organization in a certain type of position, and the five-degree relationship

*AmountOfSalesByToDuring*
    *(seller:Agent, buyer:Agent, TimeInterval, ProductType,
    revenue:Money)*

which indicates how much of a certain product was sold by a particular seller to a particular buyer during a particular time interval.

In Cyc, these two predicates are defined as an instance of #$*FunctionalPredicate*, which is not a predicate, but rather an entity type. The instances of #$*FunctionalPredicate* are predicates that are functional in at least one argument (in *HasPositionIn*, a person can have only one position in an organization; in *AmountOfSalesByToDuring*, there can be only one amount of revenue for a given seller, buyer, time interval, and product type). More examples are presented below.

Let us see what would happen if meta relationship types were relationship types. Consider the following meta relationship type:

> *BinaryRelationshipType*
> *(participant1:EntityType, participant2:EntityType)*

whose instances are all binary relationship types. However, in conceptual modeling, no two instances of the same relationship type can have the same participants. Therefore, we could not have the relationship types

> *Lives* (*Person, Town*)
> *Works* (*Person, Town*)

as two instances of *BinaryRelationshipType*, because they have the same participants (*Person, Town*). One solution would be to give *BinaryRelationshipType* a third participant with the name of the relationship type (*Lives, Works*). However, the instances of a ternary relationship type would then be binary relationship types, and similar problems would appear.

For this reason, *BinaryRelationshipType* is usually defined as an entity type whose instances are relationship types with two participants.

Class relationship types, which have been described above, are sometimes confused with meta relationship types. However, the difference is clear: the instances of a class relationship type are not relationship types (concepts), but rather relationships.

## 17.4.2 Logical Representation

Chapter 3 discussed the logical representation of the instances of a relationship type in a monolevel information base. In essence, an instance of a relationship type $R$ of degree $n$ is represented by a formula $R(A_1, \ldots, A_n)$, where $R$ is the predicate of the relationship type, which is defined in the schema, and $A_1, \ldots, A_n$ are the symbols that denote the participating entities.

In multilevel information bases, we cannot represent $R$ as an instance of a meta relationship type $MR$ with a formula such as

*MR(R)*

because *R* would be both a predicate and a term. This is the same problem that we encountered when we attempted to classify entity types as meta entity types.

One solution is to represent all binary relationship types using a single ternary predicate, which we shall call *InBinaryRT*. Thus,

*InBinaryRT(A,B,R)*

means that entities *A* and *B* are the participants in an instance of *R*. To represent *R* as an instance of *MR*, we would write

*In(R,MR)*

where *In* is the predicate defined in Sect. 17.1.5.

We would do the same for ternary relationship types, using a predicate such as *InTernaryRT*, and for any other degrees required.

The main drawback of this form of representation is that relationship types do not have associated predicates. If we need them, they must be defined as derived. For example, if we need a predicate that corresponds to the relationship type *LivesIn*, we must define a new derived predicate such as *P_LivesIn* using the following derivation rule:

*P_LivesIn(person,town)* ↔ *InBinaryRT(person,town,LivesIn)*

where *LivesIn* is a constant that denotes a relationship type called "*LivesIn*."

When relationship classifications are expressed using the *InBinaryRT* predicate, the logical representation of the specialization *R IsA S*, where both *R* and *S* are binary relationship types, is the following formula:

*InBinaryRT(a,b,R)* → *InBinaryRT(a,b,S)*

## 17.4.3 Representation in UML

UML is not well suited to representing meta relationship types and their instances in multilevel information bases. The only way to do so is by using stereotypes, as explained later on in this chapter. However, stereotypes provide only limited expressiveness.

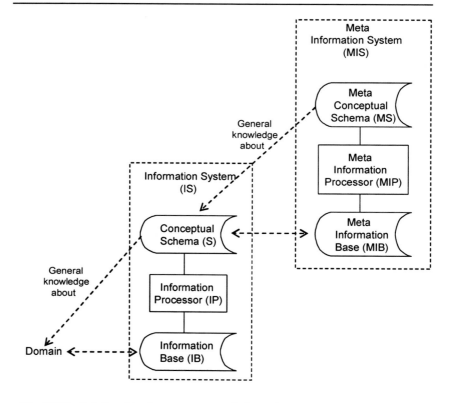

**Fig. 17.10.** Relationships between a meta information system and an information system

## 17.5 Metaschemas

### 17.5.1 Definition

We know that a conceptual schema is a representation of general knowledge about a domain. Domains are normally organizations or parts of them, but they may also take many other forms. In particular, a domain may be the conceptual schema of an information system. A *metaschema* is a schema that represents general knowledge about a domain that consists of a schema.

Figure 17.10 shows the difference between a schema and a metaschema and introduces some related concepts. The figure shows an information system *IS* that consists of three components: an information processor *IP*, a conceptual schema *S* and an information base *IB*. The information base *IB* contains a representation of the state of the domain; that is, *IB* contains a representation of all the entities in the domain and their relationships. The schema *S* contains a representation of the general knowledge about the domain (entity types, relationship types, constraints, domain events, etc.). The processor *IP* receives external messages and changes *IB* and/or produces an output.

Let us assume that we have another information system *MIS* that, among other functions, maintains a representation of the schema *S*. The right-hand side of Fig. 17.10 shows the three components of *MIS*:

- The information base *MIB* contains a representation of *S*.
- The conceptual schema *MS* contains a representation of the general knowledge about the domain that consists of *S*. The schema *MS* is the metaschema of *S*. Also, *S* is an instance of *MS*.
- The processor *MIP* receives external messages and changes *MIB* and/or produces an output.

Figure 17.10 also shows a relationship between the domain and *IB*. This is a representation or denotation relationship, which indicates that the instances and relationships in the domain are represented by symbols in *IB*. By virtue of this relationship, the domain corresponds to *IB*.

Similarly, there is a representation or denotation relationship between *S* and *MIB*, which indicates that the instances and relationships in *S* are represented by symbols in *MIB*. By virtue of this relationship, *S* corresponds to *MIB*.

The schemas *S* and *MS* may be written in the same conceptual model and language or in different ones. For example, *S* may be represented graphically in the ER model, *MS* may be represented in the FOL model and language, or *S* and *MS* may both be written in UML.

## 17.5.2 Example of a Metaschema

In order to illustrate the meaning of the concepts shown in Fig. 17.10, let us analyze a specific example of a metaschema *MS*. Figure 17.11 shows the entity and relationship types of a metaschema fragment in UML.

The entity types in *MS* are:

- *EntityType*. This is a level-2 meta entity type whose instances are the entity types of a schema *S*. Each instance of *EntityType* has a value for the attribute *name*, which is the name of the corresponding entity type.

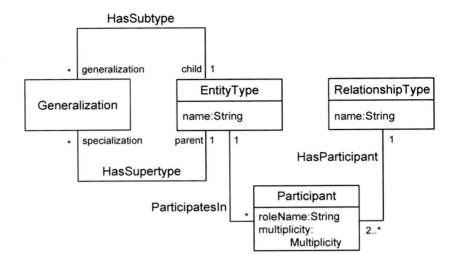

**Fig. 17.11.** Fragment of a metaschema

- *RelationshipType*. This is a level-2 entity type whose instances are the relationship types of a schema *S*. Each instance of *RelationshipType* has a value for the attribute *name*, which is the name of the corresponding relationship type.
- *Participant*. This is a level-1 entity type; therefore, its instances are not concepts. The instances of *Participant* define the roles and entity types of the participants in a relationship type. The attributes *roleName* and *multiplicity* give the name of the role and its multiplicity, respectively.
- *Generalization*. This is described below.

Normally, a metaschema *MS* is much smaller than its schema instances *S*. In a schema *S*, there are many instances of the entity types shown in Fig. 17.11.

Figure 17.12 shows a relationship type (*LivesIn*) in the schema *S* and its representation in the meta information base *MIB* as a UML object diagram. There is a correspondence between *LivesIn* and the single instance of *RelationshipType*. Because *LivesIn* is binary, there are two instances of *Participant* in the *MIB* (*p*1 and *p*2).

The correspondence rules between *S* and *MIB* are the following:

- There is a 1–1 correspondence between the entity types in *S* and the instances of *EntityType* in *MIB*. The name of an entity type in *S* is the value of the attribute *name* in *MIB*.

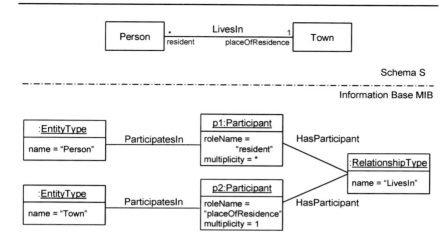

**Fig. 17.12.** Example of a relationship type (*LivesIn*) in the schema *S* and its representation in the information base *MIB*

- There is a 1–1 correspondence between the relationship types in *S* and the instances of *RelationshipType* in *MIB*. The name of a relationship type in *S* is the value of the attribute *name* in *MIB*. The relationship type in *S* has a participant for each instance of *Participant* in the corresponding *RelationshipType* in *MIB*. The name of this participant is the value of the attribute *roleName* of *Participant*. The multiplicity of this participant is the value of the attribute *multiplicity* of the participant. The participant entity type is given by the association *ParticipatesIn*.

Naturally, the metaschema *MS* must include the integrity constraints that its instances must satisfy (in *MIB*). These constraints are sometimes called meta integrity constraints, although this may cause confusion because these constraints are not concepts and do not have instances. Nevertheless, this is an acceptable name because these constraints are defined in metaschemas. These constraints are also sometimes called *well-formedness rules*. A *well-formedness rule* is a term used in the normative UML metamodel specification to describe a set of constraints written in OCL that helps to define a metamodel element.

Figure 17.11 defines graphically the referential and cardinality constraints of *MS*. The additional constraints are (in OCL)

```
context EntityType inv nameIsUnique:
  EntityType.allInstances()->isUnique(name)
context RelationshipType inv nameIsUnique:
  RelationshipType.allInstances()->isUnique(name)
```

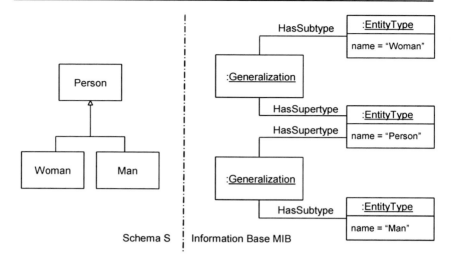

**Fig. 17.13.** Examples of generalizations in the schema *S* and their representation in the information base *MIB*

```
context RelationshipType inv rolesHaveDifferentName:
  participant->isUnique(roleName)
```

The metaschema example shown in Fig. 17.11 illustrates again that meta relationship types are entity types. In this figure, the entity type *RelationshipType* is a meta relationship type because its instances are relationship types in *S*.

Figure 17.13 shows a generalization (*Person Gens Man, Woman*) in the schema *S* and its representation in the information base *MIB* through an object diagram. The two instances of *Generalization* correspond to the *IsA* of schema *S*. The correspondence is simple: if in *S* there is a *B IsA C*, then in MIB there is an instance of *Generalization*, *g*, such that

- *g.subtype* = the instance of *EntityType* with *name* = "*B*"
- *g.supertype* = the instance of *EntityType* with *name* = "*C*"

The most important constraint related to *Generalization* is that an *EntityType* cannot be a direct or indirect generalization of itself. Formally,

```
context EntityType inv noCycles:
  not self.allParents()->includes(self)
```

where *allParents*() is a helper operation defined as

```
context EntityType:
  def allParents():Set(EntityType) =
    self.generalization.parent->
      union(self.generalization.parent.allParents())->asSet()
```

### 17.5.3 Levels of a Meta Information Base

The first section of this chapter explained that information bases may be monolevel or multilevel. Let us now determine what kind of meta information base is shown in Fig. 17.12, assuming that its metaschema is the one shown in Fig. 17.11.

*MIB* is monolevel. It contains classifications of level-1 entity types into level-2 entity types (such as *Person InstanceOf EntityType*) and classifications of level-0 entities into level-1 entity types (such as *p*1 *InstanceOf Participant*), but no entity type is classified as an instance of another entity type.

*MIB* also contains several instances of ordinary relationship types. For example, Figure 17.12 shows the value of the attribute *roleName* of *Participant p*1.

*MIB* contains several instances of class relationship types. One is

*ParticipatesIn* (*EntityType*, *Participant*)

The instances of this type have a level-1 participant (an entity type, such as *Town* in Fig. 17.12).

### 17.5.4 The Importance of Metaschemas

Metaschemas are the schemas of meta information systems. These systems are normally integrated into larger development environments. Meta information systems perform functions that are very useful to designers. These functions include the following:

- Maintaining a consistent representation of the schema in the meta information base. Conceptual modelers tell the meta information processor the changes they want to make to a schema, and the meta information processor records them in the meta information base. The meta information processor verifies that the schema is correct by checking all relevant constraints defined in the metaschema.
- Providing information about a schema on demand and in the appropriate form.

- Supporting schema validation by generating prototypes, paraphrasing a schema in a language understood by the relevant audience, or providing additional explanations.
- Integrating two or more schema fragments.
- Automatically generating (part of) the system code.

### 17.5.5 Conceptual Models versus Metaschemas

Now that we have examined the concept of metaschemas, let us review the terms introduced in Chap. 1 and relate them to the ones used in this chapter.

In Chap. 1, we defined "conceptualization" as the set of concepts used in a specific domain, and a "conceptual schema" (or ontology) as the specification of a conceptualization in some language. We also defined a "conceptual model" as a way to observe domains.

By analogy, therefore, a *metaconceptualization* is a set of concepts used in conceptualizations. Therefore, a conceptual model is a metaconceptualization. A metaconceptualization consists of two essential concepts: entity types and relationship types. However, the fact that there are many other concepts and variations makes conceptual models highly diverse.

A metaschema is a specification of a conceptual model in a particular language. For example, the fragment of the metaschema shown in Fig. 17.11 specifies, in UML, a fragment of a conceptual model that conceptualizes domains in terms of entity types, relationship types, and generalizations of entity types. This conceptual model does not include integrity constraints, reifications, generalizations of relationship types, or attributes.

When highly precise usage of terms is not required, metaschemas and conceptual models may be considered as synonyms.

### 17.5.6 The UML Metaschema

The UML metaschema is a schema that represents general knowledge about models that may be defined in UML. The UML metaschema was specified and adopted by the Object Management Group (OMG) as a standard in 1997. Since then, it has been continuously reviewed and improved. The UML metaschema is the reference source that expert modelers and meta information processor designers use to clarify the meaning of the language constructs. The UML metaschema is very large

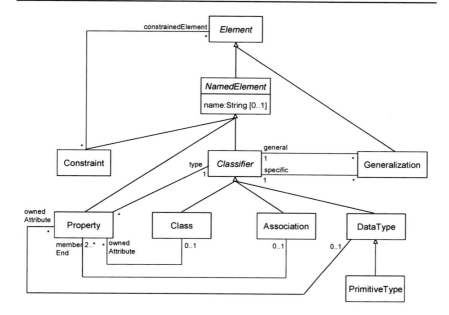

**Fig. 17.14.** Fragment of the UML metaschema (simplified)

because UML deals not only with conceptual schemas but also with other kinds of software model.

The UML metaschema includes hundreds of entity types. Figure 17.14 shows a few of the entity types that are most relevant to conceptual modeling, which are:

- *Class*. The instances are entity types.
- *DataType*. The instances are data types.
- *PrimitiveType*. A predefined data type such as *Boolean* or *String*.
- *Association*. The instances are associations.
- *Property*. The instances are attributes of entity types, data types or association participants.
- *Classifier*. An abstract entity type that groups classes, data types, associations and other model elements.
- *Generalization*. There is an instance of this entity type for each *IsA* relationship between two classifiers.
- *Constraint*. The instances are constraints.

- *NamedElement*. An abstract entity type that groups all model elements that have a name. Note that the instances of *Generalization* have no name.
- *Element*. An abstract entity type that groups all model elements.

The two associations between *Classifier* and *Generalization* are similar to those shown in Fig. 17.11. The association between *Constraint* and *Element* gives the elements constrained by a constraint. The association between *Property* and *Classifier* defines the type of the attribute or participant. An integrity constraint forces the type to be a *Class* or a *DataType*. The associations between *Class* or *DataType* and *Property* define the attributes of a class or a data type, respectively. Finally, the association between *Association* and *Property* gives the participants of an association.

The UML metaschema includes many constraints, which are defined formally in OCL. For example, one constraint states that a constraint cannot be applied to itself. In OCL,

```
context Constraint inv cannotBeAppliedToItself:
   not constrainedElement->includes(self)
```

## 17.6 Stereotypes

### 17.6.1 Definition

UML has a mechanism called *profiles* for adapting metaschemas with constructs that are specific to a particular domain, platform, or method. For example, a profile for conceptual modeling might consist of constructs for defining particular entity types (such as events), associations (such as materializations) or constraints (such as permanent).

A profile consists essentially of one or more stereotypes. A *stereotype* is a class whose instances extend the characteristics defined in a model element. These new characteristics are additional information that may be used for many different purposes.

For example, we can annotate a model element (that is, an instance of *Element*, shown in Fig. 17.14) with the name of the author and the date when the element was defined. UML does not provide constructs for defining this information. However, we can define a stereotype, which we shall call *Authorship*, using two attributes, *author* and *date*, as indicated in Fig. 17.15. Stereotypes are defined by means of a class symbol (a rectangle) with the keyword «*stereotype*». The arrow from *Authorship* (the stereotype) to *Element* indicates that the stereotype applies to instances of

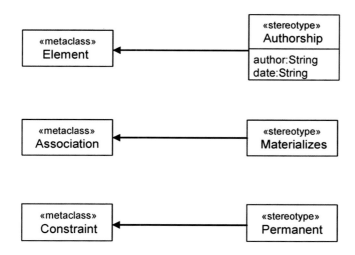

**Fig. 17.15.** Definition of stereotypes *Authorship, Materializes* and *Permanent*

*Element.* We write the keyword *«metaclass»* above *Element* to indicate that it is an entity type of the metaschema. Each instance of *Authorship* is related to an instance of *Element*, and the values of its two attributes give the *author* and *date* of the corresponding element. Each instance of *Authorship* extends the characteristics of an *Element*.

To indicate that we want to define the authorship information about an element, we write *«authorship»* above or before the name of the element. The values of the attributes can be shown as part of a comment symbol connected to the stereotyped element. Figure 17.16 shows an example, in which the authorship of the entity type *Production* is defined.

The application of the stereotype *Authorship* to *Production* is understood as the creation of a new instance of a class called *Authorship*,

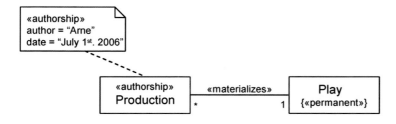

**Fig. 17.16.** Examples of application of stereotypes *Authorship, Materializes,* and *Permanent*

which is related to a single instance of *Element* (*Production* in this case), and whose attributes are additional information about the stereotyped element (*Production*).

*Materializes* is another stereotype shown in Fig. 17.15. Each instance of it is related to an association, and it means that the association is a realization of the generic relationship type *Materializes*, which was described in Chap. 7. Figure 17.16 shows the application of this stereotype to the relationship between *Production* and *Play*. In this case, the instances of *Materializes* have no attributes.

The last example shown in Fig. 17.15 is *Permanent*. Each instance of it is related to a constraint, and it means that the constraint is permanent, which was described in Chaps. 2 and 3. Figure 17.16 shows the application of this stereotype to the constraint defined in *Play*. As in the above example, the instances of *Permanent* have no attributes.

## 17.6.2 Stereotypes in the Metaschema

Now we shall describe the placement of stereotypes in the UML metaschema. Figure 17.17 shows an adaptation and simplification of the fragment of the metaschema that deals with stereotypes.

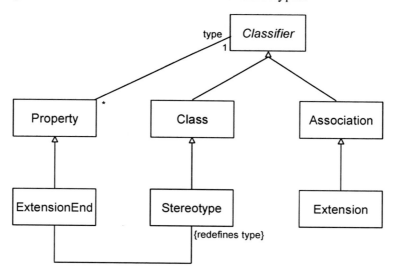

**Fig. 17.17.** Fragment of the UML metaschema that deals with stereotypes

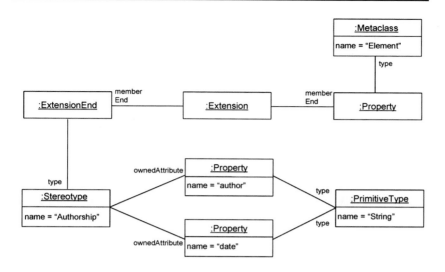

**Fig. 17.18.** Representation in the meta information base of the stereotype *Authorship*

The stereotypes that we define are instances of *Stereotype*, which is a subtype of *Class*. Therefore, an instance of *Stereotype* is a class. Like classes, stereotypes may have attributes. The three stereotypes shown in Fig. 17.15 are instances of *Stereotype*, one of which (*Authorship*) has attributes.

The relationship type between a stereotype and the element that it extends is an instance of *Extension*, a subtype of *Association*. The three associations shown in Fig. 17.15 are instances of *Extension*. The metaschema includes a constraint that requires instances of *Extension* to be binary associations. The constraint is defined in OCL as follows:

```
context Extension inv isBinary:
  self.memberEnd->size()= 2
```

One participant of an extension must be a stereotype. The other one must be a meta entity type defined in the metaschema. The participant that is a stereotype is an instance of *ExtensionEnd*. Figure 17.17 defines that the *type* of an extension end must be a stereotype. The other participant of an extension is an ordinary *Property*, but its *type* must be an instance of *Metaclass*. This cannot be shown in Fig. 17.17 because *Metaclass* is a meta meta entity type. The instances of *Metaclass* are the meta entity types of the metaschema.

An instance *R* of *Extension* is a class relationship type because

- *R* is a relationship type; and
- the instances of *R* are relationships in which one of the participants is an entity type.

Figure 17.18 shows the instantiation of Fig. 17.17 for the stereotype *Authorship*. The stereotype is an instance of *Stereotype* with the name "Authorship". A stereotype is a class, and a class is a *NamedElement*, whose instances may have a name. *Authorship* has two attributes named *author* and *date*, which are both of type *String*. The instance of *Extension* has two participants (*memberEnd*). One is an *ExtensionEnd* and the other is a *Property*. The type of the former is *stereotype*, whereas the type of the latter is *Element*, which is an instance of *Metaclass*.

Figure 17.19 shows the representation in the meta information base of the schema defined in Fig. 17.16. An instance of the stereotype *Authorship* extends the entity type *Production*. An instance of the stereotype *Materializes* extends the association between *Production* and *Play*. An instance of *Permanent* extends the constraint that constrains the entity type *Play*.

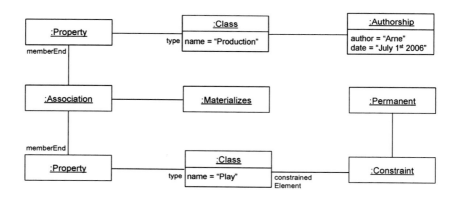

**Fig. 17.19.** Representation in the *MIB* of the schema shown in Fig 17.16

## 17.7 Bibliographical Notes

KEE (Fikes and Kehler 1985) and Proteus (Rusinoff 1989) were two of the first knowledge representation languages that made it possible to define classification hierarchies of entity types. In the field of conceptual modeling of information systems, the first language that provided the constructs needed to define unbounded classification hierarchies was Telos (Mylopoulos et al. 1990), a successor to RML (Greenspan et al. 1982). The ConceptBase system made it possible to define schemas in a variant of Telos and manage the corresponding multilevel information base; see (Jeusfeld et al. 1998) for an overview of the system.

Atkinson and Kühne (2001) introduced the concept of a classification level (potency). Atkinson et al. (2000) discussed the causes of confusion between *InstanceOf* and *IsA* and proposed transitivity analysis as a means of distinguishing between them.

Odell (1994) defined powertypes and analyzed their relationship to *IsA*. Dahchour et al. (2002) discussed the relationship between powertypes and materialization.

Motschnig-Pitrik and Mylopoulos (1992) provided a complete survey of the various aspects of classification. Martin and Odell (1995, Chap. 22) presented an introduction to metamodeling.

The idea of metaschemas was introduced in an ISO report (Griethuysen 1982). Since then, many metaschemas have been defined and published. One of the most recent was UML 2.1 (OMG 2006a). Bernstein (2003) described several functions of meta information systems and presented several operators that manipulate schemas. Atzeni et al. (2006) described an implementation of ModelGen, an operator that transforms schemas from one metaschema to another.

Gogolla and Henderson-Sellers (2002) analyzed the definition and use of stereotypes in UML 1.4.

## 17.8 Exercises

**17.1** Visit a website containing the Cyc ontology, and:

1. Identify a concept that is a meta entity type, and at least two of its instances.
2. Identify a concept that is a meta meta entity type, and at least two of its instances. Identify at least two instances of each of these two instances.
3. Identify a concept that is a meta relationship type and at least two of its instances.

**17.2** In general, we cannot infer from *A IsA B* and *B InstanceOf C* that *A InstanceOf C*. However, there are particular cases in which such an inference would be valid. Give an example.

**17.3** Consider a system that records information about the employees of a company. Each employee has a name and a category. There are three categories of employee: *Salesperson*, *Engineer*, and *Manager*. Each category has a different salary and weekly working hours. All employees of a given category have the same salary and weekly working hours. A salesperson sells a set of products. An engineer works on a set of projects. A manager manages a set of projects. Design the structural schema of this system in two variants: with and without powertypes. Each variant should include all relevant constraints, expressed in OCL if needed. Compare the two variants.

**17.4** Give the instantiation of the UML metaschema indicated in Fig. 17.14 that corresponds to the relationship type (association) shown at the top of Fig. 17.12.

**17.5** Find out the placement of the association classes in the current version of the UML metaschema and extend Fig. 17.14 to deal with them.

# 18 The MOF and XMI

Just as a schema is an instance of a metaschema, so is a metaschema an instance of a meta-metaschema. Meta-metamodeling is concerned with the definition and use of meta-metaschemas. The best-known meta-metaschema is the Meta-Object Facility (MOF), which is introduced in Sect. 18.1. Many metaschemas can be defined as an instance of the MOF. However, the MOF can also be used as a conceptual model (that is, a metaschema) for a restricted subset of schemas, as we show in Sect. 18.2.

The MOF is also the basis of XML Metadata Interchange (XMI), an important standard that enables the exchange of data about schema instances (entities and relationships) between systems and, in particular, the exchange of schemas between conceptual modeling tools. We examine XMI in Sect. 18.3. In that section, we assume that the reader has an elementary knowledge of XML.

## 18.1 Meta-Metaschemas

### 18.1.1 Definition

We know that a schema is a representation of general knowledge about a domain. In the preceding chapter, we saw that a metaschema is a schema that represents general knowledge about a domain consisting of a schema. If we move up a level, we find meta-metaschemas. A *meta-metaschema* is a schema that represents general knowledge about a domain consisting of a metaschema.

Figure 18.1, an extension of Fig. 17.10, shows the difference between a metaschema and a meta-metaschema. A meta-meta information system (*MMIS*) is a system that, in addition to other functions, contains a representation of a metaschema (*MS*). The upper right-hand part of Fig. 18.1 shows the three components of *MMIS*:

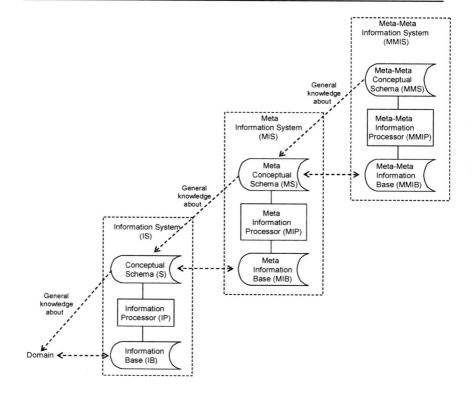

**Fig. 18.1.** Relationships between a meta-meta information system and a meta information system

- The information base (*MMIB*), which contains a representation of *MS*.
- The conceptual schema (*MMS*), which contains a representation of the general knowledge about the domain consisting of the *MS*. *MMS* is the metaschema of *MS*, and *MS* is an instance of *MMS*.
- The processor (*MMIP*), which receives external messages and changes *MMIB* and/or produces an output.

Figure 18.1 also shows a relationship between *MS* and *MMIB*, indicating that the instances and relationships in *MS* are represented by symbols in *MMIB*. By virtue of this relationship, there is a correspondence between *MS* and *MMIB*. *MS* and *MMS* may be written in the same language or a different language.

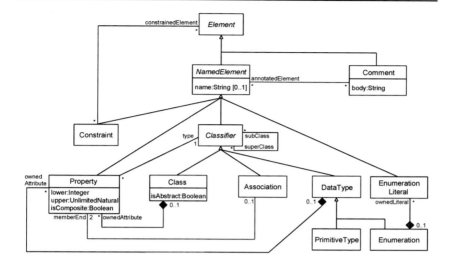

**Fig. 18.2.** Simplified version of the MOF

## 18.1.2 The MOF

The best-known meta-metaschema is the Meta-Object Facility (MOF) specified by the OMG. The MOF acts as a meta-metaschema for several metaschemas (it corresponds to *MMS* in Fig. 18.1). The UML metaschema is an instance of the MOF, but the metaschema of other languages can also be defined as an instance of the MOF.

The MOF reuses a subset of UML concepts that makes the MOF a stand-alone conceptual modeling language (a metaschema) that is suitable for certain applications. We shall describe this use of the MOF in Sect. 18.2.

The MOF is also the basis of XMI, a widely used standard that is described in Sect. 18.3.

The MOF is much smaller than the UML metaschema, but it is still too large to be covered in this book. Instead, we shall describe a simplified version of it that provides an intuitive understanding of its relationship with the UML metaschema and its role in XMI.

Figure 18.2 shows the simplified version of the MOF that will be used in this chapter. In this section, we describe the main relationships between the simplified MOF and the UML metaschema. We illustrate these rela-

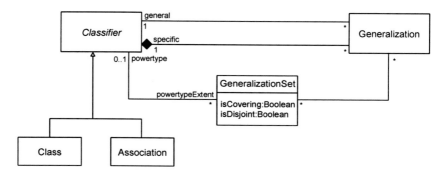

**Fig. 18.3.** Fragment of the UML metaschema

tionships using the fragment of the UML metaschema (Fig. 18.3) that deals with generalizations, generalization sets, and powertypes.

Instances of *Class* in the MOF are entity types in the metaschema. These types have a *name* and may be *abstract*. Figure 18.3 shows five instances of *Class*, whose names are as follows: "Classifier", "Class", "Association", "Generalization", and "GeneralizationSet". Of these, only the first is abstract (*isAbstract = True*). This is shown by writing the name in italics. *Classifier*, *Class*, and *Association* occur both in the MOF and in the metaschema, but they are different concepts. For example, instances of *Class* in the MOF are entity types in the UML metaschema, while instances of the UML metaschema *Class* are entity types in UML schemas.

The five instances of *Class* shown in Fig. 18.3 are types, because they may have instances in a schema. For example, the *IsA* relationships that exist in a schema are instances of *Generalization*.

Instances of the MOF recursive association *subclass–superclass* are *IsA* relationships in the metaschema. Figure 18.3 shows two examples: *Class IsA Classifier* and *Association IsA Classifier*.

Instances of *Association* in the MOF are binary relationship types in the metaschema. These types also have a *name*. Figure 18.3 shows four instances of this *Association*, whose names (not shown in the figure) are as follows: "general–generalization", "specific–generalization", "powertype–powertypeExtent", and "generalizationSet–generalization".

A relationship type in the metaschema involves three instances of MOF types. One is an instance of *Association*, and the other two are instances of *Property*. The names of the instances of *Property* are the names of the participants in the relationship type, and the values of the attributes *lower* and *upper* give the minimum and maximum cardinalities of the participants. If the value of the attribute *isComposite* is true, then the association is a composition.

For example, consider the relationship type *specific–generalization* in Fig. 18.3. This type is an instance of *Association* in the MOF. Each of its two participants is an instance of *Property* in the MOF, whose names are "specific" and "generalization", respectively. The values of the *lower* and *upper* attributes of the first property are both 1. The value of the *isComposite* attribute of the first property is *true*. The value of the *lower* attribute of the second property is 0, while that of *upper* is unlimited. The value of the *isComposite* attribute of the second property is *false*.

An instance *a* of *Property* that is an *ownedAttribute* of an instance *c* of *Class* and whose *Property::type* is the *Classifier t* is an attribute of *c* of type *t* in the metaschema. The name of the attribute *a* is the value of *a* for the attribute *Property::name*. Figure 18.3 shows two examples: the attributes *GeneralizationSet::isCovering* and *GeneralizationSet::isDisjoint*. Both are of *Boolean* type, which is an instance of *PrimitiveType*.

The instances of *Comment* are the comments that form part of the UML metaschema specification. Each comment annotates named elements of the metaschema. For example, the UML metaschema specification includes the following comment:

> Each Generalization is a binary relationship that relates a specific Classifier to a more general Classifier (i.e., from a class to its superclasses). Each GeneralizationSet defines a particular set of Generalization relationships that describe the way in which a general Classifier (or superclass) may be divided using specific subtypes (…)

This string is the value of the attribute *body* of an instance of *Comment* in the MOF that annotates the instance of *NamedElement* in the MOF that corresponds to *GeneralizationSet* in the UML metaschema.

The instances of *Constraint* in the MOF are the constraints of the UML metaschema. Each constraint constrains a number of metaschema elements. For example, the UML metaschema includes the following constraint:

> Every Generalization associated with a particular GeneralizationSet must have the same general Classifier.

This constraint is an instance of *Constraint* in the MOF that constrains the instance of *Element* in the MOF that corresponds to *GeneralizationSet* in the UML metaschema.

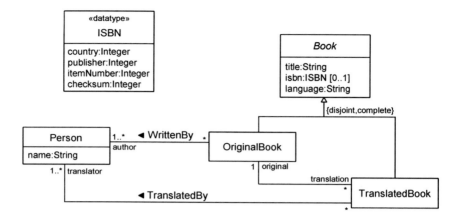

**Fig. 18.4.** Fragment of a UML schema

## 18.2 The MOF as a Conceptual Modeling Language

We have just seen that the MOF is a meta-metaschema, that is, a schema whose instances are metaschemas. However, since a metaschema is also a schema, a question naturally arises: can the MOF be used as a metaschema? Or, given that a metaschema is a conceptual modeling language, can the MOF be used as a conceptual modeling language?

The answer is both yes and no: the MOF can be used as a conceptual modeling language for some fragments of a schema, such as the one shown in Fig. 18.4, but it cannot be used as a conceptual modeling language for full-fledged information system schemas, because it lacks important features, such as association classes and state transition diagrams.

In this section, we briefly present the use of the MOF as a conceptual modeling language and describe some of its limitations.

In general, the MOF can define many (but not all) structural schemas that consist of entity types, data types, attributes, associations, etc. Figure 18.4 shows an example of a schema that can be fully expressed in the simplified version of the MOF shown in Fig. 18.2:

- *Book*, *OriginalBook*, *TranslatedBook*, and *Person* are instances of *Class*. The value of the attribute *isAbstract* of *Book* is *true*, whereas it is *false* in the other three classes.
- *String* is an instance of *PrimitiveType*.

- *ISBN* is an instance of *DataType*.
- The relationships *OriginalBook IsA Book* and *TranslatedBook IsA Book* are instances (links) of the MOF association *subClass–superClass*.
- The three associations *WrittenBy*, *TranslatedBy*, and *original–translation* are instances of *Association* in the MOF. The participant entity types are given by the instances of the association *property–type* of the corresponding instances of *Property*. The role names and multiplicities are the values of the *name*, *lower*, and *upper* attributes of the corresponding instances of *Property*.
- Similarly, the three attributes of *Book*, the attribute of *Person*, and the four attributes of *ISBN* are instances of *Property*.

However, many elements of complete information system schemas cannot be expressed as instances of MOF elements. These include:

- *n*-ary associations. The instances of *Association* in the MOF must be binary.
- Association classes. The MOF includes no concept (classifier) whose instances are both a class and an association.
- The covering and disjointness constraints on *IsA* relationships. The MOF includes no type whose instances are these particular classes of constraint. However, they can be expressed as general constraints (see Exercise 18.3).
- Use cases. The MOF includes no concept whose instances are use cases (such as *Add a new book* or *Give the translators of a book*).
- State transition diagrams.

### 18.2.1 The MOF as an ω-metaschema

In the preceding chapter, we explained that there are types, called *ω*-types, whose instances have several classification levels. The MOF is akin to an *ω*-type and can be considered as an *ω*-metaschema. An instance of the MOF may be a metaschema (as described in Sect. 18.1.2) or a schema (as described above). In fact, the MOF can be defined as an instance of itself. The left-hand side of Fig. 18.5 shows the complete MOF/UML instantiation hierarchy; the right-hand side shows some examples of elements in each layer.

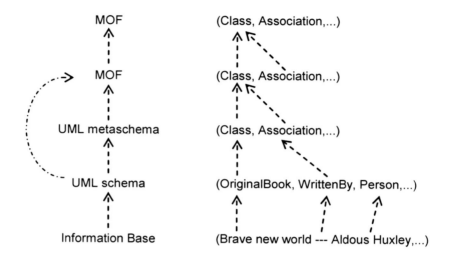

**Fig. 18.5.** MOF/UML instantiation hierarchy

## 18.3 XMI

A schema defines the types of entities and relationships that exist in a domain, in addition to a number of other things. However, a schema does not define how specific entities and relationships should be physically represented. For example, a schema may define that a domain includes the types *OriginalBook*, *Person*, and *WrittenBy*, but it does not define how to physically represent the fact that the book entitled *Brave New World* was written by the person named Aldous Huxley.

Each information system stores and displays entities and relationships in the formats chosen by its designers and users. Two different systems with the same schema may represent particular entities and relationships in different formats.

When two or more systems need to exchange data about particular entities and relationships, their designers must reach a twofold agreement on the types of entities and relationships of interest, and on how to format the data about the instances of these types. The agreement on the types (that is, on the schema) is unavoidable, and it is documented using a conceptual modeling language such as UML. The agreement on the format would be unnecessary if there were a standard way of formatting data about the instances of types.

UML uses object diagrams, which can show particular entities with their attributes and associations, as described in Sect. 3.2.3. However, this is not practical for exchanging data about many entities. Furthermore, the graphical characteristics of the diagrams are not standardized.

XML Metadata Interchange (XMI) is an OMG standard for representing data about instances of types of MOF schemas in XML. Using XMI, two systems that share the same MOF schema can exchange data about its instances in a standard way, and no further explicit agreement is required.

Since an MOF schema may be a schema or a metaschema, XMI can serve two different purposes: to represent instances of the entities and relationships that exist in a domain, or to represent schemas. Taking the schema example of Fig. 18.4, XMI can be used to represent specific instances of *OriginalBook*, *TranslatedBook*, *Person*, their attributes and associations, or the schema itself.

A complete presentation of XMI and its applications is worthy of a book of its own. In the next section, we describe only the essentials of XMI, which should provide an intuitive understanding of it and of its use in conceptual modeling.

### 18.3.1 XMI Representation of Entities and Relationships

XMI uses a set of rules to represent instances of MOF schemas in XML. In this section, we introduce these rules and use them to represent a few instances of the entity types shown in the schema in Fig. 18.4. Figure 18.6 shows the XMI representation.

The overall structure of an XML document that represents entities and their relationships is

```
<xmi:XMI xmi:version = "2.1"
      xmlns:xmi = "http://www.omg.org/XMI">
<!-- Entities and their relationships -->
</xmi:XMI>
```

The XML element *XMI* is the root element of the XML document. This element has two attributes: *version*, which must have the value of the version of the XMI standard used (in this case, 2.1), and *xmlns*, which declares the *xmi* namespace. Other namespaces may be declared as well.

Each entity *e* (that is, each instance *e* of an instance *E* of *Class* in the MOF) is represented by an XML element. The tag name of the element is the name of *E* (the class of *e*). In Fig. 18.6, there is one instance of *OriginalBook*, two instances of *TranslatedBook*, and three instances of *Person*.

```
<xmi:XMI xmi:version = "2.1"
    xmlns:xmi =  "http://www.omg.org/XMI">
  <OriginalBook xmi:id = "B1" title = "Brave new world"
    language = "english" author = "P1"
      translation = "B2 B3">
    <isbn nil = "true"/>
  </OriginalBook>
  <TranslatedBook xmi:id = "B2" title = "Un món feliç"
    isbn = "84,7279,124,6" language = "catalan"
    translator = "P2" original = "B1" />
  <TranslatedBook xmi:id = "B3" title = "Un mundo feliz"
    language = "spanish" translator = "P3"
    original = "B1">
    <isbn nil = "true"/>
  </TranslatedBook>
  <Person xmi:id = "P1" name = "Aldous Huxley"
    originalBook = "B1"/>
  <Person xmi:id = "P2" name = "Ramon Folch"
    translatedBook = "B2"/>
  <Person xmi:id = "P3" name = "Ramón Hernández"
    translatedBook = "B3"/>
</xmi:XMI>
```

**Fig. 18.6.** XMI representation of some instances of the schema in Figure 18.4

XMI uses three attributes to identify XML elements so that they may be associated with each other. The most important (and the only one described here) is the attribute *id*, which has the type ID. The XML semantics requires that the values of this attribute be unique within an XML document. In the present example, the single instance of *OriginalBook* has an attribute *id* with a value *B*1.

The attribute values of an entity are normally represented using XML attributes in the corresponding XML element. However, they can also be represented by nested XML elements whose tag name is the name of the attribute. When the attribute is multivalued or has a null value, the value must be represented by an XML element.

In the example, we declare that the original book *B*1 has the title *Brave New World* and is written in *English*. The value of the attribute *ISBN* of books *B*1 and *B*3 is unknown and is represented by a nested XML element whose tag name is *isbn*:

```
<isbn nil = "true"/>
```

Figure 18.4 defines that the type of the attribute *isbn* is *ISBN*, a data type with attributes. In order to preserve the ability to represent data types in XML as simple strings, the value of a data type with attributes is represented as a single string, with the values of the attributes of the data type separated by a comma. Figure 18.6 shows an example in the value of the attribute *isbn* of book *B2*.

Let $R(p_1:E_1,p_2:E_2)$ be a binary relationship type defined as a UML association. In XMI, the instances of $R$ are normally represented by two XML attributes of type *IDREFS*: one with a name $p_2$ in the XML element corresponding to an instance of $E_1$, and the other with a name $p_1$ in the element corresponding to an instance of $E_2$. The value of each attribute consists of the identifiers of the XML elements corresponding to the referenced entities, separated by spaces.

In the example, we declare that the author of book *B1* is *P1*, and that its translations are the books *B2* and *B3*. We also declare that *B1*:

- is the originalBook of *P1*,
- is the original of *B2*, and
- is the original of *B3*.

When the association is a composition, the representation is somewhat different, as described in the next section.

## 18.3.2 XMI Representation of UML Schemas

XMI rules can be applied to obtain an XML representation of any set of instances of entity types, attributes and associations of any schema whose entity types, attributes, and associations are instances of the corresponding MOF classes.

Since the UML metaschema is a schema whose entity types, attributes and associations are instances of the corresponding MOF classes, the instances of the UML metaschema can be represented using XMI. That is, we can use XMI rules to achieve a standard XML representation of UML schemas. Representing UML schemas in a standard format is of the utmost importance because it enables system interoperability. Many development tools for conceptual modeling allow schemas to be imported and exported from and to XMI.

In this section, we illustrate the XMI representation of UML schemas by applying XMI rules to an example. The example is the schema shown in Fig. 18.4. This schema is an instance of the UML metaschema that we studied in the preceding chapter. For convenience, Fig. 18.7 shows a fragment of this metaschema.

The overall document structure is

```
<xmi:XMI xmi:version = "2.1"
   xmlns:xmi = "http://www.omg.org/XMI"
   xmlns:cmof="http://schema.omg.org/spec/MOF/2.0/cmof.xml">
... UML schema (see below) ...
</xmi:XMI>
```

The *ISBN* data type and its four attributes (Fig. 18.4) are instances of *DataType* and *Property*, respectively (Fig. 18.7). Therefore, the XMI representation of the *ISBN* data type is

```
<DataType xmi:id = "D1" name = "ISBN">
   <ownedAttribute xmi:id = "A1" name = "country" lower = 1
            upper = 1 isComposite = "false">
      <type xmi:type="cmof:PrimitiveType"
            href="doc#Core-PrimitiveTypes-Integer"/>
   </ownedAttribute>
   <ownedAttribute xmi:id = "A2" name = "publisher"
            lower = 1 upper = 1 isComposite = "false">
      <type xmi:type="cmof:PrimitiveType"
            href="doc#Core-PrimitiveTypes-Integer"/>
   </ownedAttribute>
   <ownedAttribute xmi:id = "A3" name = "itemNumber"
            lower = 1 upper = 1 isComposite = "false">
      <type xmi:type="cmof:PrimitiveType"
            href="doc#Core-PrimitiveTypes-Integer"/>
   </ownedAttribute>
   <ownedAttribute xmi:id = "A4" name = "checksum"
            lower = 1 upper = 1 isComposite = "false">
      <type xmi:type="cmof:PrimitiveType"
            href="doc#Core-PrimitiveTypes-Integer"/>
   </ownedAttribute>
</DataType>
```

In Fig. 18.7, the association *dataType–ownedAttribute* is a composition. In this case, the XMI rules state that the part entities are defined as nested elements inside the composite element. The tag name of these elements is the name of the part role. In UML, the parts of a composite cannot belong to two composites at the same time. In the example above, *D*1 is the whole of the parts *A*1, *A*2, *A*3, and *A*4, which are defined inside the XML element *D*1. The name of the part role is *ownedAttribute*.

When the entity to which an entity is related is defined in another XML document, it must be represented by a nested XML element. One example is the *type* of the four *ISBN* attributes. They have been represented using the following XML element:

```
<type ...  href="doc#Core-PrimitiveTypes-Integer"/>
```

This declares that the *type* is the XML element with the identifier *Core-PrimitiveTypes-Integer* located in the XML document *doc*.

According to Fig. 18.7, the *type* of a *Property* is an instance of *Classifier*. However, since *Classifier* is an abstract class, we have to specify the subclass of which it is an instance. The XML attribute *xmi:type* indicates

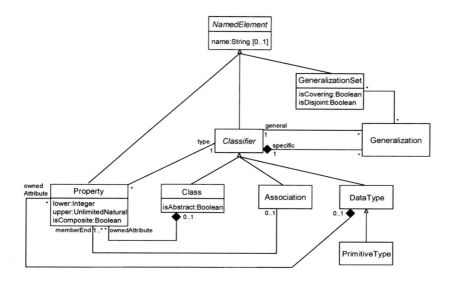

**Fig. 18.7.** Fragment of the UML metaschema (simplified)

that the *type* of the attribute is an instance of *PrimitiveType*, a subclass of *Classifier*:

```
<type xmi:type = "comof:PrimitiveType"
    href="doc#Core-PrimitiveTypes-Integer"/>
```

Similarly, the XMI representation of *Book* is

```
<Class xmi:id = "B1" name = "Book" isAbstract = "true">
    <ownedAttribute xmi:id = "A5" name = "title" lower = 1
            upper = 1 isComposite = "false">
        <type xmi:type="cmof:PrimitiveType"
            href="doc#Core-PrimitiveTypes-String"/>
    </ownedAttribute>
    <ownedAttribute xmi:id = "A6" name = "isbn"
            lower = 0 upper = 1 isComposite = "false">
        <type xmi:type="cmof:DataType" href="#D1"/>
    </ownedAttribute>
    <ownedAttribute xmi:id = "A7" name = "language"
            lower = 1 upper = 1 isComposite = "false">
        <type xmi:type="cmof:PrimitiveType"
            href="doc#Core-PrimitiveTypes-String"/>
    </ownedAttribute>
</Class>
```

The type of the attribute *isbn* is the instance of *DataType* that we have specified in the same document with identifier *D1*.

The XMI representation of *Person* is simple:

```
<Class xmi:id = "P1" name = "Person" isAbstract = "false">
   <ownedAttribute xmi:id = "A8" name = "name" lower = 1
         upper = 1 isComposite = "false">
      <type xmi:type="cmof:PrimitiveType"
            href="doc#Core-PrimitiveTypes-String"/>
   </ownedAttribute>
</Class>
```

The XMI representation of *OriginalBook* and *TranslatedBook* and their generalization into *Book* is

```
<Class xmi:id = "B2" name = "OriginalBook"
     isAbstract = "false">
   <generalization xmi:id = "G1" general = "B1"/>
</Class>
<Class xmi:id = "B3" name = "TranslatedBook"
     isAbstract = "false">
   <generalization xmi:id = "G2" general = "B1"/>
</Class>
```

The three associations are

```
<Association xmi:id = "As1" name = "WrittenBy"
   memberEnd = "Pr1 Pr2"/>
<Association xmi:id = "As2" name = "TranslatedBy"
   memberEnd = "Pr3 Pr4"/>
<Association xmi:id = "As3" name = "original-translation"
   memberEnd = "Pr5 Pr6"/>
<Property xmi:id = "Pr1" name = "originalBook"
   lower = 0 upper = * isComposite = "false"
   type = "B2" association = "As1"/>
<Property xmi:id = "Pr2" name = "author"
   lower = 1 upper = * isComposite = "false"
   type = "P1" association = "As1"/>
<Property xmi:id = "Pr3" name = "translatedBook"
   lower = 0 upper = * isComposite = "false"
   type = "B3" association = "As2"/>
<Property xmi:id = "Pr4" name = "translator"
   lower = 1 upper = * isComposite = "false"
   type = "P1" association = "As2"/>
<Property xmi:id = "Pr5" name = "original"
   lower = 1 upper = 1 isComposite = "false"
   type = "B2" association = "As3"/>
<Property xmi:id = "Pr6" name = "translation"
   lower = 0 upper = * isComposite = "false"
   type = "B3" association = "As3"/>
```

## 18.4 Bibliographical Notes

The current official description of the MOF is that given by the OMG (2006b). The latest version of the XMI standard is also defined by the OMG (2005a). Grose et al. (2002) provided a detailed explanation of XMI and its applications.

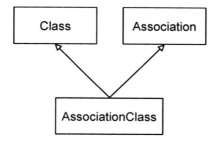

**Fig. 18.8.** Fragment of the UML metaschema that defines association classes

## 18.5 Exercises

**18.1** Figure 18.8 shows the fragment of the UML metaschema that defines the association classes: an instance of an association class is both a class and an association. Explain how this fragment is an instance of the simplified MOF shown in Fig. 18.2.

**18.2** Assume that the schema fragment shown in Fig. 18.4 also includes the following constraint: "The language of a translated book must be different from that of its original." Explain how this constraint is an instance of the simplified MOF shown in Fig. 18.2.

**18.3** Assume that you are using the MOF as a conceptual modeling language in a schema that includes the specializations *A IsA B* and *C IsA B*, and that you want to define *A* and *C* as disjoint. Define this constraint in OCL and explain how it is an instance of *Constraint* in the MOF.

**18.4** Use an UML object diagram to represent the entities and relationships whose XMI representations are given in Fig. 18.6. Compare the two representations in terms of human and machine readability.

**18.5** Since the MOF is an instance of itself, the MOF can be represented in XMI. Write the XMI representation of the simplified MOF shown in Fig. 18.2.

# References

Abiteboul S, Hull R (1987) IFO: A formal semantic database model. ACM Trans. Database Syst. 12(4):525–565.

Abrial JR (1974). Data semantics. In: Klimbie JW, Koffeman KL (eds) Data management systems. North–Holland, pp 1–59.

ACM (1994) Special issue on intelligent agents. Commun. ACM 37(7).

ACM (1996) Special issue on data mining and knowledge discovery in databases. Commun. ACM 39(11).

Ackermann J, Turowski K (2006) A library of OCL specification patterns for behavioral specification of software components. CAiSE 2006, LNCS 4001:255-269.

Adolph S, Bramble P (2003) Patterns for effective use cases. Addison-Wesley.

Alexander IF, Maiden N (eds) (2004) Scenarios, stories, use cases through the systems development life-cycle. Wiley.

Analyti A, Spyratos N, Constantopoulos P (1997) Property covering: A powerful construct for schema derivations. ER 1997, LNCS 1331:271–284.

ANSI (1975) ANSI/X3/SPARC study group on data base management systems. Interim report. FDT, Bulletin of ACM SIGMOD 7(2).

Armstrong W (1974) Dependency structures of database relationships. IFIP Congress 1974:580–583.

Artale A, Franconi E, Guarino N, Pazzi L (1996) Part–whole relations in object–centered systems: An overview. Data Knowl. Eng. 20:347–383.

Artz JM (1997) A crash course in metaphysics for the database designer. J. Database Manag. 8(4):25–30.

Assenova P, Johannesson P (1996) Improving quality in conceptual modelling by the use of schema transformations. ER 1997, LNCS 1157:277–291.

Atkinson C, Kühne T (2001) The essence of multilevel metamodeling. UML 2001, LNCS 2185:19–33.

Atkinson C, Henderson–Sellers B, Kühne T (2000) To meta or not to meta – That is the question. JOOP 13(8):32–35.

Atzeni P, Parker DS (1988) Formal properties of net–based knowledge representation schemes. Data Knowl. Eng. 3:137–147.

Atzeni P, Cappellari P, Bernstein PA (2006) Model–independent schema and data translation. EDBT 2006, LNCS 3896:368–385.

Balaban M, Shoval P (1999) Resolving the "weak status" of weak entity types in Entity-Relationships schemas. ER 1999, LNCS 1728:369-383.

Bancilhon F, Ramakrishnan R (1986) An amateur's introduction to recursive query processing strategies. SIGMOD Conference 1986:16–52.

Batini C, Ceri S, Navathe SB (1992) Conceptual database design: An entity–relationship approach. Benjamin/Cummings.

Berardi D, Calvanese D, De Giacomo G (2005) Reasoning on UML class diagrams. Artif. Intell. 168(1-2):70-118.

Bergamaschi S, Sartori C (1992) On taxonomic reasoning in conceptual design. ACM Trans. Database Syst. 17(3):385–422.

Bernstein PA (2003) Applying model management to classical meta data problems. CIDR 2003:209–220.

Bicarregui J, Ritchie B (1995) Invariants, frames, and postconditions: A comparison of the VDM and B notations. IEEE Trans. Software Eng. 21(2):78–89.

Biskup J, Menzel R, Polle T, Sagiv Y (1996). Decomposition of relationships through pivoting. ER 1996, LNCS 1157:28–41.

Bodart F, Pigneur Y (1993) Conception assistée des systèmes d'information. Masson.

Bodart F, Patel A, Sim M, Weber R (2001) Should optional properties be used in conceptual modelling? A theory and three empirical tests. Inf. Syst. Res. 12(4):384–405.

Boman M, Bubenko JA Jr, Johannesson P, Wangler B (1997) Conceptual modelling. Prentice Hall.

Bonner AJ, Kifer M (1998) The state of change: A survey. In: Freitag B, Decker H, Kifer M, Voronkov A (eds) Transactions and change in logic databases, LNCS 1472:1–36.

Booch G (1991) Object–oriented design with applications. Benjamin/Cummings.

Booch G, Rumbaugh J, Jacobson I (1999) The Unified Modeling Language user guide. Addison-Wesley.

Borgida A (1985a) Features of languages for the development of information systems at the conceptual level. IEEE Software 2(1):63–72.

Borgida A (1985b) Language features for flexible handling of exceptions in information systems. ACM Trans. Database Syst. 10(4):565–603.

Borgida A (1995) Description logics in data management. IEEE Trans. Software Eng. 7(5):671–682.

Borgida A, Greenspan SJ (1980) Data and activities: Exploiting hierarchies of classes. Workshop on Data Abstraction, Databases and Conceptual Modelling 1980: 98–100.

Borgida A, Mylopoulos J, Wong HKT (1984) Generalization/specialization as a basis for software specification. In: Brodie et al. (eds) pp 87–117.

Borgida A, Greenspan S, Mylopoulos J (1985) Knowledge representation as the basis for requirements specifications. IEEE Computer 18(4):82–91.

Borgida A, Mylopoulos J, Schmidt JW (1993) The TaxisDL software description language. In: Jarke M (ed) Database application engineering with DAIDA. Springer, pp 63–84.

Borgida A, Mylopoulos J, Reiter R (1995) On the frame problem in procedure specifications. IEEE Trans. Software Eng. 21(10):785–798.

Bosak R, Clippinger RF, Dobbs C, Goldfinger R, Jasper RB, Keating W, Kendrick G, Sammet JE (1962) An information algebra: phase 1 report - language structure group of the CODASYL development committee. Commun. ACM 5(4):190–204.

Bracchi G, Furtado A, Pelagatti G (1979) Constraint specification in evolutionary data base design. In: Schneider HJ (ed) Formal models and practical tools for information systems design. North–Holland, pp 149–165.

Brachman RJ (1983) What IS-A is and isn't: An analysis of taxonomics links in semantic networks. IEEE Computer 16(10):30–36.

Brachman RJ, Levesque HJ (eds) (1985) Readings in knowledge representation. Morgan Kaufmann.

Brachman RJ, Schmolze JG (1985) An overview of the KL–ONE knowledge representation system. Cognitive Sci. 9(2):171–216.

Brodie ML (1981) Association: A database abstraction for semantic modelling. ER 1981, North–Holland, pp 577–602.

Brodie ML, Zilles SN (1981) (eds) Proceedings of the workshop on data abstraction, databases and conceptual modeling. ACM SIGMOD Record, 11(2).

Brodie ML, Mylopoulos J, Schmidt JW (eds) (1984) On conceptual modelling: Perspectives from artificial intelligence, databases and programming languages, Springer.

Bubenko JA Jr (1977) Validity and verification aspects of information modeling. VLDB 1977:556–565.

Bubenko JA Jr (1980) Information modeling in the context of system development. IFIP Congress 1980:395–411.

Business Rules Group (2000) Defining business rules – What are they really? Final Report, July 2000, http://www.businessrulesgroup.org/ first_paper/ br01c0.htm

Cabot J, Raventós R (2006) Conceptual modelling patterns for roles. J. Data Semantics V:158–184.

Calvanese D, Lenzerini M (1994) On the interaction between ISA and cardinality constraints. ICDE 1994:204–213.

Ceri S, Fraternali P (1997) Designing database applications with objects and rules: The IDEA methodology. Addison-Wesley.

Chaffin R, Herrmann DJ (1988) The nature of semantic relations: A comparison of two approaches. In: Evens MW (ed) Relational models of the lexicon, Cambridge University Press, pp 289–334.

Chaffin R, Herrmann DJ, Winston M (1988) An empirical taxonomy of Part–Whole relations: Effects of Part–Whole relation type on relation identification. Language and Cognitive Processes 3(1):17–48.

Champeaux D de, Lea D, Faure P (1993) Object-oriented system development. Addison-Wesley.

Chen PPS (1976) The Entity–Relationship model: Towards a unified view of data. ACM Trans. Database Syst. 1(1):9–36.

Chen P (1983) English sentence structure and entity–relationship diagrams. Inf. Sci. 29(2–3):127–149.

Chomicki J, Saake G (eds) (1998) Logics for databases and information systems. Kluwer Academic.

Cockburn A (2001) Writing effective use cases. Addison-Wesley.

Codd EF (1979) Extending the database relational model to capture more meaning. ACM Trans. Database Syst. 4(4):397–434.

Coleman D, Hayes F, Bear S (1992) Introducing objectcharts, or how to use statecharts in object–oriented design. IEEE Trans. Software Eng. 18(1):9–18.

Constantine LL, Lockwood LAD (1999). Software for use. Addison–Wesley.

Cook S, Daniels J (1994) Designing object systems: Object–oriented modelling with Syntropy. Prentice Hall.

Costal D, Gómez C (2006) On the use of association redefinition in UML class diagrams. ER 2006, LNCS 4215:513–527.

Costal D, Olivé A, Sancho M-R (1997) Temporal features of class populations and attributes in conceptual models. ER 1997, LNCS 1331:57-70.

Costal D, Olivé A, Teniente E (2001) Relationship type refinement in conceptual models with multiple classification. ER 2001, LNCS 2224:397–411.

Costal D, Gómez C, Queralt A, Raventós R, Teniente E (2006) Facilitating the definition of general constraints in UML. MoDELS 2006, LNCS 4199:260-274.

Couger JD (1973) Evolution of business system analysis techniques. ACM Comput. Surv. 5(3):167–198.

Crane ML, Dingel J (2005) UML vs. classical vs. Rhapsody statecharts: Not all models are created equal. MoDELS 2005, LNCS 3713:97–112.

Dahchour M, Pirotte A, Zimányi E (2002) Materialization and its metaclass implementation. IEEE Trans. Knowl. Data Eng. 14(5):1078–1094.

Dahchour M, Pirotte A, Zimányi E (2005) Generic relationships in information modeling. J. Data Semantics IV:1–34.

Dalianis H, Johannesson P (1997) Explaining conceptual models - An architecture and design principles. ER 1997, LNCS 1331:215-228.

Dardenne A, van Lamsweerde A, Fichas S (1993) Goal–directed requirements acquisition. Sci. Comput. Program. 20:3–50.

Davis AM (1988) A comparison of techniques for the specification of external system behavior. Commun. ACM 31(9):1098–1115.

Davis AM (1993) Software requirements: Objects, functions and states. Prentice Hall.

Davis R, Shrobe H, Szolovits P (1993) What is a knowledge representation? AI Magazine 14(1):17–33.

DeMarco T (1979) Structured analysis and system specification. Prentice Hall.

De Troyer O, Meersman R, Verlinden P (1988) RIDL* on the CRIS case. In Olle et al (eds) pp 375–459.

Dey D, Storey VC, Barron TM (1999) Improving database design through the analysis of relationships. ACM Trans. Database Syst. 24(4):453–486.

Dignum F, Kemme T, Kreuzen W, Weigand H, Riet R van de (1987) Constraint modelling using a conceptual prototyping language. Data Knowl. Eng. 2:213–254.

D'Souza DF, Wills AC (1999) Objects, components and frameworks with UML: The Catalysis approach. Addison-Wesley.

Dubitzky W, Büchner AG, Hughes JG, Bell DA (1999) Towards concept–oriented databases. Data Knowl. Eng. 30:23–55.

Dubois E, Hagelstein J, Lahou E, Ponsaert P, Rifaut A, Williams F (1986) The ERAE model: A case study. In: Olle et al. (eds) pp 87–105.

Dullea J, Song I-Y (1999) A taxonomy of recursive relationships and their structural validity in ER modeling. ER 1999, LNCS 1728:384–398.

Dullea J, Song I-Y, Lamprou I (2003) An analysis of structural validity in entity–relationship modeling. Data Knowl. Eng. 47:167–205.

Elmasri R, Navathe SB (2003) Fundamentals of database systems. Addison-Wesley.

Embley DW, Kurtz BD, Woodfield SN (1992) Object–oriented systems analysis. Yourdon Press.

Engels G, Gogolla M, Hohenstein W, Hülsmann K, Löhr–Richter P, Saake G, Dieter HD (1992) Conceptual modelling of database applications using an extended ER model. Data Knowl. Eng. 9:157–204.

Eshuis R, Jansen DN, Wieringa R (2002) Requirements–level semantics and model checking of object–oriented statecharts. Requir. Eng. 7:243–263.

Evermann J, Wand Y (2005) Ontology based object–oriented domain modeling: Fundamental concepts. Requir. Eng. 10:146–160.

Fagin R (1977) Multivalued dependencies and a new normal form for relational databases. ACM Trans. Database Syst. 2(3):262–278.

Ferrentino AB, Mills HD (1977) State machines and their semantics in software engineering. In: Proceedings of the First International Software and Applications Conference (COMPSAC 77), IEEE Computer Society, pp 242–251.

Fikes R, Kehler T (1985) The role of frame–based representation in reasoning. Commun. ACM 28(9):904–920.

Formica, A (2002) Finite satisfiablity of integrity constraints in object–oriented database schemas. IEEE Trans. Knowl. Data Eng.14(1):123–139.

Formica A, Frank H (2002) Consistency of the static and dynamic components of object–oriented specifications. Data Knowl. Eng. 40:195–215.

Fowler M (1997) UML distilled. Addison-Wesley.

Fry JP, Sibley EH (1976) Evolution of data–base management systems. ACM Comput. Surv. 8(1):7–42.

Furtado A, Casanova MA, Tucherman L (1987) The CHRIS consultant. ER 1987, North–Hollland, pp 515–532.

Gane C, Sarson T (1979) Structured systems analysis: Tools and techniques. Prentice Hall.

Gemino A, Wand Y (2005) Complexity and clarity in conceptual modeling: Comparison of mandatory and optional properties. Data Knowl. Eng. 55:301–326.

Glinz M (2000) A lightweight approach to consistency of scenarios and class models. ICRE 2000:49–58.

Godfrey P, Grant J, Gryz J, Minker J (1998) Integrity constraints: Semantics and applications. In: Chomicki and Saake (eds) pp 265–306.

Gogolla M (2000) Identifying objects by declarative queries. In Papazoglou MP, Spaccapietra S, Tari Z (eds) Advances in object-oriented data modeling. MIT Press, pp 255-277.

Gogolla M, Henderson–Sellers B (2002) Analysis of UML stereotypes within the UML metamodel. UML 2002, LNCS 2460:84–99.

Gogolla M, Bohling J, Richters M (2005) Validating UML and OCL models in USE by automatic snapshot generation. Software and System Modeling 4(4):386-398.

Goldstein RC, Storey V (1994) Materialization. IEEE Trans. Knowl. Data Eng. 6(5):835–842.

Goldstein RC, Storey V (1999) Data abstractions: Why and how? Data Knowl. Eng. 29:293–311.

Greenspan S, Mylopoulos J, Borgida A (1982) Capturing more world knowledge in the requirements specification. ICSE 1982, IEEE, pp 225–235.

Greenspan S, Mylopoulos J, Borgida A. (1994) On formal requirements modeling languages: RML revisited. ICSE 1994, IEEE Computer Society/ACM Press, pp 135–147.

Griethuysen JJ van (ed) (1982) Concepts and terminology for the conceptual schema and the information base. ISO TC97/SC5/WG3.

Grose TJ, Doney GC, Brodsky SA (2002) Mastering XMI. Java programming with XMI, XML and UML. Wiley.

Gruber TR (1993) A translation approach to portable ontology specifications. Knowl. Acquis. 5:199–220.

Guarino N, Giaretta P (1995) Ontologies and knowledge bases: Towards a terminological clarification. In: Mars NJI (ed) Towards very large knowledge bases. IOS Press, pp 25–32.

Gulla JA (1996) A general explanation component for conceptual modeling in CASE environments. ACM Trans. Inf. Syst. 14(3):297–329.

Gustaffsson MR, Karlsson T, Bubenko JA Jr. (1982) A declarative approach to conceptual information modeling. In: Olle et al. (eds) pp 93–142.

Hainaut J-L (1996) Specification preservation in schema transformations - Application to semantics and statistics. Data Knowl. Eng. 19(2):99–134.

Halper M, Geller J, Perl Y (1998) An OODB Part–Whole model: Semantics, notation and implementation. Data Knowl. Eng. 27:59–95.

Halpin T (2001) Information modeling and relational databases: From conceptual analysis to logical design. Morgan Kaufmann.

Halpin TA, Proper HA (1995a) Subtyping and polymorphism in object–role modelling. Data Knowl. Eng. 15:251–281.

Halpin TA, Proper HA (1995b) Database schema transformation and optimization. OOER 1995, LNCS 1021:191–203.

Hammer M, McLeod D (1981) Database description with SDM: A semantic database model. ACM Trans. Database Syst. 6(3):351–386.

Harel D (1987) Statecharts: A visual formalism for complex systems. Sci. Comput. Program. 8(3):231–274.

Harel D, Gery E (1997) Executable object modeling with statecharts. IEEE Computer 30(7):31–42.

Harel D, Kupferman O (2002) On object systems and behavioral inheritance. IEEE Trans. Software Eng. 28(9):889–903.

Harel D, Naamad A (1996) The STATEMATE semantics of statecharts. ACM Trans. Software Eng. Methodol. 5(4):293–333.

Hartmann S (1998) On the consistency of int–cardinality constraints. ER 1998, LNCS 1507:150–163.

Hartmann S (2001) Decomposing relationship types by pivoting and schema equivalence. Data Knowl. Eng. 39:75–99.

Henderson–Sellers B, Barbier F (1999) What is this thing called aggregation? Tools29, IEEE Computer Society Press, pp 216–230.

Hofstede AHM ter, Weide, TP van der (1993) Expressiveness in conceptual data modelling. Data Knowl. Eng. 10:65–100.

Hofstede AHM ter, Proper HA, Weide TP van der (1997) Exploiting fact verbalisation in conceptual information modeling. Inf. Syst. 22(6/7):349–385.

Hopcroft JE, Motwani R, Ullman JD (2001) Introduction to automata theory, languages, and computation. 2nd edn. Addison-Wesley.

Hull R, King R (1987) Semantic database modeling: Survey, applications, and research issues. ACM Comput. Surv. 19(3):201–260.

IEEE (1999) IEEE standard for conceptual modeling language syntax and semantics for IDEF1X97 (IDEFobject). IEEE Std 1320.2–1998.

Imam IF, Kodratoff Y (1997) Intelligent adaptive agents. AI Magazine 18(3):75–80.

Insfrán E, Pastor O, Wieringa R (2002) Requirements engineering-based conceptual modelling. Requir. Eng. 7:61–72.

Iris MA, Litowitz BE, Evens M (1988) Problems of the part–whole relation. In: Evens MW (ed.) Relational models of the lexicon, Cambridge University Press, pp 261–288.

Jackson M (1983) System development. Prentice Hall.

Jackson M (2001) Problem frames: Analyzing and structuring software development problems. Addison-Wesley.

Jacobson I (2004) Use cases – yesterday, today and tomorrow. Software and Systems Modeling 3(3):210–220.

Jardine DA (1984) Concepts and terminology for the conceptual schema and the information base. Computers & Standards 3:3–17.

Jarke M, Mylopoulos J, Schmidt JW, Vassiliou Y (1992) DAIDA: An environment for evolving information systems. ACM Trans. Inf. Syst. 10(1):1–50.

Jarrar M, Heymans S (2006) Unsatisfiability reasoning in ORM conceptual schemes. EDBT Workshops 2006, LNCS 4254:517–534.

Jeusfeld MA, Jarke M, Nissen HW, Staudt M (1998) ConceptBase: Managing conceptual models about information systems. In: Bernus P, Mertins K, Schmidt G (eds) Handbook on architectures of information systems. Springer, pp 265–285.

Johannesson P (1995) Representation and communication – a speech act based approach to information systems design. Inf. Syst. 20(4):291–303.

Jones T, Song I-Y (1996) Analysis of binary/ternary cardinality combinations in entity–relationship modeling. Data Knowl. Eng. 19 (1):39–64.

Katasonov A, Sakkinen M (2006) Requirements quality control: a unifying framework. Requir. Eng. 11(1):42-57.

Kent W (1978) Data and reality. North-Holland.

Kim W, Banerjee J, Chou HT, Garza JF, Woelk D (1987) Composite object support in an object–oriented database system. OOPSLA 1987:118–125.

Kim W, Bertino E, Garza JF (1989) Composite objects revisited. SIGMOD Conference 1989:337–347.

Kowalski R (1978) Logic for data description. In: Gallaire H, Minker J (eds) Logic and data bases. Plenum Press, pp 77–103.

Kung CH (1984) A temporal framework for database specification and verification. VLDB 1984:91–99.

Kung CH, Sølvberg A (1986) Activity modeling and behavior modeling. In Olle et al. (eds) pp 145–171.

Lakoff G (1987) Women, fire, and dangerous things. What categories reveal about the mind. University of Chicago Press.

Lambrix P (2000) Part–Whole reasoning in an object-centered framework. LNAI 1771, Springer.

Langefors B (1974) Information systems. IFIP Congress 1974. North-Holland, pp 937–945.

Larman C (2002) Applying UML and patterns. Prentice Hall.

Larman C (2005) Applying UML and Patterns: An Introduction to object–oriented analysis and design and iterative development. 3rd edn. Prentice Hall.

Le Moigne J–L (1978) La théorie du système d'information organisationnel. Informatique et Gestion, 102:28–31.

Lenzerini M (1987) Covering and disjointness constraints in type networks. ICDE 1987:386–393.

Lenzerini M, Nobili P (1990) On the satisfiability of dependency constraints in entity–relationship schemata. Inf. Syst. 15(4):453–461.

Lenzerini M, Nardo D, Simi M (1991) Inheritance hierarchies in knowledge representation and programming languages. Wiley.

Liddle SW, Embley DW, Woodfield, SN (1993) Cardinality constraints in semantic data models. Data Knowl. Eng. 11:235–270.

Lindland OI, Sindre G, Sølvberg A (1994) Understanding quality in conceptual modeling. IEEE Software 11(2):42–49.

Ling T (1985) A normal form for entity–relationship diagrams. ER 1985:24–35.

Lipeck UW (1986) Stepwise specification of dynamic database behaviour. SIGMOD Conference 1986:387–397.

Loucopoulos P (1992) Conceptual modeling. In: Loucopoulos P, Zicari R (eds) Conceptual modeling, databases and CASE: An integrated view of information systems development. Wiley, pp 1–26.

Loucopoulos P, Karakostas V (1995) System requirements engineering. McGraw–Hill.

Lundberg B (1983) On correctness of information models. Inf. Syst. 8(2):87-93.

Lunn T, Neff SA (1992) MRP: Integrating material requirements planning and modern business. McGraw-Hill.

Marca DA, McGowan, CL (1988) SADT: Structured analysis and design technique. McGraw–Hill.

Martin J, Odell J (1995) Object–oriented methods: A foundation. Prentice Hall.

McAllister AJ (1998) Complete rules for *n*–ary relationship cardinality constraints. Data Knowl. Eng. 27(3):255–288.

McAllister AJ, Sharpe D (1998) An approach for decomposing n–ary data relationships. Softw., Pract. Exper. 28(2):125–154.

McCarthy J, Hayes P (1969) Some philosophical problems from the standpoint of artificial intelligence. In: Meltzer B, Michie D (eds.) Machine Intelligence 4: 463–502.

McMenamim SM, Palmer JF (1984) Essential systems analysis. Yourdon Press/Prentice Hall.

Meyer B (1997) Object–oriented software construction. Prentice Hall.

Moody DL (1998) Metrics for evaluating the quality of entity relationship models. ER 1998, LNCS 1507:211–225.

Moody DL, Sindre G, Brasethvik T, Sølvberg A (2003) Evaluating the quality of information models: Empirical testing of a conceptual model quality framework. ICSE 2003:295–307.

Motro A (1989) Integrity = validity + completeness. ACM Trans. Database Syst. 14(4):480–502.

Motro A (1994) Intensional answers to database queries. IEEE Trans. Knowl. Data Eng. 6(3):444–454.

Motschnig-Pitrik R (1993) The semantics of parts versus aggregates in data/knowledge modelling. CAiSE 1993, LNCS 685:352–373.

Motschnig-Pitrik R, Kaasboll J (1999) Part–Whole relationship categories and their application in object–oriented analysis. IEEE Trans. Knowl. Data Eng. 11(5):779–797.

Motschnig-Pitrik R, Mylopoulos J (1992) Classes and instances. Int. J. Cooperative Inf. Syst. 1(1):61–92.

Motschnig-Pitrik R, Storey VC (1995) Modelling of set membership: The notion and the issues. Data Knowl. Eng. 16:147–185.

Mylopoulos J (1998) Information modeling in the time of the revolution. Inf. Syst. 23(3/4):127–155.

Mylopoulos J, Levesque HJ (1984) An overview of knowledge representation. In: Brodie et al. (eds): 3–17.

Mylopoulos J, Bernstein PA, Wong HKT (1980) A language facility for designing database–intensive applications. ACM Trans. Database Syst. 5(2):185–207.

Mylopoulos J, Borgida A, Jarke M, Koubarakis, M (1990) Telos: Representing knowledge about information systems. ACM Trans. Inf. Syst. 8(4):325–362.

Nicolas JM (1982) Logic for improving integrity checking in relational data bases. Acta Informatica 18:227–253.

Nicolas JM, Gallaire H (1978) Data base: Theory vs. interpretation. In: Gallaire H, Minker J (eds) Logic and data bases. Plenum Press, pp 33–54.

Nicolas JM, Yazdanian K (1978) Integrity checking in deductive data bases. In: Gallaire H, Minker J (eds) Logic and data bases. Plenum Press, pp 325–344.

Nijssen GM, Halpin TA (1989) Conceptual schema and relational database design. Prentice Hall.

Norrie MC, Steiner A, Würgler A, Wunderli M (1996) A model for classification structures with evolution control. ER1996, LNCS 1157:456–471.

Nuseibeh B, Easterbrook S (2000). Requirements engineering: a roadmap. ICSE–Future of SE Track 2000:35–46.

Oberweis A, Sander P (1996) Information system behavior specification by high–level Petri nets. ACM Trans. Inf. Syst. 14(4):380–420.

Odell J (1994) Power types. JOOP 7(2):8–12.

Olivé A (1999) Relationship reification: A temporal view. CAiSE 1999, LNCS 1626:396–410.

Olivé A (2000a) An introduction to conceptual modeling of information systems. In: Piatini M, Díaz O (eds) Advanced database technology and design. Artech House, pp 25–57.

Olivé A (2000b) Time and change in conceptual modeling of information systems. In: Brinkkemper S, Lindencrona E, Sølvberg A (eds) Information systems engineering. State of the art and research themes. Springer, pp 289–304.

Olivé A (2002) Representation of generic relationship types in conceptual modeling. CAiSE 2002, LNCS 2348:675–691.

Olivé A (2003a) Derivation rules in object–oriented conceptual modeling languages. CAiSE 2003, LNCS 2681:404–420.

Olivé A (2003b) Integrity constraints definition in object-oriented conceptual modeling languages. ER 2003, LNCS 2813:349–362.

Olivé A (2005) Conceptual schema–centric development: A grand challenge for information systems research. CAiSE 2005, LNCS 3520:1–15.

Olivé A, Raventós R (2006) Modeling events as entities in object–oriented conceptual modeling languages. Data Knowl. Eng. 58(3):243–262.

Olivé A, Teniente E (2002) Derived types and taxonomic constraints in conceptual modeling. Inf. Syst. 27:391–409.

Olivé A, Costal D, Sancho M–R (1999) Entity evolution in IsA hierarchies. ER 1999, LNCS 1728:62–80.

Olle TW, Sol HG, Verrijn–Stuart AA (eds) (1982) Information systems design methodologies: A comparative review. North-Holland.

Olle TW, Sol HG, Tully CJ (eds) (1983) Information systems design methodologies: A feature analysis. North-Holland.

Olle TW, Sol HG, Verrijn–Stuart AA (eds) (1986) Information systems design methodologies: Improving the practice. North-Holland.

Olle TW, Sol HG, Bhabuta, L. (eds) (1988) Computerized assistance during the information systems life cycle. North-Holland.

OMG (2005a) MOF 2.0/XMI Mapping Specification, v2.1 formal/05–09–01.

OMG (2005b) OCL 2.0 Specification. Version 2.0, ptc/2005–06–06.

OMG (2006a) Unified Modeling Language: Superstructure. Version 2.1, ptc/06–01–02.

OMG (2006b) Meta Object Facility (MOF) Core Specification. Version 2.0 fomal/06–01–01.

Opdahl AL, Henderson–Sellers B, Barbier F (2001) Ontological analysis of whole–part relationships in OO–models. Information and Software Technology, 43:387–399.

Papazoglou MP (1995) Unraveling the semantics of conceptual schemas. Commun. ACM 38(9):80–94.

Parent C, Spaccapietra S, Zimányi E (2006) Conceptual modeling for traditional and spatio–temporal applications: The MADS approach. Springer.

Parsons J (1996) An information model based on classification theory. Management Science, 42(2):1437–1453.

Parsons J, Wand Y (1997) Choosing classes in conceptual modeling. Commun. ACM 40(6):63–69.

Parsons J, Wand Y (2000) Emancipating instances from the tyranny of classes in information modeling. ACM Trans. Database Syst. 25(2):228–268.

Pastor JA, Olivé A (1995) Supporting transaction design in conceptual modelling of information systems. CAiSE 1995, LNCS 932:40-53.

Pastor O, Gómez J, Insfrán E, Pelechano V (2001) The OO–Method approach for information systems modeling: From object–oriented conceptual modeling to automated programming. Inf. Syst. 26:507–534.

Peckham J, Maryanski F (1988) Semantic data models. ACM Comput. Surv. 20(3):153–189.

Pernici B (1990) Objects with roles. SIGOIS Bulletin, ACM Press 11(2/3):205–215.

Pirotte A, Zimányi E, Massart D, Yakusheva T (1994) Materialization: A powerful and ubiquitous abstraction pattern. VLDB 1994:630–641.

Poulovassilis A, McBrien P (1998) A general formal framework for schema transformation. Data Knowl. Eng. 28(1):47-71.

Queralt A, Teniente E (2006) Specifying the semantics of operation contracts in conceptual modeling. J. Data Semantics VII:33–56.

Queralt A, Teniente E (2006b) Reasoning on UML class diagrams with OCL constraints. ER 2006, LNCS 4215:497-512.

Qian X (1993) The deductive synthesis of database transactions. ACM Trans. Database Syst. 18(4):626-677.

Quillian R (1968) Semantic memory. In: Minsky M (ed) Semantic information processing. MIT Press, pp 227–270.

Ram S, Khatri V (2005) A comprehensive framework for modeling set–base business rules during conceptual database design. Inf. Syst. 30:89–118.

Reiter R (1992) What should a database know? J. Log. Program. 14(1,2):127–153.

Richters M, Gogolla M (2000) Validating UML models and OCL constraints. UML 2000, LNCS 1939:265–277.

Riddle WE, Wileden JC, Sayler JH, Segal AR, Stavely AM (1978) Behavior modelling during software design. Proc 3rd. Intl Conf On Software Engineering, pp 13–22.

Robinson KA (1979) An entity/event data modelling method. The Computer Journal, 22(3):270–281.

Robinson K, Berrisford G (1994) Object–oriented SSADM. Prentice Hall.

Rochfeld A, Negros P (1993) Relationships of relationships. Data Knowl. Eng. 9: 205–221.

Rolland C, Cauvet C (1992) Trends and perspectives in conceptual modelling. In: Loucopoulos P, Zicari R (eds) Conceptual modeling, databases and CASE: An integrated view of information systems development. Wiley, pp 27–48.

Rolland C, Prakash N (2000) From conceptual modelling to requirements engineering. Ann. Software Eng. 10:151–176.

Rolland C, Proix C (1992) A natural language approach for requirements engineering. CAiSE 1992, LNCS 593:257–277.

Rolland C, Richard C (1982) The REMORA methodology for information systems design and management. In: Olle et al. (eds) pp 369–426.

Rolland C, Ben Achour C, Cauvet C, Ralyté J, Sutcliffe A, Maiden NAM, Jarke M, Haumer P, Pohl K, Dubois E, Heymans P (1998) A proposal for a scenario classification framework. Requir. Eng. 1:23–47.

Rosenthal A, Reiner D (1994) Tools and transformations – rigorous and otherwise– for practical database design. ACM Trans. Database Syst. 19(2):167–211.

Rumbaugh J, Blaha M, Premerlani W, Eddy F, Lorensen W (1991) Object–oriented modeling and design. Prentice Hall.

Rumbaugh J, Jacobson I, Booch G (2005) The Unified Modeling Language reference manual. Addison–Wesley.

Rusinoff DM (1989) Proteus: A frame–based nonmonotonic inference system. In Kim W, Lochovsky FH (eds) Object–oriented concepts, applications, and databases, Addison-Wesley, pp 127–150.

Schrefl M, Stumptner M (2000) On the design of behavior consistent specializations of object life cycles in OBD and UML. In: Papazoglou MP, Spaccapietra S, Tari Z (eds) Advances in object-oriented data modeling. MIT Press, pp 65–104.

Schrefl M, Stumptner M (2002) Behavior–consistent specialization of object life cycles. ACM Trans. Softw. Eng. Methodol. 11(1):92–148.

Schreiber G, Akkermans H, Anjewierden A, Hoog R de, Shadbolt N, Van de Velde W, Wielinga B (2000) Knowledge engineering and management: The CommonKADS methodology. MIT Press.

Selic B, Gullekson G, Ward PT (1994) Real-time object-oriented modeling. Wiley.

Sendall S, Strohmeier A (2000) From use cases to system operation specifications. UML 2000, LNCS 1939:1–15.

Shipman DW (1981) The functional data model and the data language DAPLEX. ACM Trans. Database Syst. 6(1):140–173.

Shlaer S, Mellor SJ (1992) Object lifecycles. Modeling the world in states. Yourdon Press.

Siau K, Wand Y, Benbasat I (1997) The relative importance of structural constraints and surface semantics in information modeling. Inf. Syst. 22(2/3):155–170.

Smith EE (1988) Concepts and thought. In: Sternberg RJ, Smith EE (eds) The psychology of human thought. Cambridge University Press, pp 19–49.

Smith EE, Medin DL (1981) Categories and concepts. Harvard University Press.

Smith JM, Smith DCP (1977) Database abstractions: Aggregation and generalization. ACM Trans. Database Syst. 2(2):105–133.

Snoeck M, Dedene G (1998) Existence dependency: The key to semantic integrity between structural and behavioral aspects of object types. IEEE Trans. Software Eng. 24(4):233–251.

Sølvberg A, Kung DC (1985) On structural and behavioral modeling of reality. DS-1, North-Holland, pp 205-221.

Sommerville I, Sawyer P (1997) Requirements engineering: A good practice guide. Wiley.

Sowa JF (ed) (1991) Principles of semantic networks: Explorations in the representation of knowledge. Morgan Kaufmann.

Steimann F (2000) On the representation of roles in object–oriented and conceptual modelling. Data Knowl. Eng. 35(1):83–106.

Stillings NA, Weisler SE, Chase CH, Feinstein MH, Garfield JY, Rissland EL (1995) Cognitive science: An introduction. MIT Press.

Storey VC (1993) Understanding semantic relationships. The VLDB Journal, 2(4): 455–488.

Sundgren B (1975) Theory of data bases. Petrocelli.

Teichroew D, Hershey EA (1977) PSL/PSA: A computer–aided technique for structured documentation and analysis of information processing systems. IEEE Trans. Software Eng. 3(1):41–48.

Teichroew D, Sayani H (1971) Automation of system building. Datamation, August: 25–30.

Teisseire M, Poncelet P, Cichetti R (1994) Dynamic modelling with events. CAiSE 1994, LNCS 811:186–199.

Thalheim B (1992) Fundamentals of cardinality constraints. ER 1992, LNCS 645:7–23.

Thalheim B (2000) Entity–relationship modeling. Springer.

Theodoulidis C, Wangler B, Loucopoulos P (1992) The Entity–Relationship–Time model. In: Loucoupulos P, Zicari R (eds) Conceptual Modeling, Databases and CASE: An integrated view of information systems development. Wiley, pp 87–115.

Tsichritzis DC, Klug A (1978) The ANSI/X3/SPARC DBMS framework: Report of the study group on data base management systems. Inf. Syst. 3(3):173–191.

Tsichritzis DC, Lochovsky FH (1982) Data models. Prentice Hall.

Ullman JD (1988) Principles of database and knowledge–base systems, Vol. 1. Computer Science Press.

Van Der Straeten R, Jonckers V, Mens T (2004) Supporting model refactorings through behaviour inheritance consistencies. UML 2004, LNCS 3273:305–319.

Veloso PAS, Furtado AL (1985) Towards simpler and yet complete formal specifications. Proc. IFIP WG 8.1 WC on Theoretical and Formal Aspects of Information Systems, pp 175–189.

Verrijn–Stuart AA, Olle TW (eds) (1994) Methods and associated tools for the information systems life cycle. IFIP Transactions A–55. North-Holland.

W3C (2004) XML Schema Part 2: Datatypes, 2nd edn. Available online at http://www.w3.org/TR/xmlschema-2/.

Wand Y, Weber R (1988) An ontological analysis of some fundamental information systems concepts. Proc. of the 9th Annual Intl Conf on Information Systems, pp 213–225.

Wand Y, Storey VC, Weber R (1999) An ontological analysis of the relationship construct in conceptual modeling. ACM Trans. Database Syst. 24(4):494–528.

Warmer J, Kleppe A (2003) The Object Constraint Language: Getting your models ready for MDA, 2nd edn. Addison-Wesley.

Wegner P (1987) The object–oriented classification paradigm. In: Shriver B, Wegner P (eds) Research directions in object–oriented programming. MIT Press, pp 479–560.

Wieringa RJ (2003) Design methods for reactive systems. Yourdon, Statemate and the UML. Morgan Kaufmann.

Wieringa R, Jonge W de, Spruit P (1995) Using dynamic classes and role classes to model object migration. TAPOS 1(1):61–83.

Wieringa R, Meyer JJ, Weigand H (1989) Specifying dynamic and deontic integrity constraints. Data Knowl. Eng. 4:157–189.

Wieringa R, Weigand H, Meyer J-J, Dignum (1991) The inheritance of dynamic and deontic integrity constraints. Ann. Math. Artif. Intell. 3(2-4):393-428.

Winston ME, Chaffin R, Herrmann D (1987) A taxonomy of part–whole relations. Cognitive Science 11(4):417–444.

Woods WA (1991) Understanding subsumption and taxonomy. A framework for progress. In: Sowa (ed) pp 45–94.

Young JW, Kent HK (1958) Abstract formulation of data processing problems. The Journal of Industrial Engineering 9(6):471–479.

Yourdon (1993) Yourdon systems method: Model–driven systems development. Yourdon Press.

Zave P (1997) Classification of research efforts in requirements engineering. ACM Comput. Surv. 29(4):315–321.

# Index

Lightning Source UK Ltd.
Milton Keynes UK
UKOW051909170513

210852UK00002B/19/P